ADVANCED EXCEL™

ADVANCED EXCEL™

IBM PC,® PS/2,® AND COMPATIBLES

Ruth Ashley

Judi N. Fernandez

WILEY

JOHN WILEY & SONS, INC.
New York • Chichester • Brisbane • Toronto • Singapore

Publisher: Stephen Kippur
Editor: Therese A. Zak
Managing Editor: Ruth Greif
Editing, Design, and Production: G&H SOHO, Ltd.

This publication is designed to provide accurate and authoritative information in regard to the subject matter covered. It is sold with the understanding that the publisher is not engaged in rendering legal, accounting, or other professional service. If legal advice or other expert assistance is required, the services of a competent professional person should be sought. FROM A DECLARATION OF PRINCIPLES JOINTLY ADOPTED BY A COMMITTEE OF THE AMERICAN BAR ASSOCIATION AND A COMMITTEE OF PUBLISHERS.

Copyright © 1989 by John Wiley & Sons, Inc.

All rights reserved. Published simultaneously in Canada.

Reproduction or translation of any part of this work beyond that permitted by section 107 or 108 of the 1976 United States Copyright Act without the permission of the copyright owner is unlawful. Requests for permission or further information should be addressed to the Permission Department, John Wiley & Sons, Inc.

TRADEMARKS

Excel, Microsoft, MS-DOS, MultiPlan, and the Microsoft logo are registered trademarks of Microsoft Corporation.
CompuServe is a registered trademark of CompuServe Information Service.
dBASE, dBASE II, and dBASE III are registered trademarks of Ashton Tate Corporation.
IBM, IBM PC, and IBM AT are registered trademarks of International Business Machines Corporation.
1-2-3, Lotus, and Symphony are registered trademarks of Lotus Development Corporation.
PostScript is a registered trademark of Adobe Systems, Inc.
Wordstar is a registered trademark of MicroPro International Corporation.

Library of Congress Cataloging-in-Publication Data

Ashley, Ruth.
  Advanced Excel.

  Bibliography: p.

  1. Microsoft Excel (Computer program). 2. IBM Personal Computer—Programming. 3. Business—Data processing. I. Fernandez, Judi N., 1941
II. Title.
HF5548.4.M523A84 1989   005.36′9   88-28039
ISBN 0-471-61576-5

Printed in the United States of America

89 90 10 9 8 7 6 5 4 3 2 1

CONTENTS

Introduction 1

1 WINDOWS, EXCEL, AND FILES 3

Excel and Your System 3
Installation Notes 4
Communicating with Excel 4
Starting Excel 4
    With Full Windows   5
    With Run-Time Windows   6
The Excel Application Window 6
The Document Window 8
Mouse Basics 9
Keyboard Basics 10
Keyboard Shortcuts 10
Mouse and Keyboard Equivalences 11
Menus 11
The Control Menus 13
Dialog Boxes 13
Help in Excel 15
    The Help Index Command   16
    The Help Keyboard Command   17
Using Files in Excel 18
    Opening an Existing File   19
    Opening a New Empty Worksheet   20
    Closing Files   21
    Deleting Files   21
    Saving Files   22
    Saving the Workspace   23
    Terminating Excel   24
Summary 26

2 CREATING WORKSHEETS — 27

- Designing a Worksheet — 27
- Entering Data — 28
    - Formula Bar Editing — 29
    - Types of Values — 30
    - Number Values — 30
    - Text Values — 31
- Entering Formulas — 31
    - Using Functions — 32
    - Pointing for References — 33
- Selecting Ranges — 33
- Changing Column Width and Row Height — 35
- Using the Edit Menu — 38
- Filling Adjacent Cells — 39
- Copying Cells — 40
    - Undoing a Copy or Fill — 41
    - Efficient Data Entry — 42
- Cutting Cells (Moving) — 42
- Selective Pasting — 42
- Emptying Cells — 44
    - Clearing a Cell or Range — 44
    - Removing a Cell or Range — 45
- Inserting Rows or Columns — 46
- Changing Calculation Time — 47
- Menu Lengths — 48
- Summary — 49

3 POLISHING THE WORKSHEET — 50

- The Format Menu — 50
    - Aligning Entries — 50
    - Justifying Text — 52
- Formatting Numbers — 54
    - Format Symbols — 55
    - Hiding Values — 58
    - Custom Formats — 58
- Date and Time Formats — 58
- Modifying Onscreen Appearance — 60
- Borders — 61

CONTENTS vii

Modifying the Display ... 62
   Formulas   64
   Gridlines   64
   Row and Column Headings   65
   Zero Values   65
Using Fonts ... 65
   Printer Fonts   68
   Examples   68
Summary ... 70

4 WORKSHEET SELECTION FEATURES ... 71

References to Cells ... 71
   Relative References   71
   Absolute References   72
   Using the R1C1 Style   73
   Moving to a Cell   73
Ranges ... 73
   Multiple Selection   74
   Moving within a Range or Multiple Selection   75
Names ... 76
   Establishing Names   77
      One Name at a Time   77
      Many Names at Once   78
   Editing or Deleting Names   80
      Using Names   80
   Applying Names to References   82
   Moving to a Named Cell or Range   83
Cell Notes ... 83
   Creating Notes   84
   Editing Notes   85
   Deleting Notes   85
   Printing Notes   85
Cell Information ... 85
   The Info Menu   86
   Scrolling through the Info Windows   88
   Printing Info Window Data   89
   Precedents and Dependents   89
Finding Data in the Worksheet ... 90
Finding Other Things ... 91
Summary ... 94

5 EXCEL FORMULAS AND FUNCTIONS   95

Formulas   95
    Operators in Formulas   96
    Entering Formulas   97
    Viewing Formulas   98
    Printing Formulas   99

Functions   99
    Arguments   99
    Using Functions   100
    Date Functions   101
        Using Date Functions   103
    Financial Functions   105
        Depreciation Functions   105
        Investment and Annuity Functions   106
        Rate of Return Functions   107
    Information Functions   108
        Logical Returns   108
        Cell Information   109
    Logical Functions   111
        Assigning Logical Values   111
        Making Decisions   112
        Logical Operators   113
    Mathematical Functions   115
    Statistical Functions   117
        Basic Statistics   117
        Variance and Standard Deviation   118
        Advanced Statistics with Curve Fitting   118
    Text Functions   119
    Trigonometric Functions   122

Summary   122

6 PRINTING AND PAGE LAYOUT   124

Printer Setup   124
Basic Printing   126
    Printed Appearance   128
    Using Preview   128
    Magnification without a Mouse   131

Setting up the Page	131
Headers and Footers 132	
Margins 133	
Row and Column Headers 133	
Gridlines 133	
Using Print Options	134
Set Print Area 134	
Set Print Titles 135	
Set Page Break 135	
The Print Spooler	137
Summary	138

7 MANAGING WINDOWS AND LINKS — 139

Multiple Open Worksheets	139
Multiple Views of a Single Worksheet	140
Multiple Areas in a Worksheet 140	
Multiple Windows 140	
Why Use Multiple Windows? 141	
Window Panes 142	
Creating Panes 143	
Locking Titles on Screen 143	
Linking Data and Worksheets	145
External Reference Names 146	
External References 146	
Locating External References 147	
Identifying Supporting Worksheets 147	
Establishing Links 147	
Using Paste Link 148	
Establishing Complex Links 149	
Using Names in References 149	
Using Values Rather than References 150	
Saving Linked Worksheets 150	
Opening Linked Worksheets 150	
Removing Links 152	
Handling Links to Different Directories 152	
Redirecting Links 153	
Transfering Data to and from Other Applications	153
Writing to Disk in Other Formats 154	
Reading from Disk in Non-Excel Formats 156	

Transfering Data among Windows Applications 156
   Using the Clipboard 156
   Using Dynamic Data Exchange (DDE) 157
Summary 158

8 HANDLING DATABASES 159
What Is a Database? 159
Designing a Database 160
   Worksheet Layout 161
Creating a Database 161
   Define the Database 162
Using Data Forms 163
   Adding Records 164
   Deleting Records 165
   Finding Records 165
   Data Forms Summary 166
Sorting Records 167
   Sort Sequence 168
   Starting a Sort 169
   Rearranging Columns 170
   When to Sort 171
Using the Criteria Range 172
   Simple Criteria 173
   Computed and Complex Criteria 174
   Compound Criteria 175
   Criteria References Outside the Database 175
Using Data Find 176
Extracting Records 177
   The Extract Range 177
   Extracting to a Different Worksheet 179
Deleting Selected Records 179
Using Database Functions 180
   The Database Functions 181
   Examples 182
Summary 184

9 USING CHARTS — 185

Basic Charting — 185
Chart Creation — 185
    Making the Selection — 186
    Including Names in the Selection — 187
Chart Geography and Terminology — 189
    The Elements of a Chart — 189
    Selecting Chart Elements — 190
    The Chart Menu Bar — 191
Types of Charts — 192
    Area Charts — 192
    Bar Charts — 194
    Column Charts — 194
    Line Charts — 197
    Pie Charts — 199
    Scatter Charts — 199
    Combination Charts — 202
    Setting a Preferred Chart Type — 204
Modifying the Chart Layout — 204
Printing Charts — 206
Summary — 206

10 CUSTOMIZING CHARTS — 207

Before You Customize — 207
Legends — 208
Font Formatting — 209
Changing Patterns — 211
Modifying Markers — 213
Axes — 214
Gridlines — 217
Text in Charts — 217
    Attached Text — 217
    Unattached Text — 220
    Using Arrows — 221
    Linking Text to a Worksheet Cell — 222

Converting Customized Charts	222
Handling Overlays	223
The Series Formula	224
Series Name Argument 224	
Categories Argument 225	
Values Argument 226	
Plot Order Argument 226	
Creating a New Series Function 227	
Summary	227

11 USING DATA SERIES, TABLES, AND ARRAYS — 228

Data Series	228
Using Numeric Data Series 230	
Using Date Data Series 230	
Data Tables	231
A One-Input Table 231	
Adding to the Table 233	
A Two-Input Table 234	
Lookup Tables	237
Defining Lookup Tables 237	
HLOOKUP and VLOOKUP Functions 238	
The LOOKUP Function 240	
The MATCH Function 241	
The INDEX Function 242	
Lookup Table Summary 243	
Arrays in Excel	243
Using Array Ranges in Basic Applications 244	
Using Array Formulas 245	
Mathematical Arrays and Matrix Functions 245	
Summary	247

12 RECORDING AND USING MACROS — 248

Types of Macros	248
Macro Sheet	249
Macro Functions	250
Command Macros	251

The Macro Recorder	251
Relative and Absolute Recording 252	
Recording a Basic Macro 253	
Examining the Recorded Macro 254	
Another Macro 255	
Running a Macro	256
Editing a Macro	257
Controlling Recorded Macro Placement	258
Controlling Macro Sheets 259	
Setting the Recorder Range 259	
Starting Macro Placement 260	
Macro Naming	260
Formatting the Macro Sheet	261
Displaying Dialog Boxes through Macros	262
Referencing Other Worksheets	263
Macro Running Errors	264
Sample Recorded Macros	265
Summary	267

13 MACRO DEVELOPMENT   269

Macro Functions	269
Function Macros	274
Designing a Function Macro 275	
Customizing Command Macros	278
Naming in Macros	278
User Input	279
Using INPUT Function Values 280	
Communicating with the User	281
The ALERT Function 281	
The MESSAGE Function 283	
The BEEP Function 283	
Macro Example 283	
Macro Application	284
The Sample Data 285	
Setting Up Labels 285	
Creating Labels 289	
Printing Labels 292	
Summary	295

14 CUSTOMIZED EXCEL APPLICATIONS — 296

Customized Boxes — 296
The Dialog Editor — 298
   Selecting Objects   299
   Adding Text to Objects   301
   Selecting, Moving, and Sizing Objects   302
   Using the Dialog Editor Edit Menu   302
   Saving the Dialog Box   305
   Converting a Range to the Dialog Editor   305
The Custom Range — 305
   Screen Measurement Units   308
   Positioning   308
   Sizing Objects   309
Custom Box Design — 309
Preparing Custom Data Forms — 310
   Developing Custom Data Forms   312
   Testing Custom Data Forms   312
   Using the Custom Data Form   313
Custom Dialog Boxes — 314
Using the Object Types — 315
   OK and Cancel Buttons   315
   Text and Edit Boxes   316
   Option Buttons and Check Boxes   318
   Text List Boxes   320
   Icon Graphic   322
   Handling Files, Drives, and Directories   322
Developing a Customized Dialog Box — 324
   Testing the Cutomized Dialog Box   325
   Processing Customized Dialog Box Input   326
Customized Help — 327
Other Customizing — 329
Summary — 330

15 PROTECTING AND CONTROLLING DOCUMENTS AND CELLS — 331

Protecting Documents — 331
   Preventing Document Access   331
   Passwords   332

CONTENTS

    Accessing a Protected File   333
    Removing Document Protection   334
    Protecting a Document from Changes   334
    Protecting without Passwords   335

Controlling Cell Protection   336
    Unlocking Cells   336
    Allowing Selected Changes   337
    Protecting Charts   338

Using Excel Control Functions   339
    Running the Clipboard   340
    Running the Control Panel   341
        Adjusting Control Panel Fields   341
        Control Panel Installation Options   342
        Control Panel Setup Options   343
        Control Panel Preferences   343
    Macro Translation   346

Summary   348

Appendix   MACRO FUNCTIONS   349

Index   357

INTRODUCTION

Spreadsheets have become almost as ubiquitous as word processors in most business and personal computer environments. Microsoft® Excel incorporates one of the most sophisticated spreadsheet programs around, with database and chart functions to rival any specialized programs you may find.

With Excel you can create and manipulate spreadsheets and databases on a single worksheet or on separate ones. You can create and customize charts to meet your own needs or to be included in reports or documents. Excel even includes text-handling functions so you can include text in your printed output.

How you use Excel depends on what you want it to do for you and how much effort you are willing to put into learning its features. The documentation provided with the software is primarily for reference. The online tutorial and feature guide that you can access through Excel's Help menu give you a quick introduction to basic data entry and an overview of Excel features.

This book assumes that Excel is installed on your IBM PC compatible computer and that you can start it up. It even assumes you have tried out the tutorial and feature guide using the Help menu. But it then takes you further into Excel. Each chapter includes one or more suggested exercises that guide you through real solutions using Excel. You'll make mistakes but you'll learn to correct them through Excel's messages or through the hints in each exercise. If you have started using Excel at any level, feel free to modify the exercises to perform similar operations on your own worksheets.

By the time you finish reading this book and doing the exercises, you'll be able to use most of Excel's features. Practice and the motivation of real problems to solve are all you'll then need to become an Excel user *par excellence*.

1 WINDOWS, EXCEL, AND FILES

Microsoft® Excel is a super worksheet. In fact, it is any number of super worksheets and a great deal more. Excel not only lets you develop the spreadsheets, databases, and charts you need, but also lets you link them together to keep them up to date and share data between them. Excel lets you create and maintain spreadsheets and databases, generate and manipulate charts, and link them all as needed. You can develop macros—predefined sequences of commands that Excel executes at your command. You can customize menus and dialog boxes to meet the needs of your applications.

Microsoft Excel includes an excellent basic online tutorial; if you haven't been through it yet, take time to do so before going on to later chapters in this book. While this chapter reviews many of the basic commands and underlying concepts of Excel and Windows, the tutorial gives you practice and information you may need. If you are already familiar with Windows, you may be able to just skim parts of this chapter.

Because Excel can do so much it is very complex. You'll learn to use Excel at a basic level very easily. But it has many features, and many advanced applications of its basic features, that you won't learn unless you keep exploring. Don't give up on Excel. If something seems awfully difficult, there may be an easier way.

EXCEL AND YOUR SYSTEM

Excel is a Microsoft Windows application; that means it runs under Windows, specifically under Windows 2.0 (or later versions) or Windows/386. Windows, in turn, runs under DOS or OS/2. If you already have an appropriate version of Windows installed, you can install Excel in the same or a separate directory to run as an application under Windows. If you don't have Windows as a separate package, you can use the partial version included in the Excel software package; this "run-time" version lets you run Excel but not any other Windows applications. Just follow the installation instructions in the Excel documentation. When you are finished, you have a form of Windows that can run Excel but nothing else. While you start Excel differently with the full version and the run-time Windows, once Excel is started everything looks and acts the same. Running under the full Windows program gives you added advantages if you have additional Windows applications since you can transfer data back and forth among them. Most of the instructions and examples in this book apply to both forms of Excel installation; where they apply to only one form, this is clearly stated.

INSTALLATION NOTES

The Excel documentation includes excellent installation instructions. Before you start, though, be sure you know what type of monitor, printer, and mouse you have. Know the port connections of your printer and mouse as well. A parallel printer generally uses LPT1. A mouse may have a separate connection or be connected to any serial (COM) port. If you have a serial printer and a serial mouse, they are connected to different ports; be sure you know which component is connected to which port.

COMMUNICATING WITH EXCEL

You can enter Excel and Windows commands with a mouse, a keyboard, or a combination of both. For many functions, a mouse is easier. For others, the keyboard is more convenient. We'll cover both techniques in more detail later in this chapter. For now, just keep in mind that the mouse uses only the left button. Click means to press the left button once and release; double click means to press and release the left button twice in succession, rather quickly. On the keyboard, you can use the ALT key to activate menus and select commands. The notation ALT+ means to hold down the ALT key while pressing the key that follows. The directional arrows on the keyboard duplicate many mouse features within an Excel document.

STARTING EXCEL

Once Excel is installed, you want to start it up and see if it works. The method is different depending on whether you have run-time Windows or the full version.

With Full Windows

To start up Excel with the full version of Windows, you must first start up Windows. If you don't have a special startup file, change to the directory that includes Windows (usually \windows) and type WIN. You'll see the Microsoft title screen followed by the Windows control screen labeled MS-DOS Executive, as shown in Figure 1.1. This screen lists all the files in the current directory. If you placed the Excel program files in the same directory as Windows, you can just select EXCEL.EXE on the screen to run Excel. With a mouse, double click on the desired file name. Without a mouse, you can type the first letter of the desired file name; just press E until EXCEL.EXE is highlighted, then press Enter. If you placed Excel in a different directory, you have to change the displayed directory. You can do that by clicking (with a mouse) on the directory name. Without a mouse, press ALT + S to activate the Special pull-down menu, then press C to change directory. In the resulting dialog box, type the name of the desired directory (such as C:\EXCEL). (Menus and dialog boxes are covered in detail later in this chapter.) Windows then shows you the listing of that directory. You can select Excel by double-clicking with the mouse on the name EXCEL.EXE; without a mouse, press E to move the cursor to the next file starting with E until EXCEL.EXE is highlighted. Then press Enter to select it. In either case, the Excel application window, shown in Figure 1.2, appears next.

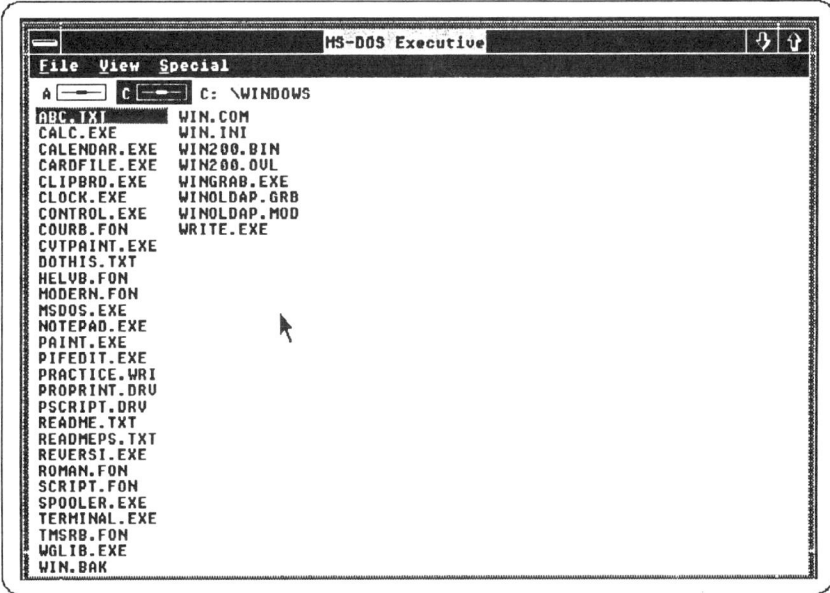

FIGURE 1.1.   Windows MS-DOS Executive Window

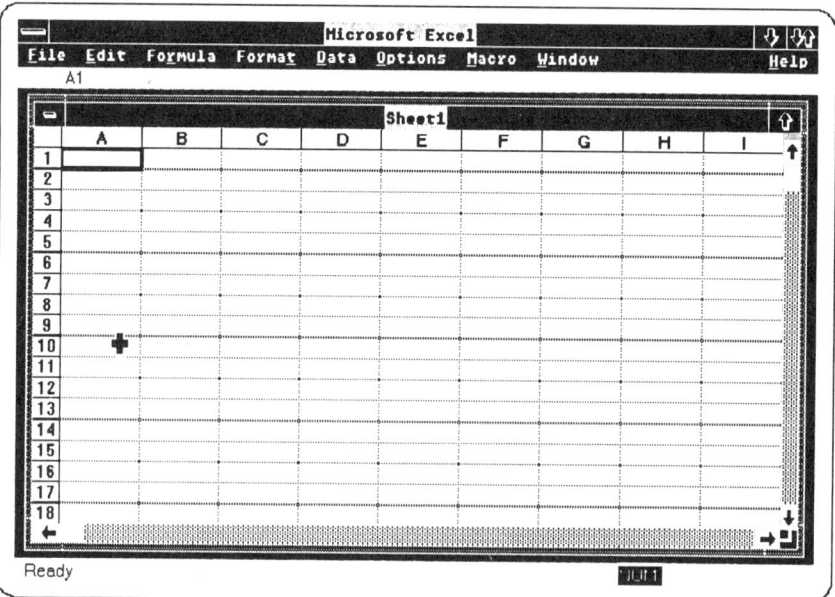

FIGURE 1.2. Excel Application Window

With Run-Time Windows

To start up Excel with the run-time version of Windows, first change to the directory that contains the Excel program. Then type EXCEL to run the program EXCEL.EXE. When the program is loaded, you'll see the Excel application window shown in Figure 1.2.

THE EXCEL APPLICATION WINDOW

The Excel application window includes features essential to using Excel. Many of these are labeled in Figure 1.3. Notice the application name (Microsoft Excel) in the application title bar at the top of the screen. On the very left of the application title bar is the application control menu icon. This menu is your gateway to the control menu, which lets you manipulate the size, shape, and appearance of the application window. The right end of the application title bar contains maximize and minimize icons; you can click on these to use the entire screen for the application (maximize) or to reduce it to an icon (minimize). Without a mouse, you can select these options from the application control menu. A menu bar appears on every Windows screen. The menus available are different for different displays. For example, if this screen didn't include a document window (a worksheet window in the example), the menu bar would

WINDOWS, EXCEL, AND FILES

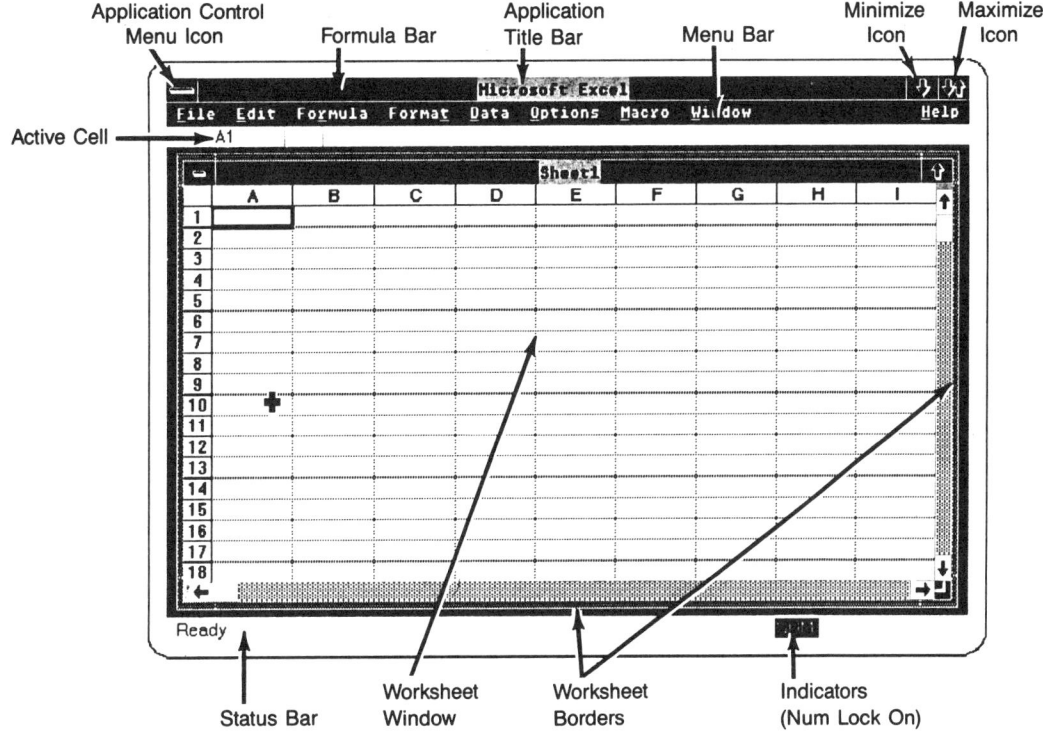

FIGURE 1.3. Application Window Features

show only the first and last menus, File and Help. You can access any menu by clicking on its name in the menu bar with the mouse or by pressing ALT + the underlined letter in the menu name. We'll cover all the menus as we progress through the book.

The line below the menu bar refers to the current portion of the active document on the screen; the active document here is a worksheet, so it shows the active cell, the intersection between the row and column where data can be entered. The space on the left gives its reference; in this case, it uses the column and row headings you see in the worksheet window. The rightmost part of the line is called the formula bar; it shows the contents of the current cell. If the value is derived from a formula, the formula appears in the formula bar. Since the current worksheet is empty, the current cell has no contents and the formula bar is blank.

The document window itself is bordered by heavy lines. Below the document window is the application status bar. The left part contains the current status or a message. In this case, it shows Ready; Excel is ready to receive data or a command. The right part of the status bar contains indicators; it shows when num lock, caps lock, or scroll lock is on.

THE DOCUMENT WINDOW

Figure 1.4 shows the same screen with document window features labeled. Excel has three types of documents, any (or all) of which can appear in the application window. The worksheet is the basic document type, however, so we've used it here. The features are similar for macro sheets and charts, the other types of documents. The labeled features all refer to the active worksheet; if several worksheets or other documents are open at once, only one is active. Notice that the name of the worksheet is in the document title bar. The document control menu icon appears on the left and the maximize icon on the right end of the bar. These positions and effects parallel those of the application title bar.

The document window can't be reduced to an icon, so it doesn't have a minimize icon. The document control menu can be accessed from the keyboard by pressing ALT+Hyphen. A cell occurs at every intersection of row and column headings. The current cell is highlighted or surrounded by a border on

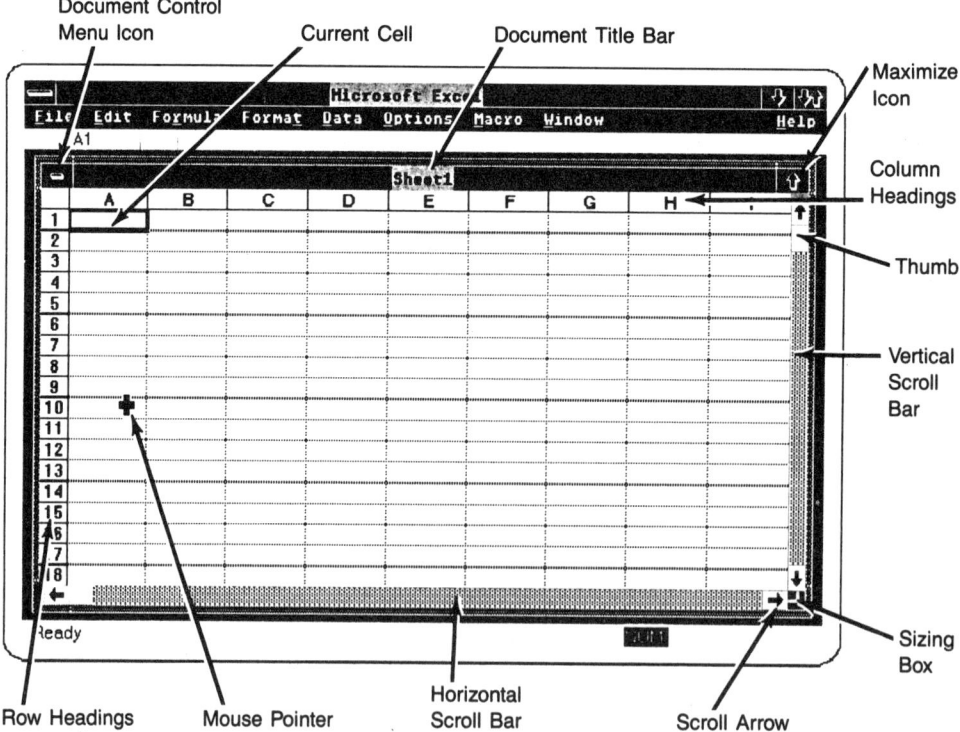

FIGURE 1.4. Document Window (Worksheet) Features

WINDOWS, EXCEL, AND FILES 9

the screen; notice that this corresponds to the reference in the application window reference area. The mouse pointer appears on the screen, even if you aren't using a mouse. The worksheet window includes vertical and horizontal scroll bars and arrows. The thumb mark in each scroll bar shows where in the used portion of the worksheet the currently displayed part is. In this case, the very beginning (upper left) corner of the worksheet is shown, so the thumbs are at the left and top of the scroll bars.

MOUSE BASICS

The mouse pointer takes on several different shapes, depending on where it is and what you have started doing. The cross icon in Figure 1.4 is the standard mouse pointer in the body of a worksheet. If you click on the worksheet, the cell containing the cross becomes the current cell. Figure 1.5 shows several other shapes the mouse can take, along with an explanation of where each occurs.

The mouse can be used to select data and manipulate windows. You select an item by clicking once with the left button. Any other buttons have no effect.

Icon	Where	What it does
◥	Menu, scroll bar, chart	Move, select
 ✛	Worksheet	Move+click to select, drag to extend
 ⧗	Anywhere	Wait a moment
 ☞	Help boxes	Select items
 I	Text boxes, formula bar	Move+click to set insertion point for edit

FIGURE 1.5. Mouse Pointer Representations

If you're left-handed, you might want to change the effect to the right button; see the Excel documentation for this. You can drag the mouse pointer by pressing the button and then moving the mouse while holding the button down. You can maximize a window by clicking on the maximize icon. You can minimize an application to an icon by clicking on the minimize icon. You can resize a window by clicking on the window border (the pointer becomes a double-headed arrow) and dragging the mouse to where you want that edge of the window to be. To move a window, click in the title bar (the pointer becomes a single-headed arrow and the border turns color) and drag a shadow border to where you want the window to be positioned. Between column or row headings, the pointer becomes a double-headed arrow; you can drag it to change the row or column size.

You can click on the scroll arrows or scroll bars to scroll through the worksheet as needed. Drag the thumb to scroll more quickly.

KEYBOARD BASICS

Even if you have a mouse, you'll find many times when you want to use the keyboard. If you need to type data, of course, you need the keyboard. The arrow keys and PageUp and PageDown keys have the same effects as the scroll bars. You can maximize, minimize, move, and size windows with the control menus and arrow keys. To select menus with the keyboard, press the ALT key with the underlined letter in the menu name; Excel doesn't care whether you use uppercase or lowercase letters in menus. We'll use uppercase in instructions, however. Use ALT+Spacebar for the application control menu, ALT+ − for the document control menu.

When you use the keyboard, you frequently have to press a series of keys. We use a system in showing you what to do. The plus sign (+) means to press the keys at the same time. If you should press them sequentially, we'll use a comma (,). So ALT+F means to hold down the ALT key while pressing F. ALT+F,O means to hold down the ALT key while pressing F, then release both and press O. With the ALT keys, you can use either upper- or lowercase letters to access menus or commands.

KEYBOARD SHORTCUTS

Excel offers many shortcuts that make using the keyboard more efficient. These shortcuts are based on function keys; you can use them at any time to replace various commands. Each function key has four different, but somewhat related, effects, one when the key is used alone and one each when it is pressed with the ALT, CONTROL, or SHIFT keys. The Excel package includes a template you can use on your keyboard to remind you of the shortcuts. And there's an instructional system (the Help menu) that includes online reminders. One very useful shortcut is F1; it brings you directly into the Help system.

In this book, we'll use the full commands in examples and in text most of the time. They are easier to remember, and you can always look at the menus to find out how to use them. But feel free to use any shortcuts you happen to remember. They have exactly the same effects as the Excel commands. In a few situations, we'll tell you the shortcut key if it is very much more convenient than the command.

Later in this book, you'll learn to develop your own shortcut commands, called macros, which can perform a whole series of commands.

MOUSE AND KEYBOARD EQUIVALENCES

Many times Excel gives you a message or asks you a question, displaying a box containing OK and Cancel buttons. You can click on the one you want with the mouse. It is often easier to press Enter for OK or Escape for Cancel. Enter always works for OK, and Escape always works for Cancel. Escape also removes menus and may change the status in the status bar.

MENUS

You select Excel's menus by clicking on the desired menu name in the menu bar or on the control menu icon. To access a menu from the keyboard press ALT + the underlined letter in the menu name or press ALT + Spacebar for the application control menu or ALT + Hyphen for the document control menu. Figure 1.6 shows the Help menu. Once the menu is displayed, you can select a command by clicking on it with the mouse or by pressing the underlined letter in the command; if you use the ALT key once the menu is displayed, it removes the menu, canceling your request. If the command name is followed by an ellipsis (three dots), a dialog box will appear in which you can provide further information; you'll also have a chance to change your mind. For example, suppose you want to know how much memory your system has. You select the Help menu, then select About by clicking or pressing A. Figure 1.7 shows the result. This box shows you how much conventional and expanded memory is available. To get rid of the box, just click OK, press Enter, or press Escape. We'll cover Excel's help system in more detail later in this chapter.

12 ADVANCED EXCEL

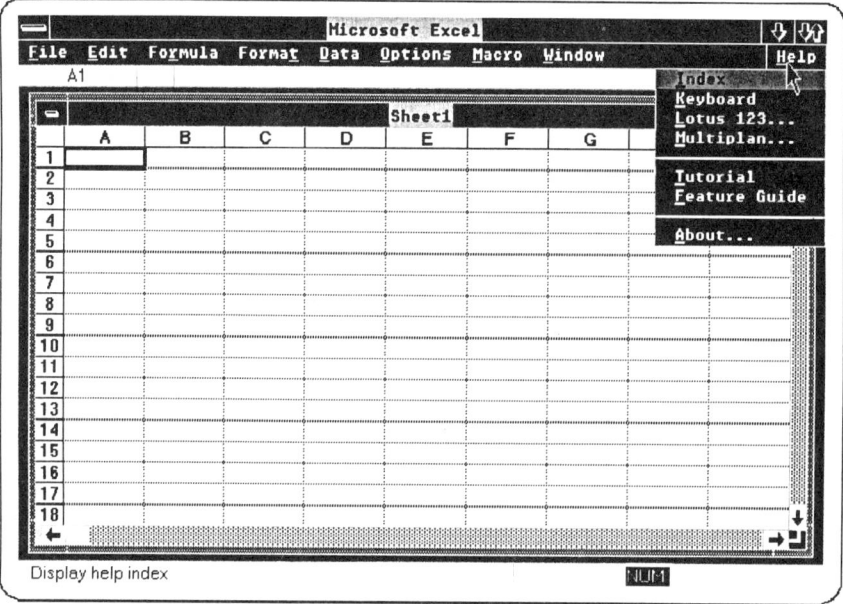

FIGURE 1.6. Help Menu

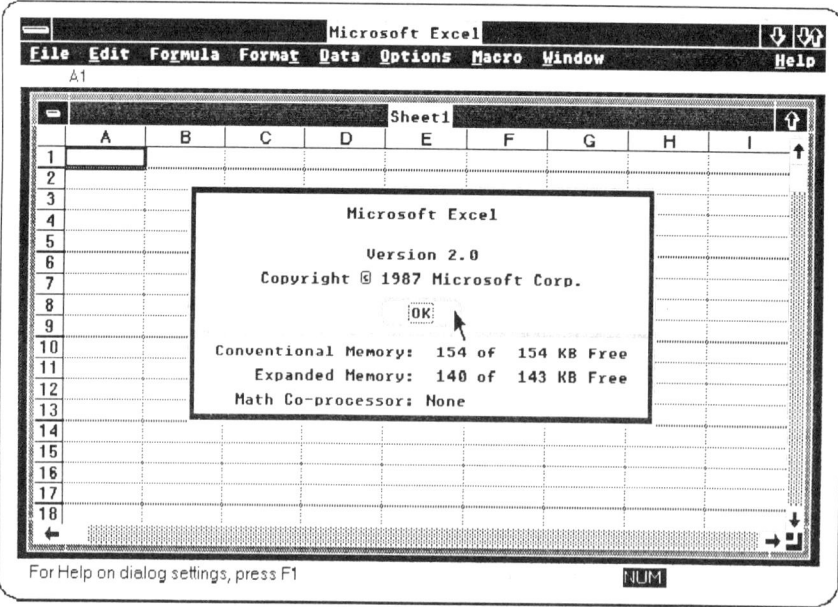

FIGURE 1.7. Help About Dialog Box

WINDOWS, EXCEL, AND FILES   13

```
         Application                Document

         Restore                    Restore
         Move                       Move
         Size                       Size
         Minimize                   Maximize
         Maximize                   Close
         Close                      Split
         Run
```

FIGURE 1.8. Control Menus

THE CONTROL MENUS

The application and document control menus are very similar; Figure 1.8 shows the commands listed on each. You access the control menu by clicking on the icon in the upper left corner of the window with the mouse or by pressing ALT + Spacebar (for the application control menu) or ALT + Hyphen (for the document control menu). The functions of most control menu commands can be performed with the mouse as well. For example, to maximize or minimize a window, you can use its icons. Selecting the commands has the same effect. You can also use the commands to move or size a window from the keyboard. Once you select the command, the arrow keys do the moving and sizing. If you maximize a document, it sort of becomes one with the application window, but you'll see two control icons in the upper left corner. The same commands access the menus.

The Restore command puts the window back in the size and position it was in before the last use of maximize or minimize. If you've maximized a document window, you must use its control menu to restore it and separate the two windows on screen. The Close command closes the document or application. If you close the application, Excel closes all open documents as well. If you've made any changes to the documents, Excel asks if you want the changes saved before it closes them.

The Run command on the application control menu lets you run the Excel control panel, the Windows clipboard, the macro translator, and the Dialog Editor (in Version 2.1). These are covered later in the book. The Split command on the document control panel lets you split the current window into panes. Use of these commands is covered later in the book.

DIALOG BOXES

Once you select a command from a menu, you may see a dialog box. Dialog boxes may just give information, as in the Help About command. In that case,

14 ADVANCED EXCEL

you just choose OK (by clicking on the OK button or pressing Enter) and continue. But dialog boxes can be much more complex. They may contain list boxes that show a list of items from which you can select. They may contain text boxes in which you can type or edit text. They may contain a set of buttons from which you can select. They may contain a set of check or toggle boxes that let you turn items on and off. You can use the tab key to move from one major area to another. Keep in mind that pressing Escape generally gets rid of a dialog box without making any further changes. It will ignore entries that haven't yet been processed.

Figure 1.9 shows a typical dialog box; this one results from the File Open command that you use to open a document stored as a file on one of your disks.

The File Open dialog box contains two list boxes, one for files and one for directories. It also contains one toggle box; you can set Read Only on or off. The File Name text box is to contain the name of the file to be opened. At the moment, it contains a generic name (*.XL*) that represents all the files in the current directory with an extension beginning with XL. The wildcard character usage here matches that in DOS or OS/2. The information below the text box shows the current directory name.

You can select anything in a dialog box with either the mouse or the keyboard. To use the mouse, just move the pointer and click. For example, to scroll through the file names in the Files list box, just click in the list box scroll

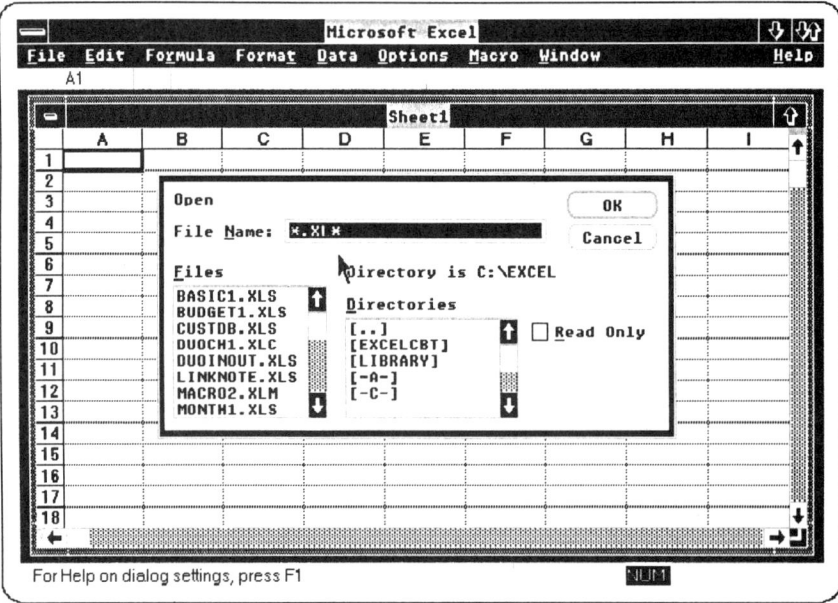

FIGURE 1.9. File Open Dialog Box

bar. When you see the file you want, click or double click on it. If you use a single click, you can then click on OK to complete the operation. With the keyboard, use ALT+F (from Files) to activate the list box, then use the arrow keys to select the file. When it is selected, choose OK or press Enter. To change to the LIBRARY directory, move the mouse pointer to LIBRARY in the Directories list box and double click, or click once on LIBRARY and once on OK. The first click puts the path in the File Name text box; the second click or OK displays files from that directory in the Files list box. With the keyboard, press Tab, or ALT+ the underlined letter, to activate a list box, then repeatedly press its first letter or use the arrow keys to select the desired item in the list. If you like, you can use ALT+N (from File Name) to activate the File Name field text box, then just type the file name. If you press ALT+R or click on Read Only, an X appears in the small box; this means the field is turned on and you won't be able to make changes in the file selected until the field is reset.

When the File Name field contains the name of the file you want to open, choose OK by clicking or pressing Enter. Excel opens the file as a document and puts it in a window on the screen. Or you can choose Cancel by clicking or pressing Escape.

As you see additional dialog boxes, or encounter them in your own explorations of Excel, you can apply the same general rules.

HELP IN EXCEL

The built-in instructional system can be of great assistance as you work with Excel. You've already seen the pull-down Help menu (Figure 1.6) and the dialog box that results from choosing the Help About command (Figure 1.7). The other commands on the Help menu give you much more information. The Tutorial and Feature Guide provide completely self-explanatory online instruction. If you haven't worked through them yet, do so at your first opportunity. The Lotus 1−2−3® and Multiplan® commands let you enter a command or select an option from the designated program; Excel then provides detailed information about how to accomplish the same thing using Excel commands. The Keyboard and Index commands give more detailed information about Excel itself.

The F1 key brings you directly into the Help system from wherever you are in Excel. If a command is already selected when you press F1, you'll get information about that command. SHIFT+F1 brings up a question mark on the screen; the next item or command you select brings up information specific to that item. These shortcuts are very useful while you are learning the basics of Excel.

16 ADVANCED EXCEL

The Help Index Command

The Help Index command results in a multilevel index, beginning with a window like the one shown in Figure 1.10. This is a window rather than a dialog box, because it includes a menu bar, title bar icons, and the other features of windows. You can select items from the menu bar just as from other windows.

Each Help window contains four commands in the menu bar. You can select Index from any non-index window. Selecting Print causes the current help topic to be printed; you'll see an alert box that gives you a chance to cancel the print. The Back and Next commands let you page through the Help system; they give information on adjacent topics or return you through the screens you've already read. Use PageUp and PageDown to page through an individual topic that takes more than one page.

The window in Figure 1.10 contains the top level of the index. You can select any item with the mouse or keyboard to see the next level of index until you reach the definition level. Even then, you can select any underlined words in the definition for further information. With the mouse, just click on the desired item. With the keyboard, use Tab or SHIFT+Tab to move among underlined items, then press Enter when the one you want is selected. In a list,

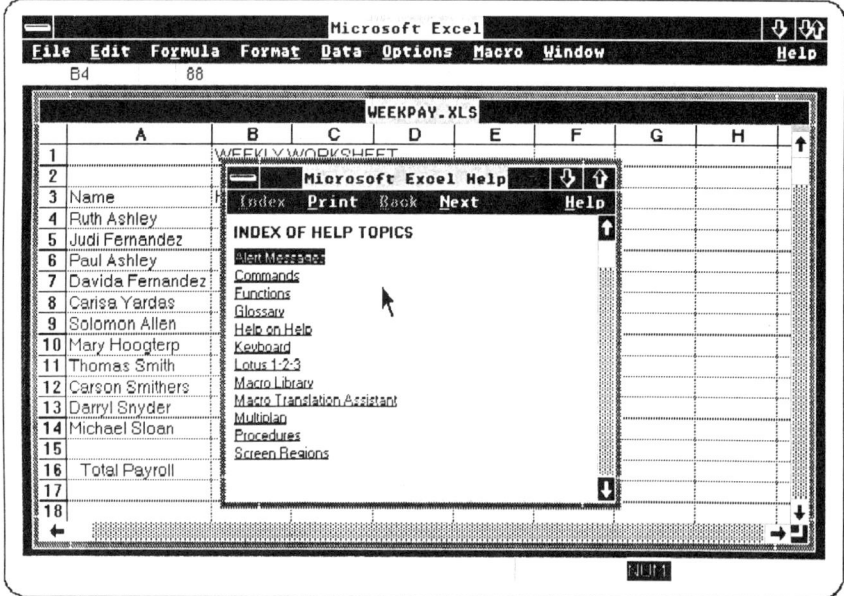

FIGURE 1.10. Help Index—Top Level

WINDOWS, EXCEL, AND FILES

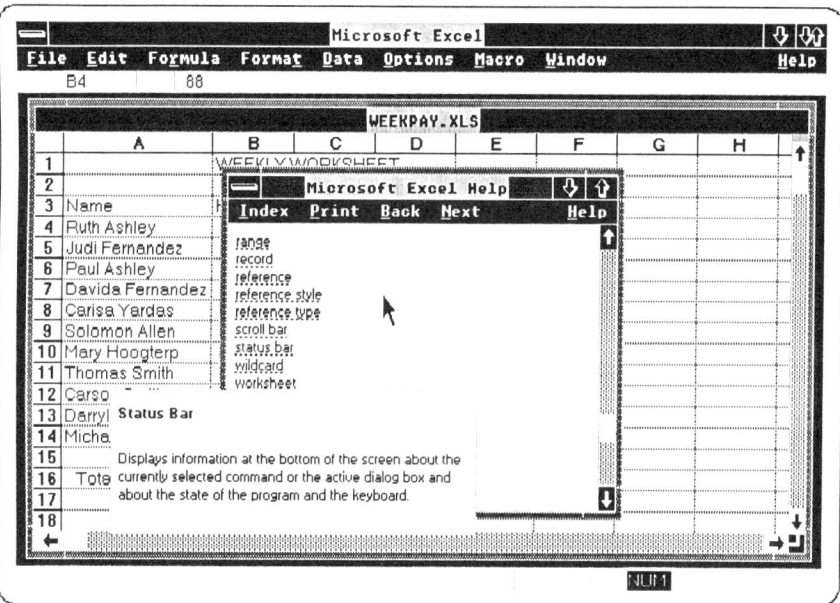

FIGURE 1.11. Help Index Glossary Window

as in Figure 1.10, you can type the first letter in the item to move to it directly. For example, pressing M selects Macro Library; pressing M again selects Macro Translation Assistant. Just press Enter when the item you want is selected. Use the scroll bar or the PageUp and PageDown keys to move through the information.

If you select Glossary, you see a long list of terms; the beginning is shown in Figure 1.11. Each item in the glossary has a dotted underscore; to see information about the selected item, you have to hold down the mouse button or Enter key. The highlight disappears while you read the information, then reappears when you release the mouse button or Enter key.

The Help Keyboard Command

The Help Keyboard command results in a window much like that of Help Index. A listing of topics related to the keyboard is shown, including such topics as Function Keys, Chart Keys, and Control Key Shortcuts. It works just like Help Index, and you can switch from here to the index by selecting Index in the menu bar.

SUGGESTED EXERCISE

If Excel is not yet installed on your system, take time to do it now, using the instructions in your documentation. Then continue with the exercise. If you prefer to control your own practice sessions, take time to start up Excel, use the control menu commands, and examine the Help system before going on.

1. Start Excel.
2. Use the mouse (move then click) or keyboard (arrow keys) to change the current cell. Notice that the cell reference in the reference area changes as well.
3. Activate the Help menu.
4. Examine the Help About dialog box. Notice how much memory is available.
5. Check the Help Index. Look at several areas. Examine a few entries in the Glossary.
6. When you're finished, press Escape or click outside the Help window to remove it from the screen.
7. Examine the document control menu. Change the size or location of the SHEET1 worksheet.
8. Examine the application control menu. Use Close to put Excel away. Just abandon any changes you may have made to SHEET1.

What if It Doesn't Work?

1. If Excel doesn't come up or if the mouse doesn't work as it should, check your installation. See your dealer if necessary.
2. If you have trouble using Help, select the Help on Help option in the Help Index to get a review of how to use it.
3. If you have trouble closing Excel, just leave it open. The next part of this chapter includes another method you can use.

USING FILES IN EXCEL

When Excel first comes up on your screen, it gives you an empty worksheet named SHEET1. While Excel works with a worksheet of any kind, it keeps the entire thing in active memory. You can then save worksheets on disk to use again later. You save your work on files, to which you give names. Excel uses a system of extensions for file names. Figure 1.12 lists the standard Excel extensions.

You can use other extensions if you wish, but these are easy to use and remember. You can create as many subdirectories as you wish to hold your files;

WINDOWS, EXCEL, AND FILES

```
XLS        Worksheets
XLC        Charts
XLM        Macros
XLW        Workspaces
```

FIGURE 1.12.   Excel File Extensions

however, they must be created under DOS or OS/2. The SHEET1 worksheet has no extension because it isn't yet a file; once saved, its default name is SHEET1.XLS; you can change the name any time, however. When you open a file or save a worksheet, the extension displays in the title bar as well. You'll use the File menu, shown in Figure 1.13, to perform most file operations. Notice the last command is Exit; you'll use that to get out of Excel. It has much the same effect as selecting Close on the application control menu.

Opening an Existing File

The File Open command lets you select an existing file from any directory and bring it to the screen. You saw the File Open dialog box in Figure 1.9. You'll use this command a great deal. You can change among the directories here as needed. Whatever directory you leave selected will be selected next time you

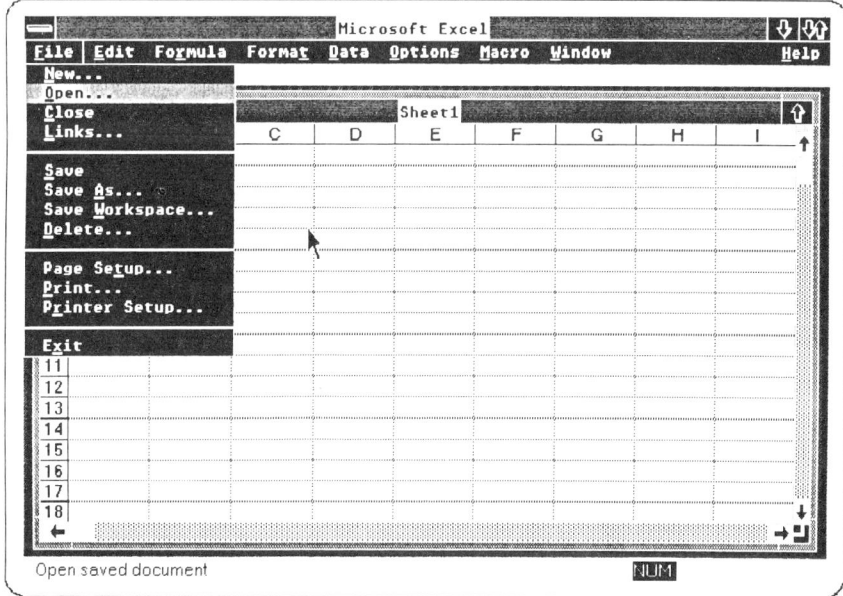

FIGURE 1.13.   File Menu

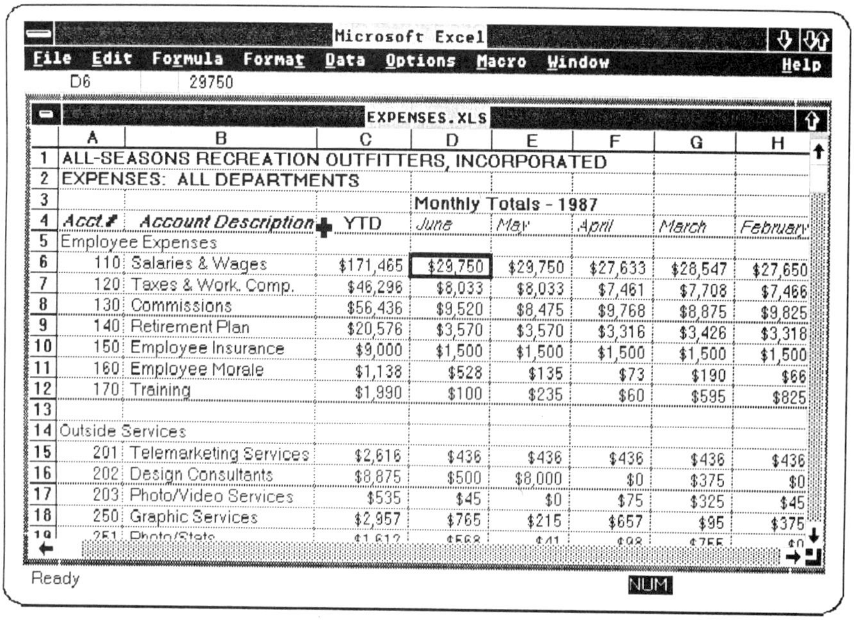

FIGURE 1.14. Opened Worksheet

enter this box or a similar one, such as File Delete. You can also change the generic file name shown in the File Open dialog box. By default, Excel uses *.XL* as the generic file name to display all files in Excel format. If you want to bring in files with other extensions, you can type the entire name or change the generic name to display more files.

When you locate your file and select it, choose OK. Excel reads the file into memory and puts it in a document window on the screen. That window is made active, which means you can use all the commands and features. Figure 1.14 shows a freshly opened worksheet. The active cell is the same one that was active when the file was last saved. Once the file is displayed, you can use the mouse or keyboard to examine cells and move around in the worksheet.

Opening a New Empty Worksheet

The File New command produces a dialog box like the one shown in Figure 1.15. Just select the type of new document you want; at this point we've only talked about worksheets, but you can create a new chart or macro sheet here as well. Only one of the three can be selected at a time; if you select Chart, the Worksheet button turns off. The new worksheet receives default name SHEET2, SHEET3, or whatever, depending on what you've done so far in the session.

WINDOWS, EXCEL, AND FILES

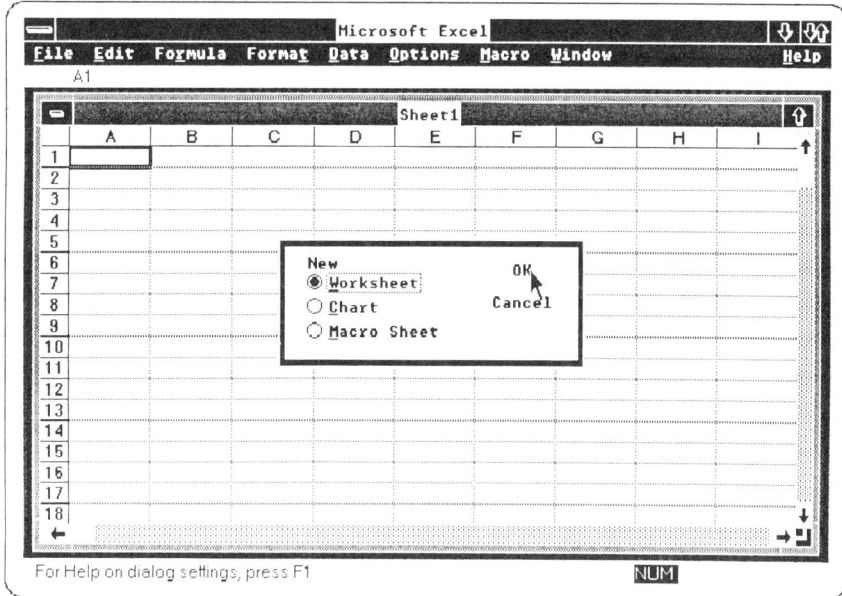

FIGURE 1.15. File New Dialog Box

When you add a new window, it becomes the active one; the menu bar refers to the active window.

Closing Files

You can close the active worksheet or file by selecting Close on the File menu. It works just like Close on the window's control menu. If changes have been made since it was saved, Excel asks if you want to save it first. Selecting Exit on the File menu terminates Excel. But Excel first closes all open worksheets, asking you if you want any changes saved. If you want to close all the files at once, hold the shift key down while selecting the File menu; the command will show Close All. You'll still get a chance to save each.

When a file or worksheet is closed, Excel removes it from memory and from the screen. You can open a saved file again later if you need it.

Deleting Files

Excel lets you delete files using a command on the File menu. When you select Delete on the File menu, you see a dialog box much like the one you see for File Open. Figure 1.16 shows the File Delete dialog box.

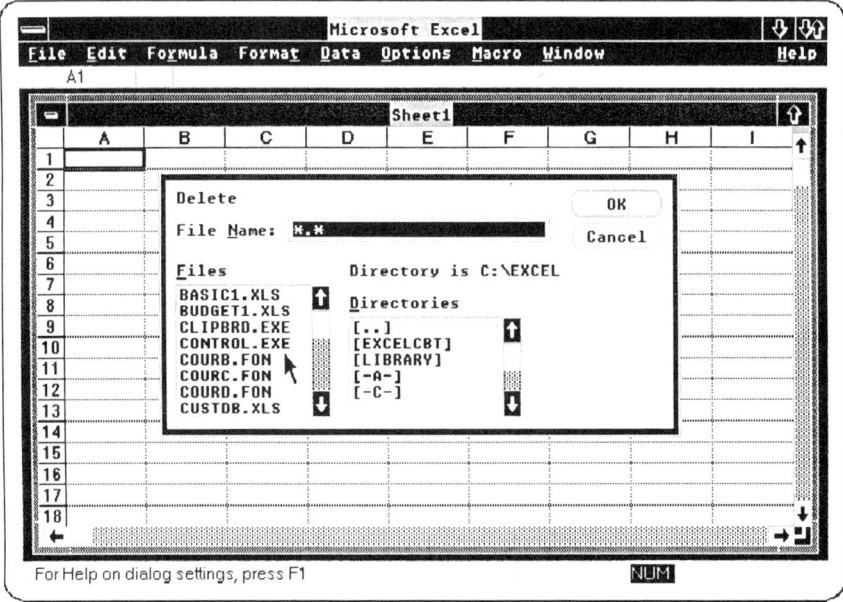

FIGURE 1.16. File Delete Dialog Box

You can manipulate the directories to locate the file you want to delete, then select it and choose OK. Excel presents you with a warning box asking if you really want to delete the selected file. When you choose Yes, it's gone, just as if you deleted under DOS or OS/2. The File Delete dialog box stays on screen in case you want to delete more files. Just choose Cancel or press Escape to get rid of it. This doesn't undo the deletions, but it doesn't delete any more files either.

Saving Files

When Excel saves files, it updates them on disk but keeps them on the screen. You've already seen that Excel asks if you want to save files when you close a file. If you decline the opportunity, the file on disk isn't changed from when you opened it. If you accept, the new version overlays the old.

Three more commands on the File menu let you save files. When you choose File Save, the active file is updated on disk, using the same path and name it had before; if a new document is active, Excel treats it as if you selected File Save As, since it doesn't have a file name as yet.

When you choose File Save As, Excel provides a dialog box like the one shown in Figure 1.17. It may be a bit different for other types of documents. Excel provides a default file name, using the document name with the appropriate extension or the current file name. You can edit or change it as you like.

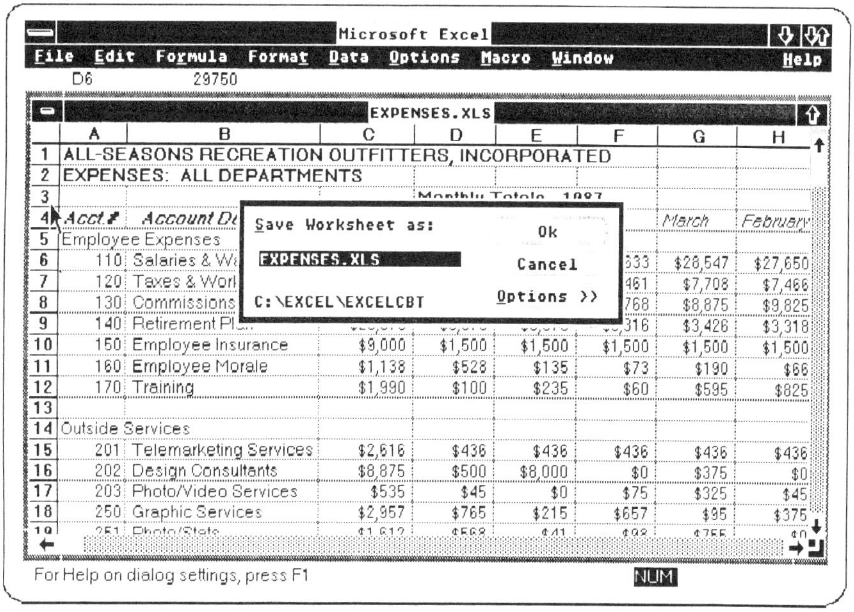

WINDOWS, EXCEL, AND FILES

FIGURE 1.17. File Save As Dialog Box

When you like the name, choose OK and the file is saved under the new name. The new name then appears in the title bar for the window on the screen.

The Options button lets you save the file in a different format; you won't need it most of the time. Figure 1.18 shows the dialog box after Options is selected. Notice that Normal is selected; normal means standard Excel format, which is what you usually want. The other formats are for creating files compatible with other programs. They are covered in Chapter 7. If you assign a password here, you'll need to specify it to open the file later. Use a password to protect a file from view by others. You'll have to specify the password when you try to access the file again, so be sure to keep a note of it somewhere besides in the document. If you want a backup file created, check that box. Then every time you save that file, Excel changes the old name to have a BAK extension and saves the new one. If you are concerned about backup files, you might want to check this box for each new worksheet you save. Once turned on, the backup field remains checked for that document until you change it.

Saving the Workspace

The workspace is the complete memory/screen layout, including the files that are open, where they are on screen, what cells and windows are active, and so forth. If you frequently work with the same set of windows on screen, you may

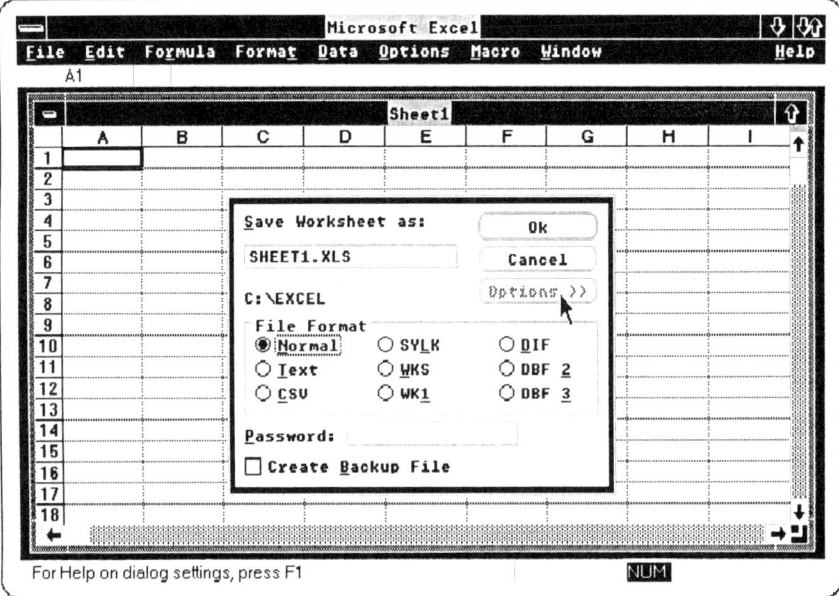

FIGURE 1.18. File Save As with Options Displayed

want to save the workspace description so you can open the whole set at once. When you select Save Workspace, Excel creates a new file to hold the workspace information. You'll see a dialog box like the one in Figure 1.19. Excel always provides the name RESUME.XLW as a default; you can replace it with the name you want. When you choose OK, the workspace description is saved, as are all the files currently in memory. The screen remains the same, however, and you can continue working. Eventually, you can save and close each file independently. The workspace file appears in the file listing in the File Open dialog box; when you select it for opening, the screen and memory are recreated as before. If you delete the workspace file, only the workspace description is deleted; the individual files aren't touched.

Terminating Excel

The Exit command on the File menu tells Excel to terminate. You'll be asked if you want to save any files that have been changed. You respond to each question individually. When all have been checked, Excel terminates. If you are running under the full Windows, you still have to close it; use the control menu and select Close.

WINDOWS, EXCEL, AND FILES

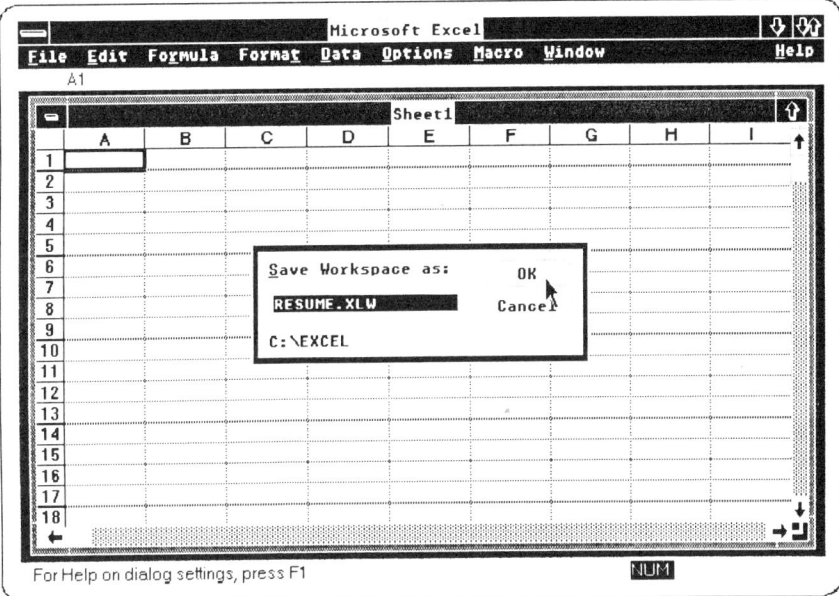

FIGURE 1.19. File Save Workspace Dialog Box

SUGGESTED EXERCISE

If you prefer to direct your own practice sessions, take time to try using the File menu to open and save worksheets. Delete any new files you create, but don't delete any existing ones. If you would prefer guided practice, follow the instructions below.

1. Bring up Excel if it isn't on your screen already.
2. Use the File Open command. Switch to the LIBRARY directory, and select file INCOME.XLS. Enlarge the worksheet to fill the space below the formula bar.
3. Use the File New command to open a new worksheet window. Type your name in the active cell, then use File Save As to save it. Use any currently unused file name with .XLS as the extension.
4. Notice the file name in the title bar. Close this worksheet.
5. Use the File Delete command to erase the file you just created.
6. Type a character or two in the active cell of the INCOME.XLS worksheet and press Enter, then select File Close. When asked if Excel should save changes, respond No.
7. If you haven't been through the Excel tutorial yet, do it now.
8. Use Exit to terminate Excel.

What if It Doesn't Work?

1. If you have trouble in the Open File dialog box, check the Help function. Double clicking on directories and files is more efficient than single clicking followed by OK. Remember that pressing Enter is OK.
2. Any time Excel asks if it should save changes, you have to answer Yes or No. If you don't recall making any changes, answer No.

SUMMARY

In this chapter, you've learned to start Excel using your system. The control menu or mouse lets you resize or relocate windows on screen. Close from the control menu or Exit from the File menu lets you terminate Excel. You can activate menus and use dialog boxes with either the mouse or the keyboard to communicate with Excel.

You've learned to use the online Help system from the Help menu to get more information about how to use Excel. And you've learned to use commands from the File menu to handle opening, closing, and deleting of files. You are likely to use both Help and file manipulation in every Excel session from now on.

2 CREATING WORKSHEETS

Most of your time in Excel will be spent creating and editing worksheets, which are the basic document in Excel. Charts are based on worksheet data. Macros work on worksheets or charts. Worksheets can include text, numbers, and other values. This chapter covers basic data entry and editing. You'll learn to use Excel's default formats and features as you enter data. You'll learn to enter simple but common formulas and functions. Later chapters in this book cover formatting and more complex entries.

Editing is essential to even the most basic worksheets. No worksheet remains unchanged forever. Most are updated on a daily or weekly basis. You'll learn to use most of the Edit menu commands in this chapter, as well as some commands from other menus, such as Format and Options. You'll also learn to make editing changes in the formula bar.

DESIGNING A WORKSHEET

Before you start to develop a worksheet, it helps to give it a bit of thought. Decide what information you have and what you need. Decide where to place the data on Excel's worksheet. Decide what text to use. Any text should be concise enough so as not to waste space on screen, but clear enough that you and other users know what is intended. Think of other people who will use this worksheet or reports drawn from it.

A worksheet can contain many small- to medium-sized spreadsheets; they don't even have to be related. Most worksheets are used for a single purpose, since Excel lets you link them together if you need to use the same data in several worksheets. It makes sense to locate data near the upper left corner of the worksheet to save energy while working with it. This also saves memory, since Excel needs space in memory for all rows and columns through the last that contain values; if you start your worksheet in column Z, the 25 blank columns also must be retained in memory.

In addition to how the spreadsheet will look on screen, you have to consider any reports that will be printed from it. While we aren't covering printing in detail until Chapter 6, keep the reports in mind as you design your worksheet. You can print the entire worksheet or any section of it.

ENTERING DATA

Entering data in Excel is simple. Just select the cell you want to hold the data and type. Excel places what you type in the cell as well as in the formula bar. Figure 2.1 shows the formula bar in use.

The formula bar becomes active when you start typing data or press F2 while a cell is selected. The reference area shows the currently selected cell. The large area to the right shows the contents being typed or stored in the cell. The Cancel and Enter boxes are visible only when the formula bar is active. You can click on the Cancel box (the X) to cancel the entry or on the OK box (the check mark) to process it. As in other places, Escape has the same effect as Cancel, and Enter has the same effect as OK. While you're typing data, you'll find it

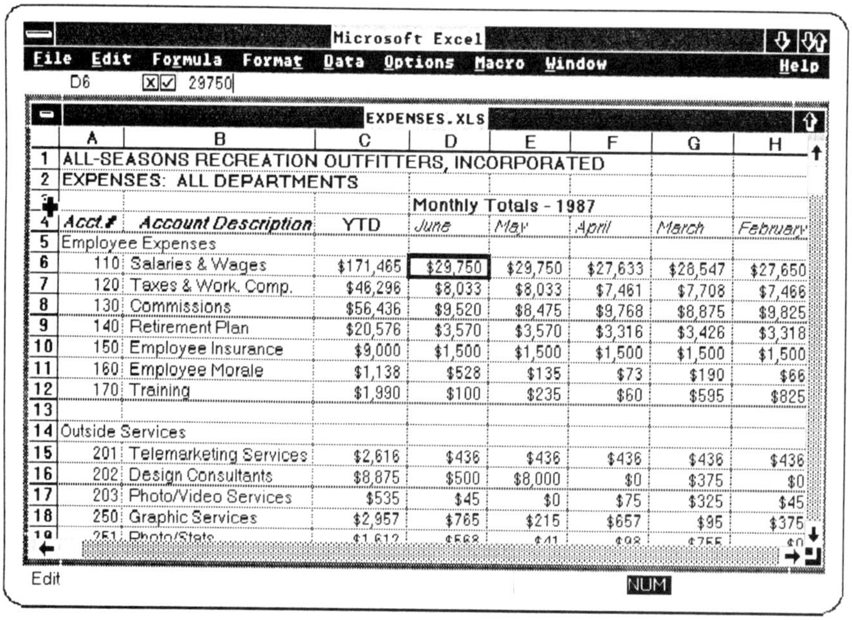

FIGURE 2.1. Formula Bar

easier to press Enter or Escape than to click. If you typed a number or text value, Excel puts it directly in the cell. If you typed a formula or function, Excel puts its value in the cell. If you typed something invalid, Excel puts an error message in the cell. If you're going to type in another cell next, you can press an arrow key or Tab instead of Enter; either one will enter the value into the cell and then move the highlight to the next cell.

Formula Bar Editing

If you start typing while a cell that contains a value is active, the value is erased and the new data appears in the formula bar; if that wasn't what you intended, just press Escape to restore the previous contents immediately. To edit an existing value rather than replace it, press F2 first. The formula bar becomes active with an insertion point at the end of the value, as in Figure 2.1. The insertion point is a flashing vertical bar that indicates where the next character you type will appear. You can move the insertion point with the arrow keys. You can do fairly extensive editing in the formula bar. Figure 2.2 shows the effects of the various editing keys. Notice that you can do most functions that can be done in a word processor. In most cases, you'll find that backspace, delete, and the arrow keys take care of your formula bar editing.

```
Key                 Effect

Home                Beginning of line
CONTROL+Home        Beginning of formula bar
End                 End of line
CONTROL+End         End of formula bar
Arrow               Move one character
CONTROL+Arrow       Move one word

SHIFT+ above        Extends selection

                    Selected characters       Insertion Point
Delete              Deletes them              Deletes char to right
SHIFT+Delete        Cuts                      Deletes char to right
Backspace           Deletes last char         Deletes char to left
SHIFT+Insert        Pastes cut or             Pastes cut or copied
                      copied over sel.          at insertion point
CONTROL+Delete      Delete entire sel.        Delete to end of line
CONTROL+Insert      Copies selection          No effect

CONTROL+;           Insert date in formula bar
CONTROL+:           Insert time in formula bar
```

FIGURE 2.2. Formula Bar Editing Keys

Types of Values

Excel has specific rules that determine whether a value is a number; we'll get to these rules next. Any value that begins with an equal sign (=) is a formula or function. Any value that begins with the pound sign (#) is generated by Excel as a message. If Excel can't tell what the value is, it treats the value as text. Figure 2.3 shows several number and text values.

Number Values

A number value may include the digits 0 through 9, as well as a plus or minus sign, parentheses at the beginning and end only, the letter E or e, commas, and a decimal point. These values are all numbers to Excel: 57, −59.8, (456.009), 14E−23, 4,333.12, and 0. Excel removes any commas and changes parentheses to a minus indicator.

By default, Excel uses a general format for numbers, aligning them on the right. The general format doesn't display any leading zeros before the decimal point or trailing zeros after it. If a numeric value in general format is too large to fit in the cell, Excel converts it to scientific notation; a value such as

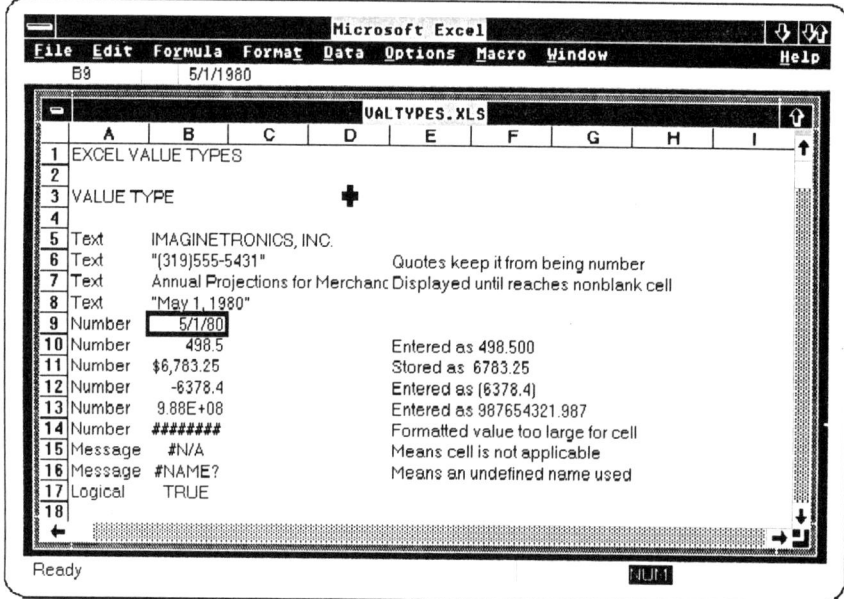

FIGURE 2.3. Text and Number Values

1234567890 appears in the cell as 1.23E+09. You'll learn to change the alignment and formats of values in Chapter 3.

Dates are stored internally as five-digit serial numbers. Date value 00001 represents January 1, 1900. Times are stored as decimal fractions, each representing the time elapsed between the beginning of the day (midnight is 0) and the specified time. For example, .5 is noon and .75 is 6:00 P.M. These internal values allow direct arithmetic to be done with date and time values. Both dates and times are displayed in built-in formats, both in cells and in the formula bar. Calculations using dates and times always use the internal value, however.

Text Values

Typical text entries are worksheet headings, categories, names, and addresses. You can even include longer text passages such as descriptions in a single cell. Excel treats as text any value that doesn't start with an equal sign (=) or pound sign (#) or doesn't meet the criteria for a number. By default, text values are aligned on the left. Excel limits text to about 250 characters. As you type text, the formula bar enlarges. When a line is filled, a new line is added at the bottom. When it can't take any more, you'll see a warning box telling you that the text is too long. You can move the cursor during data entry with arrow keys if you want to do some editing before placing the value in the cell.

If a text value is too long to fit into a cell, Excel lets it extend over cells to the right if they are empty; if the cells to the right contain data, only the first part of the text will display in the cell. You can see examples of both in Figure 2.3. In Chapter 3, you'll learn to justify and rearrange text values in cells.

ENTERING FORMULAS

Formulas are entered a bit differently than text or number values. First type an equal sign (=) to tell Excel a formula is coming. Then type the formula. Formulas can be very simple; you can use =A4 to use the same value as in cell A4. You can use =B4+7 to take the value in cell B4 plus 7. You could use =1.06*C12 to multiply the value in cell C12 by 1.06 and place the result in the current cell. You can use absolute values, such as 7 or 1.06, and cell references as needed. You can use the same arithmetic symbols you use on any calculator. Chapter 5 covers formulas in more detail, including how to use keyboard selection and pasting from other sources in the worksheet. We'll just do the very basic ones in this chapter, so you can get started on your own worksheets.

```
                          Microsoft Excel
File  Edit  Formula  Format  Data  Options  Macro  Window            Help
     D4              =B4*C4
                              WEEKPAY.XLS
         A          B        C        D       E      F      G      H
  1              WEEKLY WORKSHEET
  2
  3  Name         Hours    Wage     Pay
  4  Ruth Ashley      56     24.6    1377.6
  5  Judi Fernandez   36     22.5     810
  6  Paul Ashley      27      7       189
  7  Davida Fernandez 12      6        72
  8  Carisa Yardas    23      6       138
  9  Solomon Allen    40     12       480
 10  Mary Hoogterp    38     10.75    408.5
 11  Thomas Smith     42     10.75    451.5
 12  Carson Smithers  25      9.25    231.25
 13  Darryl Snyder    27      8       216
 14  Michael Sloan    14      7.5     105
 15
 16  Total Payroll                   4478.85
 17
 18
Ready                                                          NUM
```

FIGURE 2.4. Sample Worksheet

When you press Enter after typing a formula, the calculated value appears in the cell. The formula itself remains displayed in the formula bar.

The worksheet in Figure 2.4 uses formulas to calculate values in column D. Each row with hours and wage values uses a formula to multiply the two and place the result in column D. For example, the formula for cell D4 is =B4*C4.

Using Functions

Excel provides more than a hundred built-in functions you can use in worksheets to calculate common values. One of the most used is SUM, which adds values in the specified cells. You can use functions as complete formulas or as parts of more complex formulas. Cell D16 in Figure 2.4 uses the SUM function to add up the individual pay values.

Each function includes a list of arguments or values it needs to calculate a result. SUM can use either values or references. For example, you could use =SUM(5,10,19.8) to add the three values in the parentheses or =SUM(D4,D5,D6,D7,D8,D9,D10,D11,D12,D13,D14) to add up the values in all the named cells. (We'll cover functions in detail in Chapter 5.) To make them really useful, functions can refer to a range of cells. It would be much easier to tell EXCEL to add up all the cells between D4 and D14; you do that by

CREATING WORKSHEETS

connecting the two extremes with a colon as in D4:D14. This reference is called a range. This form of the function reads =SUM(D4:D14) and adds the values in the cells. It even ignores any text cells that get in the way.

Pointing for References

So far, we've covered only the typing of data as a means of getting values into cells. You can also use selection or pointing during typing to make sure the references are correct. Pointing involves selecting cells on the screen while typing in the formula bar. For example, suppose you want to type the SUM function to refer to values in cells B6 and D6.

Steps	Formula Bar contains
Start typing the function.	=SUM(
Select one of the cells with the mouse or keyboard.	=SUM(B6
Type comma (,).	=SUM(B6,
Select the other cell.	=SUM(B6,D6
Type) and press Enter.	=SUM(B6,D6)

Use pointing to make sure references in formulas or functions are correct. You can also use pointing to select ranges.

SELECTING RANGES

Many operations in Excel require you to select a range of adjacent cells; the cells can be in one or more rows or columns, but they must form a rectangular set of cells. As you know, a cell reference may look like A1 or C6. A range reference specifies the cells in the upper left and lower right corners of the rectangle. It is expressed as two cell references connected by a colon; A1:C6 refers to the rectangle with cell A1 at the upper left and C6 at the lower right; it contains 18 cells in all. The range B2:B6 includes five cells; C3:D8 contains 12 cells.

You can select a range with the mouse or the keyboard; in either case, start by making the cell in any corner active. With the mouse, hold down the button and drag until the entire desired range is selected. Then release. With the

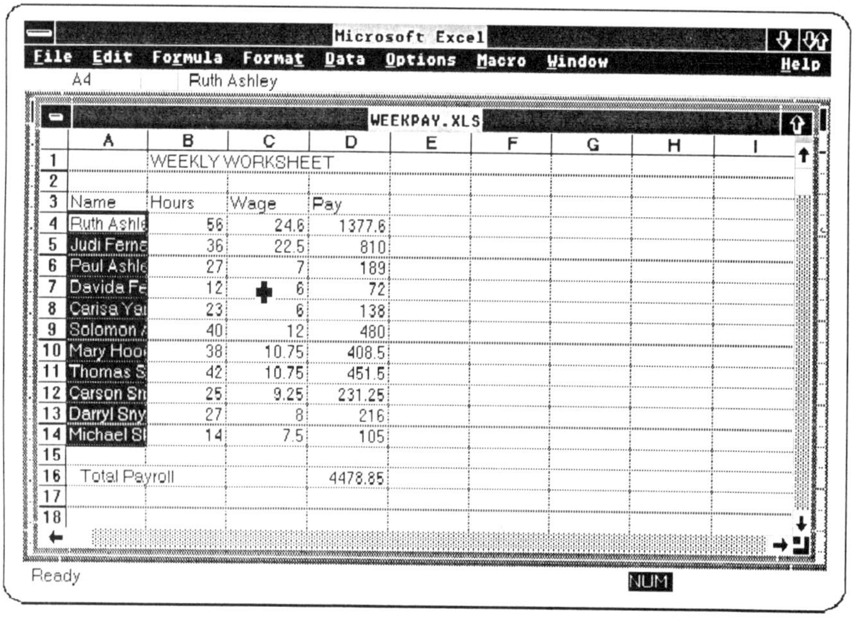

FIGURE 2.5. Range Selected

keyboard, hold down the SHIFT key and use the arrow keys to select the desired range. Alternatively, you can press F8 to turn on the Extend function, then select the range with the arrow keys; press F8 again to turn Extend off. The range is highlighted, and the current cell is still indicated; it is the one at the corner where you started selecting the range. Figure 2.5 shows a range selected on a worksheet.

You can select a range while editing in the formula bar by selecting the first corner and extending the selection. Watch how it reads in the formula bar itself.

To change the active cell within the range with the keyboard, use Tab to move to the right, SHIFT+Tab to move to the left. Use Enter to move down, SHIFT+Enter to move up. With these keys, the active cell won't leave the selected range. If you use an arrow key or PageUp or PageDown, however, the range selection is lost.

To change the active cell within the range with the mouse, hold down the control key while you click. If you click without pressing the control key, the range is deselected and lost.

Excel has a way of letting you select nonadjacent cells at the same time; this is called a multiple selection. Multiple selections can contain any number of individual cells and ranges; they are covered in Chapter 4.

CREATING WORKSHEETS

SUGGESTED EXERCISE

1. If Excel isn't up, bring it up so the SHEET1 worksheet is displayed.
2. Enter data in the form of the worksheet in Figure 2.5. Use a title and column headings. Enter a name, an hours value, and a wages value for at least five people, real or imaginary. Just enter the text and number values first.
3. Select a range containing only the names. Use Tab or CONTROL+click to change the active cell. Next select a range containing all the numbers. Move within it to get the feel of it.
4. Enter a formula to find the product of the hours and wages and place the value in the row with the first name.
5. Enter a function to find the total number of hours worked by all names. Place the value in the row below the last data values you placed.

What if It Doesn't Work?

1. Don't worry if the full text value doesn't appear in the cell. You'll learn to adjust column width next.
2. If your formula and function don't work, check the format. Did you use a leading equal sign? Are your cell references right?
3. If you have trouble selecting ranges or moving within them, use the Help system. Select Keyboard from the Help menu, then select Worksheet Keys. From that list, select Moving Within a Selection.

CHANGING COLUMN WIDTH AND ROW HEIGHT

When you open a new worksheet, as in SHEET1, all the columns are the same width and the rows the same height. For example, suppose you want a name in a column, as in the exercise. You'll need more than the standard width to fit in a name like John Fitzgerald Kennedy. Or suppose a column will contain one-letter codes. It wastes space on the screen to use the standard width. You can change the width of a column; you have to change the entire column, throughout the entire worksheet, to keep it consistent. You can also change the height of a row. Instead of leaving a blank row after your headings, for example, you might have a double height row for the first person to leave space. You'll learn more reasons for changing row height in Chapter 3.

One of the early things you'll want to do is change the default column width in a worksheet. This is done through the Format menu, shown in Figure 2.6. The Row Height and Column Width commands work in much the same way. To

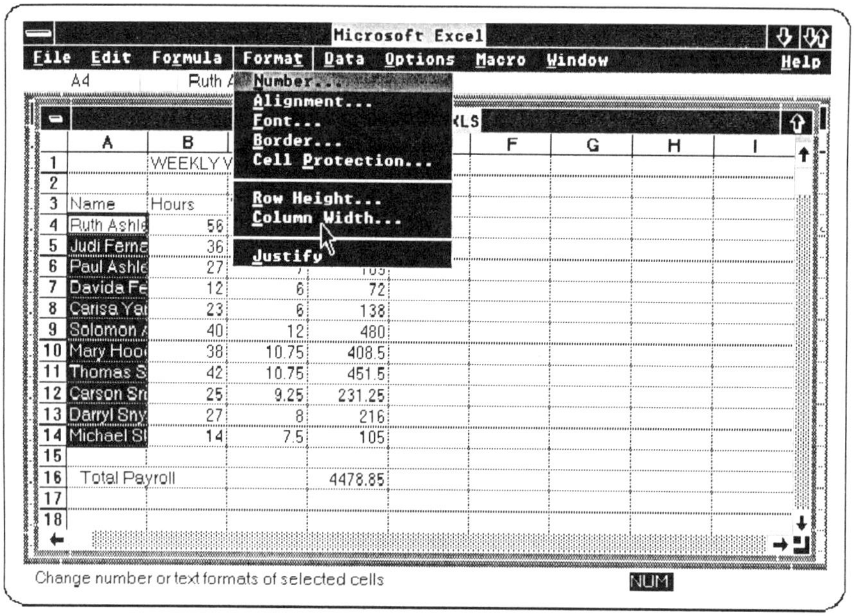

FIGURE 2.6. Format Menu

adjust one row or column, just select a cell in that row or column. Then select Format Column Width or Format Row Height. We'll focus on Format Column Width here. When you select it, you see the dialog box shown in Figure 2.7.

The current column width for the selected cell is shown in the text box. Since the Excel program uses proportional width characters by default, the default width is represented as 8.43; this allows 8 characters to fit comfortably. When you change it, you can use a whole number for convenience. To return to the standard width, turn on the check box in the Standard Width field. When you've entered the value you want, press Enter or click OK. The column is adjusted. The row height is adjusted in the same way. Figure 2.8 shows two worksheets with the same values. The upper one has had the column width and row height adjusted for easy reading.

You can adjust the column width and row height as often as necessary. If a single cell is selected, you can adjust either its width or height; any changes affect the entire column or row. You can select a complete column by pressing CONTROL + Spacebar, then adjust its width or the height of every row. You can select a complete row by pressing SHIFT + Spacebar, then adjust its height or the width of every column. To adjust the width of several columns at once, select cells in those columns as a range (SHIFT + arrow keys) before selecting the Format Column Width command. To adjust the height of several rows at

CREATING WORKSHEETS

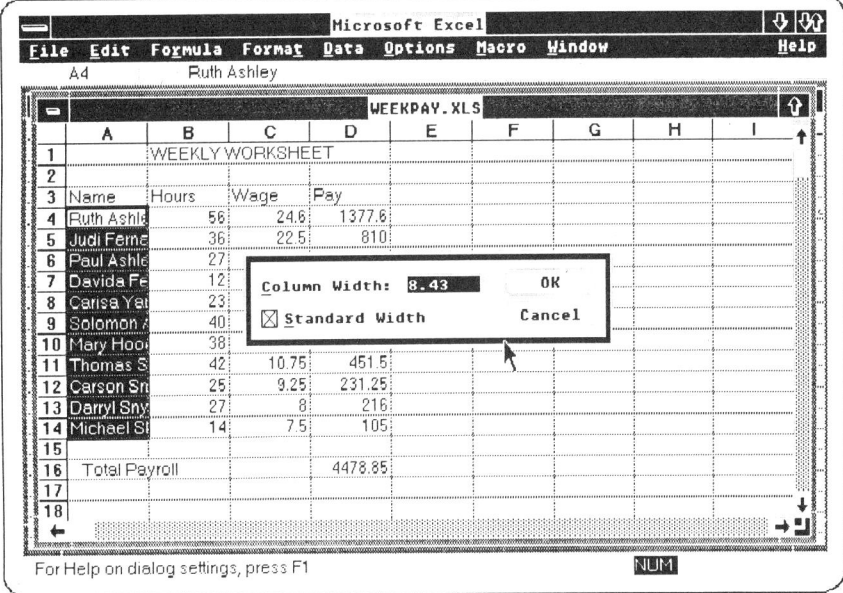

FIGURE 2.7. Column Width Dialog Box

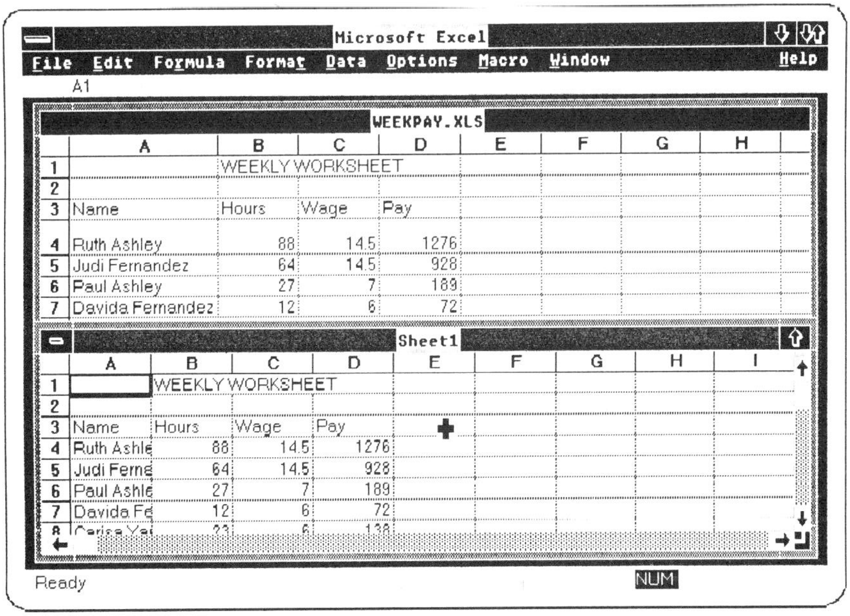

FIGURE 2.8. Adjusted Columns and Rows

38 ADVANCED EXCEL

once, select cells in those rows as a range before selecting the Format Row Height command. The measurement box is blank if cells of several different heights or widths are selected.

For example, suppose you want to use narrower columns for columns B, C, and D in the WEEKPAY.XLS worksheet. Select a range in any row that includes columns B, C, and D. Then select Format Column Width. Enter a smaller number in the column width text box, such as 6, then choose OK. All three columns are adjusted.

USING THE EDIT MENU

Excel's Edit Menu includes commands you can use to rearrange, duplicate, and remove values and cells from your worksheet. Figure 2.9 shows the menu. We'll cover all the commands except Paste Link in this chapter. The top two commands vary depending on the editing you have just done. If Undo is available, it reverses the action you have just taken. If you have just pasted something into the worksheet, Undo Paste appears; if you have just performed a sort, Undo Sort appears; if you have just entered data, Undo Entry appears. When you

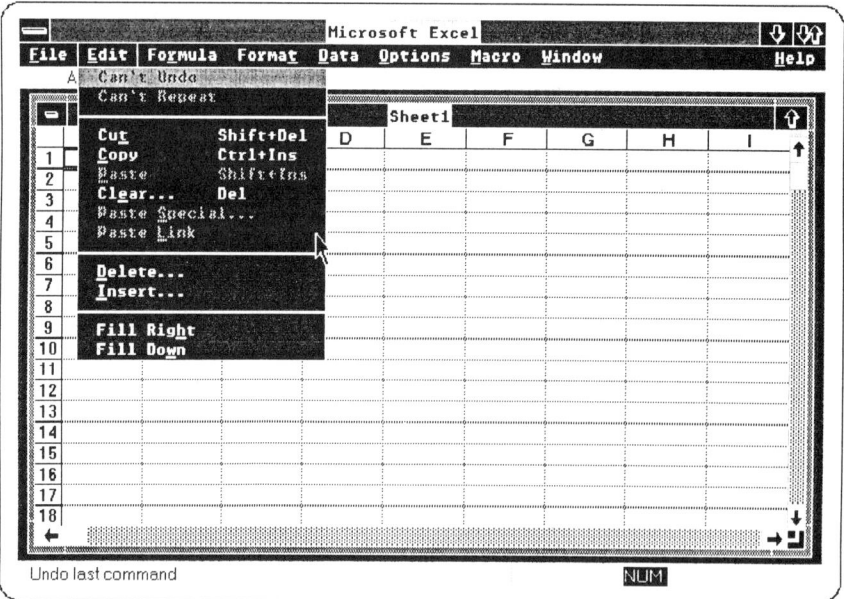

FIGURE 2.9. Edit Menu

CREATING WORKSHEETS

select Undo, the former operation is undone. If the previous action can't be undone, the menu contains Can't Undo and the command isn't available. The Repeat command works much the same way. If the last action can't be repeated, Can't Repeat appears in the menu and the command isn't available. If Repeat Entry, Repeat Sort, or a similar command is in the menu, selecting it causes the mentioned action to be repeated.

All the Edit commands require that you select the cells to be acted upon before selecting the command. For example, if you want to copy cells, you must first select them, then use Edit Copy.

FILLING ADJACENT CELLS

It is often necessary to copy a value from one cell to adjacent ones. For example, suppose every employee in your company worked 40 hours. You could type 40 in the first hours cell, then tell Excel to fill the rest with the same value. To do that, you first type the single value, then select the range that includes the value to be copied and the cells to which it is to be copied. Then select the Edit Fill Down command. Figure 2.10 shows how the screen looks at this time.

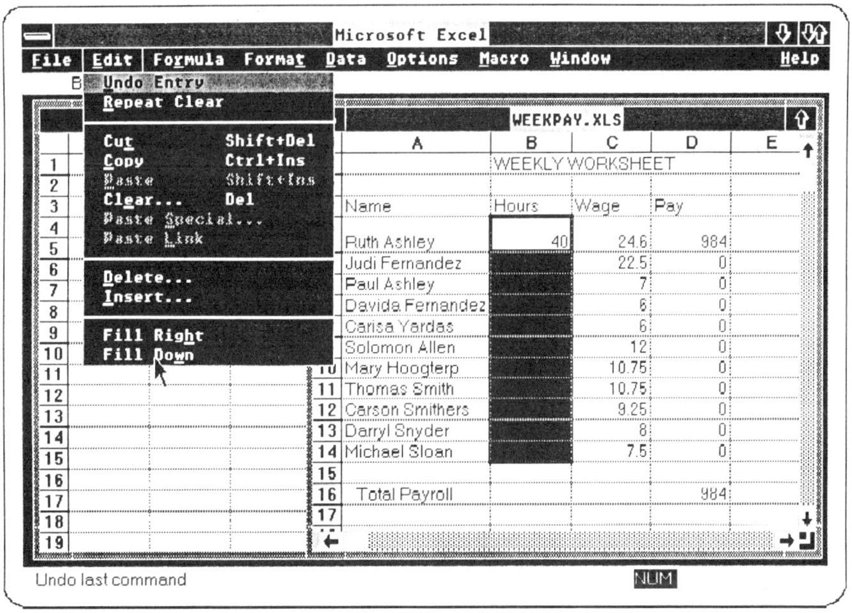

FIGURE 2.10. Filling Adjacent Cells

When you choose the command or press Enter, the cells are immediately filled with the same value. Our value to be copied was at the top of the range, so we selected Edit Fill Down. If the value to be copied was at the left and the range extended to the right, we could use Edit Fill Right. These two options cover most filling situations. If you happen to have to fill up (from the bottom cell of a range) or to the left (from the rightmost cell in a range), hold down the shift key while selecting the edit command. The menu will show Fill Left and Fill Up as the last two commands.

The range selected for an Edit Fill command can include more than one row or column; values from the appropriate cells are used to fill the selected cells. To fill a range with a single value, first fill the cells to the right or down, then use the other command; the original value is placed in every selected cell.

COPYING CELLS

When you copy a cell to another location, Excel puts another copy of it there without affecting the original location. Suppose you need another set of the names from a worksheet in a second location. You can select the already entered set as a range and copy it to the other spot.

The first step is to select the cell or range to be copied. Then select the Edit menu, shown earlier in Figure 2.9. Then select Copy. The menu disappears and the selected cell or range is surrounded by a moving marquee, much like flashing theater lights. The message "Copy (Select destination and press Enter or choose Paste)" appears in the status bar. Figure 2.11 shows the screen at this point.

Then use either the keyboard or the mouse to select the destination; you can select a single cell to represent the upper left corner of the range. If you select the complete range, it must be the same size and shape as the copied range. Finally, press Enter or select Edit Paste.

If the data to be copied is text or numbers, it is copied unchanged. Formulas might be adjusted to suit their new location. A cell reference such as B16 or D8 is a relative reference; Excel determines the target cell's actual location from the location of the cell containing the reference. When a formula containing such a reference is moved or copied to another location, Excel adapts the reference so that it refers to the same relative cell, maintaining the same relationship between the original cell reference and its target as between the newly located cell reference and its target. Suppose cell G7 contains the formula =D7*2. Cell G7 is three cells to the left of D7, in the same row. If you copy cell G7 to cell G10, Excel modifies the formula so that it becomes =G7*2;

CREATING WORKSHEETS

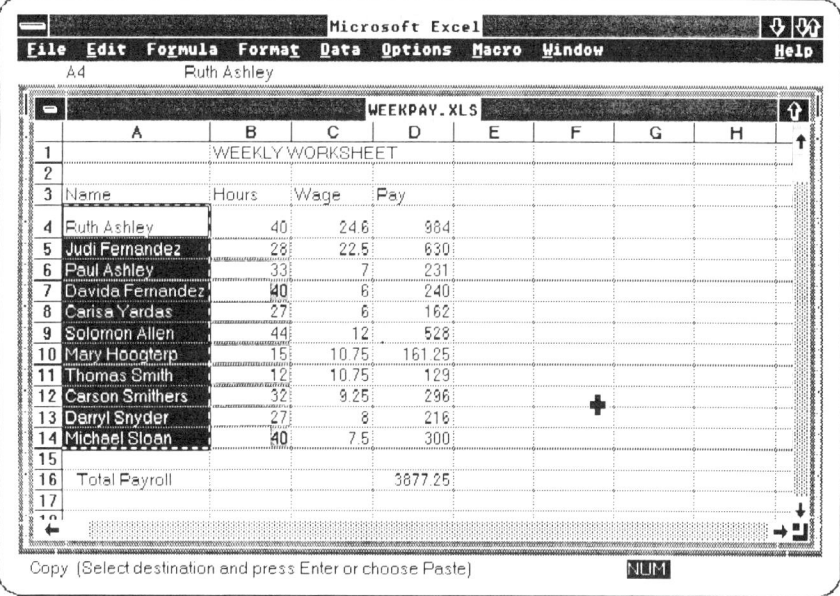

FIGURE 2.11. Copying a Range

it then refers to a cell in the same relative location as that referred to in the original reference.

You can copy a single constant value to a range of cells; Excel places the value in each target cell. If you copy a single formula to a range of cells, Excel converts it appropriately for every target cell. If the target cells contain values prior to the move or copy, the earlier values are overlaid and destroyed in the process. Be sure you don't need the former data before you do this. Undo copy can rescue the situation, but you must do it immediately, before any other undoable action.

It makes a difference whether you press Enter or select Paste to complete a copy. If you press Enter, the copy is done, the marquee disappears, and the operation is over. If you select Edit Paste, the marquee remains and you can paste the range in another location as well. When you press Enter or Escape, Excel returns to ready mode and you can't paste the data again.

The Edit Copy command also works when you are editing in the formula bar, as does Edit Paste.

Undoing a Copy or Fill

Excel lets you change your mind after a copy or fill operation is done. Just select Edit Undo; at this point it reads Undo Copy or Undo Paste. The data is removed from the new location and restored in its original location. Undo also restores any data that was overlaid in the process.

Efficient Data Entry

If you know in advance a value or formula will be copied to adjacent cells, you can do the initial entry and copy in a single step. First select the range of cells that must contain the same value. Type the value or formula in the active cell. Then press CONTROL + Enter instead of just Enter. The value appears in each cell of the selected range.

CUTTING CELLS (MOVING)

Sometimes you don't want to copy data but move it completely. You can select the part of the formula, the cell, or the range you want to move or cut from its current location. Then select Edit Cut. When the marquee appears around the cells to be removed, select the new location. If you are cutting a range, you can select just the upper left corner of the destination location. If you select a destination range, it must be the same size and shape as the original range. Once you select a new location, the selected cell(s) disappear from their original location and occupy the new one.

You can undo a cut just as you undo copy. If you select Edit, you'll see Undo Paste on the menu; select it and the cells are removed from where you pasted them and put back where you cut them from. To cut cells and paste them in several locations, you can use a multiple selection for the paste area. Multiple selections are covered in Chapter 4.

SELECTIVE PASTING

So far, you've been using the Edit Paste command to copy data to new locations. Excel also has the Edit Paste Special command. This command is available only after Copy; you can't use it following a Cut command. Figure 2.12 shows the resulting dialog box. You can use this command to paste selectively or to perform operations on the values in cells during the paste. The

CREATING WORKSHEETS 43

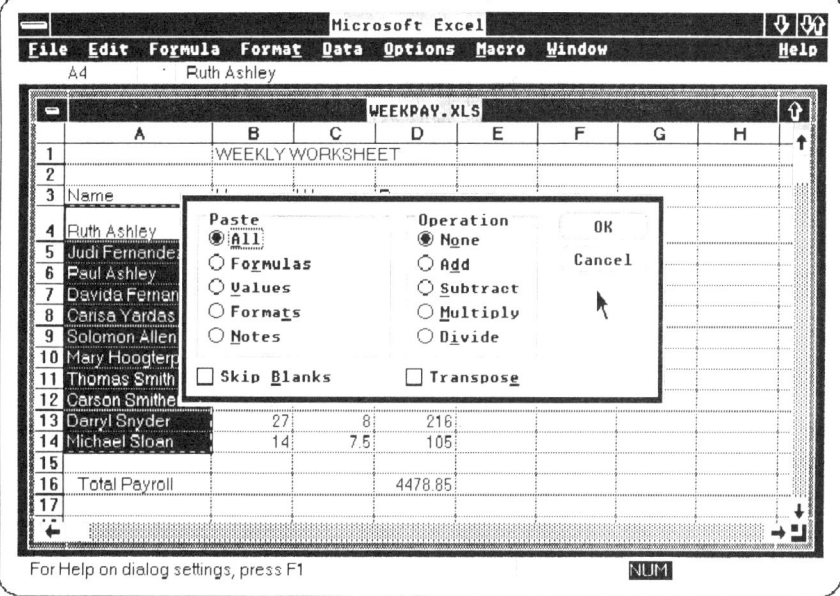

FIGURE 2.12. Edit Paste Special Dialog Box

default Paste operation, None, has the same effect as the basic Edit Paste command. If you select Formulas, Values, Formats, or Notes, just the selected component is pasted in the destination cells. The most useful one here is Values; you could copy the current values from a set of cells that contain formulas. The current values will be placed in the new locations but the formulas themselves won't be. This can be useful in creating summary reports, for example.

The operation options work differently; if you select anything except None, the operation will be applied to the current values in the target cells. For example, if you have a range that contains a year-to-date salary value for each employee, you might copy the monthly values to that range with the Add operation. The monthly values you are copying will be added to the current values in the destination range instead of overlaying them. While this is effective, it doesn't leave any documentation trail; other users may not be able to figure out where you got the values in your worksheet.

The Skip Blanks field tells Excel not to bother with blanks in the copy area while pasting; that means the paste won't change target cells that were blank in the source area so those corresponding cells will be unchanged in the destination area. The transpose field tells Excel to reverse the row/column orientation of the range in pasting. That means to put what were rows in the copied area vertically in the destination area.

EMPTYING CELLS

Excel offers several ways to empty out cells; all work with the current selection, whether that is a cell, a range, or more. The methods have different effects, so you have to consider what effect you want. Do you want the cell to be empty? Use the Edit Clear command. Do you want the cell to go away completely so that other cells slide over to fill the space? Use the Edit Delete command.

Clearing a Cell or Range

To empty a cell, select the Edit Clear command or press the Delete key. You'll see the dialog box shown in Figure 2.13. You can turn on any one of the listed choices. The default, Formulas, erases anything that appears in the formula bar for the cell or selection. The Formats choice removes any format set for the cell. The Notes choice removes any notes attached to the cell. If you select All, the formula, format, and notes are all gone. Generally, you'll just want to remove Formulas. That also takes care of constant values. If you later put a different value in the cell, you'll probably want the same format. Notes are covered in detail in Chapter 4.

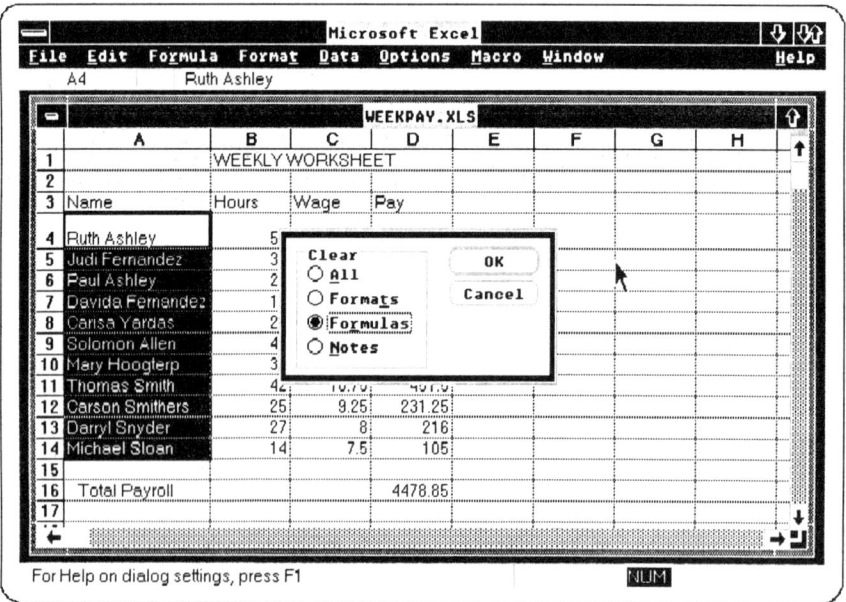

FIGURE 2.13. Edit Clear (Del Key) Dialog Box

CREATING WORKSHEETS 45

Removing a Cell or Range

To remove a cell or range completely, select the cell or range, then select the Edit Delete command. This results in the dialog box shown in Figure 2.14. When Excel deletes cells with this command, the cells and their contents are completely gone. Since we can't have a blank space with no cells in the middle of the worksheet, you have to specify what cells should shift over to fill the space. They must come from the outer edge of the worksheet; cells can shift left or up. If you select entire rows (SHIFT + Spacebar, followed by SHIFT + arrow keys to extend it), Excel automatically shifts cells up. If you select entire columns (CONTROL + Spacebar, followed by SHIFT + arrow keys to extend it), Excel automatically shifts cells to the left. If you select just part of a row or column, though, you may get a mess. Be sure you know what you are asking. If you remove a range that includes several rows and a few columns of a worksheet, with active cells adjacent, you probably don't want to use Edit Delete. Figure 2.15 shows the effect of using Edit Delete on a range in a worksheet. We deleted the numeric data but left the column headings so you can see what happened. Notice that the data no longer can be used as a coherent worksheet. The process doesn't change any column width effects, as you can see.

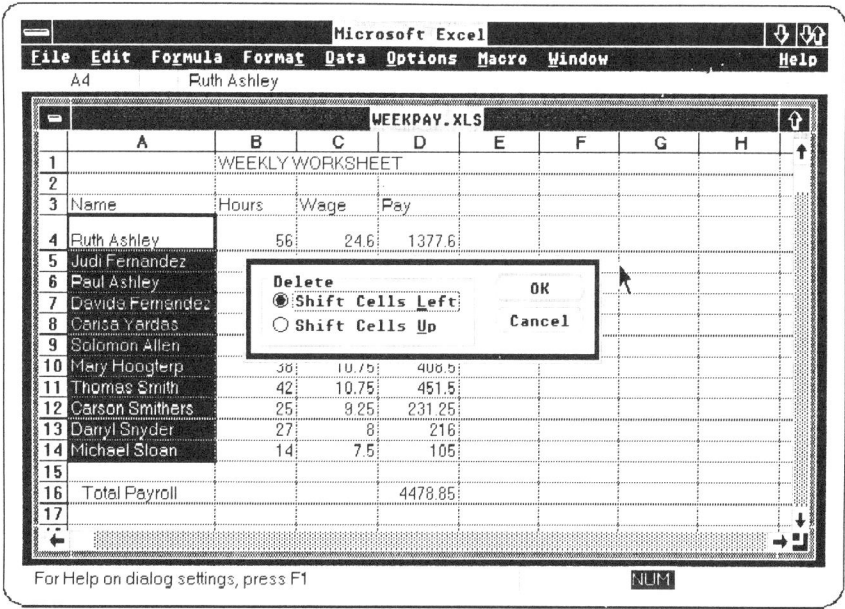

FIGURE 2.14. Edit Delete Dialog Box

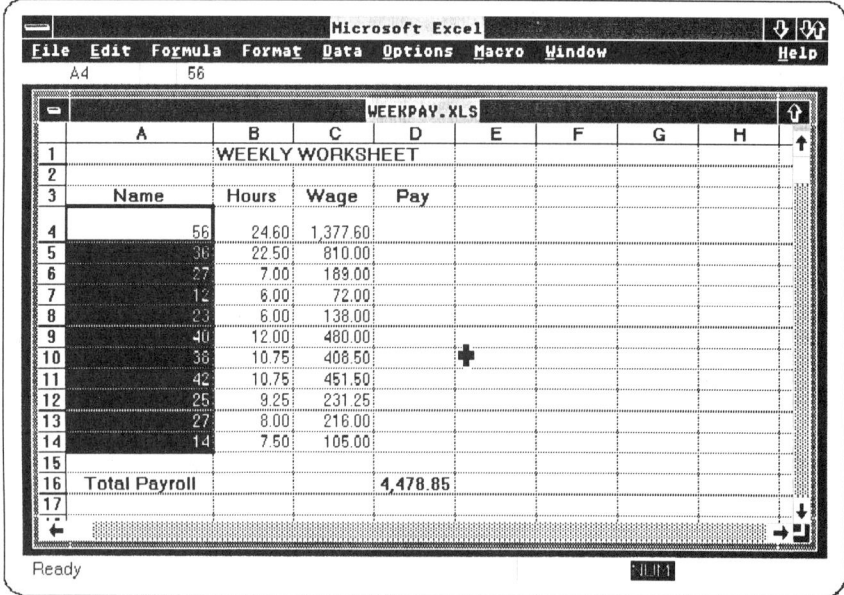

FIGURE 2.15. Worksheet with Cells Deleted

INSERTING ROWS OR COLUMNS

Excel lets you insert rows or columns using the Edit Insert command. The resulting dialog box is similar to that for Edit Delete, but the effect is different. If you want to insert a complete new row in the middle of a worksheet, select the row with the number you want to insert. To insert a new row 4, use SHIFT+Spacebar to select the current row 4. Then select Edit Insert. A blank row 4 appears and the other rows are shoved down. To insert 5 blank rows above the current row 4, use SHIFT+Spacebar to select row 4, then use SHIFT+downarrow to extend the selection four more rows before you choose Edit Insert. Blank rows 4 through 8 are inserted and the other rows are shoved down.

If you select less than a full row or column, you have to select the direction in which cells should be shifted to make room for the insert. You won't generally use less than a full row unless you have several separate spreadsheets on the same worksheet. While this is legitimate, it can cause problems if you have to add or remove rows and columns from the separate areas.

CREATING WORKSHEETS

CHANGING CALCULATION TIME

Excel calculates formulas when you enter them; normally, it continually recalculates the worksheet as you work with it. Excel is intelligent about this; it only recalculates the cells that are affected by a new value. But the recalculation may slow you down occasionally. For example, suppose you have a large worksheet containing budget data for several hundred categories. These are summed at the bottoms of columns and at the ends of rows. When you are entering new values, you may want to tell Excel to wait before calculating. To do that, select the Calculation command from the Options menu. Figure 2.16 shows the resulting dialog box. One of the upper three buttons is always on. The default is automatic, as you've seen. Manual means that Excel calculates only when you tell it to. We'll cover the other commands later in the book.

Once manual calculation is set, you have to tell Excel when to calculate the worksheet. When you do, it recalculates the entire thing. The Options Calculate Now command has the desired effect. Any time you find that your worksheet doesn't show correct calculated values, check the calculation setting. You may have set it to manual.

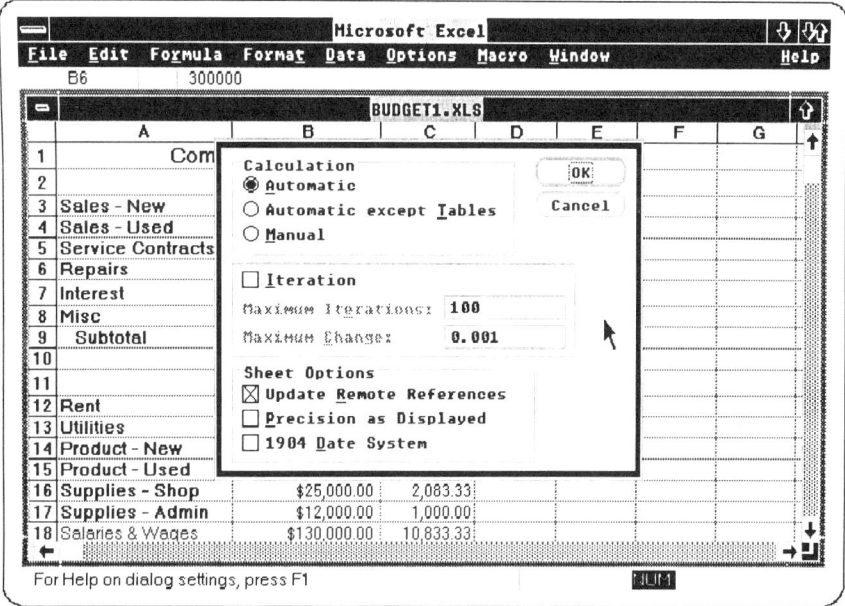

FIGURE 2.16. Options Calculation Dialog Box

MENU LENGTHS

You can tell Excel to show you short or full menus. We've been acting under the assumption that you have the full menus on your system. If you do not, check the Options menu. The last command is either Full Menus or Short Menus, whichever is not in effect at the moment. Some people prefer to work with Short Menus. Most people don't find that seeing the extra commands gets in their way. In fact, they may remind you of other Excel features that you haven't tried.

SUGGESTED EXERCISE

1. Bring up your worksheet. Adjust the column widths so you can see all your values.
2. Change the row height on one of the rows to see the effect. Then reset it to standard height.
3. Copy the set of names to a position lower on the worksheet.
4. Use Edit Fill Down to copy the single formula you entered to calculate total pay to the rest of the appropriate cells.
5. Use Edit Copy to copy the pay values to the column next to the new set of names. Use Paste to place the same set of values in several different locations. Then use Undo Paste to remove the last one.
6. Use Edit Clear to remove extra values from the worksheet.
7. Insert two new blank rows between the last name row in your first worksheet section and the row that contains the SUM function. Examine the SUM function and notice that the cell reference has changed. Then delete the new blank lines.
8. Practice with editing in the formula bar, cut, and copy some more until you feel comfortable with them.

What if It Doesn't Work?

1. If you have trouble with fill, cut, copy, and paste, check the Help system. And try again. Remember to select the item to be affected first.
2. If you have trouble inserting rows, remember to select an entire row (SHIFT+Spacebar), then use SHIFT+arrow to extend it before using Edit Insert. The active selected row is pushed down.
3. Work on these if you have troubles; the edit functions covered in this chapter are essential to Excel operations.

SUMMARY

This chapter covered the basics of entering and editing data in Excel worksheets. You learned to enter text and number values as well as simple formulas and functions. You also learned to handle such editing functions as selecting, copying, cutting, pasting, inserting, deleting, and filling cells. You've learned to work with both individual cells and ranges for all the covered functions.

By now, you should be comfortable with the basics of Excel. You can create a worksheet, modify it, and manipulate it. The next chapter treats formatting and modifying the onscreen display in more detail.

3 POLISHING THE WORKSHEET

Formatting data and arranging the display are crucial to efficient worksheet manipulation. In this chapter, you'll see how to use and manipulate the standard formats, as well as how to create others in order to better meet your needs. You'll learn to manipulate text and numbers, in a single cell and over a range of cells. You'll see how to use borders and shading to focus attention on a part of the worksheet, in this way creating the ideal display or printouts for you and your audience. Various other display options, including additional fonts, can also enhance the presentation of your data.

Excel also has special ways of storing and displaying times and dates. You'll see how to handle the default formats and how to define your own.

THE FORMAT MENU

The Format menu allows you to arrange the format of text and numbers in worksheet cells. Figure 3.1 shows the menu. You've already learned to use the Row Height and Column Width commands. In this chapter we will cover the rest of the Format menu commands, except for Cell Protection, which is covered later. Alignment and Justify apply mostly to text entries. Number applies to number entries, including dates and times; it can also be used to add text to number entries. Border and Font can apply to any cell.

Aligning Entries

By default, data in cells is aligned according to a general alignment formula. Text is aligned on the left, numbers on the right; this means that text entries start at the left edge of the cell and numbers start at the right. If you have text data that looks like numbers, such as phone numbers or zip codes, Excel aligns it on the right like all numbers; you might want to align it on the left so it

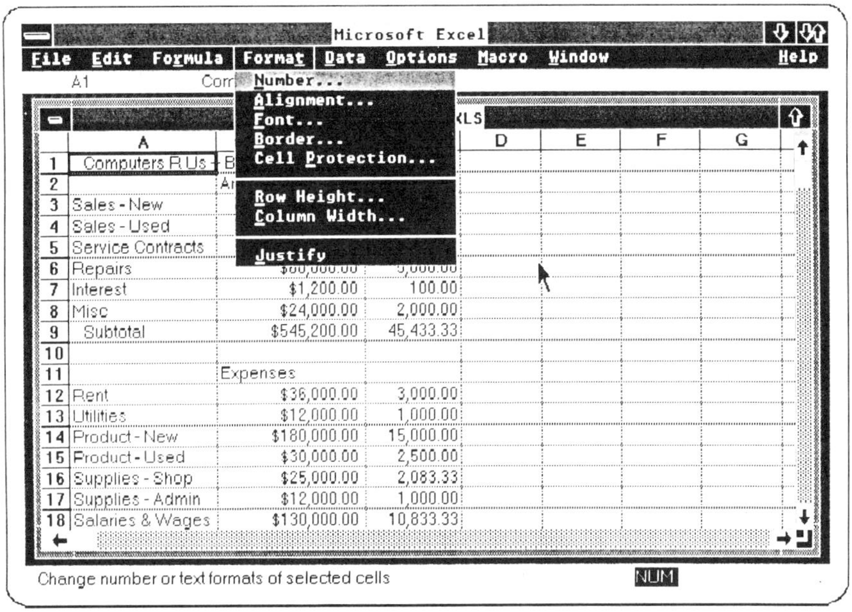

POLISHING THE WORKSHEET

FIGURE 3.1. Format Menu

matches the other text data. You can change the alignment for a single cell or a range without affecting the value that is stored in the cell by selecting the cell(s) to be realigned, then selecting Format Alignment. Excel presents you with the dialog box shown in Figure 3.2.

Just choose the alignment you want for the selected data; only one option is valid per selection. Left or Right leaves spaces on the right or left respectively. If you center a value in a cell that has empty cells adjacent on each side, the centered value may display into both adjacent cells. If a cell on either side contains values, the data is still centered in the original cell, but it extends only on the side with an empty cell.

If you choose Fill, Excel truncates the display or repeats the value in the cell to fill it. If the value is too long for the cell, selecting Fill causes only what fits in the cell to display, even if the adjacent cells are empty. If the value is too short for the cell (or the selection), it is repeated to fill it. If selected cells to the right are empty, they too are filled by the Format Alignment Fill command. But formatting doesn't change the stored value. If cell A3 contains only an asterisk (*) and you want a row of asterisks to appear, you can select cells A3:F3, then select Format Alignment Fill. A complete six-column-wide string of asterisks appears on the screen, but the formula bar still shows one asterisk in cell A3 and no contents in cells B3:F3. If you then add data to one of those filled cells, say C3, whatever you add becomes the contents of that cell, and it is filled to

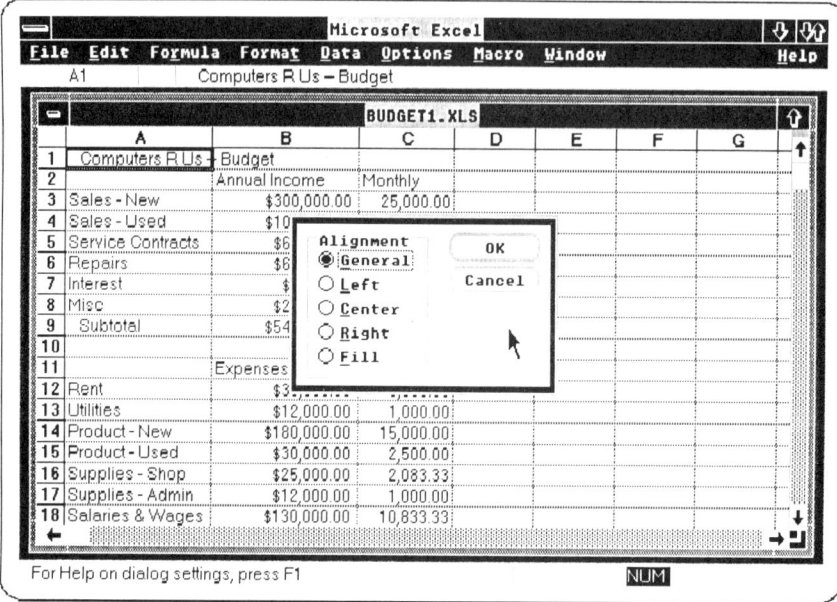

FIGURE 3.2. Format Alignment Dialog Box

the end of the original selection. You'll have to change the alignment to get rid of the fill effect.

None of the alignment options have any effect on what is actually stored in the cells; they affect only how it displays. And since the data prints as it displays, the alignment options also affect the print. So you can use alignment options to arrange headings, labels, and data. For example, you can center a heading over a worksheet range by entering the data approximately in the center cell, then using Format Alignment Center to arrange it. Formatting never changes the actual data in the cell.

Justifying Text

Normally, Excel places text in the active cell. You may want to spread a block of text, such as a paragraph of explanation, across a range of cells. You can arrange this by first entering the text in a single cell or vertical series of cells. Figure 3.3 shows an example. The top row is all contained in A3, the next row in A4, and so forth. Don't worry if it doesn't all display; notice that the contents of A6 and A8 run off the screen in the figure.

The Format Justify command takes text in the leftmost cells in a range and distributes it evenly among the selected range so that each line is as long as possible within the range. Figure 3.4 shows the text from Figure 3.3 after it has

POLISHING THE WORKSHEET

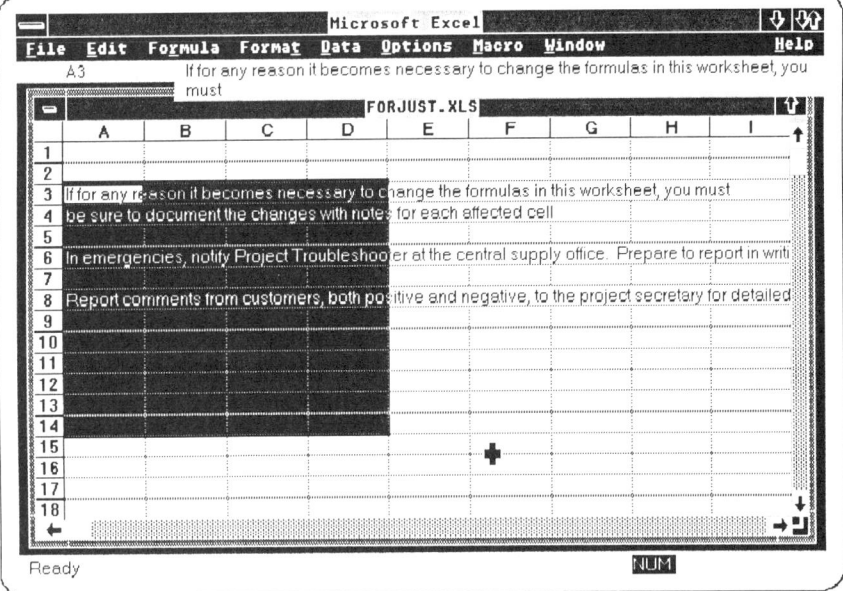

FIGURE 3.3. Text to Be Justified

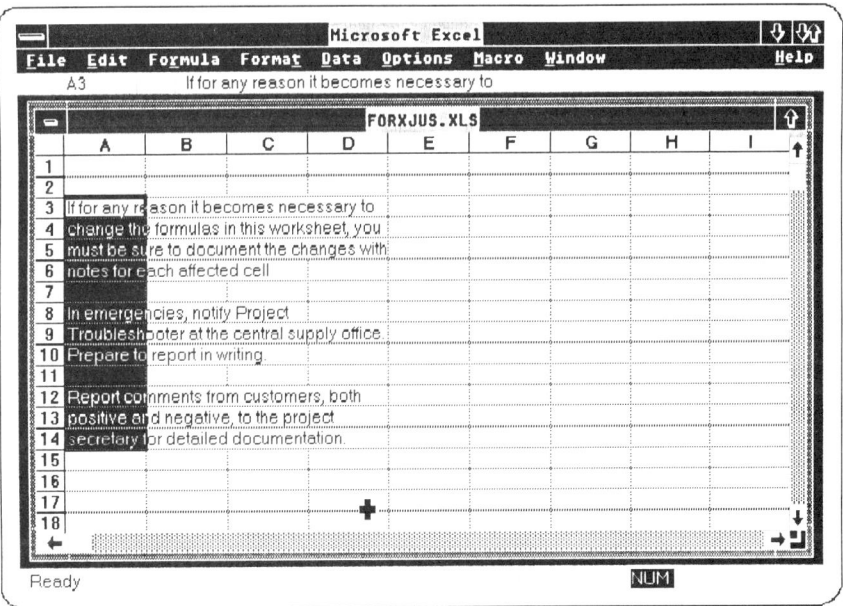

FIGURE 3.4. Justified Text in a Range

been justified. In the process Excel moved text values from one cell to the adjacent vertical cell.

Before the Format Justify command is used, the leftmost cells in the selected range must contain text or be blank; the others cells in the range can contain anything, but the contents will be destroyed in the justification process. After justification, the first column of cells in the justified range contain text or are blank; all other cells in the range are blank. Where a blank cell appeared in the leftmost column in the original layout, Excel leaves a blank line and starts a new paragraph. Text in cells is combined into a single paragraph until a blank cell in the first column appears. Then Excel starts another paragraph after a blank cell in the leftmost column.

If you select a range too short for the justified result, Excel asks if it is OK to extend below it. Be careful before you say Yes; justified text overlays current data and destroys it. You can Undo or Repeat a justification, just like many other commands. However, once you've done something else, the justification can't be undone.

FORMATTING NUMBERS

Excel uses a default general format for number entries. It also has default formats for dates and times; the default it uses depends on how you enter the number, date, or time. In this section, we'll look at the default and built-in number formats you can use and see how you can define new ones. As with most commands, you first select the cells to be affected. You can select a single cell, a range, or even the entire worksheet, but all selected cells will be set to the same format. When you select Format Numbers, you see the dialog box shown in Figure 3.5. You select the format from the list box and choose OK. The selected cell formats are changed. Formatting doesn't change what is actually stored, just how it appears on screen.

Each format shown in the list box is a character string that represents a specific style in which values will be displayed. In the General format, numbers are displayed with no leading zeros before the decimal point or trailing zeros after it. If the value is too large for the cell, it is shown as precisely as possible. Decimal places may be dropped or the value may be displayed in scientific notation. If that won't fit either, the cell is filled with pound signs (#). Any time calculations are done, Excel uses the internal stored value unless you tell it otherwise. If text is entered in a cell formatted for numbers, it displays as general text, aligned on the left.

POLISHING THE WORKSHEET   55

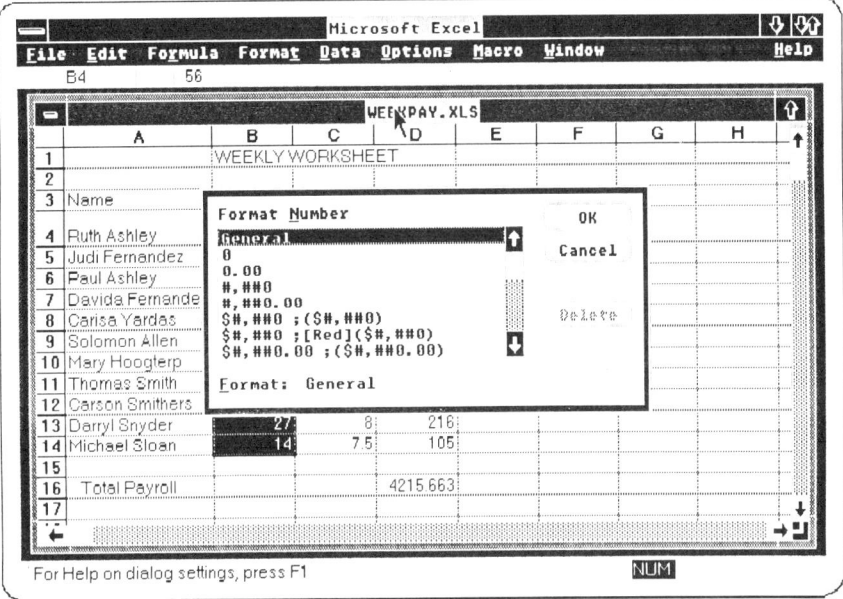

FIGURE 3.5.   Format Numbers Dialog Box

Format Symbols

With just a bit of information, you'll be able to interpret the built-in formats and customize your own. These are the most common symbols Excel uses to show a picture of a format:

marks a digit position; leading or trailing zeros are not displayed. A format of #.# displays the value zero as blank, 2.2 as 2.2, 2. as 2, and 0.2 as .2.

0   also marks a digit position with leading or trailing zeros displayed. The value 0 displays. A picture of 0.0 always results in at least one digit on each side of the decimal point. The value 2. displays as 2.0, the value .2 displays as 0.2.

.   marks the decimal point. Excel aligns the value's decimal point with the decimal point in the format for display. If digits on both sides are not displayed as in #.# with value 0, the decimal point is suppressed as well.

%   means to convert the value to a percent and display it with the percent symbol. Excel multiplies the value by 100 in any calculation.

separates thousands. If the comma does not have a displayed digit to its left, it is suppressed. You can use two commas in a row or a comma followed by a period to scale numbers. For example, ###,. causes the value 789654 to be displayed as 790.; the value is scaled to the nearest thousand and rounded. The picture ###,, causes the same value to be displayed as 1 (rounded to the nearest million).

E− E+ which could also be shown as e− e+, indicates scientific notation. The number of digit positions (0 or #) to the right of the symbol determines the number of digits in the exponent. A minus sign displays only if the exponent is negative. A plus sign displays a plus sign or minus sign, whichever is appropriate for the value. If you aren't familiar with scientific notation, don't worry about it. If it appears on your worksheet and you want to get rid of it, use Format Column Width to widen the column and allow a normal numeric display.

You can use additional symbols in a format. If you use a dollar sign ($), a colon (:), a plus (+) or minus sign (−), a space, or parentheses (to indicate a negative value), it is displayed as requested. You can insert any other character by enclosing it in double quotes or preceding each character with a backslash (\). You can include standard format symbols such as − or ( ) in the same way, by using quotes or preceding each with a backslash. Wherever you put the character in the number picture, the inserted character appears in the display.

For example, the number picture "Account #: "00-0000 causes the entered value 456456 to be displayed as Account #: 45-6456, aligned at the right. To cause a string of ten digits to be displayed as a phone number in the form (000)000-0000, use the picture \(000\)000\-0000. If an inserted character, such as a dollar sign, precedes a string of # characters, it is inserted immediately before the first displayed digit. If it precedes a string of 0 characters, zeros may follow the inserted character.

Another character you can use in a picture is the asterisk (*). This tells Excel to repeat the next character to fill the column width. Only one asterisk can appear in a format. A picture of ##,###*− causes the value 763 to appear in a standard width column as 763−−−−−−−. If the format is ##,###*−+, the value appears as 763−−−−−+.

You can also use a color indicator in a format to cause the number to be displayed in the named color. Your choices are RED, BLACK, WHITE, GREEN, BLUE, YELLOW, MAGENTA, and CYAN. Just enclose the color with square brackets as the first item in the picture. The format [green]$##,##0.00 causes the value to appear in green. The colors are useful for

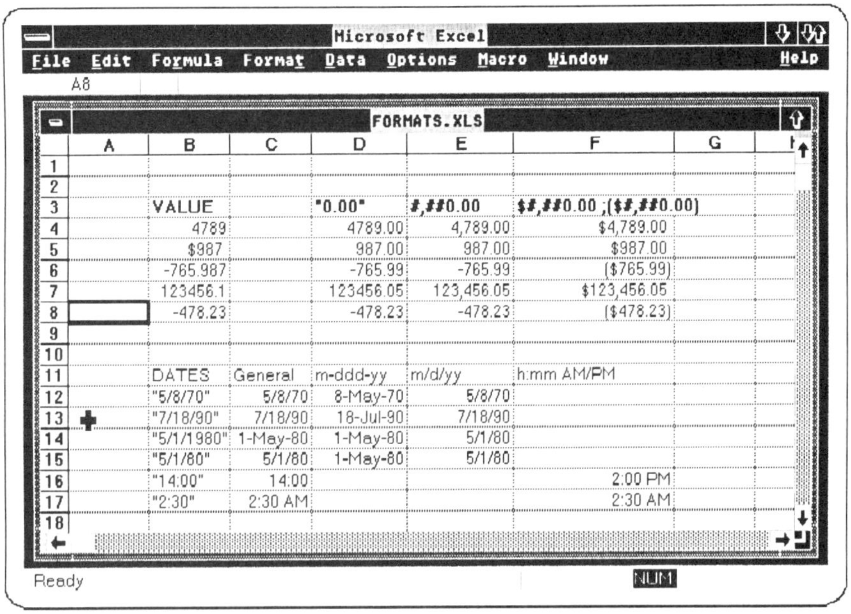

POLISHING THE WORKSHEET

FIGURE 3.6. Format Picture Effects

negative values, of course, but they are also handy to make values stand out on the screen. You might want to use bright colors to show up totals or fields that are more important than others. The colors on the screen don't affect the printed result (unless you have a color printer).

Figure 3.6 shows how various built-in formats cause values to be displayed or printed. The date and time formats are covered a bit later.

The formats examined so far have only one section; actually a format can contain up to four sections. Each section is followed by a semicolon before the next.

One section: Any number
Two sections: Positive numbers and zeros; negative numbers
Three sections: Positive numbers; negative numbers; zero
Four sections: Positive numbers; negative numbers; zero; text

Suppose you want to suppress leading and trailing zeros for positive values, show 0.0 for a zero value, and show minus values in red enclosed in parentheses with leading and trailing zeros for negative values. If the value contains text, you want the message "NUMERIC?" to appear in the cell. Here's the format definition you could use:

##,###.##;[RED](00,000.00);0.0;"NUMERIC?"

In many cases, a single format is sufficient. Excel differentiates between positive and negative numbers with + or − signs. A zero value will print if you use 0 and not if you use #. If you want to use parentheses to indicate negative, define the format with a separate picture for negative values; use the same format as for positive but enclose it in parentheses. Be sure to include an extra space following the semicolon in the positive value so the positive and negative values will align. You can see some examples of this in the built-in format list.

The symbol @ tells Excel to use any entered text, even if the format has fewer than four sections. If text follows @ in the format, it is inserted into the cell following any typed text. Without @, the text in the format replaces any text that is entered. For example, the format might be 00000 ; ; ; not Numeric. The format causes any positive text to be displayed as a five-digit number with leading zeros if necessary; negative or 0 values aren't displayed. And any text is replaced with the message "Not Numeric."

Hiding Values

You can use special formats to cause values to be hidden from the worksheet; they'll still appear in the formula bar, however. The easiest format is simply two semicolons (;;). When you define this format and assign it to cells, no numeric values in the cells will display, but text still displays. A format of ;;; suppresses text data as well.

Custom Formats

You can define a custom format by editing one that already exists or by starting from scratch. Excel never actually changes or deletes the built-in formats, so you can't hurt them. Just select the Format Text entry box in the Format Number dialog box and edit or start your format. Remember to use double quotes around any text or inserted characters or precede each with a backslash.

Once a custom format is defined, it appears at the end of the format list in the dialog box; you can use it with that worksheet whenever you want. It will not be present when any other worksheet is active. You can delete custom formats at any time, but you can't delete built-in formats.

DATE AND TIME FORMATS

The Format Numbers dialog box includes formats for date and time values. Excel uses a format close to what you enter when it recognizes that you have

POLISHING THE WORKSHEET

entered a date or time value. Date or time formats generally include a single section, applied to either date or time. Excel lets you include both in a single cell, if you use a space to separate the formats. Here is a list of format symbols for date and time values.

d	Indicates the day of the month. It will display without a leading zero. Use dd to include a leading zero.
ddd	Indicates the three-letter abbreviation for the day of the week. Use dddd to have the day spelled out.
m	Indicates the number of the month. It displays without any leading zero. Use mm to include a leading zero. If m or mm follows h or hh, it means minutes rather than month.
mmm	Indicates the three letter abbreviation for the month. It displays with an initial capital letter. Use mmmm to have the month spelled out.
yy	Indicates the last two digits of the year. You can use yyyy to display the entire year.

You can define custom formats with characters such as / or – inserted directly into the date. The picture m\/d\/yy displays October 5, 1989 as 10/5/89. To insert a space, enclose it in double quotes. If you use the picture mmmm" "d", "yyyy the same date displays as October 5, 1989.

h	Indicates the hour without a leading zero; hh includes the leading zero. If AM/PM is not included, this indicates a 24-hour clock.
m	If it follows h, this indicates the number of minutes, without leading zeros. Use mm to include leading zeros.
ss	Indicates the number of seconds, with leading zeros.

In time values, you can insert a colon (:) where needed. Use AM/PM or A/P (upper- or lowercase) as the last characters to force a 12-hour clock and the appropriate indicator.

You can include date and time in the same cell if you like. Just use both in the format, separated by a space. The last built-in format shows this technique.

If appropriate, you can include colors in date and time format pictures. Remember that these don't appear in print.

SUGGESTED EXERCISE

1. Bring up your worksheet and center each column heading in its cell.
2. Change the format for the pay amounts to one that will print two digits after the decimal place. Continue to suppress leading zeros.
3. Enter today's date in the format of 5/8/89 in a cell. Notice how the date appears in the formula bar and in the cell. Try it in the format 8 May 89.
4. Add a new column heading to the right labeled "Phone." Format the entire column to take a phone number in the format you want, with the area code included. You want to be able to type just the digits and have it display nicely. Try it out in a few cells.
5. Create a four-part format that will display the positive values as dollars and cents, negative values to three decimal places, and zero values as 0.0. If the value is text, add the message "Check" to it.
6. Format any other cells you want on your worksheet. Experiment with any features you expect will be useful to you.

What if It Doesn't Work?

1. Remember to select the cells to be affected first. Don't worry if you select too many; you can always reformat a cell or two.
2. Try out a set of values to see what happens. Make small changes in the formats. Remember to use a space before a semicolon.
3. Try this format: $#,###.## ;0,000.000 ;0; @"Check". The @ causes the message to be added to the text rather than to replace it.

MODIFYING ONSCREEN APPEARANCE

Excel provides several methods of enhancing or modifying your display in addition to the formats. You can use different fonts on the screen, you can display formulas instead of values, you can show or suppress gridlines, row and column headings, and zero values. You may be able to change the colors used in your headings and gridlines. You can also use borders and shading in your worksheet. Some of these affect only the display; others affect any print output as well. None has any effect on how Excel actually stores the data.

POLISHING THE WORKSHEET   61

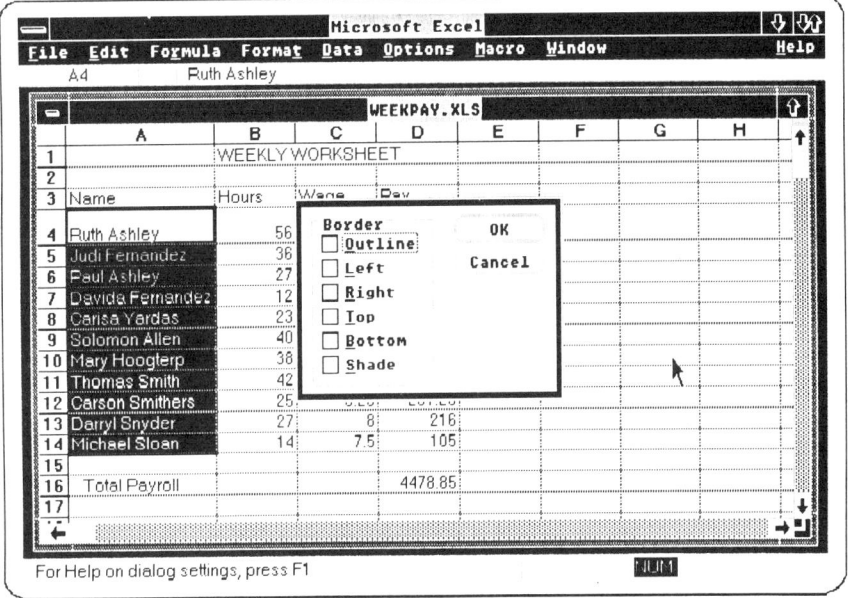

FIGURE 3.7.   Format Border Dialog Box

BORDERS

The Format menu allows you to select the Borders command, resulting in the Border dialog box, as shown in Figure 3.7. In this box, you can set the desired borders or shading. What you select here affects the currently selected cell or range on the screen and appears in print output as well.

If you select Outline, a single border outlines the selected cell or range. You can achieve the same effect by selecting Left, Right, Top, and Bottom. Or you can select any of the four sides by itself or in combination with any others. A line appears on the appropriate edge of the cell. Adjacent cells share borders; you get the same effect from a bottom border on A1 as a top border on A2; using both doesn't create a thicker or darker border. However, you can make a double line appear by drawing a border at the right of one column, inserting a blank column and bordering it on the right as well. Then adjust the column width to create the double line. Figure 3.8 shows an example in which double borders are created by adjusting both column width and row height; both were set to 4.

When you select an entry in the Borders dialog box, it is marked. When you access the box while a bordered cell is selected, the bordering is shaded in the

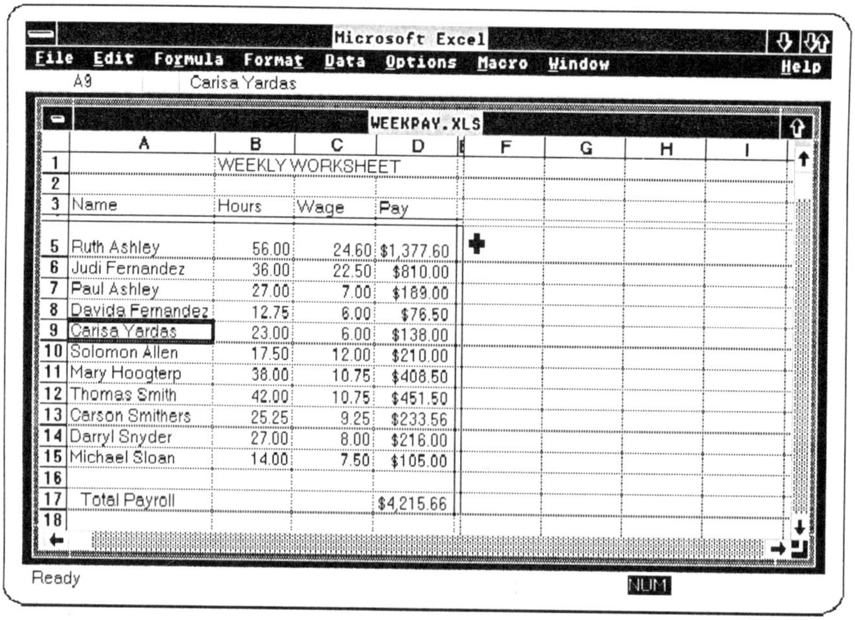

62 ADVANCED EXCEL

FIGURE 3.8. Using Borders

dialog box. You can select it again to remove the border. If a selected cell or range is outlined completely, the shading appears in the four directional boxes. You'll have to turn off all four sides to remove the border.

When you select Shade in the Borders dialog box, the selected cell or range is shaded. You don't have any choice of darkness or density of shading. The shading appears both on the screen and in any printout. Figure 3.9 shows how shading appears on the screen. It also affects the printout; exactly how depends on your printer.

MODIFYING THE DISPLAY

The Options Display command results in the Display dialog box, shown in Figure 3.10. The colors that appear are appropriate to your system. If Automatic is in effect, you can change the color of the gridline and headings only through the Control Panel.

By default, Excel displays values rather than formulas, has gridlines turned on, shows all row and column headings, and displays 0 when a value is zero. (Some early versions don't display a zero value.)

POLISHING THE WORKSHEET

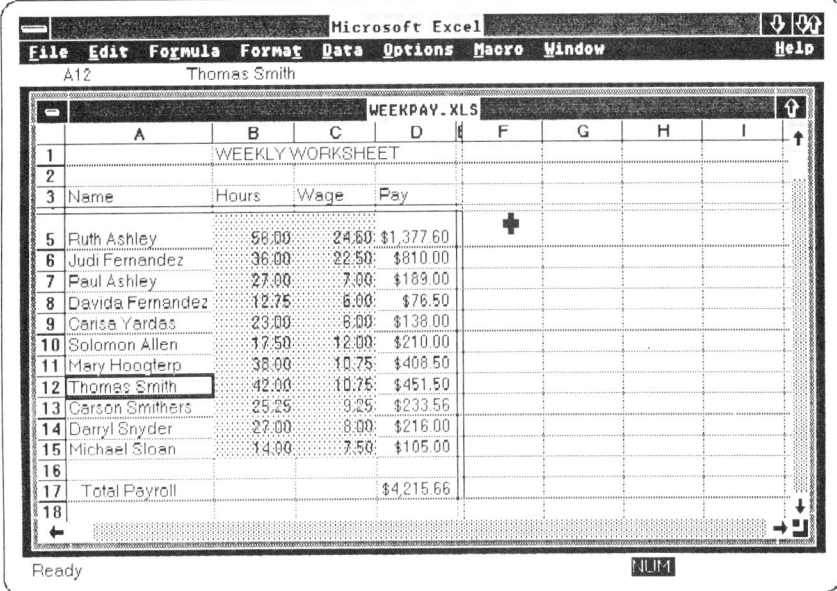

FIGURE 3.9. Using Borders and Shading

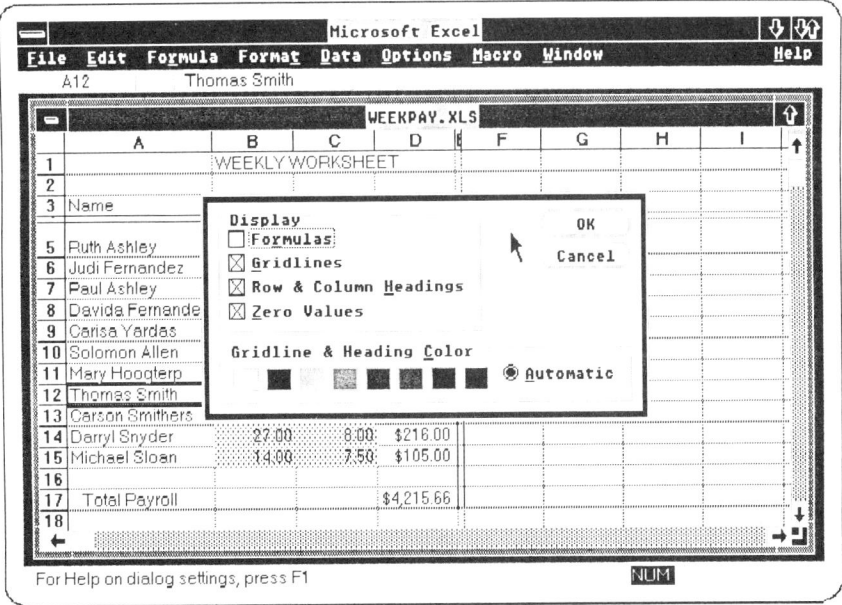

FIGURE 3.10. Options Display Dialog Box

Formulas

It's convenient to display formulas rather than values in the worksheet when you are trying to locate the source of an error. Normally, you can see only one formula at a time, in the formula bar. If you turn Formulas on in the Options Display dialog box, then a formula appears in every cell that has one. Whatever appears in the formula bar when the cell is active appears in the cell itself. For dates and times, you'll see the actual serial number that Excel uses internally to represent the date. Excel automatically widens the columns when formulas are displayed. You might want to view two copies of the same worksheet and display formulas in one and values in the other. This can be a great help in troubleshooting or in auditing your work. Chapter 7 covers that technique.

Gridlines

Gridlines are useful in data entry, but you may want to remove them later, when the worksheets are in use. If you lay out the worksheet appropriately, with labels and borders to show where data should be entered, you may find that the gridlines are a distraction. Figure 3.11 shows a worksheet with gridlines turned off.

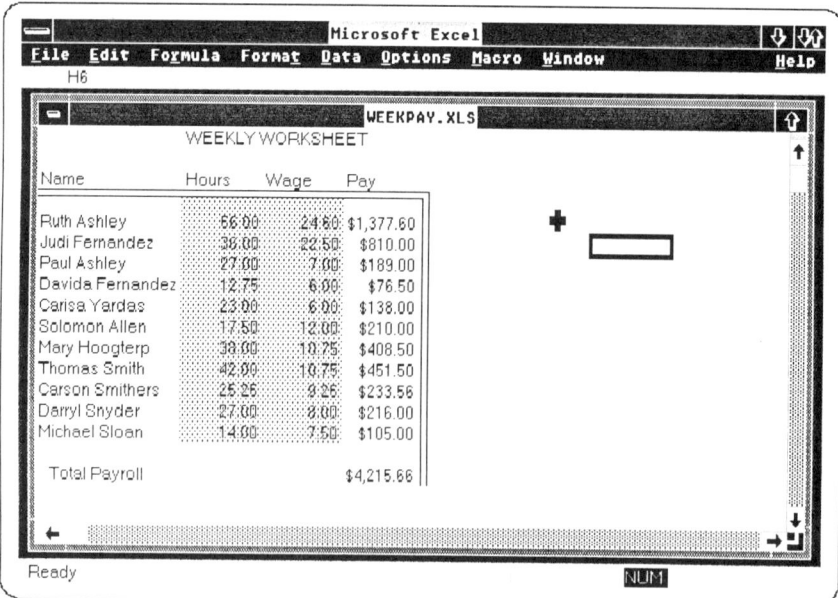

FIGURE 3.11. Gridlines Off

If you turn gridlines off for print as well, the printed result will resemble the screen.

Row and Column Headings

Like gridlines, row and column headings are useful in designing worksheets and in data entry, but may get in the way of other users. If you have a well-designed template, you can turn the row and column headings off. The text values on the screen will tell users where to enter data or what the values mean. Figure 3.11 shows this effect.

Zero Values

You may want to suppress or display zero values for the entire worksheet. The Options Display Zero Values check box indicates that they are to be displayed. To suppress them in the entire worksheet, select any cell, then turn the Zero Values check box off. Cells that contain zero display as blank, although 0 still shows in the formula bar. When Zero Values is on, you can still suppress zeros with a format of #.#; but if Zero Values is turned off, you can't force individual zero values to display.

USING FONTS

A font is a typeface in a specific size and style. Figure 3.12 shows several different fonts. Notice that variations in the typeface (Courier or Helvetica), the size (10 point or 24 point), and the style (bold or italic) all create a different font. The fonts that are available depend on your software and your hardware. Your screen can handle certain fonts; your printer can handle certain ones. They may or may not be able to handle the same ones. If you specify printer fonts for display, Excel gets as close as it can. If you print with screen fonts, again Excel does the best it can. You may want to experiment to find out which fonts show well in both media.

The size of fonts is given in points, which represent the height of the characters. The point size is measured from the highest tall letter (ascender) to the lowest dropped letter (descender). Each point is 1/72 inch, so 72-point type is one inch high. Ten-point type is 10/72 inch tall. Point size reflects character height, not width. All 10-point fonts are not the same width. Most of the Excel

Helvetica 10

Helvetica 10 bold

Helvetica 10 italic

Courier 10

Courier 12 bold

Courier 8 italic

Times Roman 8

Times Roman 10 bold

Times Roman 10 italic

Times Roman 24 bold

FIGURE 3.12.   Font Examples

fonts are proportionally spaced; some letters are wider than others. Some fonts are called fixed width because they use the same width for each character, as on a typewriter. The most common fixed-width font is Courier; it can be used in several widths, including the standard 10 characters per inch (called Courier 12) and 12 characters per inch (called Courier 10).

Excel limits you to four fonts per worksheet. The default screen fonts for an EGA monitor are shown in Figure 3.13 in the Fonts dialog box accessed by the Format Fonts command. The fonts may be different for different monitor types, but the concepts involved are the same.

Excel uses the Helvetica (Helv) font by default for EGA screen display. Notice that 10-point type is specified. Helvetica is a proportional font, so the characters are of different widths. Without changing the default, you can use bold, italic, or combined bold and italic, as well as the standard font. All data entry is done in the first listed font, number 1. You can change any of the listed fonts to other fonts supported by your system. The Fonts dialog box lists the fonts you can use. As with many other commands, you must select the cells to be affected before you use the command to modify the format.

You can change the available four fonts by selecting replacements from the font listing, reached by selecting the Fonts >> button in the dialog box. Figure 3.14 shows the result.

This box lists the available fonts for the monitor. Notice that one font and

POLISHING THE WORKSHEET 67

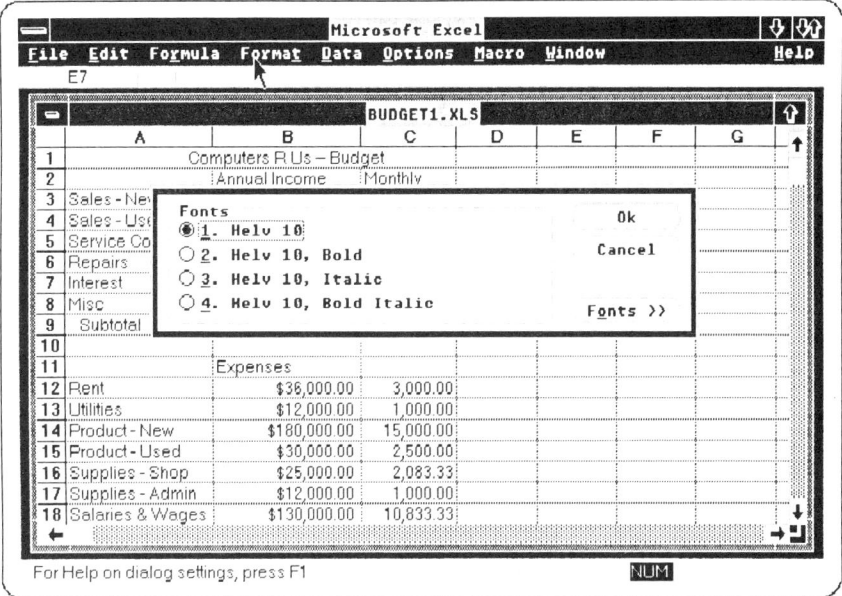

FIGURE 3.13. Format Fonts Dialog Box

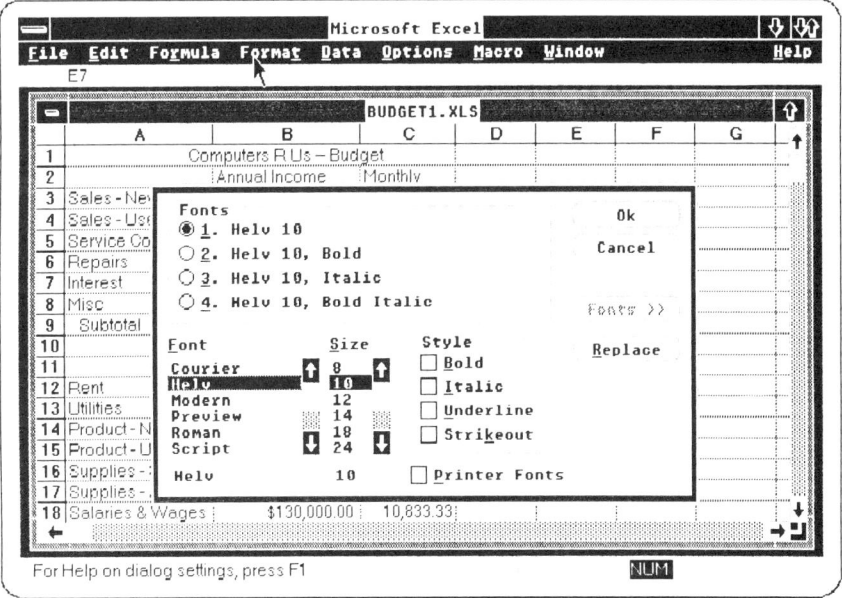

FIGURE 3.14. Fonts Dialog Box with Screen Font Listing

size are highlighted; this matches the selected font in the upper part of the box. You can change the current font for any of the four; the lower part reflects the current selection. Notice also that the Printer Fonts box is not checked; this means that the font list represents what is available for the screen. When you check the Printer Fonts box, you see the available printer fonts rather than the available screen fonts. We'll look at that effect shortly.

The fonts listed are primarily proportional. Courier and System are not. The proportional fonts take less space on screen, but you can switch to one of the others if you prefer. The largest point size for screen display is generally 24-point for the proportional fonts and 12-point for the fixed ones.

To replace one of the four default fonts, first select the font to be replaced in the upper part of the dialog box. Then set the font, size, and style characteristics you want in the lower part. Then select Replace to replace the font definition. Or select OK to replace it and remove the box. Any cells that used the changed font are automatically changed to the new one.

If you change the size of the first listed font, Excel automatically adjusts the column width and row height to display the same number of characters. If you choose a 24-point font, for example, each cell will be quite large. If you change fonts 2, 3, or 4, Excel may adjust the row height but you'll have to adjust the column width yourself.

Printer Fonts

When the Printer Fonts box is selected, the font list shows the fonts that can be handled by the currently selected printer. (Chapter 6 covers changing to a different installed printer.) Some printers, such as laser printers with PostScript, have many fonts. Others, such as the IBM Proprinter, have only a few. The printer fonts might not match the screen fonts. If not, Excel uses the closest font it can. If you select printer fonts for your worksheet, they might not look perfect on screen, but they will print perfectly. If you select screen fonts and print the worksheet, the characters won't look quite the same. You'll want to experiment or else review your lists to find what font/size/style combinations appear on both.

Examples

Figure 3.15 shows a worksheet portion that contains several different fonts.

POLISHING THE WORKSHEET

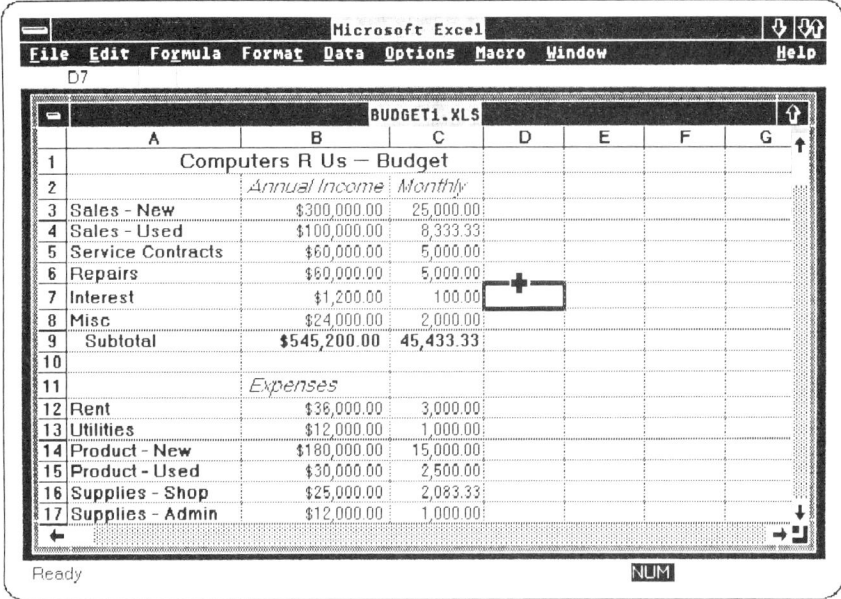

FIGURE 3.15.   Worksheet Fonts

SUGGESTED EXERCISE

1. Before you change anything in your own worksheet, look at a few of the sample programs provided with your Excel software.
   MONTHCAL.XLS for borders with gridlines off
   AMORTIZ1.XLS for border usage with gridlines off
   Try several others. Notice where additional fonts are used.
2. Change the title in your worksheet to use a different, larger font. Then change the column headings to use a still different format.
3. Check the printer fonts. Change your first listed font to a large, unusual sounding font. Then see how it looks on screen.
4. Try using borders to create a double line all the way around your basic worksheet. You'll have to add a few columns before column A to allow room to play with the column width.

What if It Doesn't Work?

1. If you have trouble finding other worksheets in your system, change to another

directory. LIBRARY and EXCELCBT both contain several .XLS files, most of which use borders and more than one font.
2. If you can't get more than one font on your screen, your system may be limited. Check your dealer.

SUMMARY

This chapter covered various ways of polishing the appearance and functionality of your spreadsheets. You can use different formats to make values easier to read and work with. You can manipulate gridlines and borders to make the display more attractive and highlight important parts. You can also shade certain cells to highlight them.

In addition, you can now use all the fonts available in your system to further enhance your display. The font changes are reflected in print output.

4 WORKSHEET SELECTION FEATURES

This chapter looks at data; you'll see how you can refer to it, how you can name it, how you can find it, even some more ways you can create it and rearrange it. The chapter goes beyond the basics in each area to show you how Excel's capabilities are applicable to your needs and how to most easily make use of these capabilities.

REFERENCES TO CELLS

Excel provides two styles for referencing cells. The default is the A1 reference style, in which each cell is referenced based on the lettered column (from A to IV) and the numbered row (from 1 to 16384). The column reference appears first, so cell references range from A1 to IV16384. You can use the R1C1 reference style instead, in which the row reference appears first and both rows and columns are represented by numbers. The lower right corner of the worksheet in this style is R16384C256. You can switch styles by selecting the Options menu, then the Workspace command. The resulting dialog box is shown in Figure 4.1. Just turn on the R1C1 Display field. The columns will then be represented by numbers instead of letters on your screen and all cell references appear in the R1C1 style. Any references already in the worksheet are automatically converted to the selected reference style. If cell B10 is active when you change to the R1C1 style, the reference in the status bar changes to R10C2.

Relative References

Each cell reference, in either style, can be either relative or absolute. A relative reference is defined in relationship to the current cell. If the current cell is C2 and it contains the formula =A2*2, that means the value in the cell in the same row two columns to the left, times 2. If the formula in cell C2 is copied to cell

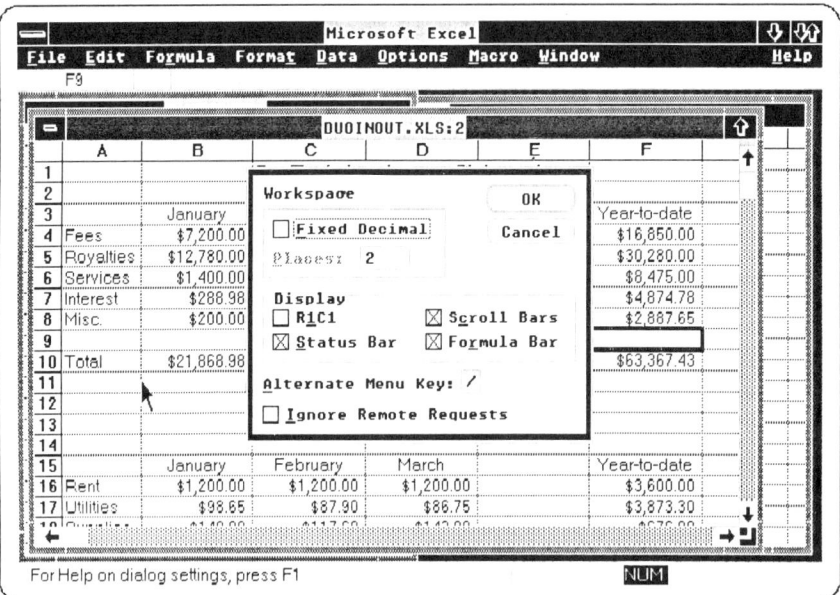

FIGURE 4.1. Options Workspace Dialog Box

D2, it is changed to =B2*2, so that it still refers to the cell in the same row, two columns to the left. When you select cells for formulas while the formula bar is active, Excel uses the relative form of the cell reference. You'll probably use the relative form yourself while you type A1 style references.

Absolute References

You can use an absolute reference to keep a reference from changing when it, or a formula containing it, is copied or moved to another cell. You fix a cell reference by typing $ before each component. For example, $A$2 refers to the cell in the A2 position, no matter which cell is referencing it. Once you have typed a relative cell reference, you can change it to an absolute one by selecting the Formula Reference command or by pressing F4; this highlights the cell reference at the cursor in the formula bar and changes it to an absolute reference by inserting a $ before each component. If you repeatedly press F4, A2 changes first to $A$2, then A$2, then $A2, then returns to the relative form of A2. As this indicates, you can mix absolute and relative references in a cell reference. Here $A2 refers to the cell in the first column, with the row relative to the location of the cell that contains the reference.

Using the R1C1 Style

In the R1C1 reference style, R2C2 is an absolute cell reference; it always refers to the cell in the second row and second column. Relative references are indicated with brackets. R[2]C[2] refers to the cell that is 2 rows down and 2 columns to the right. If you use Options Workplace to switch a standard worksheet from A1 style to R1C1 style, you will see that the references in formulas have been changed to a relative form; a reference to B5 becomes R[5]C[2].

In the R1C1 style, you can omit the R or C letter and number to indicate the same column or row as the referring cell; RC2 means the cell in the same row, column 2. Use negative values, such as R[-3]C[-2] to refer to areas above and to the left of the referring cell. For example, suppose cell B10 contains the formula =SUM(B4:B8) when you change reference styles. The cell becomes R10C2 and the formula becomes =SUM(R[-6]C:R[-2]C) as a relative reference.

Most people stick with the A1 reference style in worksheets. But in macros, you'll find the R1C1 style used.

Moving to a Cell

You can move to a given cell by moving the mouse there and clicking or by moving the cursor through all the intervening cells. You can also move to a cell directly with the Formula Goto command. In the resulting dialog box, shown in Figure 4.2, the Reference field is active; just enter the reference of the cell, using the current style of the worksheet. The F5 function key brings up the Formula Goto menu; you'll find this a very useful shortcut, well worth using to move quickly through your worksheets.

RANGES

In Excel, you deal with cells and ranges. A cell is the intersection of a row and a column; each cell is referenced in either A1 or R1C1 style. A range is a rectangular section containing two or more cells. It is referenced with two cell references representing two opposite corners of the rectangle, connected with a colon; A2:C5 represents a range containing 12 cells.

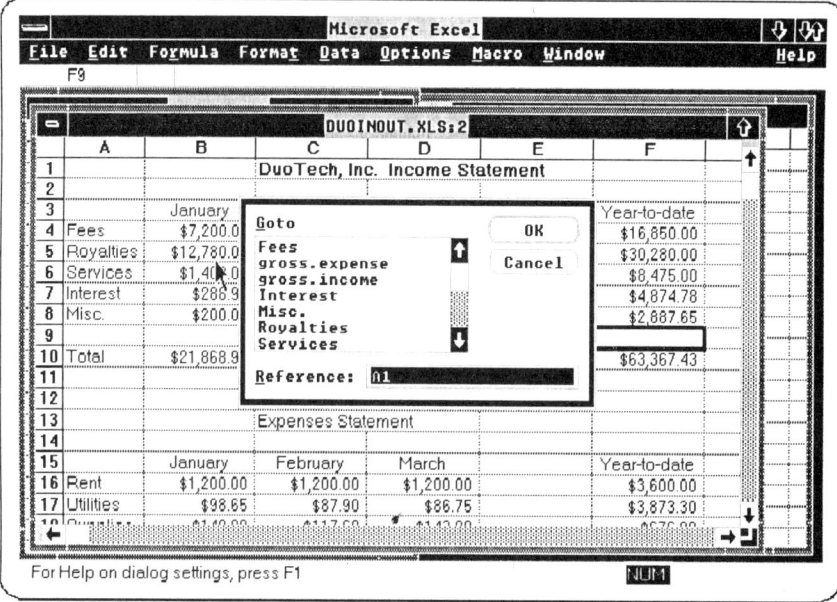

FIGURE 4.2. Formula Goto Dialog Box

Multiple Selection

In most situations in Excel where you can select a cell, you can also select a range. In fact, you can also make a multiple selection that includes several noncontiguous single cells or ranges or any combination of cells and ranges. This allows you to select, for example, all the cells that need a particular format and set the format only once. You select a cell by making it active; the current cell is always active and selected. You select a range by first making the cell at one of its corners active. Then use SHIFT and the arrow keys to extend it, using the keyboard or dragging the mouse to complete the rectangle.

To make a multiple selection, start by selecting the first cell or range. Then press SHIFT + F8 on the keyboard to tell Excel you'll be extending the selection. Then move the cursor to the next area to select and click or press F8 to select the next part, as before. If you need a third piece, press SHIFT + F8 again, and continue until the multiple selection is ready. Be sure to use SHIFT with the arrow keys to make selections after pressing SHIFT + F8 or the area is all "deselected." With a mouse, you don't need the function key; just press the control key while adding to your selection. Figure 4.3 shows a multiple selection. This one contains two ranges and two single cells.

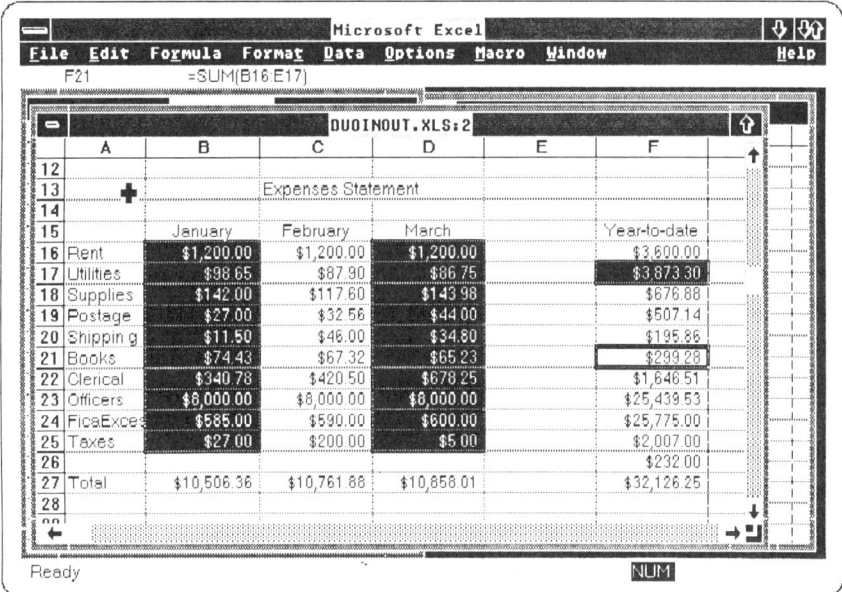

FIGURE 4.3. Multiple Selection

Moving within a Range or Multiple Selection

When you press an arrow key or click the mouse button, a range or multiple selection is deselected. Press the control key on the keyboard before a mouse click to select a cell. The keyboard commands for moving within a selected area are shown in Figure 4.4.

You move the cursor within a selected area by pressing Tab to go to the right or SHIFT + Tab to go to the left. Use Enter to go down or SHIFT + Enter to go up in the selection. Both Tab and Enter will eventually move to each cell in a range or multiple selection, jumping to the next row or column when one is finished. CONTROL + Period moves directly from one corner of a range to another. If you have multiple selections, you can use CONTROL + Tab or SHIFT + CONTROL + Tab to move directly from one selected range to a separate one. These commands cycle through the disconnected portions of the multiple selection. It takes practice to avoid using the arrow keys while in a selected range. If you provide names for your ranges or multiple selections, you'll be able to reselect them again quickly if you should deselect them accidentally!

76 ADVANCED EXCEL

```
Down one cell              ENTER
Up one cell                SHIFT+ENTER
Right one cell             TAB
Left one cell              SHIFT+ENTER
Next corner of area        CONTROL+.
Next area                  CONTROL+TAB
Previous area              SHIFT+CONTROL+TAB
```

FIGURE 4.4. Moving within a Selected Area

NAMES

Excel lets you give names to individual cells, ranges, and multiple selections, as well as to values and formulas that aren't placed in cells. Once an entity has a name, you can use the name in formulas. This makes your worksheet easier to read and understand. The formula "=gross.income-gross.expenses" is much more meaningful than "=f27-f42." Using names rather than cell references also minimizes errors and saves time. The techniques for defining, referencing, and manipulating all these named entities are the same. The commands you use are located on the Formula menu, shown in Figure 4.5.

You use Define Name and Create Names to establish new names for each worksheet. Apply Names converts existing references to their equivalent

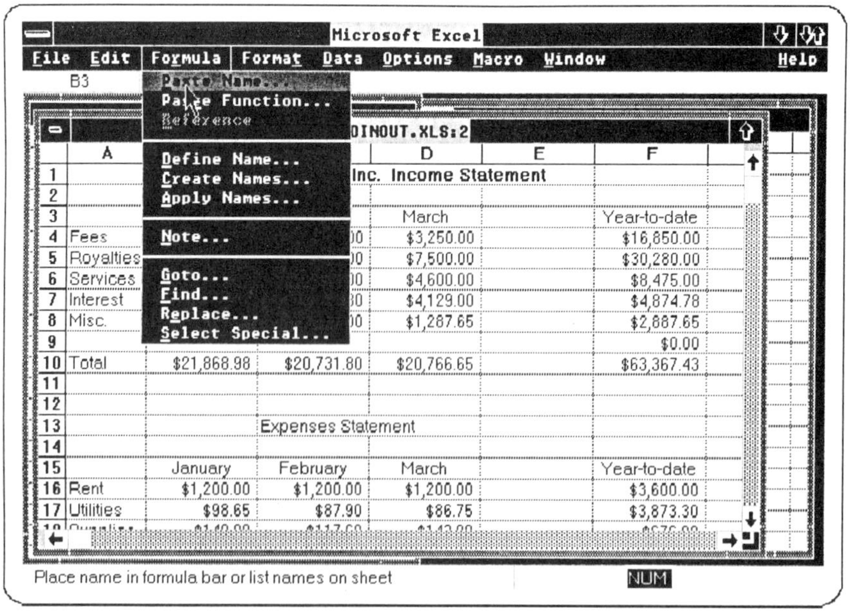

FIGURE 4.5. Formula Menu—Name Manipulation

names. Paste Name lets you select a name for use in a formula, rather than typing it. And the Goto command lets you select and move directly to any entity that has a name.

Establishing Names

Excel offers two commands for naming. Define Name lets you specify a name for a single reference, value, or formula. You supply the name and tell Excel what it refers to. Create Names lets Excel provide names for a selection of cells, using text in the specified adjacent cells as the names. To define a single name, you may select the area to be named before beginning the command. If you want Excel to create the names, you must select the range first.

The names themselves must adhere to certain rules. Each must start with a letter and be made up of letters, numbers, periods (.), and underline (_) characters. You can't include spaces; the period takes up less space on screen than does the underline, but you can use either to connect parts of a name. Each name can contain up to 255 characters; you'll want to keep them short enough to be useful, yet long enough to be meaningful. The only other restriction on names is that they can't look like a cell reference; "R2D2" and "A444" are not valid names, for example. You can use either upper- or lowercase letters; Excel treats them the same in names.

Each name in a worksheet must be unique. If you use the same name to define another entity, the earlier one is overlaid. Excel doesn't alert you if you reuse a name, so be sure to check the name list.

One Name at a Time. Suppose you want to name a cell "subtotal" and use its value in formulas. First make that cell active. Then select the Formula Define Name command. The dialog box in Figure 4.6 shows the result. The list box on the left contains the names currently defined for the worksheet. The insertion point is in the Name field; if the active cell already has a name, that name appears by default. If an adjacent cell contains text, that text will appear in the Name field, because Excel tries to suggest an appropriate name for you. The Refers to field contains the absolute cell reference for the active cell. You can accept a proposed name or type your own; here you'd type "subtotal" to name the cell. If you neglected to select the cell first, you can overtype the current value in the Refers to field. Be sure to keep the = symbol before a reference or formula. When you approve of both fields, choose OK. The new name is added to the list and the box goes away. You can change both name and reference as well. If you want to provide a name for a cell that isn't active, just overtype the reference in the Refers to field.

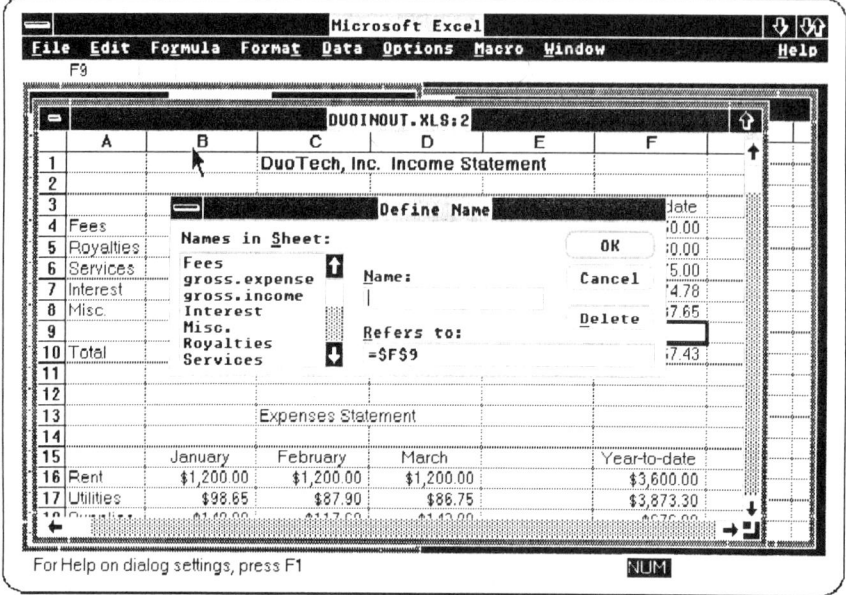

FIGURE 4.6. Formula Define Name Dialog Box

You can define a named value using the same method. To set the value of "inflation" at .065, select Formula Define Name, type the name in the Name field and the value as = .065 in the Refers to field. To use a formula, just type a formula in the Refers to field. If you use cell references in a formula, try to use absolute references. If the formula contains relative references, they will refer to different cells every time the formula is used. If you really need relative references, however, you can use them.

One advantage of naming a value or formula that isn't in a cell is that it can be easily changed; the changed value here affects all references to the name. You'll see how to edit names and references shortly.

Many Names at Once. In some situations, Excel can create names for a range of cells. If the cells you want to name have text in the immediately adjacent cells, you can tell Excel to use that text to name the cells. For example, suppose your worksheet includes a column for each month, with the month name at the top of the column, as shown in Figure 4.7. Notice that the row of names is selected as part of the range. The next step is to select Formula Create Names, which results in the dialog box shown in Figure 4.8.

Now you just have to click on the box that represents the location of the names you want to use. After choosing OK, the name January applies to cells B4 through B8; the row containing the names is not part of the actual named

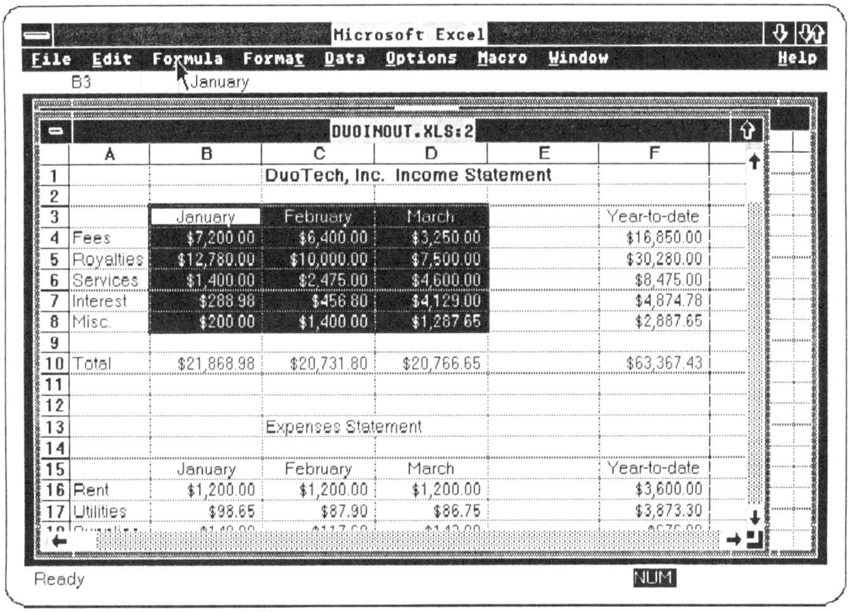

WORKSHEET SELECTION FEATURES

FIGURE 4.7. Sample Worksheet Selection

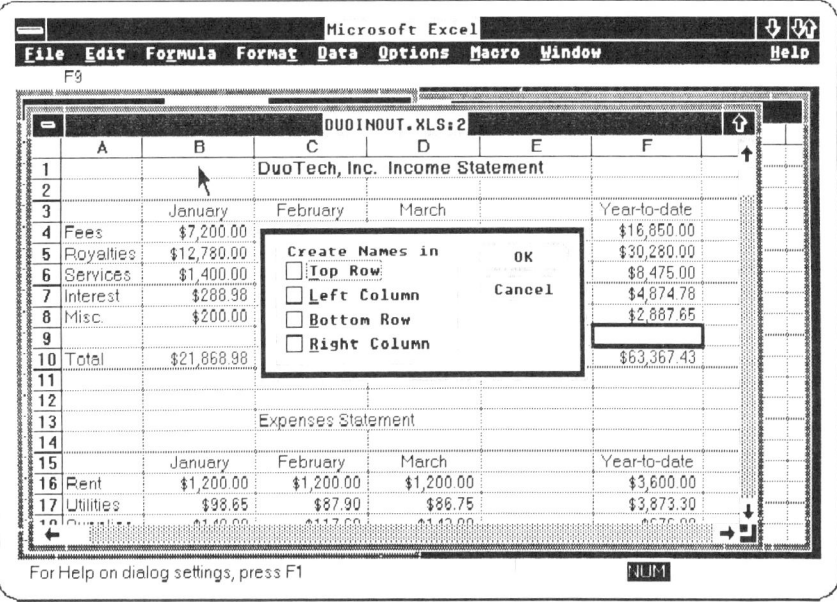

FIGURE 4.8. Formula Create Names Dialog Box

range. If our selection included cells A3:A8, we could select both Top Row and Left Column. Then the name Fees, for example, refers to B4 through D4.

Editing or Deleting Names

You can edit or delete any names through the Define Names dialog box. To remove a name from the list, just select it in the list box, so that it appears in the Name field. Then select the Delete button (see Figure 4.6). The name is gone from the list and the dialog box remains for you to do more work. If you delete a name that is in use in some cells, the error message #NAME? appears in each affected cell.

To make changes to a name or a reference, select the name in the list box. Once it and its definition appear in the Name and Refers to fields, select the part you want to edit. The same editing rules apply here as in the formula bar. Remember to precede references with = and use absolute references where possible.

If you press Cancel while working in the Define Name dialog box, it doesn't cancel any editing or deletions you have already done. It merely removes the dialog box without processing any changes currently in progress. Once you have deleted a name it is gone; you can redefine it to reuse the name.

Using Names. You can use names instead of definitions to call up formulas or references throughout Excel worksheets. If you have named the value .065 "interest," you can use =B5*interest as a formula. If you have named cell B5 "price," you can use =price*interest as a formula. If you have named a range "January," you can use =January*interest as a formula; Excel uses the value of January that is in the same row or column as the formula. If you use a name that you haven't defined, Excel gives you an error message.

You can also select names from a list for pasting into formulas. Start the formula you want in the formula bar, then select Formula Paste Name. The dialog box that results is shown in Figure 4.9. Just select the name you want in your formula and choose OK. It is added to the formula and you can continue typing in the formula bar.

The dialog box also gives you the chance to paste the complete name list into a cell. This gives a permanent onscreen list of the defined names that you can keep in an out-of-the-way place in the worksheet; you can refer to your list or to the Define Names list box while typing formulas. First decide where you want the list to appear; select a cell below or to the right of the active worksheet area. Then select Formula Paste Name and select the Paste List button. The complete list of names for that worksheet, along with their definitions, appears beginning at the active cell. Figure 4.10 shows an example.

WORKSHEET SELECTION FEATURES

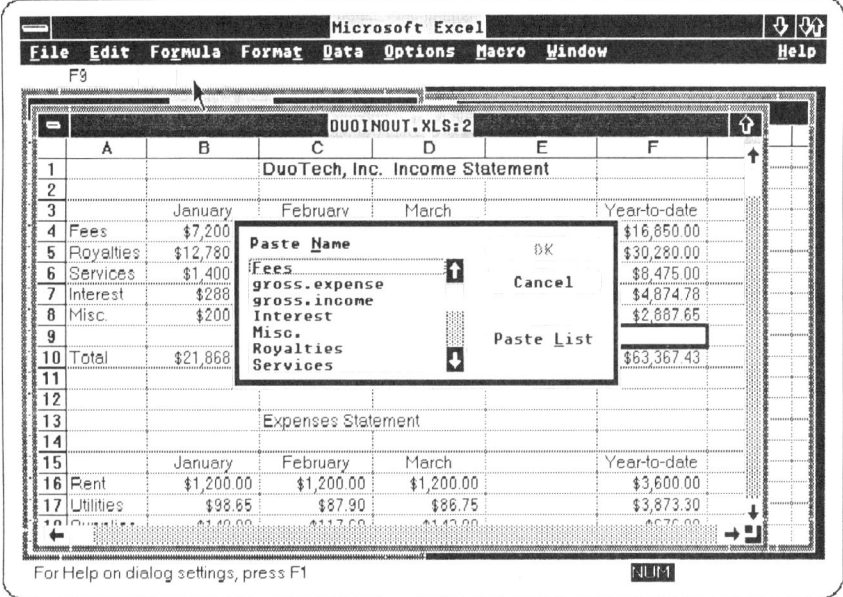

FIGURE 4.9. Formula Paste Name Dialog Box

FIGURE 4.10. List of Names Pasted in Worksheet

Applying Names to References

Sometimes you define names after you've already used the cell references in formulas. You can tell Excel to search the worksheet and replace cell references with specified names. First you have to select the range; that is generally the entire active worksheet, or the part you have entered data into or are working with. Then select Formula Apply Names. Figure 4.11 shows the resulting dialog box. The figure shows the dialog box with options selected. By default, Excel goes through the selected range and changes all references to the selected names whether they are relative or absolute. That means a formula =B5*B12 might be changed to =interest*B12, with interest being defined as $B$5. If you want Excel to pay attention to the relative/absolute status of the cell, turn Ignore Relative/Absolute off; then Excel will only apply the name to a cell reference if the reference is exactly the same as the definition of the name.

If you used both row and column names to refer to the same cells, you might have to deal with the rest of the options. By default, Excel uses both, omitting the column name if the reference is in the same column and the row name if the reference is in the same row. And if it uses both, it uses the row first, then the column in the A1 reference style. These are the standard ways Excel and most other worksheets function. You won't want to change any of these options unless you have a very nonstandard worksheet or the R1C1 reference style.

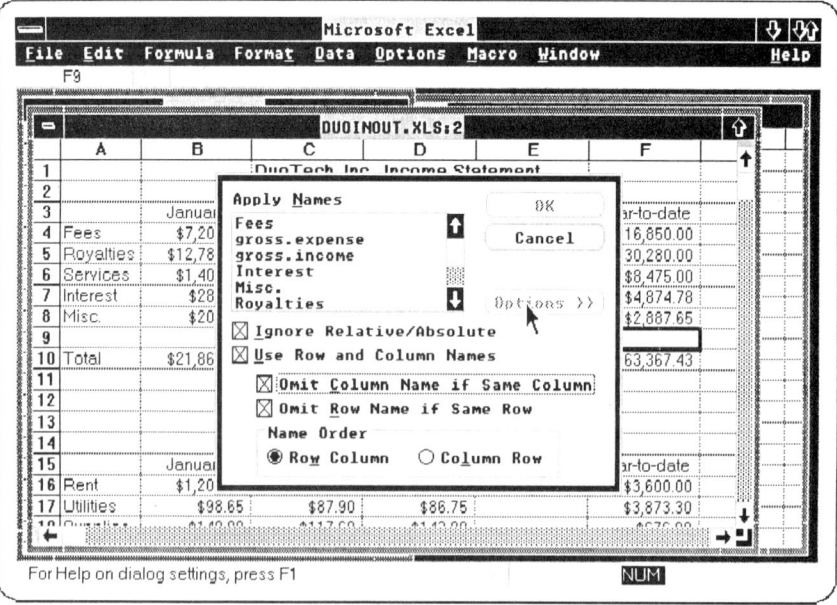

FIGURE 4.11. Formula Apply Names Dialog Box

WORKSHEET SELECTION FEATURES **83**

Once the options are as you want them, select the name or names to be applied in the selected range. To select more than one name with a mouse, press SHIFT while you click on each name you select. On the keyboard, use CONTROL and the appropriate arrow key; press the space bar to select or deselect a name.

Moving to a Named Cell or Range

You can move directly to a named cell or select and move directly to a named range or multiple selection by using the Formula Goto command or pressing F5. The resulting dialog box was shown in Figure 4.2. Just select the name you want and choose OK. The reference field shows you the target of the name for reference only; you can't change it here.

SUGGESTED EXERCISE

1. Define a value called raise and give it the value 10%.
2. Add a column to your worksheet headed "New Wages." Use a formula using the name "raise" to calculate new pay based on the old value. Use any technique to get the formula in all the appropriate cells.
3. Give the name "Hours" to each hours value. Then use the Formula Apply Names command to convert the formulas you use for calculating pay.
4. Examine the Define Names box. Change the name of "raise" to "increase" and change its value to 12%. See how this affects the worksheet.
5. Give a name to the entire worksheet.
6. Examine the file named CALENDAR.XLS in the LIBRARY directory. See what names are defined for it. Check the formulas in the worksheet to see how these names are used.

What if It Doesn't Work?

1. Try looking up "names" in the Help system. Press F1 while the Define Name dialog box is displayed.
2. Define a name for one simple value. Then put =name in a cell. If the value doesn't appear, check to see if you have formulas turned on in Options Display.

CELL NOTES

Excel provides you with a facility for adding notes to any or all cells in a worksheet. The notes can serve as reminders or can document the worksheet.

84 ADVANCED EXCEL

You can use them to provide a guided tour of the entire active worksheet or to give guidance to others who might view or use your worksheet. Notes can be scanned while viewing the worksheet or can be printed out, either along with the worksheet or separately. You can view them through the same note facility you use to enter them or through the Info system, covered later in this chapter. You might use notes to document where data came from originally. Or you could use the various codes placed in a field in a note that users can refer to during data entry. Notes can serve any purpose at all.

You can create or access notes through the Formula Note command, which results in the dialog box shown in Figure 4.12.

The reference of the active cell appears in the upper left. The box on the left lists all cells in the active worksheet that currently contain notes. The box in the center contains the text of the current note. To add a note, you just type it in here; the editing rules are the same as for the formula bar.

Creating Notes

To create a note for any cell, it must first be identified in the reference field in the upper left corner of the Cell Note dialog box. If that cell wasn't active when you selected Formula Note, you can select the Cells field and overtype the reference shown. Don't press Enter after it, but select the Note box and begin

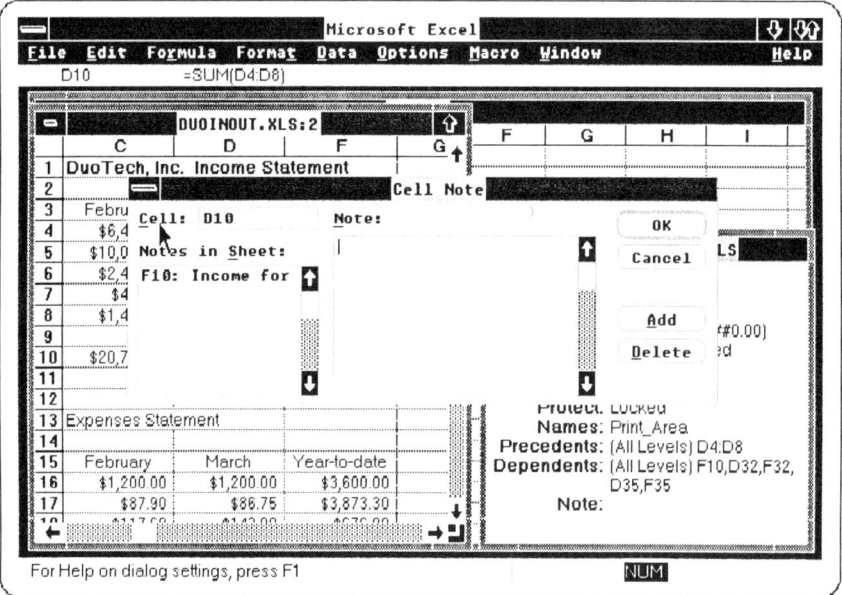

FIGURE 4.12. Formula Note Dialog Box

typing the note. Don't use Enter while typing a note, since that immediately adds the note and clears the dialog box. Excel wraps words to the next line as needed. You can use CONTROL+E to start a new line if that becomes necessary, however. When the note is ready, you can press Enter or OK to add the note and remove the dialog box. If you select the Add button, the note is added and appears in the list box, but the dialog box remains; the Cell field is selected so you can enter another cell reference to add another note.

Editing Notes

Once a note is attached to a cell, you can change it while it is displayed in the Formula Note dialog box. Just select the Note box and move the insertion point as in the formula bar. All the techniques you use there work in note editing as well.

Deleting Notes

You can also remove notes through the Formula Note dialog box. Just select the note you want to delete in the list and select the Delete button. Excel asks you to confirm or cancel the deletion since this action can't be undone.

If you select the Cancel button, it doesn't cancel any additions, changes, or deletions that you have done. All it does is cancel any operation you have started but not completed and remove the dialog box without adding another cell note.

Printing Notes

Printing is covered in detail in Chapter 6. You can print notes as part of the worksheet or as separate entities. Even if printed in conjunction with a worksheet, the notes start at the top of a page.

CELL INFORMATION

Sometimes you want to know more about a cell than you can tell by just looking at it. Excel, of course, knows all about it; it uses a different document from a worksheet to show you cell information. You can access the information by selecting Show Info on the Window menu to see the Info window for the

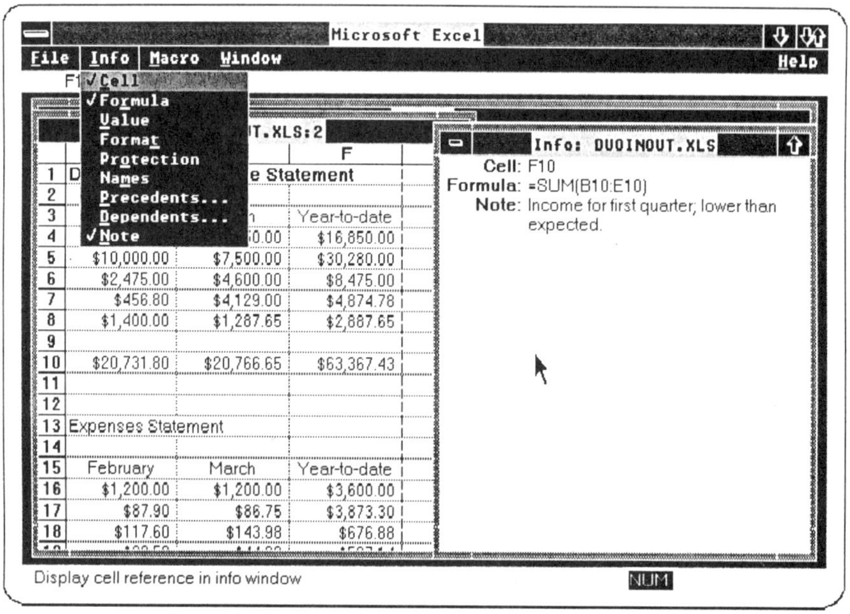

86 ADVANCED EXCEL

FIGURE 4.13. Default Info Window

current cell. You can keep the info window on screen while you work with your worksheet. You can arrange it by moving, sizing, or "tiling" (Window Arrange All) so that you can always see the inside information on the active cell. You can examine just the basic information or all that Excel has. Figure 4.13 shows the default Info window and the initial Info menu.

Excel provides a different menu bar while the Info window is active. The Info window control menu (ALT + Hyphen) includes the usual Close command, with which you can remove the window. The File menu is the same as for worksheets. The Macro and Window menus are only slightly changed. The Info menu contains commands that you can select to change the types of information shown in the Info window. Figure 4.14 shows the Info menu along with a maximum information Info window.

The Info Menu

Each command on the Info menu corresponds to a piece of information in the Info window.

> **Cell** Provides the reference of the cell; it is included in the default Info window.

WORSHEET SELECTION FEATURES

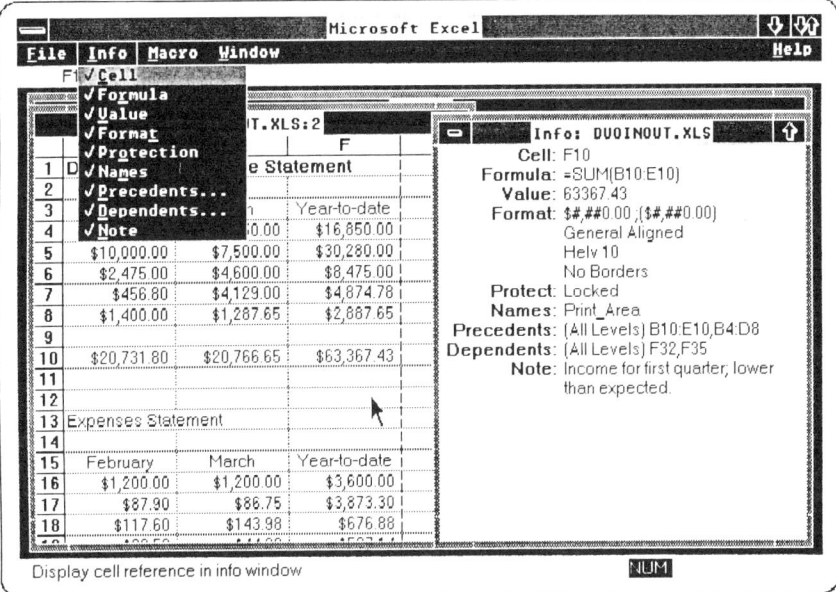

FIGURE 4.14.   Maximum Information Info Window

Formula   Gives the underlying formula; it is included in the default Info window. You can remove it from the window via the Info menu.

Value   Gives the current value in the cell; it's not included in the default window information. It shows the internal stored value rather than the displayed value; you'll see all the decimal places that are stored with the cell.

Format   Shows the format in effect for the cell; this includes a number format, alignment, font in use, and any borders or shading.

Protection   Shows the protection; even if the protection shows Locked, that doesn't mean it really is. You must use the Options Protect Document command to put the locking into effect. Protection is covered later in this book. If the formula of the cell is hidden, that shows here as well.

Names   Lists any names that include the active cell. This could include a name for just that cell, a range, or even a complete print area.

Precedents   Lists any cells that must have values before this cell can be calculated. We'll cover them in more detail later.

Dependents   Lists any cells that use this cell in calculating their formulas. We'll cover them in more detail later.

Note   Gives the text of any note for this cell. It is included in the default Info window.

Once the Info window contains the information you want, you can keep it on the screen while you work with your worksheet. You can arrange the windows side by side or use Windows Arrange All to let Excel arrange the display so all windows show; this is called tiling. You can reduce the size of the Info window so that no extra space is used. For example, you may be able to narrow it by about 2/3; long entries, such as notes and lists, wrap around to lower lines. You can also shorten the box to leave more room on screen for viewing other windows. Each time you change the active cell, the contents of the Info window changes to keep up to date. You can scan notes, formats, relationships, even formulas as you work with your worksheet. Since Excel has to prepare a new display for each cell, it slows the program down a bit; the amount depends on your system speed and the amount of memory available to Excel.

Scrolling through the Info Windows

To make it easy to scroll through Info windows for specific cells in the worksheet, you can use the Formula Select Special command to automatically include all cells that contain a certain feature in a multiple selection. Figure 4.15 shows the Formula Select Special dialog box.

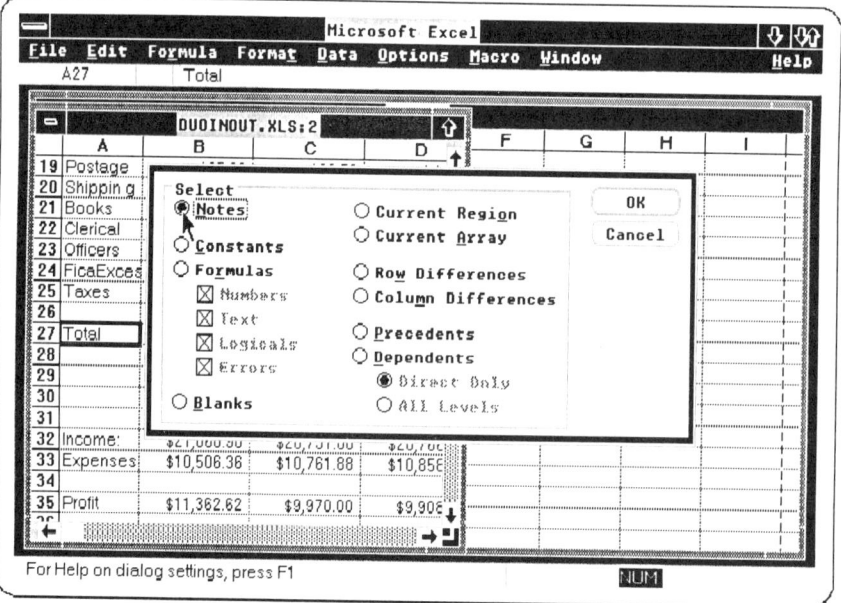

FIGURE 4.15. Formula Select Special Dialog Box

WORKSHEET SELECTION FEATURES

The most useful option here is Notes; when you select notes and choose OK, all cells that contain notes are included in a multiple selection. By using TAB to move between them, you can quickly scroll through all the notes in the worksheet. Formulas, precedents, and dependents all result in useful multiple selections for use with Info windows.

Printing Info Window Data

Excel lets you print the Info window data for the currently selected cell. If you select the entire spreadsheet and then make the Info window active before printing, values of all the categories included in the Info window are printed for each cell in the selected area. This is done in row order; if the selected area is B1:F10, the sequence is B1, C1, D1, E1, F1, B2, and so on. Even if a row or column is hidden, its information is printed. The critical thing about printing information is that the Info window must be active when you tell Excel to print. Printing is covered in detail in Chapter 6.

Precedents and Dependents

The Info window can include information on precedents and dependents of a cell. Precedents are cells that precede the given cell logically; that is, they must have values for the given cell to have a value. If you think a value in a cell is wrong, you could check its precedents to see where values in formulas came from. If cell D12 includes the formula =SUM(D4:D10), cells D4 through D10 are all precedents of D12; their values determine the value of cell D12. In fact, they are direct precedents of cell D12. If Cell D4 contains =D3*7%, D3 is a direct precedent of D4 and an indirect precedent of every cell that uses D4, including our cell D12.

Dependents are cells that depend on a given cell logically. In the example just given, cell D4 is a direct dependent of cell D3, while cell D12 is an indirect dependent of cell D3 and a direct dependent of cell D4. If you are considering changing a cell, you could check its dependents to see its effect on other cells in the worksheet.

All this becomes important when you tell Excel to include information about precedents and dependents in the Info window. It asks you to select Direct Only or All Levels. You have to decide, based on how detailed the information will be. If you select Direct Only, then Excel lists just the cells that are specified in the formula for direct precedents and just the cells that use this cell by name as direct dependents. If you select All Levels, indirect precedents and/or dependents are listed in the Info window, with (All Levels) noted before each.

You can use Formula Select Special to get a multiple selection of the precedents or dependents, either Direct Only or All Levels. Then as you use Tab, you'll see the information in the Info window.

FINDING DATA IN THE WORKSHEET

You can use the Formula Find and Formula Replace commands to locate a string of characters in formulas, values, or notes. You can tell Excel to look for the string as a whole or as part of a longer string. Figure 4.16 shows the Formula Find dialog box. You type the string you want to locate in the Find What field. Then indicate where Excel should look, in the formulas, values, or notes. If you specify Whole, the text you enter must be the entire value. To find the word "elegant" in a note, you must specify Part unless the word is the entire note. Since Excel stops the search with the first match it finds, you can look by rows or columns to control what it finds first. If no match is found, you'll get an alert message. When a match is found, that cell becomes active.

You can use the Formula Find command to locate information in the Info

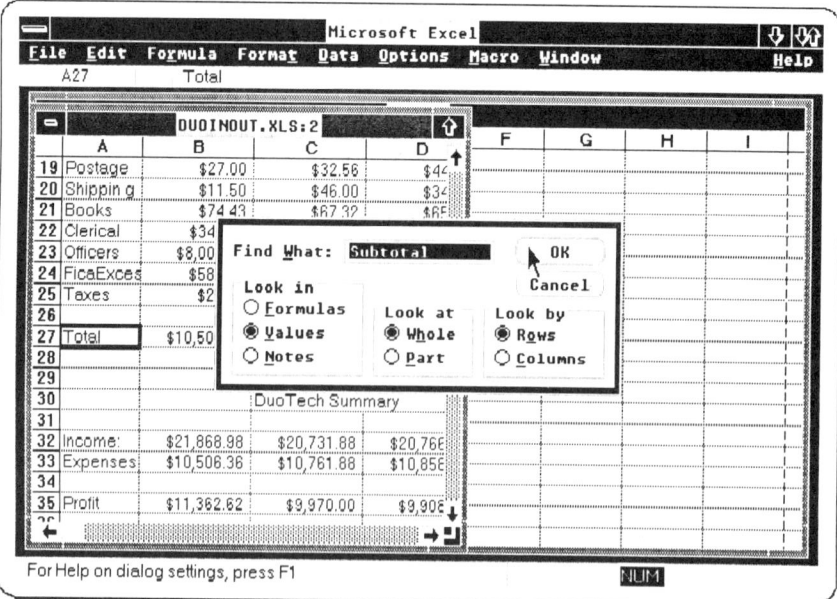

FIGURE 4.16. Formula Find Dialog Box

WORKSHEET SELECTION FEATURES

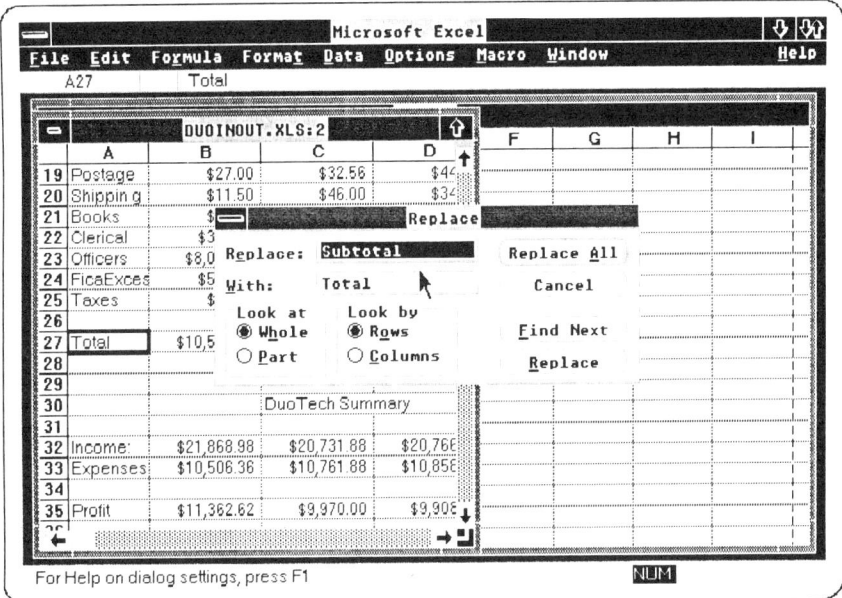

FIGURE 4.17. Formula Replace Dialog Box

window while the worksheet is active and the Info window is open. Just type the text you want to find in the Find What field and select the Notes option. The text is located and the cell containing it is made active. If the text can't be found, Excel sends you a "No match" message.

If you want to replace the found string with another, use the Formula Replace command instead. The dialog box is shown in Figure 4.17. You enter a string to find and a replacement string. As with Find, you select Whole or Part and tell Excel to search by rows or columns. Replacements never affect notes, but do affect both formulas and values. If you select Replace All, all occurrences are found and replaced automatically. If you select Find Next, Excel finds the next cell containing the string and pauses. You can select Replace to change it or Find Next to leave it alone. Then you can go on to the next match. When enough replacements are finished, select Cancel. This doesn't undo any replacements, just cancels the operation.

FINDING OTHER THINGS

Excel also lets you find other things quickly, through the Formula Select Special command. You saw earlier (Figure 4.15) how to use it to do a multiple selection of all cells that contain notes or have precedents or dependents. To use Select Special for the entire worksheet, select any single cell before using the command; to select within a certain range, select the range before using the command. Select Special lets you find cells that contain constant text, numbers, logical values, or error values. You can select all formulas that produce text, number, logical, or error values. If appropriate, you can select all cells that contain blanks.

The current region refers to the area around the active cell bounded by a blank row and column; to select it, position the active cell where you want and select Current Region. If the cursor is positioned within a numerical array, you can select the complete array with Current Array. Arrays are covered in Chapter 11.

If you select Row or Column Differences, Excel selects any cells in the selection that are different from the cells in the column or row of the active cell. The difference is based on the value or relative reference. Suppose you select the range shown in Figure 4.18, then use Formula Select Special to select the column differences. At a glance you can tell that each cell contains different values. But each cell in column C contains a formula of the same form: =B3/12 through =B9/12. Excel converts these relative formulas to R1C1 form, so each reads =RC[−1]; since the relative formulas match, they aren't selected.

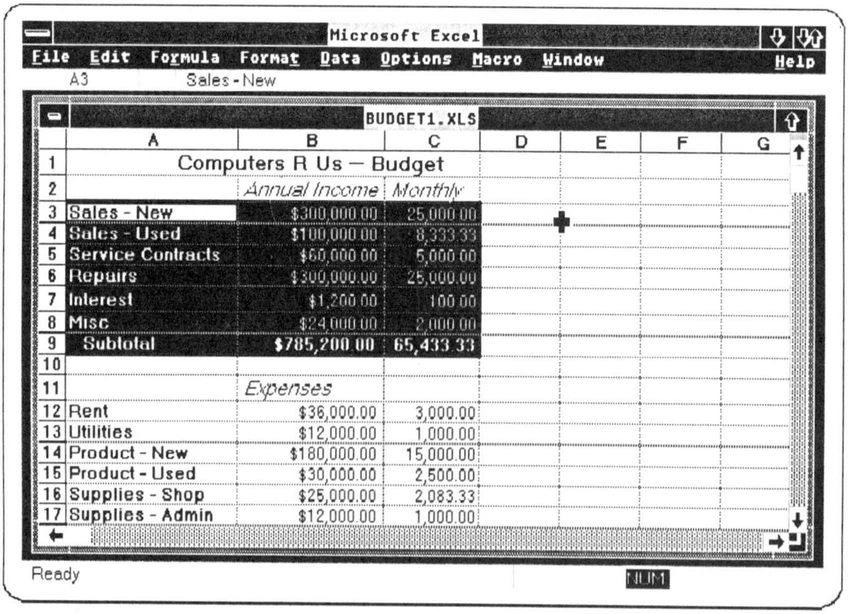

FIGURE 4.18. Before Column Differences Selection

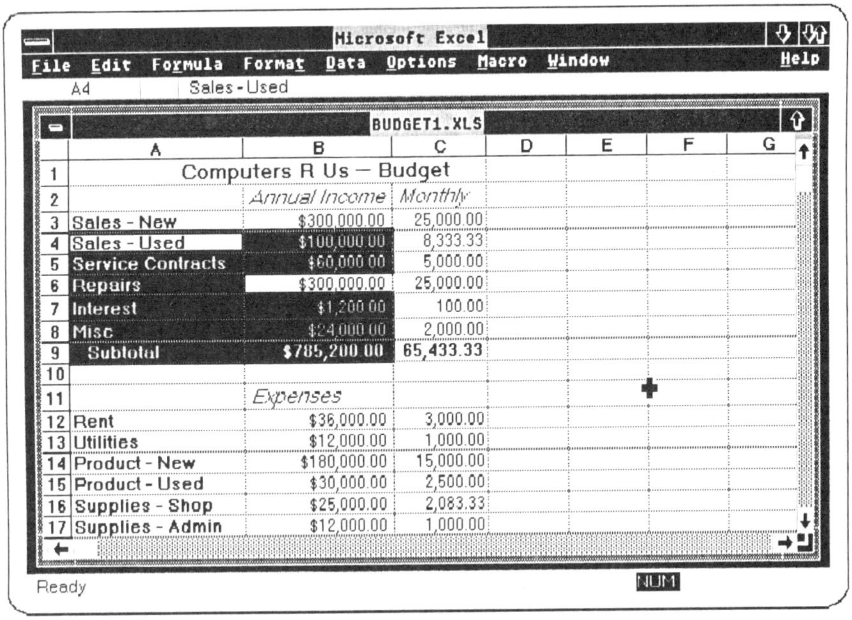

WORKSHEET SELECTION FEATURES

FIGURE 4.19. After Column Differences Selection

The result is shown in Figure 4.19. The active cell is the upper-left selected cell. The comparison cells (those in the first row in Figure 4.18) aren't selected, and neither are any cells from the third column. One cell in the center column is not selected because it matches the comparison cell in that column. The selection can be a range or a multiple selection; the active and comparison cells need not be within the selection. Comparison cells are never included in the final selection resulting from Row or Column Differences in the Formula Select Special command.

SUGGESTED EXERCISE

1. Use the Formula Note command to add notes to at least three cells in your practice worksheet.
2. Examine the cell information for a cell that has a note.
3. Close the SHEET1 worksheet, then use Window Arrange All so you can see your worksheet and the Info window at the same time. Make your worksheet active and change the active cell. Notice how the Info window changes.
4. Add more information to the Info Window. Turn on each feature listed on the Info Menu.
5. On your worksheet, make active a cell that contains a formula; notice the Info window contents.

6. On your worksheet, try to locate values. Use something you know is in several cells. Use Find Next to locate another one. Try replacing something in the text.
7. Select all cells that contain text constants. Then select all cells that contain number formulas. Try selecting all blank cells.
8. Examine the worksheet EXPENSES.XLS in the EXCELCBT directory. Check the notes and Info window for several cells.

What if It Doesn't Work?

1. You shouldn't have any trouble with notes and the Info window. If you do, check the Help system.
2. Finding is somewhat tricky. Be sure to specify "Part" if you don't give the entire cell contents to find. Be sure to completely erase previous items to find.

SUMMARY

This chapter focused on selection of cells and data, as well as on cell information. You can now set up and manipulate cells, ranges, and multiple selections. You can assign names to cells, ranges, values, and formulas; you can also manipulate and manage those names. You can use commands to move directly to any cell or to select by name or reference.

You can create and page through cell notes as needed. You can use the Info window to examine information about cells in a worksheet. You can also use various Formula commands to find data and conditions in the worksheet.

5 EXCEL FORMULAS AND FUNCTIONS

Values in cells can be derived from constants, references, or formulas. You have already learned to use constants and references, as well as basic formulas. Formulas can include constants, functions, operators, and so on. A thorough acquaintance with formula constraints is essential to developing efficient worksheets. This chapter begins with a review of the rules for developing formulas.

Excel offers more built-in functions than most of us will ever use. You've already seen some very common functions, such as SUM. This chapter overviews most of the functions that can be used in worksheets. Extra information is provided for functions you can use to make decisions or place new values in cells. For example, you'll see how to use various date functions in developing a generic monthly calendar. We'll spend some time with the IF function too, so you'll learn to tell worksheets to make decisions during calculations.

Functions that apply specifically to databases, lookup tables, arrays, and macros are covered in the appropriate chapters. All the worksheet functions can be used in macros as well; we'll cover macros starting in Chapter 12.

FORMULAS

A formula is made up of values, cell references, names, functions, and operators; it is contained in a cell and results in a single value. You enter the formula in the formula bar; it appears in the cell as well until you end it by pressing Enter or moving to another cell. Then the resulting value appears in the cell unless you have turned on Options Display Formulas; in that case, formulas also appear in the cells. If the formula isn't valid, a message box may appear. After you choose OK to remove the message box, the formula is selected so that you can correct it. Other formula errors result in a message in the cell rather than the value; these messages appear if you used an undefined name or referenced a cell that can't be found or is the wrong type, for example. The message gives some clue as to the problem.

Every formula begins with an equal sign (=); no embedded spaces can appear except as an operator or as part of a quoted text constant. You can type formulas directly, use pointing to pull in references, or use Edit Paste Names to insert defined names into formulas. If there is an error in formula construction, a message dialog box appears on the screen.

Operators in Formulas

You are already familiar with values, cell references, and names. You have undoubtedly used very basic functions such as SUM and operators such as + and −. Figure 5.1 shows all the operators you can use in Excel formulas. The arithmetic operators work as you would expect. The minus sign works to negate a single value. One common error in formulas is the omission of the * that signifies multiplication. This can cause incorrect results or an error message, such as #NAME? if Excel thinks you used an undefined name or #VALUE! if Excel thinks you used an invalid numeric value.

A formula that contains only constants and references will most likely use only the arithmetic operators. If the references refer to text values, you might use the text operator; & causes two text values to be joined together to form a new value. When cell B23 contains "Doris" and cell B24 contains "Simpson," the formula =B23&" "&B24 results in the value "Doris Simpson." Notice that the space is inserted as a text constant.

The comparison operators are mostly used in a function such as IF to set up a comparison. These operators compare two values and result in a logical value TRUE or FALSE. The formula =age>21 results in the value FALSE if the current value of age is 19.

Type of Operator	Operators	
Arithmetic	+	plus
	−	minus
	/	divided by
	*	times (multiplied by)
	%	percent
	^	exponent (to the power of)
Text	&	concatenation
Comparison	=	equals
	>	greater than
	<	less than
	>=	greater than or equal to
	<=	less than or equal to
	<>	not equal to
Reference	:	range
	,	union
	space	intersection

FIGURE 5.1. Operators for Formulas

EXCEL FORMULAS AND FUNCTIONS

```
Operator                    Type
:                           Reference (range)
space                       Reference (intersection)
,                           Reference (union)
-                           Arithmetic (negation)
%                           Arithmetic (percent)
^                           Arithmetic (exponentiation)
* and /                     Arithmetic (multiply and divide)
+ and -                     Arithmetic (add and subtract)
&                           Text (concatenation)
= > < >= <= <>              Comparison
```

FIGURE 5.2. Hierarchy of Operations

The reference operators combine two references resulting in a new reference. You have already used the range reference many times. In addition to the form you are used to, you can use B:B to reference all the cells in column B or 2:2 to refer to all the cells in row 2. Similarly, A:C refers to all the cells in columns A, B, and C, while 1:3 refers to all the cells in the top three rows.

The space operator is also called the intersection operator; the intersection operator produces one reference to all cells in common between two references. The formula =B:B 1:3 produces a reference to cells B1, B2, and B3; these cells are in both references enclosing the space. The comma is often called the union operator; it produces a reference that includes all the cells in either of the two references. The formula =A4,B:B,1:3 produces a reference to cell A4, all the cells in column B, and all the cells in rows 1, 2, and 3.

Excel calculates formulas in a certain order. Figure 5.2 shows the hierarchy of evaluation among all the operators. Excel evaluates the formula =A2*B2+7 by multiplying the value in cell A2 by the value in cell B2, then adding the constant 7 to the result. You can modify the order of evaluation by using parentheses; Excel evaluates expressions inside parentheses first, so the formula =A2*(B2+7) has a different result from the one shown earlier. When a level includes more than one operator, as in =B2*C2/D2*E2, they are evaluated from left to right; in this example the value in B2 is multiplied by the value in C2, then that product is divided by the value in D2 and that result multiplied by the value in E2. Omitted or mismatched parentheses are one of the major causes of errors in formulas.

Entering Formulas

You can enter a formula by selecting a cell, then typing in the formula bar. Begin every formula with the equal sign or Excel treats it as text. You can minimize reference errors by using pointing to select cells from the active worksheet when the word "Enter" appears in the status bar. Immediately following the equal sign, an operator, a comma, or a left parenthesis, use the arrow keys to select a cell or range. A dotted marquee surrounds the selected item, its reference appears in the formula bar, and the word "Point" appears in the status bar. You can paste the selection and cancel Point mode by typing another operator, comma, or left parenthesis or by pressing Enter. The reference will be entered in relative format; you can change it to absolute in the formula bar if appropriate. If the formula includes any names or functions you can paste them in, using the appropriate Formula Paste commands.

Viewing Formulas

You can always see the formula for the active cell in the formula bar and start the edit process by pressing F2. If you want to see all the formulas in the worksheet, turn on the Formulas field in the Options Display dialog box. Excel adjusts the column width and displays formulas in all cells that contain them. Figure 5.3 shows a screen with formulas displayed.

To see the values and formulas at the same time, you can open another window on the same worksheet and view formulas in one and values in the other. This is covered in more detail later in this book.

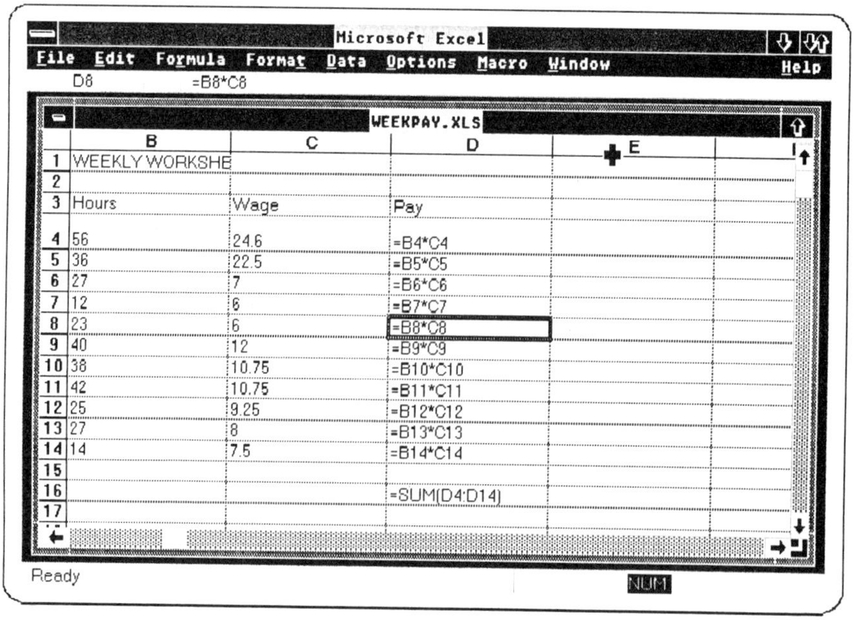

FIGURE 5.3. Displaying Formulas

Printing Formulas

When you print a worksheet, the resulting printout shows values if the display has values, formulas if the display has formulas. To print the worksheet with formulas in place, just display the formulas, then print. Another way to print formulas is to use the Window Show Info command to open the Info window; make sure the Formula is displayed, then select Print from the Info pull-down menu. You'll get a listing of the Info windows for each filled cell in the worksheet. Printing is covered in detail in Chapter 6.

FUNCTIONS

Excel provides over a hundred worksheet functions that you can use in formulas to provide values in cells or in macro definitions. The functions can be used alone or as parts of other formulas or functions. For example, you could use =SUM(A5:A20), =B20−SUM(A5:A20), or =SUM(A5:A20,COUNT(B:B)). The critical parts of a function are the function name followed by arguments in parentheses. You can use either uppercase or lowercase letters in the function and its arguments.

Arguments

Each built-in function has an argument list to be enclosed in parentheses. Arguments can be numbers, text, logical values (TRUE or FALSE), arrays, error values, or references. Any of these can be replaced by a name, a function, a formula, or a reference. The argument list for a function requires that the arguments be of certain types. For the SUM function, for example, all arguments must have number values; it ignores cells that contain other types of data.

Each function format includes an argument list that indicates the type of data expected for each argument; it also indicates which arguments are required, which are optional, and which can be repeated. The syntax used for this purpose conforms to the syntax in the Excel documentation. An argument that appears in italics is optional, one followed by an ellipsis (. . .) can be repeated. All others are required. The format SUM(number1,*number2*,. . .) indicates that the SUM function requires at least one argument, a second is optional and may be repeated, and they must all have number values.

For some functions, Excel ignores data of the wrong type. For others, Excel tries to translate arguments into the required type. For example, if a number is required and a referenced cell contains "1989" as text, Excel uses 1989 as a number in calculating the result of the formula; it doesn't change the type of data in the referenced cell, however. If the value can't be ignored or translated to the necessary type, the effect depends on the function; in most cases, you'll get an error message.

Using Functions

You are already familiar with a few functions, such as SUM. You use functions in a formula by typing them in format or by pasting them in. When you start typing, the word "Enter" replaces "Ready" in the status bar; when you see either "Ready" or "Enter," you can use the Formula Paste Function command. Figure 5.4 shows the resulting dialog box.

The list box contains all the built-in worksheet functions provided by Excel in alphabetical order. If you have created additional function macros, they'll be listed at the end (see Chapter 13). You can include a function from the list in the formula bar by selecting it here and choosing OK. To move quickly through the list, just press the initial letter of the function you want. To get SUM, press S,

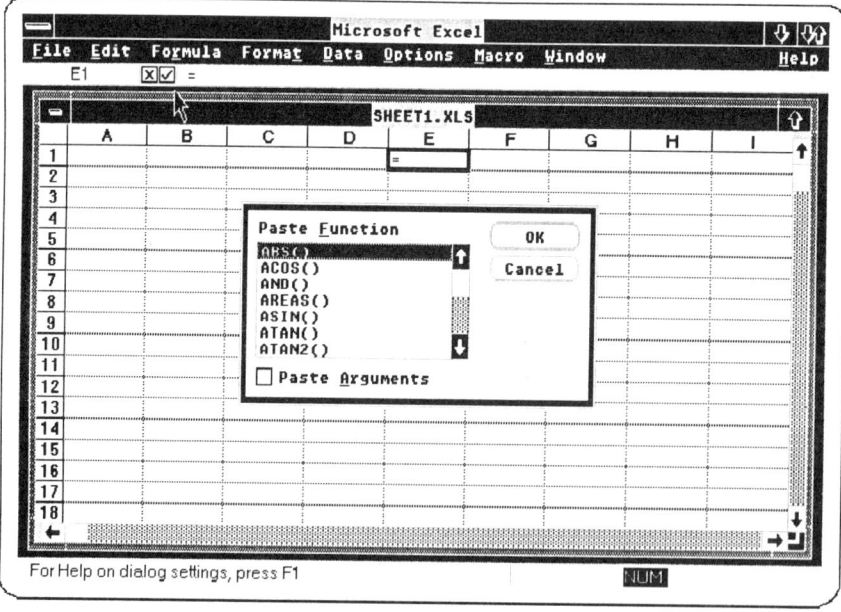

FIGURE 5.4. Formula Paste Function Dialog Box

EXCEL FORMULAS AND FUNCTIONS

then repeat S or downarrow until SUM is selected. When you choose OK, the selected function is pasted into the formula with the insertion point between the parentheses that will enclose the argument list.

If a pasted function is the first item in the formula bar, Excel includes the equal sign as well. If you want, Excel can tell you what arguments are expected. Just turn on the Paste Arguments box after selecting the function but before choosing OK. In this case, Excel inserts SUM(number1,number2,...) in the formula bar, with number1 highlighted. If you type a character before you move the cursor, it replaces the highlighted area. Then you can move the cursor to enter later argument values. Remember to remove the argument names; these are placeholders only, included to remind you of the needed values. And you can't tell which arguments are required and which are optional in the formula bar, except that if you omit a required one you'll get an error message.

The next section includes brief descriptions and examples of many of the functions provided by Excel. In the process, you'll see examples of applications of functions that you may find useful even in fairly simple worksheets.

Date Functions

The date functions extract various values from the date and time. You already know that these are stored as serial numbers; the date is a five-digit number, with 00001 representing 1/1/1900. The time is represented as a serial number separated from the date number by a decimal point; .5 means noon, .75 means 6 P.M., and so forth.

DATE(year,month,day)   Each argument here must be a number. If you use =date(1988,June,1), the active cell receives the message #NAME!. When you correct the formula to read DATE(1988,6,1), the cell contains 32295.

DATEVALUE(date_text)   This argument must be text in any of Excel's built-in date formats; it must be enclosed in quotes. You could use =DATEVALUE("June 1, 1988") to get the value 32295. A numeric value, such as 32295, results in an error message. If cell A5 contains 1–Jun–88 (stored as a serial number) and the active cell contains the formula =DATEVALUE(A5), the message #VALUE! results. On the other hand, if A5 contains "June 1, 1988" as quoted text, the function will work.

DAY(serial_number)   This argument is a five-digit number representing the date. The result is a value from 1 to 31 indicating the day of the represented month in the represented year. The function =day(32295) returns 1, since the date represented is June 1, 1988. A cell reference to a formatted date also works fine, since Excel uses the stored value in all calculations.

HOUR(serial_number) This argument corresponds to the internal stored value Excel uses; the five digits before the decimal point represent the date and any digits following the decimal point give the time on that date. The result is a value from 0 to 23 indicating the hour of the represented time.

MINUTE(serial_number) This argument is a serial number representing a date/time combination. The result is a value from 0 to 59 indicating the minute of the represented time.

MONTH(serial_number) This argument is a five-digit number representing the date. The result is a value from 1 to 12 indicating the month of the represented date. The function =month(32295) returns 6, since the date represented is June 6, 1988.

NOW() This function has an empty (null) argument list, but it still requires the parentheses. It returns the serial number of the current date and time; the result looks like 32295.65. You could use =DAY(NOW()+1) to get the day of the month for tomorrow. The DAY function ignores anything following the decimal point.

SECOND(serial_number) This argument is the serial number representing the date/time. The result is a value from 0 through 59 indicating the second in the represented time. You could use =SECOND(NOW()) as a formula to get the current second.

TIME(hour,minute,second) These arguments give the hour (between 0 and 23, the minute (between 0 and 59, and the second (between 0 and 59) of the time for which you want the serial number. The result of =TIME(12,50,2) is .534745.

TIMEVALUE(time_text) This argument must be quoted text in any of Excel's built-in time formats. The result is a five-digit serial number representing the given time. TIMEVALUE is equivalent to the DATEVALUE function.

WEEKDAY(serial_number) This argument is a five-digit serial number representing a date. The result is an integer from 1 through 7 indicating the day of the week of the represented date; 1 represents Sunday, 7, Saturday.

YEAR(serial_number) This argument is a five-digit serial number representing a date. The result is a four-digit year between 1900 and 2078 represented by the serial number.

EXCEL FORMULAS AND FUNCTIONS

Using Date Functions. Many uses of date functions are obvious. But you can create very complex uses. For example, you can create a calendar that can be tailored to any month and year; if it uses the right functions, Excel will fill in the days of the month in the right spots.

First, lay out the worksheet as in Figure 5.5. It shows row and column heads along with borders. On screen, it's more convenient to have gridlines on, but they are hard to distinguish from the borders. We've allowed six weeks, since some months need that many. The weekday names are put in as text; the month name in E3 must be added when you generate a specific calendar. The formula in cell E1 causes the year to be displayed when the name is defined; both year and month are defined names, year referring to a four-digit number and month to a value between 1 and 12. We've defined #;; as a custom format for use in all the day of the month cells; a positive value will show but others won't. The formulas in cells E4, F4, and G4 can be hidden with format ;;.

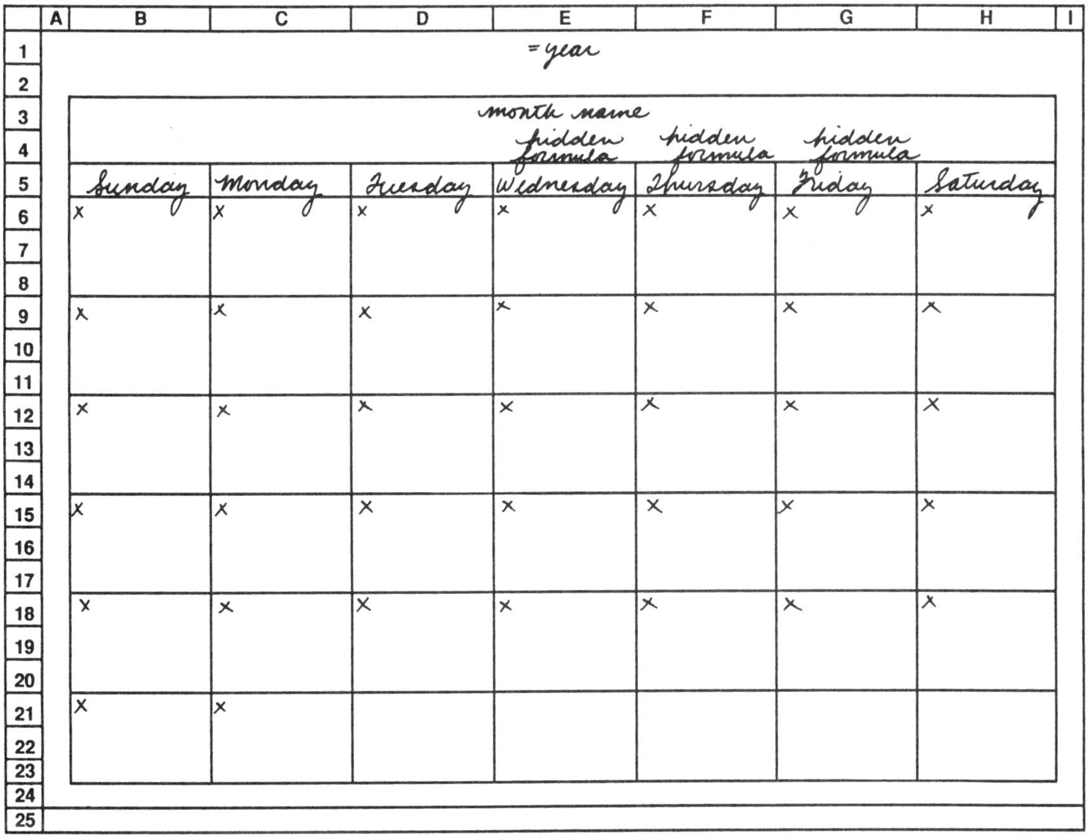

FIGURE 5.5. Monthly Calendar Layout

```
Cell       Formula
E4         =DATE(year,month,1)         (serial date for first)
F4         =WEEKDAY(E4)-1              (day of last day of last month)
G4         =DATE(year,month+1,1)-E4    (number of days this month)
B6:H6      =1-F4 through =7-F4
B9:H9      =8-F4 through =14-F4
B12:H12    =15-F4 through =21=F4
B15:H15    -22-F4 through -28-F4
```

FIGURE 5.6. Monthly Calendar Formulas

The major problem in creating the calendar is figuring out where to put the day numbers. To do that, you need to know the weekday of the first day of the month and the number of days in the month. We start by calculating the serial number for the first day of the month, using the following formula: =DATE(year,month,1); remember that year and month are defined names. We've placed this formula in cell E4 with a formula that keeps it from displaying. To find the number of days in the month, you can calculate the serial number of the first of the next month and subtract, with =DATE(year,month+1,1)−E4 as the formula. If month happens to be 12, Excel knows that month+1 refers to January and increments the year in the formula as well. Since we put this formula in cell G4, that cell now contains the number of days in the month. We still have to know the day on which the month begins, which we can find with the formula =WEEKDAY(E4)−1; we'll store this formula in cell F4.

Now we start with the first day of the first week, a Sunday, in cell B6. We calculate its day value with the formula =1−F4. If the month starts on a Sunday, F4 contains 0, so the result of =1−F4 is 1; since the format is #;; the value will display and we have started the calendar at the correct day. If the month begins on any other day of the week, the value in B6 will be 0 or negative, so nothing displays. We place the formula =2−F4 in cell C6 for Monday; again, the day will display if appropriate and not if the date isn't 1 or 2. This system continues through the first four weeks, with =28−F4 in cell H15 for the fourth Saturday. After this point, the formula must check for the end of the month; that requires functions we haven't covered yet. You'll see how to complete the calendar later in this chapter. Figure 5.6 lists the formulas currently in the first part of the calendar worksheet.

SUGGESTED EXERCISE

1. On SHEET1, try out a few functions. What day of the week was January 13, 1940? What is the date 90 days from today? Try several time functions as well.
2. Create a new worksheet for a monthly calendar of your own. Put in borders and

EXCEL FORMULAS AND FUNCTIONS

adjust the columns width so it is similar to Figure 5.5. Add in the weekday names and the name of the current month.

3. Define the month and year as names; give values of the current month and year. Use = year to put the current year in the worksheet.
4. Define hidden formulas like the ones in row 4 to establish the date and weekday of the first of the month and the number of days in the month. Use a custom format of ; to keep them from printing.
5. Enter formulas to calculate the actual dates for the first four weeks of the calendar. You'll need a custom format of #;; so that negative or zero dates don't print.
6. Try out the calendar. Change the month and year under the Define Name command to see if the calendar changes.
7. Save the calendar under a name like ONEMONTH.XLS. You'll do the last week later in this chapter. In later chapters, you'll be able to polish it some more.

What if It Doesn't Work?

1. If your dates are wrong, your system may not know what the date and time are. Check your system documentation to set them correctly.
2. If you have trouble with the calendar, examine MONTHCAL.XLS in your LIBRARY subdirectory. It is similar and may help you get yours working correctly.

Financial Functions

Excel's financial functions help you calculate values often used in banks and businesses. On a personal level, you may find them helpful in evaluating investments, in figuring out payments on a new car, or for refinancing a house. These financial functions fall into three general groupings: depreciation, annuities and investment, and rates of return. We won't cover these in any great detail; you can find more details in the Functions and Macros Reference if you need to use them.

Depreciation Functions. Three functions calculate depreciation, one does straight line, one does sum-of-years digits, and one does double declining balance for a given period. The arguments are similar in all.

Argument	What it is
cost	original cost of item
salvage	estimated worth at end of useful life
life	useful life; number of periods
period	period in question; 1st year, 5th month

Be sure to specify the life in terms of the number of periods, to correspond with the period in question. If you want depreciation by month, specify the life in terms of total months. If you want quarters, use total quarters.

DDB(cost,salvage,life,period) This function uses the formula ((cost − total depreciation from prior periods)*2)/life to calculate the double declining balance depreciation for the specified period. If your new computer cost $8,450 and has an estimated salvage value of $1,000 after a useful life of 5 years, you could get the depreciation in the first quarter of the second year with =DDB(8450,1000,20,5) which results in 555.40. Notice that we used the number of quarters in the life (20) and period (5) arguments.

SLN(cost,salvage,life) This function calculates the straight-line depreciation for one period; since it's the same for each period, you don't have to specify any given period. The straight-line depreciation of our computer for one year would be determined by =SLN(8450,1000,5) which results in 1490.

SYN(cost,salvage,life,period) This function calculates the sum-of-years digit depreciation. The result for the same period for which we used DDB is 567.62.

Investment and Annuity Functions. Several functions result in values specific to annuities and investment applications. You can calculate the present or future value of an annuity or investment. You can calculate the interest or principal component of a payment, or the periodic payment itself. You can also calculate the number of periods or the interest rate. All these functions use the same set of arguments, sometimes in a different order. Some arguments are required and some are optional, depending on the function.

Argument	What it is
fv	future value (value at end of period; value 0 for loan)
nper	number of periods
per	period in question; between 1 and nper
pmt	amount of payment; interest + principal
pv	present value; total value for loan
rate	interest rate per period
type	when due; end of period = 0, beginning of period = 1; default is 0
guess	trial interest rate; default is 10%

The values you supply for all these arguments must be numbers. Be sure to consider the same period for nper and per, and use the interest rate to corre-

EXCEL FORMULAS AND FUNCTIONS

spond. If the annual interest is 8.4% and the period is monthly, you can use .084/12 as the rate. Of course, you can use a name or a reference as well. In entering payment and value figures, use negative numbers for amounts you pay out and positive numbers for amounts that come in. A loan payment of $450 appears as −450 if you are the one who pays, and as 450 if you receive the income.

FV(rate,nper,pmt,*pv,type*) This function calculates the future value of an investment, given the interest rate, number of periods, and payment per period. Present value is assumed to be zero if you don't include it. The payment is credited at the end of the period if you don't specify otherwise.

IPMT(rate,per,nper,pv,*fv,type*) This function calculates the interest in the specific payment represented by per. You provide the interest rate, the specific payment (period) you are concerned with, the number of periods, and the total (present) value. The future value is assumed to be zero if you don't specify it; it's always zero for a loan.

NPER(rate,pmt,pv,*fv,type*) This function returns the number of periods (payments) in an investment or annuity, given the interest rate, payment, and present value.

PMT(rate,nper,pv,*fv,type*) This function returns the size of payment, given the rate, number of periods, and present value. To get the monthly payment of a $12000 five-year loan at 11%, you'd use PMT(.11/12,60,12000).

PPMT(rate,per,nper,pv,*fv,type*) This function returns the principal included in a specific payment. It is equivalent to IPMT, providing the other portion of the payment.

PV(rate,nper,pmt,*fv,type*) This function returns the present value of an investment or annuity, given the rate, number of periods, and the payment. The future value is assumed to be zero and the payments are applied at the end of each period if you don't specify otherwise.

RATE(nper,pmt,pv,*fv,type,guess*) This function returns the interest rate (per period), given the number of periods, the payment per period, and the present value. The future value is assumed to be zero and the payments are applied at the end of the period if you don't specify otherwise. The estimated interest rate (guess) starts at 10%; you can change this if no valid value is returned by the function.

Rate of Return Functions. Three financial functions use a set of values to determine values related to rates of return. You can find the internal rate of return, the modified internal rate of return, or the net present value. The arguments vary among the three, but all depend on a set of positive and negative values representing periodic cash flow. These values must be in the correct sequence, since Excel uses that sequence in calculating the result.

> **IRR**(values,*guess*)   This function calculates the internal rate of return based on uneven payments over equal-length periods. The values argument must refer to a selection that includes numbers; any text, logical, or empty cells are ignored. At least one positive and one negative value must be included in the reference. Excel uses a rate of 10% and an iterative process; if it isn't correct within .00001% after 20 tries, the function returns the error message #NUM!. You can try again with different values of guess.
>
> **NPV**(rate,value1,*value2*,...)   This function is related to IRR; IRR gives the rate for which NPV equals zero. Here you can specify a list of values. A separate cell reference counts if it is a number, text equivalent to a number, logical, or empty. Only actual values count in a range or array value. The rate gives the discount rate for one period.
>
> **MIRR**(values,finance_rate,reinvest_rate)   This function gives a modified internal rate of return, based on an array or other reference to a set of values, the cost of the investment (finance_rate), and the interest on a reinvestment in cash (reinvest_rate). Restrictions on the values are the same as for the IRR function.

Information Functions

The information functions return information about a cell or reference. The argument is generally a reference or array. There are two types of information function. One type returns a logical value (TRUE or FALSE) based on what it finds out about a reference. The others return different types of values.

Logical Returns. The functions that return a logical value all use a value as an argument. The value is generally a reference to a single cell; sometimes a range argument returns useful information.

> **ISBLANK**(reference)   This function returns the value TRUE if the referenced cell or cells are blank and FALSE if they are not. If the value is a range, the returned value is FALSE if any of the cells are not blank.
>
> **ISERR**(reference)   This function returns the value TRUE if the referenced cell or cells contain any error value except #N/A and FALSE otherwise. If the value is a range, the returned value is FALSE if any of the cells does not contain an error value.

EXCEL FORMULAS AND FUNCTIONS

ISERROR(reference)   This function returns the value TRUE if the referenced cell or cells contain any error value at all, even #N/A. It returns FALSE if any referenced cell does not contain an error value.

ISLOGICAL(reference)   This function returns the value TRUE if the referenced cell or cells contain a logical value. It returns FALSE if any referenced cell does not contain a logical value.

ISNA(reference)   This function returns the value TRUE if the referenced cell or cells contain the error value #N/A. It returns FALSE if any referenced cell does not contain #N/A.

ISNONTEXT(reference)   This function returns the value TRUE if the referenced cell or cells contain nontext values. It returns FALSE if any referenced cell contains numbers, references, errors, or logical values.

ISNUMBER(reference)   This function returns the value TRUE if the referenced cell or cells contain number values. It returns FALSE if any referenced cell contains a reference, text, error message, or logical value. No translation is done here; if a cell contains "17.2" as quoted text, the function returns FALSE, because it is text, not a number.

ISREF(reference)   This function returns the value TRUE if the referenced cell or cells contain references. It returns FALSE if any referenced cell contains a number, text, error message, or logical value.

ISTEXT(reference)   This function returns the value TRUE if the referenced cell or cells contain text. It returns FALSE if any referenced cell contains a nontext value.

Cell Information. Several functions return specific information about a cell or a reference. You can find out the column or row number, the number of disconnected areas in a multiple selection, the number of columns or rows in an array, the contents of a referenced cell, or any of various bits of information about a cell itself. In addition, you can place the value #N/A in a cell or translate a value in a cell into a number. These functions use several types of arguments.

Argument	What it is
reference	a name or cell reference
array	single array reference
value	any reference or array

AREAS(reference)   This function returns the number of areas in the named reference. You can use it to determine if a name refers to a multiple selection; a returned value of 1 indicates a single cell or range. The value returned is the total of ranges and disconnected single cells.

CELL(type_of_info,reference)   This function returns a specific type of

```
Type_of_info            Returns

"width"                 column width, rounded to nearest integer
"row"                   row number
"col"                   column number
"protect"               1 if locked, otherwise 0
"address"               reference of 1st cell as text
"contents"              value in reference

"type"                  "b" if blank
                        "l" (label) if text
                        "v" (value) if anything else

"prefix"                "'" if left aligned
                        """ if right aligned
                        "^" if centered
                        " " if anything else

"format"                "G"  General
                        "F0" 0 or #,##0
                        "F2" 0.00 or #,##0.00
                        "C0" $#,##0;($#,##0) or
                             $#,##0;[RED]($#,##0)
                        "C2" $#,##0.00;($#,##0.00) or
                             $#,##0.00;[RED]($#,##0.00)
                        "P0" 0%
                        "P2" 0.00%
                        "S2" 0.00E+00
                        plus various date formats
                        plus codes for customized formats
```

FIGURE 5.7. CELL Function Argument Values

information about the reference; if reference is omitted, the active cell is assumed. The type_of_info argument must be enclosed in quotes. Figure 5.7 lists the valid values for type_of_info, with the type of information returned. As you can tell from the argument values, you can get almost any type of information about a given cell through the function just as you can in an Info window.

COLUMN(*reference*)   This function returns the column numbers involved in reference. If reference is omitted, the number of the current column is returned.

COLUMNS(array)   This function returns the number of columns in the array. Notice that this function name ends in S. It returns the total number of columns in the array, not the actual column numbers.

INDIRECT(ref_text,*type_of_ref*)   This function returns the contents of the single cell indicated by ref_text. Ref_text is generally a name; it can be a cell reference in either A1 or R1C1 style. The referenced cell contains a reference, also in either A1 or R1C1 style. The type_of_ref argument tells Excel the format of the reference contained in that cell; if omitted or TRUE, the contained reference is in A1 style. If FALSE, the contained reference is in R1C1 style.

N(*value*)   This function returns the value translated into a number. The translation is generally automatic; this function is included just because it is needed in some other worksheet programs.

NA()   This function requires no arguments, but the parentheses must still be included. It puts the value #N/A into the active cell. This helps to eliminate blank cells that might otherwise affect calculations.

ROW(*reference*)   This function returns the row number of the reference. If you omit the row reference, it returns the current row.

ROWS(*array*)   This function returns the number of rows in the referenced array. Notice that the function name ends in S. It returns the total number of rows, not the actual row numbers.

T(*value*)   This function translates the value into text; like the N function, it isn't generally used in Excel.

TYPE(*value*)   This function returns a number corresponding to the data type of the value, which can be any data or reference; the value can even include an operator, such as + or &.

- 1   number
- 2   text
- 4   logical value
- 16 error value
- 64 array

If C12 contains a date, displayed as 1-Jun-1988, TYPE(C12) returns the value 1, reflecting the stored serial number. A function like TYPE("Mr. ") or TYPE(A3) when cell A3 contains ''Wednesday'' returns the value 2, since it contains text.

Logical Functions

Excel provides several sets of logical functions. One set simply assigns the value TRUE or FALSE to the active cell. Another lets Excel make decisions based on a condition. The third set lets you combine expressions to form complex conditions.

Assigning Logical Values. These functions let you assign logical values to cells. If you just type TRUE or FALSE in a cell, it is treated as text rather than as a logical value.

FALSE()   This function assigns the logical value FALSE to the active cell.
TRUE()   This function assigns the logical value TRUE to the active cell.

Making Decisions. The IF function has a complex format but so many uses that it is worth learning, at least at a basic level. In this function, you provide a condition and say to Excel "if this condition is true, do this, otherwise do that." So you can say something like "if the value in cell B12 is greater than 500, put 10% in the current cell, otherwise put 6% here."

> **IF(logical_test,value_if_true,value_if_false)**   This function returns value_if_true if the logical_test is true and value_if_false if the logical_test is false. The logical test is an expression such as A4⟩21 or B26 = "#N/A" or even 32 − F4⟨ = G5. The conditional operators in the next section can be included in the logical_test as well.

The IF function needs a bit more explanation. If you have done any programming, even handling merge files through your word processor, you won't have any trouble with this. Basically, you use the IF function when you want something different in a cell based on conditions at the time. If you want to subtract a discount if a total in column G in the same row is over the value named cutoff but not otherwise, you could use this function:

$$IF(G\rangle cutoff,discount,0)$$

Excel compares the value in column G in the same row to the value named cutoff. If the value is larger than cutoff, the amount named discount is placed in the cell containing the function. Otherwise, the value 0 is placed there.

Figure 5.8 shows a worksheet that uses IF to determine what is placed in a cell. Notice that the formula for the active cell is displayed in the formula bar. If the hours are 40 or less, the pay cell receives the product of hours and wage. If the hours are greater than 40, the pay cell receives the product of 40 times wage, plus the product of (hours minus 40) times wage times one and one half. The formula calculates overtime if needed.

As another example, remember the calendar we discussed earlier (Figure 5.5). The last two rows of days require the IF function to determine if the day value has exceeded the number of days in the month. Here's the function for the first day of the fifth week:

$$IF(29-F4\langle =G4,29-F4,"")$$

This function compares the day of the month (29 − F4) to the value calculated in G4, which is the number of days in the month. If a date must be printed, it is (29 − F4). If not, blank text is placed in the cell. The functions for the rest of the cells in the row are similar, using 30 − F4 through 35 − F4 as the dates compared

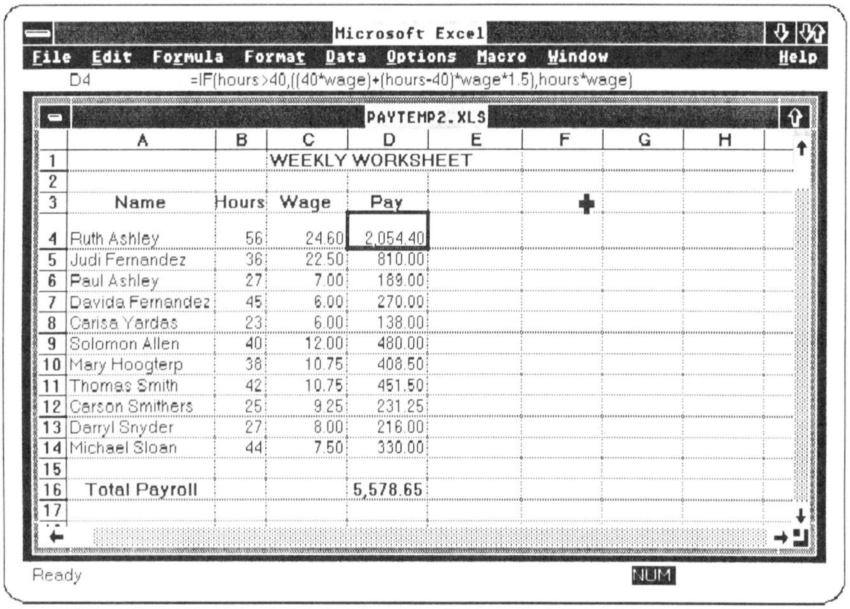

	A	B	C	D	E	F	G	H
1			WEEKLY WORKSHEET					
2								
3	Name	Hours	Wage	Pay				
4	Ruth Ashley	56	24.60	2,054.40				
5	Judi Fernandez	36	22.50	810.00				
6	Paul Ashley	27	7.00	189.00				
7	Davida Fernandez	45	6.00	270.00				
8	Carisa Yardas	23	6.00	138.00				
9	Solomon Allen	40	12.00	480.00				
10	Mary Hoogterp	38	10.75	408.50				
11	Thomas Smith	42	10.75	451.50				
12	Carson Smithers	25	9.25	231.25				
13	Darryl Snyder	27	8.00	216.00				
14	Michael Sloan	44	7.50	330.00				
15								
16	Total Payroll			5,578.65				
17								

FIGURE 5.8. IF Function in Worksheet

or printed; 36 – F4 and 37 – F4 are placed in the first two days of the last week in case the month extends beyond five weeks.

You can use IF with the logical information functions to test values and provide messages. For example, IF(ISERROR(B35),"No problem","Check B35") puts the appropriate message in the cell that contains it to alert the user to a potential problem.

IF functions can also be nested to make multiple decisions for a single cell. Here's an example:

= IF(B9<21,"Minor",(IF(B9>64,"Senior","Adult")))

In this function the basic logic test is B9<21. If that is true, the text "Minor" is placed in the cell. If not, another logic test, B9>64, is applied. If this inner condition (the value in cell B9 is greater than 64) is true, the text "Senior" is placed in the cell; otherwise, the text "Adult" is placed in the cell.

Logical Operators. In logical operations, you can use AND, OR, and NOT as operators to produce logical values from other logical values. Logical arguments must be TRUE or FALSE or numbers translatable to logical values; 1 translates to TRUE and 0 to FALSE. Any other value results in the message #VALUE!. If the reference is to an array or multicell reference, all the contents must be logical values.

AND(logical1,*logical2*,. . .) This function returns TRUE if all the logical values of the arguments are true and FALSE if any argument is false. You can use up to 14 arguments.

OR(logical1,*logical2*,. . .) This function returns FALSE if all the logical values of the arguments are false and TRUE if any argument is true. You can use up to 14 arguments.

NOT(logical) This function reverses the logical value of the argument. It returns TRUE if the argument is false and FALSE if the argument is true.

Here's an example:

= IF((AND,B9 = 0,D9>6),"Valid","Invalid")

In this function, the logic tests if the contents of cell B9 is zero and the contents of cell D9 is greater than 6. If both of these are true, then the value of the condition is true, and the text ''Valid'' is placed in the cell. If either cell B9 does not contain zero or the value in cell D9 is 6 or less, the condition is false and the value ''Invalid'' is placed in the cell. If the same function were written with OR instead of AND, only one of the logical expressions would have to be true to make the entire condition true.

Figure 5.9 shows another example of a compound condition. In this exam-

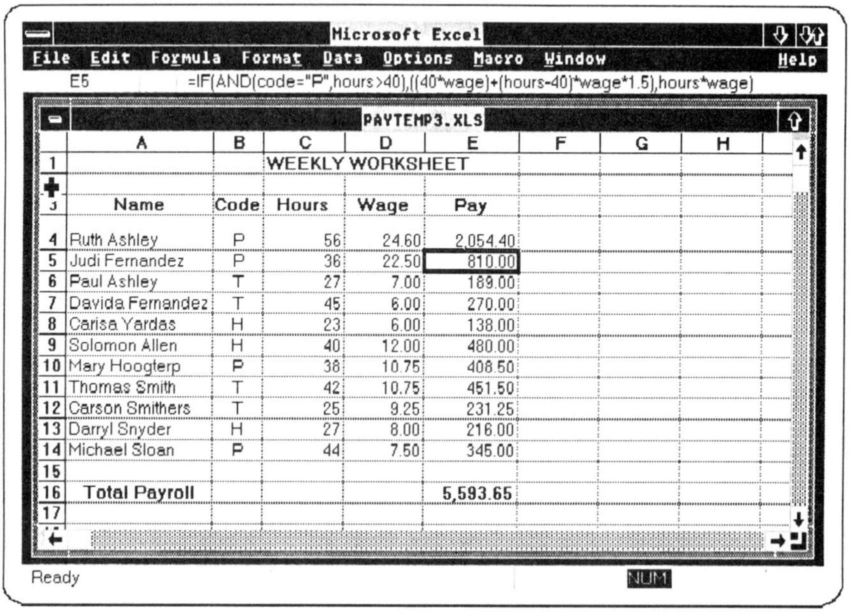

	A	B	C	D	E	F	G	H
1			WEEKLY WORKSHEET					
2								
3	Name	Code	Hours	Wage	Pay			
4	Ruth Ashley	P	56	24.60	2,054.40			
5	Judi Fernandez	P	36	22.50	810.00			
6	Paul Ashley	T	27	7.00	189.00			
7	Davida Fernandez	T	45	6.00	270.00			
8	Carisa Yardas	H	23	6.00	138.00			
9	Solomon Allen	H	40	12.00	480.00			
10	Mary Hoogterp	P	38	10.75	408.50			
11	Thomas Smith	T	42	10.75	451.50			
12	Carson Smithers	T	25	9.25	231.25			
13	Darryl Snyder	H	27	8.00	216.00			
14	Michael Sloan	P	44	7.50	345.00			
15								
16	Total Payroll				5,593.65			
17								

FIGURE 5.9. Compound Function

ple, the overtime is calculated only if the person worked more than 40 hours and is flagged as a permanent employee.

SUGGESTED EXERCISE

1. Complete your monthly calendar by adding formulas for the last two weeks. Use the IF function to determine if the last day of the month has passed yet. Try the calendar again for another month and year. Is it still correct? It should be right even in leap years.
2. Try an IF function to add a column of text values in your practice worksheet. If you have a numeric column, select its approximate midpoint and place "OVER" or "UNDER" in each cell in the new column to reflect the value in the numeric column.
3. Try some financial or information functions if you like. Check the format of a named cell. Find the monthly payment on a $13,000 car loan at 15% for four years.

What if It Doesn't Work?

1. In the calendar, check MONTHCAL.XLS again to compare your results.
2. With functions, check the use of commas, parentheses, and arguments. Use Paste Function with Paste Arguments as a reminder. The format is critical here.

Mathematical Functions

Excel offers a set of functions you can use to calculate mathematical values for cells. Many of these require a single number as an argument; the number can be represented by a constant, an expression, a cell reference, or a name. If the value doesn't meet the argument requirements, the message #NUM! appears in the cell. You probably won't have to use all of these; in fact, if you've never heard of the function, you'll most likely never need to use it.

ABS(number)   This function returns the absolute value of the number, its value without any sign. Since many functions require a positive number, the ABS function can be useful when you aren't sure if a value is positive or negative, but you want Excel to treat it as if it is positive. ABS(4*B12) returns the result of the multiplication without any sign indication.

EXP(number)   This function returns the value of e raised to the power of number. The value of e is 2.71828182845904; it is the base of the natural logarithm. If you want to raise a number to a certain power, use the ∧ operator in an expression. The LN function is the inverse of EXP.

FACT(number)   This function returns the factorial of number. FACT(6) returns the value 720 (6*5*4*3*2*1). The number specified is truncated if it is not an integer; it must not be negative. Use FACT(ABS(A4)) to find the factorial of the value in cell A4 if you aren't sure if it is positive or negative.

INT(number)   This function returns the value of number rounded down to the nearest integer. =INT(9.8) returns 9, while =INT(−9.8) returns −10. Notice that it doesn't just drop the decimal portion; the TRUNC function does that.

LN(number)   This function returns the natural logarithm of number; it is the inverse of the EXP function. Number here must be positive. If you aren't sure, you can use =LN(ABS(B7)).

LOG(number,*base*)   This function returns the logarithm of number in the base specified. If base is omitted, 10 is used. The number must be positive.

LOG10(number)   This function returns the base 10 logarithm of number. It is equivalent to LOG with the base omitted. As with log, the number must be positive.

MOD(number,divisor_number)   This function returns the remainder of dividing number by the specified divisor. MOD(29,7) returns the value 1. In noncomputer math, the example is referred to as 29 mod 7.

PI()   This function returns the value of pi, 3.14159 carried to a total of 15 significant digits. You can use it in a formula, as in =PI()*B12∧2 to calculate the area of a circle. No arguments are allowed, but the parentheses are required.

PRODUCT(number1,*number2*,...)   This function returns the product of the listed numbers. If the list refers to single elements, they can be numbers, logical values, empty cells, or text that translates to numbers. Any references to multiple cells must have only numbers in all the referenced cells. You can use up to 14 arguments.

RAND()   This function returns a random number between 0 and 1 to 6 decimal places. If you need a random two-digit nondecimal number, use =INT(RAND()*100). You have to be careful using RAND. First of all, it isn't truly random. For every Excel session, the first value is 0.711327 and later values are in a predictable sequence. And every time you use RAND again, Excel changes all the current values based on RAND. To "permanentize" a RAND value, copy it, then use Edit Paste Special to paste its value into the same cell that contains the RAND formula. At that point, the stored value will have more decimal places than you want, so you might want to use a special format for its display.

ROUND(number,number_of_digits)   This function returns the number rounded to the specified number of decimal places. If you use 0 as the number of places, the value is rounded to the nearest integer. ROUND(456.19,1) returns 456.2.

SIGN(number)   This function returns a value that corresponds to the sign of the number; 1 indicates absolute value or positive, −1 indicates negative, and 0 indicates a zero value.

SQRT(number)   This function returns the square root of number. Number must not be negative, so use SQRT(ABS(number)) if you aren't sure.

TRUNC(number)   This function returns the integer part of the number; it is not rounded up or down.

The mathematic functions work much as do their counterparts in arithmetic expressions. You can use them as needed in your worksheets.

Statistical Functions

Excel provides several functions to help you perform basic and more advanced statistical operations on your data. We've divided them into three groups. The most basic group is very straightforward; these functions may count, find the sum, the maximum, or the minimum of a group of cells. The most complex function in this group finds the arithmetic average (mean). The second group involves standard deviations and variances for a population. And the third, most advanced group involves curve fitting.

Basic Statistics. The functions in this group are useful to people who don't even consider them to be statistics. In most of them, you can include up to 14 references, each of which may be a single cell or a reference to a range or array. A "number" argument requires that all the contents must really be numbers. A "value" argument requires that the contents must be translatable to numbers, such as a logical value, an empty cell, or numerical text.

AVERAGE(number1,*number2*,. . .)   This function returns the arithmetic mean (average) of all the referenced numbers. The function =AVERAGE(D4 − B9:B18) takes D4 minus each value in the range B9:B18; the resulting ten values are added and the sum divided by 10 to get the average.

COUNT(value1,*value2*,. . .)   This function returns the integer count of the number values in the references. Nothing raises an error message here, but it only counts the cells translatable to numbers for single references and actual numbers in any multiple references.

COUNTA(value1,*value2*,...)   This function returns the integer count of cells in the references that aren't empty.

MAX(number1,*number2*,...)   This function returns the largest value among all the referenced numbers.

MIN(number1,*number2*,...)   This function returns the smallest value among all the referenced numbers.

SUM(number1,*number2*,...)   This function returns the added total of all the referenced numbers. Any nonnumbers in references are ignored.

Variance and Standard Deviation. The functions in this grouping are used to calculate the variance and standard deviation for a sample or an entire population. You can use up to 14 separate references. All the referenced cells must contain actual numbers or an error message results.

STDEV(number1,*number2*,...)   This function returns the estimated standard deviation of a population based on a sample. It uses the non-biased "n − 1" method. If you have a complete population, use STDEVP instead.

STDEVP(number1,*number2*,...)   This function returns the standard deviation of a complete population. It uses the biased "n" method. If you have only a sample rather than a complete population, use STDEV instead.

VAR(number1,*number2*,...)   This function returns the estimated variance of a population based on a sample. If you have a complete population, use VARP instead.

VARP(number1,*number2*,...)   This function returns the variance of a complete population. If you have a sample of a population, use VAR instead.

Advanced Statistics with Curve Fitting. Excel includes four functions you can use for more advanced statistics with curve fitting; these all return an array of values that you can chart or process as your application requires. We'll treat them very briefly here. If you are familiar with these statistical techniques, you can find more details in the Functions and Macros reference documentation.

GROWTH(known_y's,*known_x's,new_x's*)   This function returns values that fit a curve on an exponential trend.

LINEST(known_y's,*known_x's*)   This function returns values that fit a straight line to show parameters in a linear trend.

LOGEST(known_y's,*known_x's*)   This function returns values that fit a curve to show parameters in an exponential trend. It differs from GROWTH in containing only known values.

TREND(known_y's,*known_x's,new_x's)* This function returns values on a linear trend. It differs from LINEST in that this one includes new values as well.

Text Functions

Excel provides a set of functions for performing operations on text values. You can use them to change text, convert the case, change between formatted text and number values, even extract part of a text value for use in another cell. Be sure to enclose any text you include in the function itself with double quotation marks.

CHAR(number) This function returns the ASCII character that corresponds to number as text. Number must be from 1 to 255. CHAR(191) produces " " (a drawing character). CHAR(65) produces "A." What displays and/or prints depends a great deal on your printer and monitor; their documentation includes a complete listing.

CLEAN(text) This function returns the text with any unprintable or control characters removed. If cell B17 includes control characters and you use CLEAN(B17) in cell B18, B18 will contain the same thing as B17 with any control characters removed.

CODE(text) This function returns the number that corresponds to the ASCII character for the first character in text. If cell B17 contains "angora" and you use =CODE(B17), the result is 97.=CODE("Angry") results in 65.

DOLLAR(number,*decimals*) This function returns as text the rounded number to the specified number of decimal places, formatted as a dollar value using the format $#,##0.00;($#,##0.00). If you omit decimals, Excel uses a default of 2; that's what you generally want for dollar values. If you use a negative value for decimals, the rounding takes place to the left of the decimal point, and any positions to the right of it are dropped. If B3 contains 876.987 and you enter =DOLLAR(B3,−2) in B4, the value in B4 is "$880."

EXACT(text1,text2) This function returns a logical value depending on whether or not the two arguments are exactly the same. If they are, the result is TRUE; if not, the result is FALSE. The texts must match perfectly; this function is case sensitive and notices spaces. The function=EXACT("Ann",B2) results in FALSE if B2 contains "ANN," "Anne," "A nn," or anything other than "Ann."

FIND(find_text,within_text,*start_at_num*) This function returns the position at which it locates find_text in within_text. You can use start_ at_num to cause Excel to start looking at a position later than 1. If start_at_num is not within the range from 1 to the length of within_text, the value #VALUE! is returned. In the FIND function, case counts and you can't use wildcards. To find out if cell B12 contains "Ann," you could use =FIND("Ann",B12). If B12 contains "Anne Smithson," the returned result is 1. If it contains "Carole Annenberg," the returned result is 8. If you use =FIND("Ann",B12,3), the returned result for B12 containing "Anne Smithson" is #VALUE! because the find_text isn't located.

FIXED(number,*decimals*) This function returns the text value of number, rounded to the specified number of decimal places. As with DOLLAR, the default decimal value is 2, and a negative value causes rounding to be on the left of the decimal point. FIXED is just like DOLLAR, except that the resulting FIXED text doesn't include any dollar sign or commas.

LEFT(text,*number_of_characters*) This function returns the leftmost number_of_characters from the text. For example, you can get a three-digit random number in text form with this formula: =LEFT (FIXED(RAND()*1000000),3). You can use the initial character in B12 with =LEFT(B12), since the default is 1.

LEN(text) This function returns the number of characters in text. If the cell is empty, it returns 0. LEN is useful in determining whether a cell contains text.

LOWER(text) This function returns the same text with all letters in it converted to lowercase. It has no effect on characters that aren't letters.

MID(text,start_number,number_of_characters) This function returns the specified number of characters from text, starting at the specified starting point. It is related to LEFT and RIGHT, but you need to tell Excel where to start. The MID function returns #VALUE! if start_number is less than one. If start_number is greater than the length of text, empty text ("") is returned. If start_number plus the remaining length is greater than number_of_characters, the text from start_number to the end is returned.

PROPER(text) This function returns the same text so that all letters are lowercase except for any letter that does not immediately follow another letter. PROPER("THAT'S ENOUGH") returns "That'S Enough." IF B12 contains "JOHN B. SMITH," =PROPER(B12) returns "John B. Smith."

REPLACE(old_text,start_number,num_chars,new_text) This function returns the old text with the characters starting at start_number and extending num_chars are removed and replaced with new_text at that point. The number of characters removed need not be the same as the number in new_text. If B12 contains "JOHN B. SMITH," =REPLACE(B12,6,2,UPPER("Bartholomew")) in cell B15 results in "JOHN BARTHOLOMEW SMITH" in B15. The start_number value must be between 1 and the length of the old_text. If the sum or start_number and num_characters reaches beyond the length of the old_text, all characters to the end are removed before the insertion is done.

REPT(text,number_times)   This function results in the repetition of the specified text the given number of times. REPT("*/",4) results in "*/*/*/*/." REPT(B10,3) results in the contents of cell B10 repeated three times in the current cell.

RIGHT(text,*number_of_chars*)   This function returns the rightmost number_of_characters from the text. For example, you can get a three-digit random number in text form with this formula: =RIGHT(FIXED(RAND()*1000000),3). You can use the final character in B12 with =RIGHT(B12), since the default is 1.

SEARCH(find_text,within_text,*start_at_num*)   This function returns the position at which it locates find_text in within_text. You can use start_at_num to cause Excel to start looking at a position later than 1. If start_at_num is not within the range from 1 to the length of within_text, the value #VALUE! is returned. In SEARCH, unlike FIND, case doesn't matter and you can use ? and * as wildcards. To find out if cell B12 contains "Ann," you could use =SEARCH("Ann",B12). If B12 contains "Anne Smithson," the returned result is 1. If it contains "Carole Dannenberg," the returned result is 9. If you use =SEARCH("An?",B12,3), the returned result for B12 containing "David and Anne Smithson" is 7 because the string "and" is the first match of the find string.

SUBSTITUTE(text,old_text,new_text,*instance_number*)   This function returns the value of text with old_text removed and new_text substituted for it. If instance_number is specified, only that occurrence of old_text is substituted with new_text. Otherwise, all occurrences are substituted. A new_text of "" matches the first character. You could use =SUBSTITUTE(B12,"","*") to substitute * for the first character in the text contents of B12. SUBSTITUTE differs from REPLACE primarily in that you specify the actual text in SUBSTITUTE, while you use position and number of characters in REPLACE.

TEXT(value,format_text)   This function returns the value converted to text, using the string of format_text. The format_text must match a defined format string in the Format Number list box, except that it can be neither General nor *. The result is in text form. This function is generally automatic; that is, if Excel needs a text value and has a number, it does the necessary conversion internally.

TRIM(text)   This function returns the text with all spaces removed, except for single spaces between words. Any double spaces are converted to single. Every string of spaces is reduced to a single space.

UPPER(text)   This function returns the same text with all letters in it converted to uppercase. It has no effect on characters that aren't letters.

VALUE(text)   This function returns the number equivalent to the text, as long as the text is any format recognizable to Excel. This function is generally automatic; if Excel needs a number and the available text is convertible, the conversion is done without need for this function.

Trigonometric Functions

The last group of Excel functions are trigonometric; they are mostly used in mathematical or scientific applications. These functions are included here for completeness; if you haven't the faintest idea what they do, you can safely ignore them and skip over this section.

The first group of functions, arccosine, arcsine, and arctangent, all produce a value in radians; if your application requires degrees, Excel can convert from radians by multiplying by 180/PI(). The second group of functions, cosine, sine, and tangent, require that you specify radians.

ACOS(number)   This function returns the arccosine of a number, returning from 0 to pi radians.

ASIN(number)   This function returns the arcsine of a number, from 1 to −1.

ATAN(number)   This function returns the arctangent of a number, from −pi/2 to pi/2.

ATAN2(x_number,y_number)   This function returns the arctangent of a point. Both x and y coordinates must be specified.

COS(radians)   This function returns the cosine of the specified radians.

SIN(radians)   This function returns the sine of the specified radians.

TAN(radians)   This function returns the tangent of the specified radians.

SUMMARY

This chapter has covered the rules and regulations for using Excel's formulas and most of the built-in functions. You can now create formulas to calculate values as needed. It isn't necessary to memorize the functions, since they are all listed online in the Formula Paste Function dialog box; you can even paste the argument list in temporarily.

Take some extra time now to try out functions that you expect to use early in your Excel career. Functions are Excel's way of making your life easier. Later in the book (Chapter 13), you'll learn to create specialized functions for your own applications.

6 PRINTING AND PAGE LAYOUT

Printing in Excel can be very simple; just select File Print and it gets done. But if you want any variations on your basic setup, you have many additional steps and options available. You can print a worksheet with or without its notes, in whole or in part. You can set margins, page breaks, headers and footers to meet your needs. Excel knows what your printer can accomplish and takes that into consideration when offering you choices.

PRINTER SETUP

Before you can print anything, your printer must be installed with Excel and ready to go. But even after it is installed, you can change many of its setup features, such as orientation, paper size, resolution, and the specific printer to be used. If you have installed more than one printer, you can select the one to use. When you use the File Printer Setup command, you see a Printer dialog box like the one in Figure 6.1.

The installed printers and the port of each are shown in the list box. You can select a printer here and choose OK to use the current setup. If you choose the Setup button, you'll see a dialog box with fields related to the selected printer. Figure 6.2 shows two examples. Notice that the layout is different in each, but the type of information is the same.

The specific printer setup box shows the current printer in the top border. If the printer name could include one of several types of printers, there will be a list box containing the various options. Generally, you'll just have one of a given printer type. Current settings are shown in the various fields and boxes. With some printers, you can select a number of uncollated copies if you like; Excel prints as many as you request of the first page, then that number of the next, and so forth. If you want your copies collated, you can request extra copies through the File Print command.

PRINTING AND PAGE LAYOUT

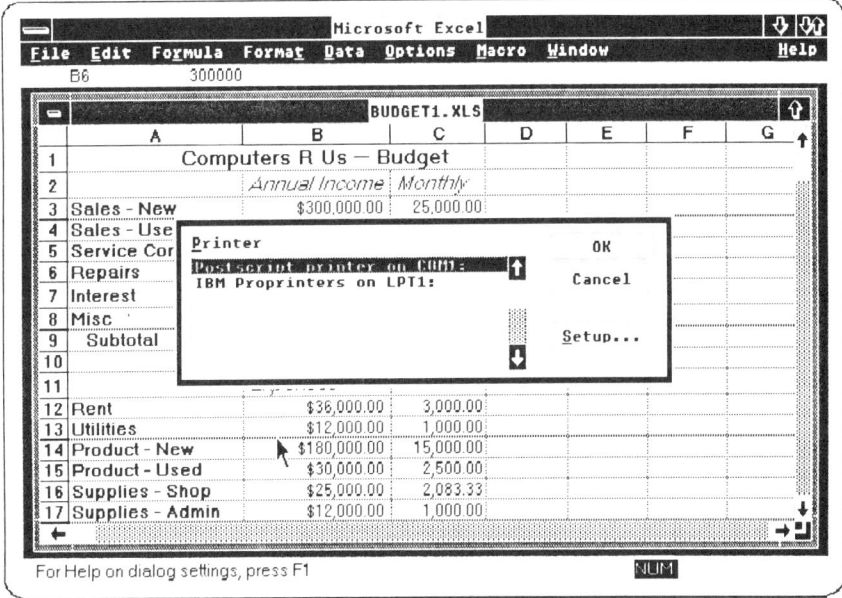

FIGURE 6.1. File Printer Setup Dialog Box

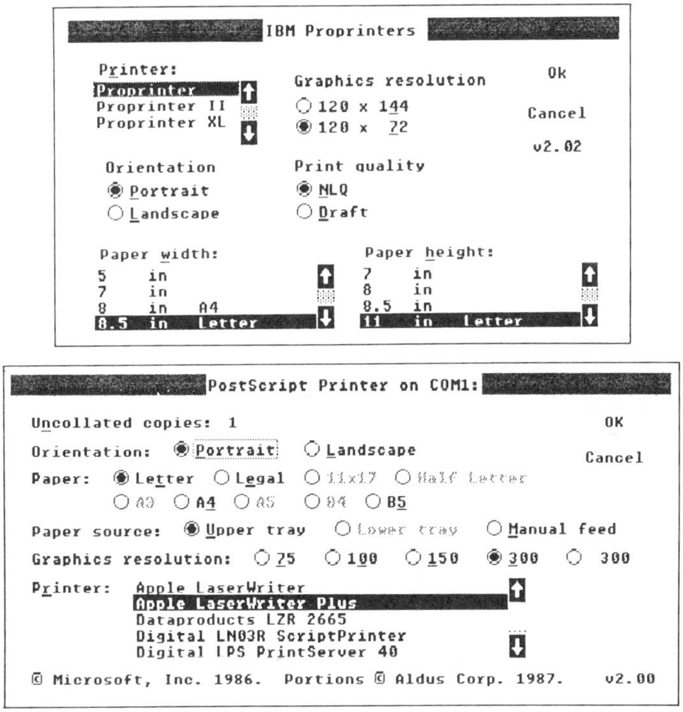

FIGURE 6.2. Specific Printer Setup Information

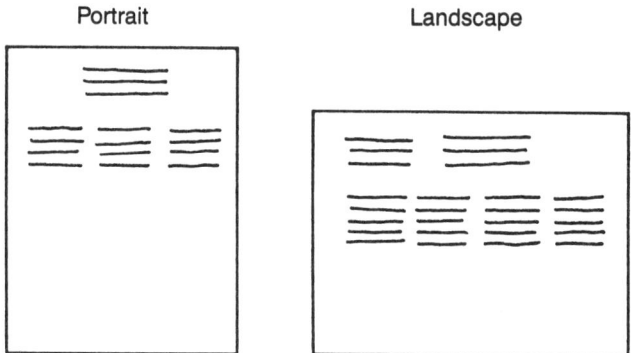

FIGURE 6.3. Portrait vs. Landscape Orientation

The paper orientation can be Portrait or Landscape for many printers; Figure 6.3 shows the difference. If a worksheet is wider than it is long, it may print more attractively in Landscape mode. Remember to set it back to restore the orientation if necessary. Changes in the printer setup stay in effect for all documents until you change them back.

The dialog box gives you the available choices for paper size, print quality, and graphics resolution. You'll only be offered the choices that are valid for your printer. You may want to experiment a bit to see the effects of the various settings.

BASIC PRINTING

You can print any displayed worksheet by selecting the File Print command, resulting in the dialog box shown in Figure 6.4, and selecting the appropriate options. Excel prints the entire worksheet that contains data if you haven't selected and set a named print area; you'll see how to do that shortly.

The dialog box shows the currently selected printer and port at the top. Anything established via the Printer Setup command is in effect. The default values print one copy of all pages of the worksheet. You can specify as many copies as you want; one complete copy is printed first, then repeated as many times as specified. You can limit the number of pages by entering a From and/or To value. If you enter a From value, but no To value, Excel prints from the specified page to the end of the Worksheet. If you enter a To value but no From value, Excel prints from the beginning of the worksheet through the specified page.

The Draft Quality field is available on some printers. On others, such as the

PRINTING AND PAGE LAYOUT

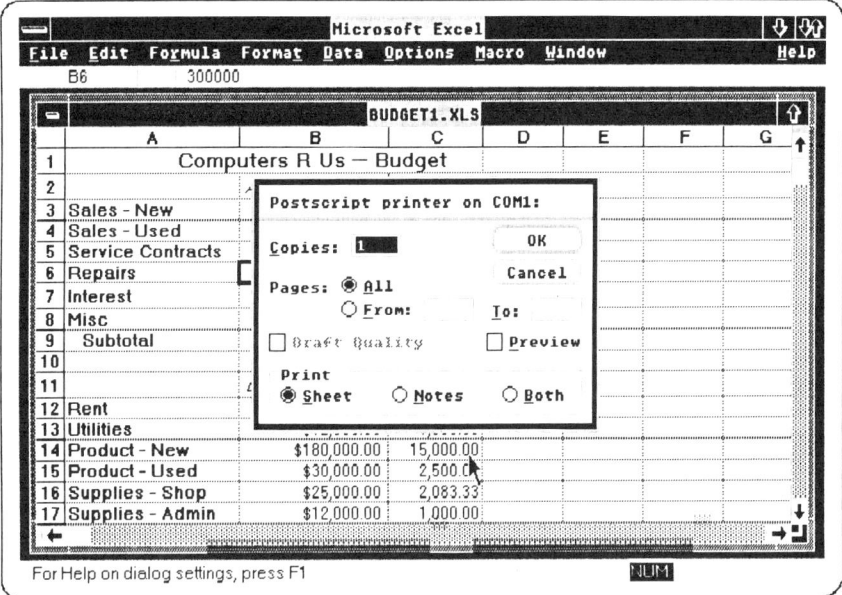

FIGURE 6.4. File Print Dialog Box

laser printer represented in Figure 6.4, this field is not available. If your printer has a draft quality, turning on this field causes faster printing of a slightly lower print quality. You might want to turn on Draft Quality for early copies of a worksheet.

You can use the bottom of the dialog box to specify what to print. By default, the worksheet itself is printed. If you specify Notes, then just the notes are printed. If you specify Both, Excel prints the worksheet, then starts the notes on the next page. Notes are printed in Row order; all notes for cells in Row 1 are printed, then those in Row 2, and so forth. The cell references are printed if the Row and Column Heading field (you'll see how to do this when we discuss the Page Setup command) is specified. Figure 6.5 shows how note printing appears. These notes show the cell references; you'll find you want the cell references printed for most notes.

Cell: B4
Note: Extra time preparing proposal for special sale.

Cell: B7
Note: First week

Cell: C14
Note: Limited so far. Raise due next month.

FIGURE 6.5.   Printed Notes

	A	B	C	D
1		WEEKLY WORKSHEET		
2				
3	Name	Hours	Wage	Pay
4	Ruth Ashley	56	24.60	1,377.60
5	Judi Fernandez	36	22.50	810.00
6	Paul Ashley	27	7.00	189.00
7	Davida Fernandez	12	6.00	72.00
8	Carisa Yardas	23	6.00	138.00
9	Solomon Allen	40	12.00	480.00
10	Mary Hoogterp	38	10.75	408.50
11	Thomas Smith	42	10.75	451.50
12	Carson Smithers	25	9.25	231.25
13	Darryl Snyder	27	8.00	216.00
14	Michael Sloan	14	7.50	105.00
15				
16	Total Payroll			4,478.85

FIGURE 6.6. Printed Worksheet

To print Info windows for a worksheet, select the cells you want information for, such as all cells with formulas, then make the Info window active and select Print. All the information for the selected cells is printed.

Printed Appearance

So what prints when you print a worksheet? That depends both on various print options and on how the worksheet appears on screen. Formats and fonts carry over to printing. If the fonts you specified aren't available on your printer, Excel gets as close as it can. If formulas are displayed when you request print, they print. Any rows or columns that are hidden (width or height zero) don't print. Figure 6.6 shows a standard printed worksheet.

Outlines, borders, and shading carry over from the screen to the printout. Gridline display and Row and Column headings can be turned on or off for print as well as for display; you can print or suppress each through Page Setup regardless of the display appearance. Excel puts in automatic page breaks where they naturally fall; you can change these with certain options. You can cause row and column titles to print on the appropriate pages with other options. You'll learn to handle all these in this chapter. To see how your document will print, you can select the Preview option in the File Print dialog box.

Using Preview

When you use the Print Preview mode, you see the pages Excel has created on-screen rather than on your printer. Figure 6.7 shows an example. You can cancel

PRINTING AND PAGE LAYOUT

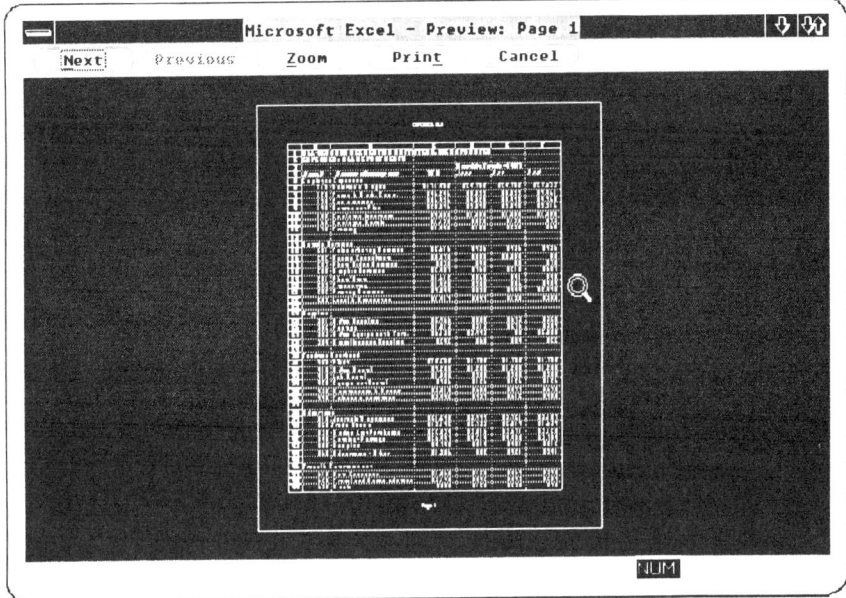

FIGURE 6.7. Print Preview

preview at any time by pressing Escape or by selecting the Cancel button. Notice that the page is smaller than normal, but all the features are shown; this page shows the margins, a header, a footer, row and column headings as well as data and gridlines.

The preview commands are shown in the menu bar. You can select Next or Previous to see the next or previous page in the document; if you are at the first page, the Previous command is grayed and selecting it has no effect. If you select Next from the last page, preview is terminated and you are returned to your worksheet. You can print the document as it is with the current settings by selecting Print, or cancel Print Preview mode and return to the worksheet itself. Figure 6.8 shows a landscape orientation in preview mode.

The pointer becomes a magnifier on the preview page; by clicking on the displayed page or selecting Zoom, you can enlarge the page and examine specific parts of it. Figure 6.9 shows the enlarged page. The Zoom button is a toggle; to return to reduced size select Zoom again or click the mouse anywhere on the displayed page. You can page through the document using Next and Previous while in Zoom mode; you'll see the same portion of each page. Use the arrow keys to move around within a preview page. If you print from preview mode, all the values already set remain in effect; the printout corresponds to what you see on the preview screen.

130 ADVANCED EXCEL

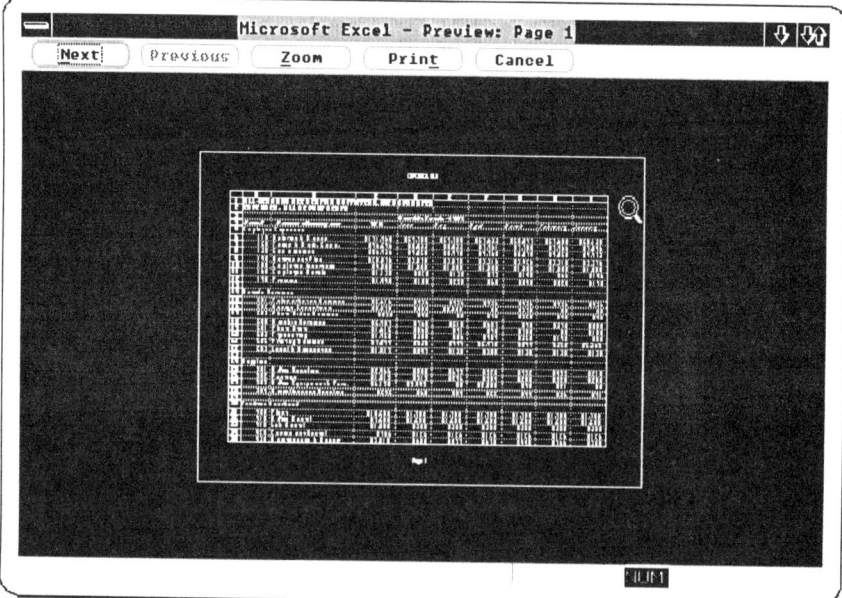

FIGURE 6.8. Preview—Landscape Orientation

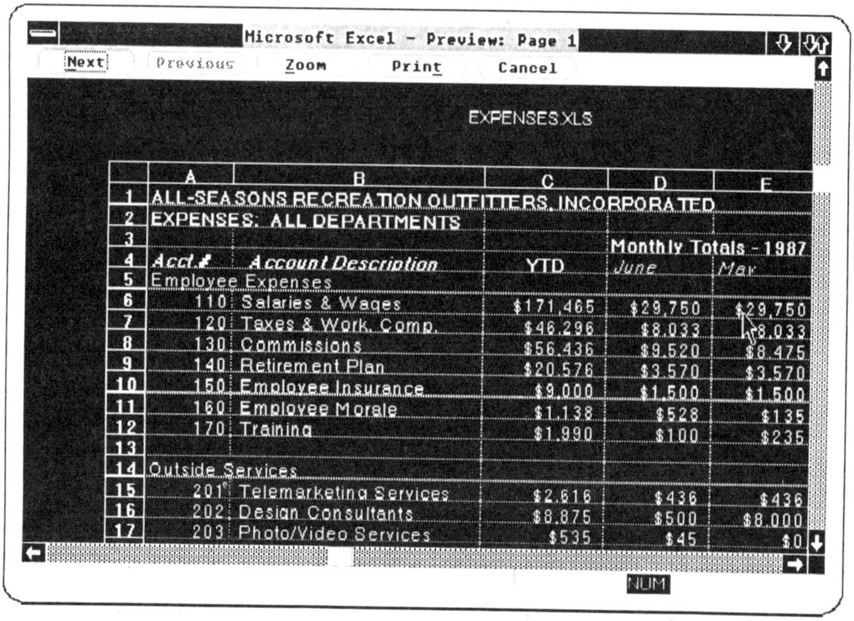

FIGURE 6.9. Enlarged Page Preview

PRINTING AND PAGE LAYOUT   **131**

Magnification without a Mouse

To use the magnification feature without a mouse, use ALT + Z to turn Zoom on and off. Once the page is enlarged, you can use the arrow keys to move around on it. The control key with the arrow keys moves the viewed portion to the appropriate edge of the page. You can use CONTROL + HOME to see the upper left corner, and CONTROL + END to see the lower right. Just press ALT + Z again to return to the reduced page.

SETTING UP THE PAGE

You have seen how to specify features specific to your printer. Excel also lets you specify features specific to the pages of your document with the File Page Setup command. Figure 6.10 shows the resulting box. This dialog box is similar for all printers, since it affects the software itself and contents and layout of the printed document. In this box you can specify a header, a footer, and margins for your printout, or you can go with the default values. You can also specify whether row and column headings (such as A, B, 1, 2, etc.) and gridlines will be printed. Any settings you change here remain with the worksheet when it is stored.

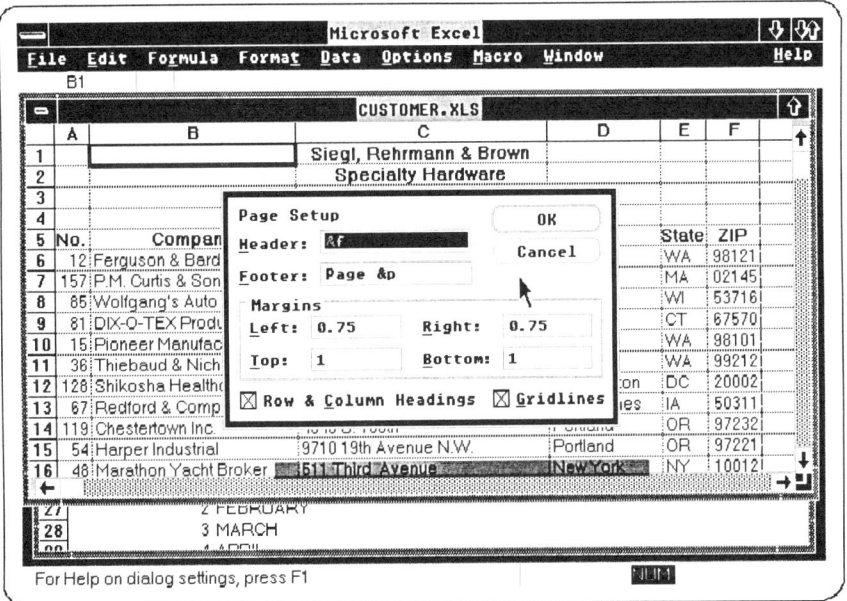

FIGURE 6.10.   File Page Setup Dialog Box

Headers and Footers

A header is a line that appears at the top of every page. A footer is a line that appears at the bottom of every page. The default header for each document is the document (or file) name; it appears centered at the top of the printed page. The default footer causes the value "Page 1" to appear centered on the first page and each page to be numbered in turn. The pages in Figures 6.7 through 6.9 show the default headers and footers.

Headers and footers can contain text and variables. Parts of headers and footers can appear in the center (default), left aligned, or right aligned. Excel provides a set of variables you can use in headers and footers. The variable for the header appears in the Page Setup dialog box for each document. Once you change it, however, your changes stay with the document.

Excel provides several additional variables you can use in headers and footers. Figure 6.11 lists them all. Notice that some are for alignment, some for styling, and some for data. You can use almost any combination, in either uppercase or lowercase. The default header is &f; this prints the file name centered at the top of the page. You can eliminate a header by deleting the characters in the header field. You can modify it by adding additional parts to the header. For example, &L&F prints the file name at the left, 3/4 inch from the edge of the page. &R&B&F prints the file name in bold at the right. &R&D&L&F prints the date on the right and the file name on the left edge of the header. To include the date at the left and your company name in bold on the right, you could use &L&D&R&BImaginetronics, Inc.

The variables work in the footer as well. The default prints the text "Page " followed by the current page number. You can start page numbering with 3 by using &P+2 to represent the page number. Alternatively, you can use the page number in the header and/or other information in the footer.

```
&L      Left align following characters
&R      Right align following characters
&C      Center following characters

&B      Use Bold for following characters
&I      Use Italics for following characters

&D      Use current Date
&T      Use current Time
&F      Use File name (document name)
&P      Use current Page number
&P+n    Add n to page number and print that
&P-n    Subtract n from page number and print that
&&      Print single &
```

FIGURE 6.11. Header and Footer Variables

Margins

You set margins for your pages in the Page Setup dialog box as well. Default margins for your printer are displayed. You can change them by typing in the number of inches you want for each margin. The header and footer appear within the top and bottom margin areas, so you need at least half an inch if you use them. Once you've looked at your preview, you may want to change the margins. You might want a larger right margin to center the data, for example, or narrower side margins to allow more data per page without reducing the font size. If you don't like where the pages break in the preview, however, you don't have to change the margins. You can use the Options Set Page Break command to do this.

Row and Column Headers

Row and column headers are the letters and numbers (in A1 reference style) or R and C numbers (in R1C1 reference style) that appear at the top and left of your spreadsheet. You can suppress them on screen with the Options Display command. If you turn the Row and Column Headings field on with the File Page Setup command (the default), they appear in your printout. Many times, you won't need these reference headings in the printed output; the row and column references are essential during development, but for final reports they may be distracting. Just click on the field to turn the row and column header printing off.

If Row and Column Headings is turned on, any printed notes are accompanied by cell references as well. If this field is turned off, no cell reference appears with a printed note; this generally makes the printed notes rather useless unless you include other references. In most cases, you'll want to be sure to turn this field on in the Page Setup dialog box before printing notes.

Gridlines

With Options Display, you can turn the gridline display on and off. This status does not affect printing however. The gridline print status is controlled by the File Page Setup command.

Gridlines are printed by default. You can turn the gridline print off to create a cleaner printed document. You'll want to use the gridlines if the worksheet is very full, with few blank lines or spacing. If regions in your worksheet are delineated by blank rows and columns, you won't need the gridlines. And if your worksheet is to be used for a calendar or otherwise uses borders to achieve an effect, the gridlines are a real disadvantage. You can try it both ways and check the result in the preview or on paper.

SUGGESTED EXERCISE

1. Print your practice worksheet and your calendar using all the defaults.
2. Reprint the calendar without gridlines or row/column headings. Use landscape mode if available for your printer.
3. Change the orientation or paper size for your other worksheet and try it under preview. Try out zoom and paging. Then see how it prints.
4. Change the status of the row and column headings and gridlines. Change the header and footer. Then preview the document and print it again.
5. Examine a longer, wider worksheet under preview. Try EXPENSES.XLS in the EXCELCBT directory. Look at the various pages. Then print it.

What if It Doesn't Work?

1. Has anything printed? Make sure your printer is installed correctly.
2. If you have trouble with headers and footers, use the examples given earlier. Once you get them to work, try creating your own.

USING PRINT OPTIONS

The Excel Options menu provides three options you can use to control how much of the worksheet prints and its style. These must all be set before the print is requested. It's a good idea to check the result in preview mode before printing the document.

Set Print Area

Excel normally prints the entire worksheet. If you want to print just part of the worksheet, you can set a specific print area for Excel to use whenever you select File Print. Just select the entire area to be printed, then select Options Set Print Area. Excel names the area "print_area" and includes that name in the official list of defined names. When you select File Print, Excel first checks for a print_area. If one exists, that area is printed, no matter what is selected.

You can change your print_area at any time; just select the desired area and use Options Set Print Area again; the new area replaces the former one. As long as a print_area is defined, Excel uses it to determine the area to print. You can remove it by selecting Formula Define Name and deleting the name print_area. Then you can print the entire worksheet or select a different print_area.

Set Print Titles

If you have row or column titles that indicate what is in the rows or columns, you can cause them to be printed on each page. To do this, select the rows and/or columns first; you can have more than one row or column, but they must be adjacent. When the parts are selected, then select Options Set Print Titles. When you select the print area, make sure the title rows and columns are not included in the print area, or they'll be printed twice on the page on which they normally appear. When you print the document, you'll find the titles repeated on every page that includes data from those rows or columns.

Setting print titles is most useful for printing documents that include only lots of data, requiring several pages to print. If your worksheet is a report in itself, you probably have built the necessary information into it.

Set Page Break

Excel automatically inserts page breaks after complete cells where it needs them to fit the maximum information on a page. You may want to break pages sooner, either horizontally or vertically. If so, you can tell Excel where to start a new page. If you set a manual page break at the bottom of page 1, Excel starts from that point to locate an automatic page break on page 2. You can also specify page break locations if your worksheet is wider than one page.

To insert a manual page break, select a cell that you want to appear at the upper left corner of a new page. Then select Option Set Page Break. Excel inserts a manual page break above that cell and to its left. If the selected cell is in the first row of the worksheet, only a vertical page break is inserted. If the selected cell is in the first column of the worksheet, only a horizontal page break is inserted.

You don't have to print or preview a worksheet to see where the page breaks are. Excel displays them on screen as dashed lines. Figure 6.12 shows how the page breaks appear on screen. Both automatic and manual breaks are indicated. On your screen, you will notice that the manual page break is darker and more noticeable than the automatic one.

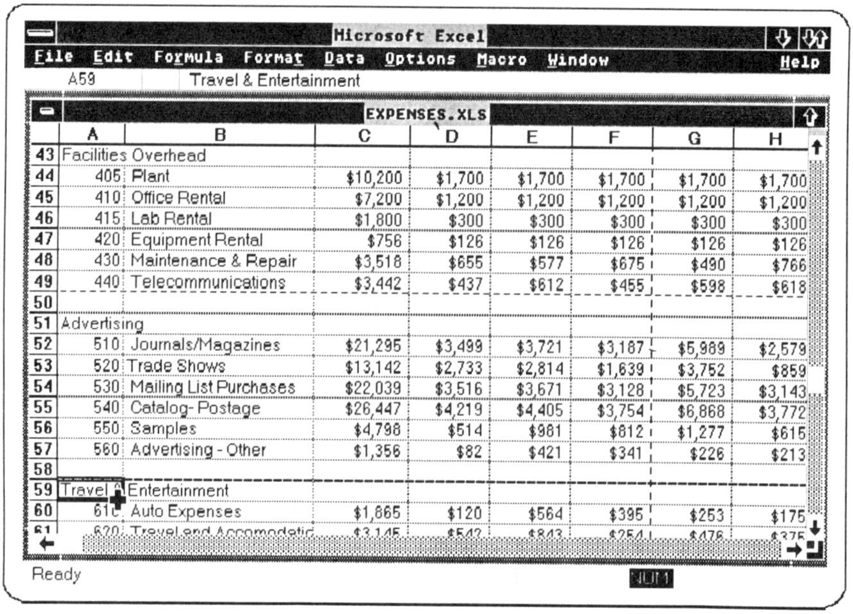

FIGURE 6.12. Automatic and Manually Set Page Breaks

What you see in the figure is the bottom of page 1 (A43:F49), all of page 2 (A50:F58), the top of page 3 (A59:F61), the lower left corner of page 4, the left edge of page 5, and the upper left corner of page 6.

When a cell is selected that borders on a manual page break, the Options menu shows Remove Page Break instead of Set Page Break; selecting Remove Page Break removes the manual page break and allows Excel to reestablish automatic ones.

SUGGESTED EXERCISE

1. Practice some more with printing larger worksheets such as EXPENSES.XLS. Set a print area and print that. Then set print titles and print again. (If you want, just do these under preview mode to see the effects.)
2. Notice where the page breaks occur when EXPENSES.XLS prints. Set manual ones a bit earlier to see the effect on screen and in printing.

What if It Doesn't Work?

1. Try again. First delete the name Print_area. Then preview the worksheet. Go back into edit and put a page break at about row 10. Preview again.

PRINTING AND PAGE LAYOUT 137

THE PRINT SPOOLER

You may have noticed that you can start using Excel again long before the printing is finished. Excel includes a utility program called Spooler that handles the printing outside of Excel itself. Spooler lets you continue using Excel while it handles printing in the background.

When you request a file print, Excel prepares it to meet your current printer setup and sends the job to Spooler. You don't have to worry about it; in fact, you generally won't even see any evidence of Spooler. But you may want to get at it. You may have ordered several print jobs and want one immediately. You may want to cancel a job. You may just want to know how many are waiting to print. You can handle all these through the Spooler window.

Normally, Spooler is represented by an icon that you never see or use. To open the icon, you can use ALT + Escape to cycle through the active icons. When the Spooler's name appears, its icon is active; double click on it or select the control menu (ALT + Spacebar) and the Restore command. The resulting window looks like the one in Figure 6.13.

The Spooler window shows the print jobs lined up (queued) for each installed printer. The commands let you change priority or operate on members of the queue. You can increase the priority to cause one job to print sooner. Or

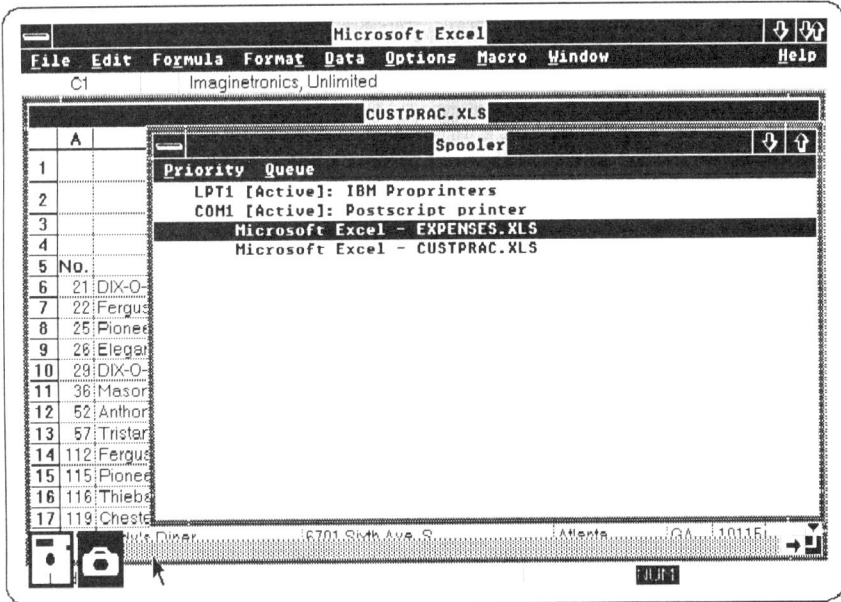

FIGURE 6.13. Print Spooler Window

you can exit the Spooler through the Priority command. The queue command lets you terminate individual print jobs, among other functions.

Spooler closes automatically when the printing is done. If you close it before then, it terminates any remaining print jobs. To continue using Excel, use ALT + Escape again until Excel is once more the active application.

SUMMARY

This chapter covered techniques for printing worksheets under Excel. Depending on your printer's capabilities, you can do all that Excel has available. You can use the various options to set up a print area, print titles, or set manual page breaks. You can set up a specific page description for the pages in the document, or specific printer information for use of your printer's features.

You can even access the print spooler to manipulate jobs waiting to be printed. All the printing information you've learned in this chapter applies to printing other Excel documents as well; you can print databases with no trouble. Even charts and macro sheets print with the same basic commands and options.

7 MANAGING WINDOWS AND LINKS

Excel really shines in its use of windows and links. Since it runs under Microsoft Windows, it has all the capabilities of Windows; you can have as many windows open on screen as you need and switch among them at will. Excel also lets you have multiple windows into the same worksheet. Or you can use panes in the same worksheet to let separated parts of the data scroll together.

Excel lets you create links between documents and keeps them current. You can transfer data from one worksheet to another or link formulas or values as needed. Changes in one worksheet affect linked worksheets or charts. You can even exchange data with other applications running under Windows.

MULTIPLE OPEN WORKSHEETS

It is no problem in Excel to use several worksheets at once. Just use the File Open command to open existing worksheets or File New to start a new document. One worksheet is always active; it is on top on the screen and has color or highlighting in the top border. You can move easily from one open worksheet to another by clicking on any open worksheet or pressing CONTROL + F6 to cycle among open worksheets. Alternatively, you can select the desired worksheet from the Windows menu.

Moving data among worksheets is simple. Use a standard Edit Copy command to copy a single cell or range from one worksheet to another. If the cell contains a constant value, the value is copied. If it contains a formula the formula is copied, with relative references adjusted as necesssary. This does NOT create a link; the copied formula refers to locations or data in the worksheet it is copied to. Techniques for creating and managing links are covered later in this chapter.

MULTIPLE VIEWS OF A SINGLE WORKSHEET

You can open several windows on a single worksheet. You may want to examine separate parts of the worksheet at once. Or you may want to keep titles on screen at all times. There are different ways you can look at parts of a worksheet, depending on how you want the cells to behave. If you want the different parts to scroll independently, you open a new window for each section. If you want the parts to scroll together, you can split a window into panes. Or you could hide columns by resizing them to 0 width or rows by resizing them to 0 height.

Multiple Areas in a Worksheet

In most applications, you'll use only one spreadsheet or database to a worksheet. If an application requires six different spreadsheets, you'll use six different worksheets. This keeps the access time to a minimum, whether you are working with one, two, or all six. But the logistics of moving back and forth may get tedious and time consuming. And more complex external references are needed to refer to data in other worksheets, as you'll see in this chapter.

You can use several different functional units on a single worksheet. This makes sense only if you have several relatively small but related pieces. If you define a range name for each separate spreadsheet, you can move to it easily and quickly. References to data in other spreadsheets on the same worksheet are made just as in a standard worksheet.

Multiple Windows

When you have a worksheet window displayed, you can select the Window New Window command. This immediately opens a new window for the active worksheet. The titles of both windows are modified to reflect where each window occurs in the sequence of open windows for the worksheet. If the active worksheet is MOSALES.XLS when you open a new window on it, the new window contains the name MOSALES.XLS:2 and :1 is appended to the name in the top border of the first window. If you open a third window, its name ends with :3, and so on.

The standard control and window commands apply to each window; you can hide, unhide, or close them. You can resize and move the windows to show the information you are working with on the screen. You can select Windows Arrange All to automatically show all the open windows on the screen. Figure

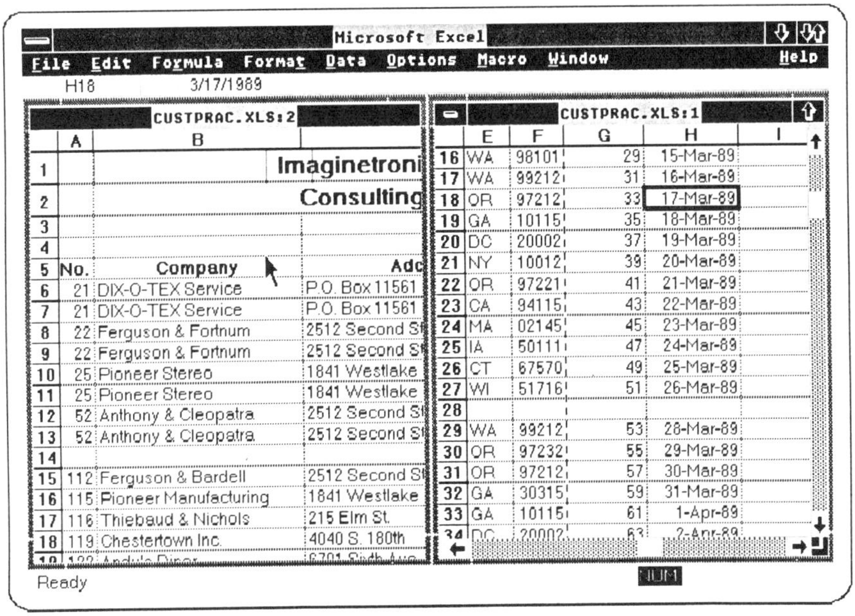

MANAGING WINDOWS AND LINKS

FIGURE 7.1. Arranged Windows in One Worksheet

7.1 shows an example. These are the only open windows; SHEET1 has been closed.

Notice the names in the title bars. Both windows open into the same data in memory. When you make changes in one window, it affects the data in memory and is immediately reflected in the other window as well. You can scroll separately in each window; each one operates independently. If you close the file through the File menu, it closes all the windows into that file. You can remove specific windows into a file by using the Close command on the document control menu; the last one you close may result in the "save changes" message box.

Why Use Multiple Windows?

The most obvious use for multiple windows into one worksheet is viewing different parts of the worksheet at the same time and being able to scroll in them independently. A less obvious use is to display different attributes. For example, you can display values in one window and formulas in another. When you change the formulas or add data you can immediately see the effects in both windows. This is especially useful while you are creating or debugging a worksheet. It also helps when trying to figure out what a worksheet someone else created does. Figure 7.2 shows an example.

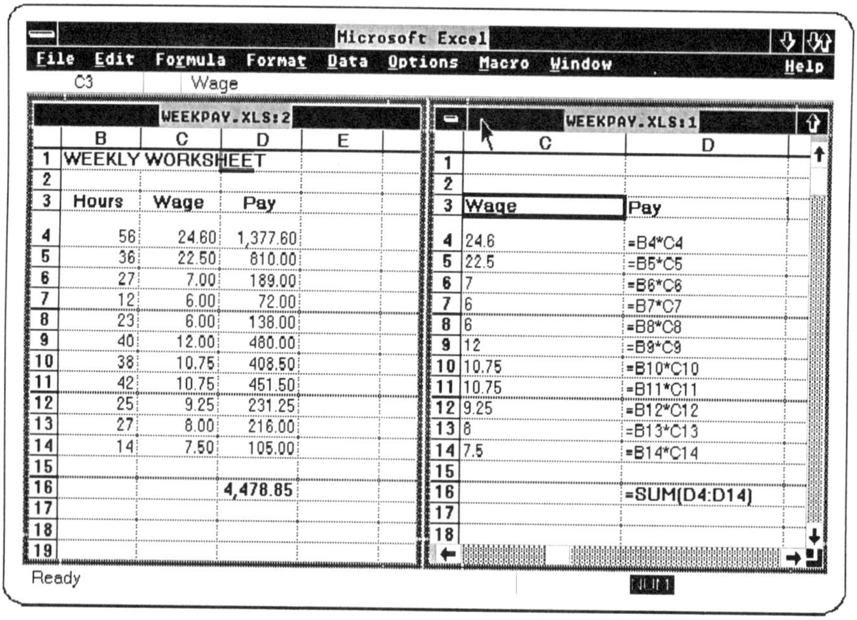

FIGURE 7.2. Viewing Formulas and Data Values

Window Panes

Sometimes you don't really need a second window into a file, you just need to see different parts of it for reference. You may want to see columns A, B, F, G, and H, for example. One way is to change the width of columns C, D, and E to zero. But restoring your worksheet then becomes a pain. You could open a second window into the worksheet, but then when you scroll from row 1 to row 43 in one window, the other just sits there. The solution is window panes. Excel lets you split the window into panes which then scroll together. If you split into vertical panes, cells on both sides of the split are in the same rows; if you scroll up or down on either side, both panes scroll. If you split the window into horizontal panes, cells above and below the split are in the same columns. If you scroll right or left, cells in both panes scroll. Figure 7.3 shows a screen split into horizontal panes.

Notice that there is a single window; the pane division (between rows 6 and 47) is marked by a gray line. Any changes in one pane may affect values in the other, since a single worksheet is involved. You can move between panes by clicking in the desired pane with the mouse or by pressing F6 or SHIFT + F6. F6 moves to the next pane, SHIFT + F6 to the previous one. If your window has only two panes, F6 and SHIFT + F6 have the same effect. A window can have four panes if it has both horizontal and vertical splits. In that case, F6 cycles clockwise and SHIFT + F6 cycles counterclockwise through the panes.

MANAGING WINDOWS AND LINKS   **143**

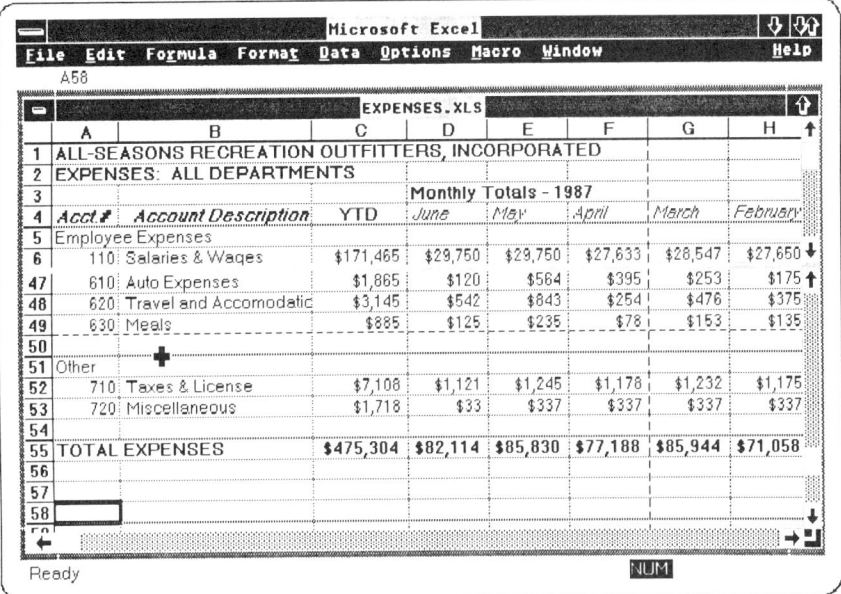

FIGURE 7.3.   Horizontal Panes

Creating Panes

You create panes in the active window with the Control Split command in the control menu (ALT + Hyphen). When you do this, the menu disappears and crosshairs appear in the upper left corner of the window. Move the cross using the mouse or arrow keys, then position the crosshairs where you want the pane split to be, and press Enter or click. Excel creates two or four panes, depending on where the bars are at the time. To remove the panes and restore a standard window, use Control Split again and move the crosshairs back to the upper left corner.

Locking Titles on Screen

Many times you will want to keep the contents of certain rows or columns on screen while you scroll around in the rest of the worksheet. This is most useful when the first few rows and/or columns contain identifying titles for the worksheet contents. You can create panes that include the titles exactly where you want them, then use the Freeze Panes command on the Options pull-down menu. Figure 7.4 shows the screen when Control Split has been selected and panes established.

Notice that the process of splitting a window into panes may repeat a row or

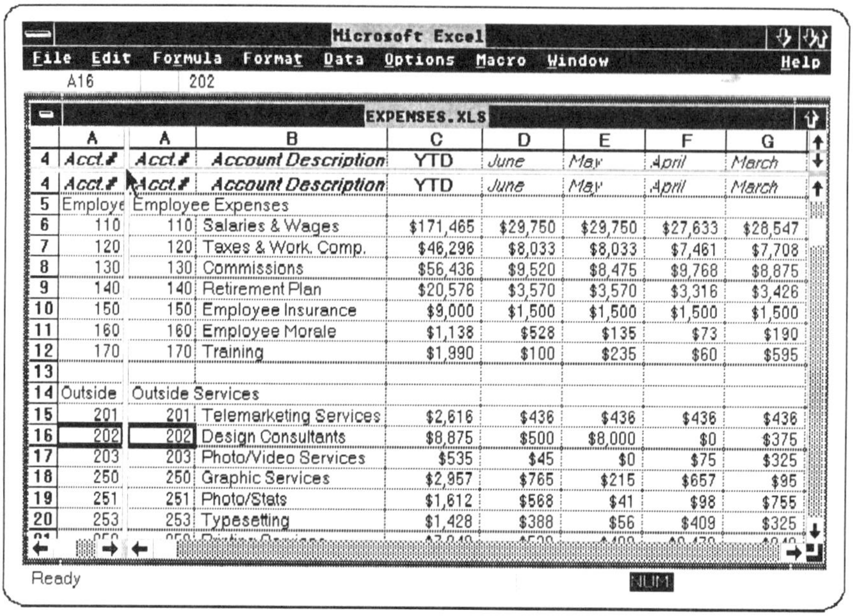

ADVANCED EXCEL

FIGURE 7.4. Title Panes Established

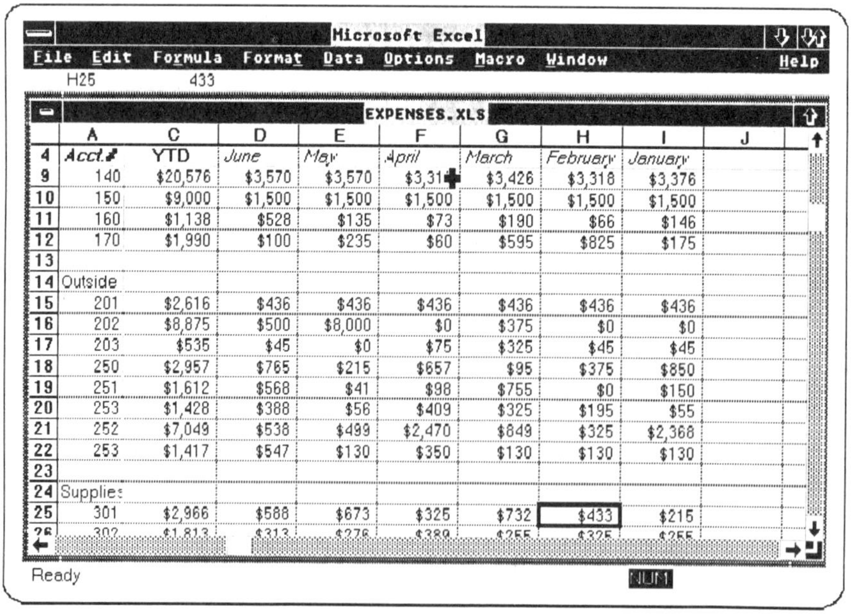

FIGURE 7.5. Titles Frozen

column in another pane. Once you freeze the titles, however, the repetition is gone. Notice also that the titles don't have to be in the first row and/or column. In the figures, we placed rows 4 and 5 at the top of the screen before establishing the split and freezing the panes. Actually, the positioning can be done at any time before you tell Excel to freeze the title panes in position. The next step is to select the Options menu and the Freeze Panes command. Figure 7.5 shows the result.

To unfreeze the titles, select Unfreeze Panes from the Options menu, then cancel the split by selecting Control Split and returning the crosshairs to the upper left corner of the window. The panes have no effect when the worksheet is printed.

SUGGESTED EXERCISE

1. Open a large worksheet such as EXPENSES.XLS (in the LIBRARY subdirectory). Open a second window into it. Then use Windows Arrange All to see the windows on screen. Close any windows other than the two EXPENSES ones and Arrange them again.
2. Close window :2 and restore the remaining EXPENSES window to full size. Divide it into vertical panes and scroll. Use F6 to move between panes. When you're finished, use Split again to remove the panes.
3. Set up Expenses so that you can freeze the row and column titles. Freeze the panes, then check it out by looking at the lower right filled cell in the worksheet.
4. Unfreeze and unsplit the window panes.

What if It Doesn't Work?

1. If you have trouble opening a new window, be sure you used the Window command rather than the File Open command.
2. If you have trouble with panes, try again. You have to use the document control menu (ALT + Hyphen) and the Split command. You can only use Freeze Panes when a split is in effect. Unfreeze is available only when panes are frozen.

LINKING DATA AND WORKSHEETS

Excel outshines most other worksheet programs in its handling of links between worksheets. You can set up your worksheets so that Excel will get data or formulas from any number of other worksheets; some of them don't even need to be open or on screen. Linking is done through external references. Much as a cell or range reference in a worksheet refers to a cell or range within it, an external reference refers to a cell or range external to the worksheet.

External references establish links between worksheets. You might want to consolidate data from several worksheets into a summary worksheet. For example, you might have a separate income/expense report for each month. When they are all correct, you can create a new worksheet under Excel that takes the final figures from each monthly worksheet and creates an annual summary report. This final worksheet would not have to be updated with changes, since you don't expect to have any changes in the supporting worksheets.

You might have several worksheets related to inventory, tracking orders, shipping, and stock. When a particular item is sold, you might add it to a value in one worksheet, then subtract it from a value in another. Links in the stock worksheet can access data values from the shipping and orders worksheets. These links use shared data and are automatically updated. If you add a value to the stock worksheet, it is immediately reflected in the links to other worksheets.

External Reference Names

An external reference relates to another worksheet, so the first part of it, naturally, names that other worksheet. The reference ACCTREC.XLS!$B$2 refers to cell B2 in worksheet ACCTREC.XLS. The exclamation point (!) connects the worksheet name to the cell. The reference above also informs Excel that the referenced worksheet is open. If it isn't open, the external worksheet name is enclosed in single quotes, as in 'ACCTREC.XLS'!$B$2. If the unopened worksheet is in a different directory from the reference, the reference must include the path name within the single quotes, as in 'C:\FINANCE\ACCTREC.XLS'!$B$2.

External References

A linked worksheet that depends on data in another worksheet is a dependent worksheet; it uses data through external references to a supporting worksheet. Changes in the supporting worksheet are reflected in the dependent worksheet.

External references can be simple or complex. A simple external reference refers to a single cell or range by absolute location or by a defined name; the name can refer to a cell or range or to a defined constant. Any other reference is complex, whether it is a relative reference to a single cell, a formula to find

```
=PAYTEMP.XLS!$F$5
=A:\EXCEL\SAVEOLD\ARCHPAY.XLS!$H$29
=PAYTEMP.XLS!F5
=PAYTEMP.XLS!$F$5*.143
=\LIBRARY\REPJAN.XLS!TOTAL+REPFEB.XLS!TOTAL+REPMAR.XLS!TOTAL
```

FIGURE 7.6.   External References

the sum of a range, or a complex mathematical expression including several functions and operators. Figure 7.6 shows several external references, both simple and complex. The distinction is important; Excel can update a simple reference even when the worksheet it refers to is not open. It can handle a complex reference only when the worksheet it refers to is open. Simple references save both time and memory.

If you move cell references in the supporting worksheets, the changes are not necessarily reflected in the dependent worksheet references. If any dependent worksheets are open, Excel updates the references. If not, it doesn't. Most external references specify absolute locations; if you move the supporting cells, be sure to verify the effect on any dependent worksheets.

Locating External References

You can locate external references in a dependent worksheet through the Formula Find command. Search for the ! character in the Formulas; it occurs only in external references. Remember that you can use ALT + Enter to repeat the last command easily to find additional external references.

Identifying Supporting Worksheets

Excel provides an easy way to identify the supporting worksheets involved in links from a dependent worksheet. Use the File Links command, which results in a dialog box like the one shown in Figure 7.7.

All the supporting worksheets are listed, even if they are already open. You can open any linked worksheet from this screen. Just select the ones you want to open and press Open. You can also make changes here to the path or location of the worksheets; that is covered later in this chapter.

Establishing Links

You establish links in a dependent worksheet by entering external references to cells or names in existing worksheets. Simple references are more efficient in terms of time and memory.

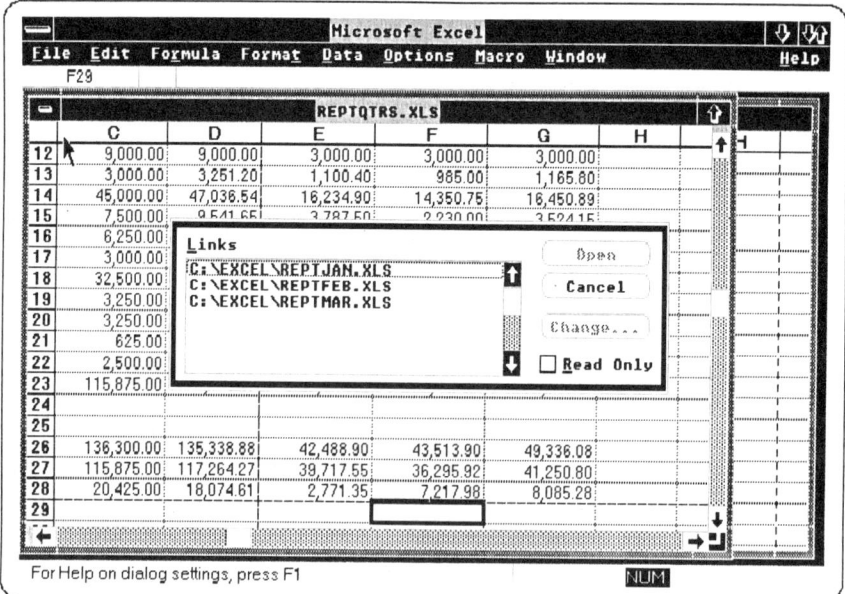

FIGURE 7.7. File Links Dialog Box

To establish a simple link to a single cell, you can use any of several methods. The basic way is to type the external reference to the supporting cell in the appropriate cell in the dependent worksheet as a formula. To use the contents of cell B6 in SHIPP.XLS in cell C9 in STOCK.XLS when both worksheets are open, activate the STOCK.XLS worksheet and select C9. Type =SHIPP.XLS!$B$6 to create a simple reference to link the two worksheets. Alternatively, you can select the link cell by pointing. Once the dependent worksheet is activated and the cell (C9) selected, activate the formula bar and type =. Then select the supporting worksheet and select the target cell (B6). When you press Enter or click the mouse, the external reference is completed with an absolute reference.

Using Paste Link

To establish a link to a range, you must use the Edit Paste Link command; this works for links to single cells as well. This method starts just like a standard copy operation. You select the range to be linked in the supporting worksheet, then use Edit Copy (CONTROL+Ins). Next you activate the dependent worksheet and select the cell at the upper left corner of the target range. To use the contents of cells B6:D12 in SHIPP.XLS in cells C9:E15 in STOCK.XLS when both worksheets are open, activate the SHIPP.XLS worksheet and select cells B6:D12. Use Edit Copy, then activate STOCK.XLS and select C9 to establish the upper left corner. Now use the Edit Paste Link command, and the link is established. The resulting reference is absolute and in the form of an array. The formula for each cell in the linked range in the dependent worksheet is the same: =SHIPP.XLS!$B$6:$D$12}. You can't change the individual formulas or any values in the range when you link them this way.

Establishing Complex Links

You can establish a complex link by typing a relative external reference to single cell in your dependent worksheet. Most complex links are a bit more involved than that, however. For example, suppose you want to use the sum of the totals in three different supporting worksheets in the dependent worksheet. You could use simple references to include the three separate ranges in the dependent worksheet. Then use the SUM function to calculate the total. Or you could use a complex function as in =SUM(east.xls!B9,west.xls!B9,north.xls!B9), and copy it to the cells in the dependent worksheet that need the value. You can't use absolute references if you're going to copy the formula to more than one place, because you want the cell references to be adjusted to access different data for different cells.

If the link references are absolute and a range is moved in the supporting worksheet, the new location won't be reflected in the dependent worksheet unless it is open at the time. If you use a name in the external reference, the dependent worksheet will always find the right cell.

Using Names in References

Excel lets you reference cells, ranges, or even constant values with names defined in the supporting worksheet. Just type the external reference using the name instead of the cell reference. If the referenced cell is moved in the supporting worksheet, the new location won't be reflected in the dependent worksheet unless it is open at the time. If you use a name in the external reference, the dependent worksheet will always find the right cell.

To establish a link to a defined constant in the supporting worksheet, use the name in the external reference. Since the constant isn't stored in a cell, you don't need any reference, either relative or absolute. Excel always uses the current value of the defined name, even if it has been changed since the link was established.

Using Values Rather than References

Some applications don't require that a link be automatically updated. A consolidation or summary worksheet may just need values from completed worksheets. You can place the values rather than the linked formulas in another worksheet with the Edit Paste Special command. First select the range to be transferred in the completed worksheet and select Edit Copy. Then activate the target worksheet and select the cell or upper left corner of the range and select Edit Paste Special.

Select the attributes of the selection you want to be pasted, and an operation to use with values already in the paste cells if appropriate. Then choose OK. If you select Values, only the values are pasted in the target worksheet. This does NOT create a link. If you make changes in the source, they won't be reflected in the target. This technique lets you use values, formulas, or whatever you need.

Saving Linked Worksheets

When you save linked worksheets, it's safest to save supporting ones first and dependent worksheets last. If you use File Save As to change the names, this technique allows the filenames to be kept up to date in references. If you save the dependent worksheet first, then use File Save As on a supporting one and change its name, that supporting worksheet won't be found next time. You can use the Options button of the File Links command to modify names or paths of any link files that Excel can't locate.

If you rename any of the files or move any to other drives or directories, the links won't work. You must be careful of your linked files. Whenever you change a filename or move a file, be aware if any links are involved. If you keep track of your files and plan any links in advance, you won't have any serious problems.

Opening Linked Worksheets

The easiest way to open a group of worksheets you need together for working is to save them as a workspace. Then when you open the workspace, they are all opened and arranged just as you left them. But that's in retrospect. What if you didn't save the set of linked files as a workspace?

When you open a dependent worksheet, Excel checks the external references. If it notes any, it displays a box as shown in Figure 7.8. If you select Yes, Excel tries to update; if No, the current values are used.

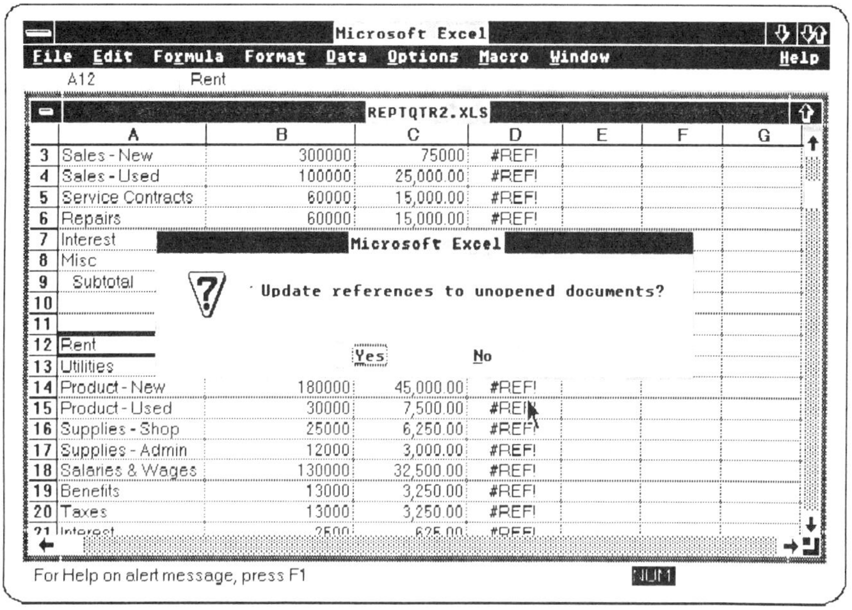

FIGURE 7.8. Update References Dialog Box

If the worksheet contains only simple external references, Excel can update them without the supporting worksheets being open. You select Yes, Excel gets the values from the files on disk. If you select No, Excel leaves the current values in the worksheet.

If the worksheet contains complex external references, Excel can't update them, even if you ask it to. The error message #REF! appears in each cell that contains a complex external reference whether you respond Yes or No to the update question. You can remove the messages by opening the supporting worksheets. Just use the File Links command while the dependent worksheet is active. Select all the supporting worksheets and press Open. They are loaded, and the complex external references are updated. If your screen is too cluttered, you can use Windows Hide to remove any supporting worksheets you won't be actively using from the screen. When you use Windows Unhide, all hidden windows are listed in a dialog box for you to place back on the screen as needed.

Once you have your required worksheets all open, you might notice different types of external references. An external reference that includes a path refers to a file that isn't open. In that case, single quotes surround the file reference. If you have supporting worksheets of the same name in different directories, you can have only one open at a time; Excel can't deal with duplicate file names in memory.

Removing Links

The easiest way to remove a link is to delete the external references from the dependent worksheet. Since this kills the values as well, it isn't always the best way, however. You can use Edit Paste Special to freeze the values and remove the formulas; just select the range or cell and use Edit Copy, then Edit Paste Special (Values) to paste the values in the same location. They are frozen and the formulas are gone. Even if they were treated as an array before, the values are now independent.

If the external reference you wish to freeze is part of a formula, you can freeze that part at the current value. First select the cell and activate the formula bar. Select the external reference itself in the formula bar and use the Options Calculate Now command; the reference is replaced with its current value and the link is broken.

You can check to see if you've broken all the links in a worksheet by using Formula Find to search for the ! character. If you find any, you have at least one more link to break.

Handling Links to Different Directories

Ideally, all linked worksheets are in the same directory. And you won't move any unless you move the entire set. In that case, Excel won't have any problems locating the links when needed. But your hard disk organization may require that you have different types of files in different directories. They may be divided by department, by time period, or in any other way. You may need to link a worksheet to data in several directories.

When saving linked worksheets for the first time after a link has been established, you'll save the supporting worksheets first, then the dependent worksheet. Use the File Save As command if they are not to be stored in the current directory. If you try to save a dependent worksheet when its supporting worksheets are not on disk where Excel expects to find them, you'll get a message and Excel gives you another chance.

If you must move a supporting or dependent worksheet to a different directory, use the File Save As command and type the complete new path. Excel will be able to find the links without your making any further changes. If you move a linked worksheet to another directory at the same level, be sure to use the complete path. If the moved worksheet has links to worksheets in a subdirectory below its own, Excel won't be able to find them. You'll have to create a new directory below the one containing the moved worksheet and move the linked worksheet to it or redirect the links through Excel.

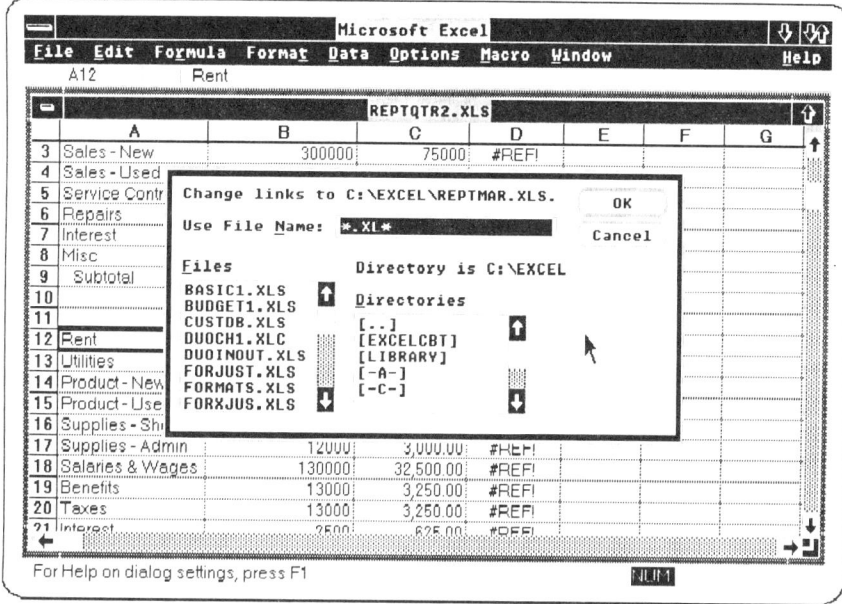

FIGURE 7.9. File Change Links Dialog Box

Redirecting Links

If Excel can't find the links when you open or save a linked worksheet, open the dependent worksheet and select File Links. Select a supporting worksheet that Excel can't find and press the Change button. Figure 7.9. shows the result. The selected supporting file name is shown at the top. You can use the list boxes here to check in the various directories to locate the file. When you find the file Excel should be using, select it; the desired name (and path if not in the current directory) displays in the Use File Name field. Then choose OK. The link is redirected to the file you selected. If you know the name and path of the file, you can type it directly in the Use File Name field; this saves a bit of time but requires that you know the file location up front.

TRANSFERRING DATA TO AND FROM OTHER APPLICATIONS

Excel can handle data from many other applications. In this section we'll cover those that are fairly straightforward, such as 1−2−3®, dBASE II®, dBASE III®, and Microsoft® Works, as well as generic ASCII or comma delimited files.

The final section shows you how to use the Clipboard and Dynamic Data Exchange (DDE), which you can use to exchange data with other programs that also run under Windows.

Writing to Disk in Other Formats

When you use the File Save As command to store a file on disk, Excel presents you with a dialog box in which you can provide the file name. If you press the Options button, you see various choices for the format of the output, as shown in Figure 7.10. The default is Normal, for standard Excel format.

Each file format provides a specific format and file extension. Figure 7.11 lists the effect of each file format. You can also provide a password for security or tell Excel to create a backup file. The formats that work with specific programs are no problem; if you need to transfer Excel data to a Microsoft Works program, for example, just Save it in the right format and open it in Works.

The Text option provides a pure ASCII file in which each row ends with a carriage return. A tab character is inserted between columns. If you read the resulting TXT file into a word processor file, it may not align correctly. You

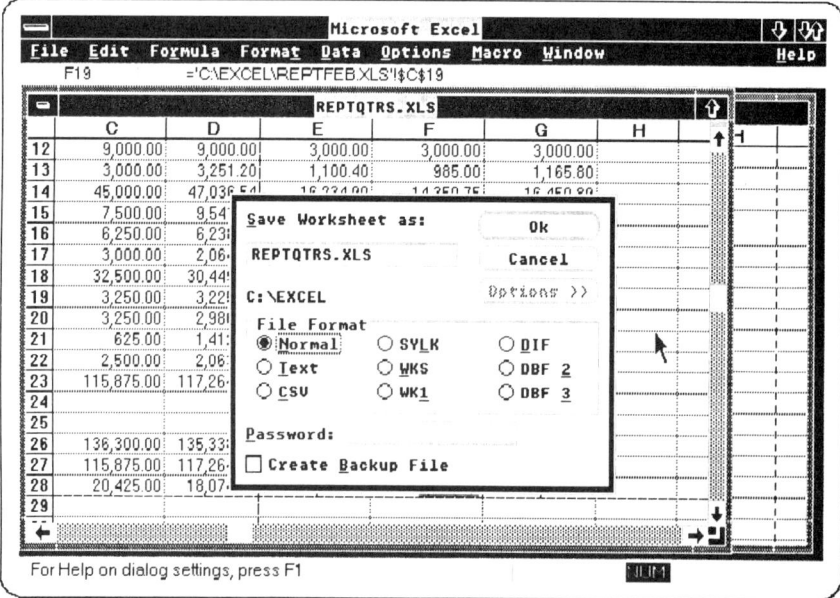

FIGURE 7.10. Save to Disk Dialog Box

MANAGING WINDOWS AND LINKS

Format	Extension	Details
Normal	XLS	Excel Worksheet
	XLC	Excel Chart
	XLM	Excel Macro sheet
	XLW	Excel Workspace listing
Text	TXT	ASCII format; each row a separate line; tabs between columns
CSV	CSV	Comma separated values; comma between columns, carriage return between rows
SYLK	SYL	Multiplan or MicroSoft Works
WKS	WKS	Lotus 1-2-3 Release 1 or Works
WK1	WK1	Lotus 1-2-3 Release 2
DIF	DIF	General low level worksheet format
DBF 2	DBF	dBASE II
DBF 3	DBF	dBASE III

FIGURE 7.11. File Save As Options

Result of TXT Save

```
          "IMAGINETRONICS, INC."

          January   February   March        April        May             Year-to-date
Fees      "$9,200.00 "         "$6,400.00 "     "$6,250.00 "     "$7,444.00 "      "$8,689.90 "
Royalties "$12,780.00 "        "$10,000.00 "    "$7,500.00 "     "$11,780.00 "     "$9,976.00 "
Services  "$5,400.00 "         "$4,475.00 "     "$4,600.00 "     "$5,245.00 "      "$4,987.00 "
Interest  "$2,288.98 "         "$2,456.88 "     "$4,129.00 "     "$3,222.00 "      "$3,198.50 "
Misc.     $875.34       "$1,400.00 "        "$1,287.65 "       $987.87      "$1,120.76 "      "$5,671.62 "

Total     "$30,544.32 "        "$24,731.88 "    "$23,766.65 "    "$28,678.87 "     "$27,972.16 "
```

Result of CSV Save

```
,"IMAGINETRONICS, INC.",,,,,
,,,,,,
,January,February,March,April,May,,
Fees,"$9,200.00 ","$6,400.00 ","$6,250.00 ","$7,444.00 ","$8,689.90 ",,
Royalties,"$12,780.00 ","$10,000.00 ","$7,500.00 ","$11,780.00 ","$9,976.00 ",,
Services,"$5,400.00 ","$4,475.00 ","$4,600.00 ","$5,245.00 ","$4,987.00 ",,
Interest,"$2,288.98 ","$2,456.88 ","$4,129.00 ","$3,222.00 ","$3,198.50 ",,
Misc.,$875.34 ,"$1,400.00 ","$1,287.65 ",$987.87 ,"$1,120.76 ",,
,,,,,,
Total,"$30,544.32 ","$24,731.88 ","$23,766.65 ","$28,678.87 ","$27,972.16 ",,
```

FIGURE 7.12. Text and CSV Options

156 ADVANCED EXCEL

may have to adjust the tab settings in your document. Be sure to adjust the "hard" tabs if your word processor has both hard and soft tabs. In the ASCII file, Excel inserts double quotes around any cell data that includes either a comma or a tab character. You can remove these in your document if you like.

The CSV option provides a comma-delimited file that you may use as input to a database or as a data file for many programs, such as WordStar®, with its merge facility. This is also a true ASCII file, but it uses commas rather than tabs to separate data from cells. As with Text, double quotes surround any cell data that includes extraneous commas. Figure 7.12 shows the same small worksheet in Text and CSV formats. You can use the format most useful for your applications.

Reading from Disk in Non-Excel Formats

Excel can open files in many other formats without any problem. If a file has any of the formats and extensions it can save to disk in, Excel will read it in that format and display it in rows and columns on the worksheet. If it has any other extension, Excel reads the file as text unless it recognizes the format. For example, Excel recognizes a 1−2−3 file even if it doesn't have the right extension. But it doesn't recognize a comma-delimited file unless it has the CSV extension. Text files are placed one line per row, in column A; additional cells are used if hard tab characters are encountered. Lines in CSV files are divided into cells at the commas. The file to be opened must have an extension; Excel appends XLS if there is no extension and then objects because the file is in the wrong format. You may have to rename files to import them correctly into Excel.

Transfering Data among Windows Applications

There are two ways you can transfer data among running Windows applications; both work only if you have the full Windows rather than just the runtime version. The first is the Clipboard, using the same techniques as when you cut or copy data among open worksheets. The second is DDE or Dynamic Data Exchange; DDE doesn't work with all applications.

Using the Clipboard. When you cut or copy cells normally, Excel stores the cut or copied information temporarily in the Clipboard. You never really have to look at it, but you can do so if you wish from the application control menu; select Run, then the Clipboard. When you want to move data to another application, just select it as usual in Excel with either Cut or Copy. Then activate the other application and Paste the data using that application's commands. No matter what you used to put the data in the Clipboard, Excel doesn't erase it from the worksheet. If you want to transfer data from another application to Excel, first cut or copy it using that application's commands. Then activate the appropriate Excel worksheet and use Edit Paste to insert it. That's all there is to it. Once the data is in Excel, you can use it as you will.

Using Dynamic Data Exchange (DDE). Dynamic Data Exchange works on some programs under Windows. You can use it to create a "hot link" between documents in different applications, much as you can link between worksheets so they are updated automatically. And as with linking worksheets, you need a special form of reference. The remote reference has three parts: the application, the topic, and the item. The format is much like an external reference:

application|topic!item

To reference Excel from another application that supports DDE you could use "Excel"|Expenses.XLS!B2:B12; the application for Excel is the quoted name, the topic is the file name, and the item is the reference. To reference another application from Excel, you use its application name, whatever it recognizes as a topic, and a reference to an item in its format.

To receive data via DDE in Excel, select the location (or the upper left corner of a range) and use Edit Paste Links. If Paste Links is not available, that means the other application doesn't support DDE.

You can find more information about DDE in the Excel documentation as well as in the documentation for other applications that support it.

SUGGESTED EXERCISE

1. First try looking at a linked set of files from the LIBRARY subdirectory. Open BREAKEVN.XLS. When the Update References box appears, answer YES.
2. Notice the #REF! entries in cells. Use File Links to open any linked worksheets.
3. Search for external references in BREAKEVN.XLS. Change a few values in CASHBUDG.XLS to see the effect in BREAKEVN.
4. Close BREAKEVN.XLS and create a worksheet that uses some values from CASHBUDG.XLS. Use both simple and complex references to make sure you can use both.
5. Save the new worksheet (the dependent one) to the main directory, then close CASHBUDG.XLS in its LIBRARY directory.
6. Close all worksheets, then open the new one. If it has any trouble finding the supporting worksheet, redirect the links.

What if It Doesn't Work?

1. Try working with BREAKEVN.XLS and CASHBUDG.XLS some more. These worksheets are fairly straightforward.
2. Try making a linked set from scratch.

SUMMARY

This chapter has covered the various ways you can manipulate and interrelate windows and documents under Excel. You should now be able to handle the optimum number of windows into a document, set up, freeze, and remove panes as you need them, and link worksheets and work with them. Be sure to take time to plan linked worksheets and keep them in the same directory if possible. Planning in advance always takes less time than trying to get organized later on.

If you run other applications under Windows as well as Excel, you can copy data from one to the other with the Clipboard or use Dynamic Data Exchange if the other applications support it. This too should be planned in advance.

8 HANDLING DATABASES

The standard Excel worksheet can also function as a database; Excel offers various database commands and functions to help you construct and maintain data for easy use as a database. All the standard worksheet commands and effects also work in a database.

Many applications are more easily handled as a database than as a spreadsheet. Sets of information about customers, stock items, employees, patients, policies, anything at all, can be constructed and manipulated as a database.

WHAT IS A DATABASE?

A database is a collection of information. It is carefully organized so that it can be edited, maintained, and used for retrieval of particular data as needed. A database, like a spreadsheet, is organized into rows and columns. Each database row contains information about one particular item; it may be a customer, an employee, an inventory item, even a time slot. The term *record* refers to a database row. Each row is treated independently. Each cell in the record represents a *field*. Each field contains a different piece of information; it may be a name, a phone number, a description, a price, even a code or comment.

Every record in a database contains the same number of fields in the same sequence. Figure 8.1 shows a diagram of a database layout.

In addition to data, the database needs field names; these are also shown in Figure 8.1. Once the database is set up on an Excel worksheet, you can search it to find specific information, form subsets for printing reports, perform various arithmetic and statistical functions on records, sort the data, and maintain up-to-date records in your database with little effort.

You can add more records to an existing database or delete records from it. You can change data in fields as needed. You can sort the records on any of the

Record Reference Number	Item Number	Item Name	Quantity on hand	Quantity on order	Unit Cost	Storage Location	Manu.	Description
Ref#	Item#	Name	On hand	On order	UnitCost	Loc.	Mfg.	Description
~~	~~	~~	~~	~~	~~	~~	~~	~~
~~	~~	~~	~~	~~	~~	~~	~~	~~
.	.	.	.	.	.	.	.	.
.	.	.	.	.	.	.	.	.
.	.	.	.	.	.	.	.	.

FIGURE 8.1. Database Diagram

fields. You can find records that contain certain values or that meet some criteria based on conditions in one or more fields. You can extract a subset of records for further processing or printing.

Excel provides several ways to process databases. You can type the data in and handle it just as in any other worksheet. You can use commands from the Data pull-down menu to perform various operations. Or you can use special customized forms that Excel develops for every database. You'll learn to use all these methods in this chapter.

DESIGNING A DATABASE

You need to design a database before you enter it into Excel. This involves deciding what information to include, what fields you need, and even what fields you don't need. For example, you should have a separate field for zip codes if you ever have to sort the records by zip code. You need a separate field for last names if you ever have to sort records alphabetically by name. But you don't need separate fields for everything. If you never think of or process a piece of data independently, it probably doesn't need a field of its own. You may use a formula to compute some fields if you want to store results in the database; if the database is large, you may want to compute values when you need them rather than store them with the database. You might want to use one extra field named COMPUTE at the end of each record; you can place whatever formula or function you need there if you want to sort or select on a computed field not normally stored with the database.

While Excel lets you use up to 255 fields (the entire worksheet width) in a database, it places the entire database in memory when you work with it. If a database needs more than 20 or so fields, you may be able to create several

HANDLING DATABASES

linked databases instead. Instead of a large database with customer numbers, customer names and mailing information, customer purchase records, and credit information, you could create three databases for the three major functions, repeating only the customer number in each. Each database is smaller and easier for Excel to handle, but linking through the customer number ensures that they are tied together if you need them. Excel can't handle more than a few thousand records efficiently. If you have more, you might consider using a dedicated database and pulling a subset of it into Excel when you need Excel's special features.

Worksheet Layout

When you have decided what to put in the database, you must decide where to put it on the worksheet. You need space for the database itself, space for specifying criteria for various operations, and space for any subset of records that Excel extracts in the process of performing functions you request. Excel calls these areas the database range, the criteria range, and the extract range.

If the database has a worksheet all to itself (the ideal condition), you might want to put the criteria range in the upper left corner (leave three or four rows and as many columns as in the database), with the database directly below it. You can place the extract range below the database proper or off to the right of it. Either location allows you to add records to the database and extract an unlimited number of records without interference. If your worksheet contains other material as well, you can place the database components in other locations.

CREATING A DATABASE

When you create a database, you first enter field names. The row directly above the first record of data is treated as field names. You can use more rows to set up titles, headings, and groupings, but the names in the row directly above the data must all be unique. Figure 8.2 shows a database with field names and one data record. Only the names in one row are actually treated as field names. The names for the fields in columns D, E, and F are HAND, ORDER, and COST.

Each field name must be text or a text formula, such as ="1940". Excel allows up to 255 characters per field name, but you'll want to keep the names fairly short for convenience in reference and to fit the column. If a field contains a company name, you can use "Company.Name" as a field name. If it

162 ADVANCED EXCEL

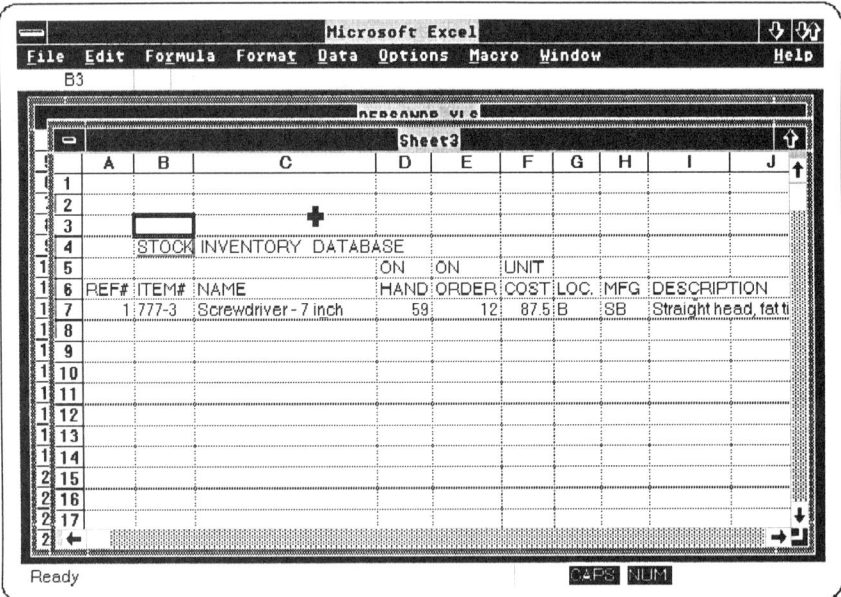

FIGURE 8.2. Field Names for Database

contains a branch number from 0 to 18, use a short name such as "BR" so as not to waste space on screen. Once you have the field names entered, adjust the width of each column for the expected data. Then enter values for the first few records. You can sort later, so don't worry about the sequence. Just get the right values in the right columns. Once you have two or three records entered, you can continue or change to another method (Data Forms) to enter the rest of the records.

If you use Formula Define Name to define your field names for the columns, you can use them in formulas. Otherwise, just use cell references for the same row. For example, if each record includes a computed field made up of the product of unit.cost and quantity, you can use =unit.cost*quantity in one record and copy it to the rest of the records in the database if the names are defined; just use C19*D19 if they aren't. Use relative references to refer to anything inside the database; use absolute references to refer to anything outside it.

Define the Database

Excel doesn't know you have a database until you tell it. You do this by first selecting the entire area of your current database, including the official row of field names at the beginning and several blank rows at the end. When the range is selected, activate the Data menu and select Set Database. Excel automatically defines the name "database" for the selected area. You can activate the area at any time by selecting Formula Goto and selecting database from the name list box. Excel allows only one database name per worksheet. If you prefer to use several databases on one worksheet, you can define unique names for each, then use the Data Set Database command to establish one active database at a time for processing.

Moving within the database is just like moving within any selected range. Use the mouse or Tab and SHIFT + Tab to move right and left. Use Enter and SHIFT + Enter to move up and down. If you touch one of the arrow keys or click outside it, the range is deselected. Several shortcuts you can use to enter data are CONTROL + ; to insert the current time, CONTROL + : to insert the current date, CONTROL + ' insert the formula from the cell above (without adjusting it), and CONTROL + " to insert the value from the cell above.

Once the database is established, you can add lines for new records in the middle; Excel automatically adjusts the database range. You can remove records from any point, except at the very end, and Excel maintains the range. You can edit the data in the records using any of Excel's techniques and commands. The database forms facility makes database maintainence easier and more convenient, however, and Excel automatically adjusts the database to correspond with your changes.

USING DATA FORMS

Excel can automatically create a data entry form for your database, using the field names you supplied. When you select the Data Form command, a dialog box appears. Figure 8.3 shows a typical database form. Excel uses your field names on the left. Notice that one letter in each name is underlined so you can select the field directly with the ALT key. Occasionally, Excel won't be able to find a unique letter and the name won't have a direct access. You can move to the adjacent field and use Tab or SHIFT + Tab to reach the desired one. The field box next to each name contains the value of the current row; that's the row that contained the current cell in the database or the first row if one of the field names was active. You can move directly to any value and change it.

Changes don't affect the record until you go on to a different record or press Enter. If you've made some changes in the form and then changed your mind, you can select the Restore button to return to the unedited current record. The up and down arrows page through the records one at a time. The

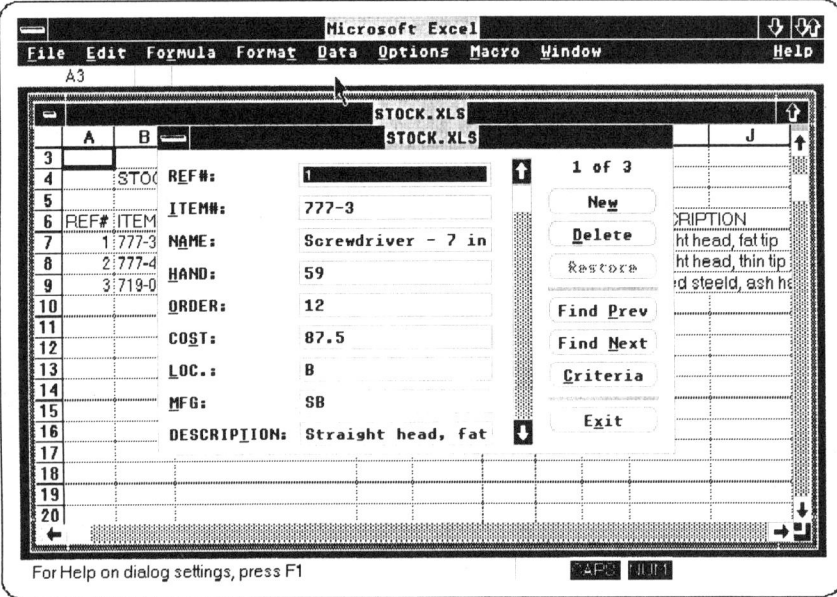

FIGURE 8.3. Database Form Dialog Box

PageUp and PageDown keys skip ten records in the appropriate direction. The Tab key moves through the displayed fields. When you press Enter any data you've entered into the form is added to the database in the worksheet.

The buttons in the panel on the right let you perform operations. Exit removes the form window and returns you to the actual database in the worksheet. Restore cancels the changes you've made since the last time you pressed Enter. Above the button panel is a message telling you where you are in the database. In Figure 8.3, we're at record 1 of 3. The scroll bar in the center of the box shows the relative position in the database.

Adding Records

You can use the New button to add records to the database. Excel places them in the blank lines you left at the bottom of the established database and adjusts the range accordingly. When you choose New, the fields in the dialog box clear. You can enter the data for each field; the shortcuts work here as well as in the worksheet. If you are using a sequential value in each record, you can enter it now or leave it blank. (In Chapter 11, you'll learn to use the Data Series command, which is useful for a sequence of numbers.) If the record contains a

HANDLING DATABASES **165**

computed field (anything using a formula), Excel automatically computes it when it can; you can't enter a computed field directly, so it doesn't appear in a text box in the form.

Press Tab after each field is ready. If you press Tab after the last field, the New button is activated. Press Enter and you'll be set up for the next new record. You can just press Enter after the last field if you prefer; Excel assumes you want to continue adding records as long as you continue entering data in the blank forms it gives you. To stop, you can press Escape or choose Exit to leave the data form or perform some other operation.

Deleting Records

To delete a record from a database using a data form, first display the contents of the record you want to delete. Use the arrow keys or PageUp or PageDown. Then select Delete. Excel gives you the message "Displayed record will be deleted permanently." If you select OK, it is gone; if you select Cancel, nothing deleted. Be sure you have a backup copy of the database if there is any chance you might want that record again.

Finding Records

Excel can locate records in the database. You tell it what records to find by setting some criteria. You might want to see record 13, any record with Name beginning with A, or any record of data with more than 12 items in stock from a particular manufacturer. For any of these, first you have to set the criteria with the Criteria button. When you choose Criteria, the dialog box changes a bit, as shown in Figure 8.4. Notice that the word Criteria appears above the button panel. And the Delete button is replaced with a Clear button. You type your condition in the appropriate field; use as many fields as you need. To find record 13, just type 13 in the REF# field and then choose either Find Prev or Find Next, depending on which way in the database you want Excel to look. If it doesn't find it in one direction, you can ask it to search in the other. Once record 13 is displayed, pressing Find Next or Find Prev results in a beep since there aren't any more.

To find records that begin with manufacturer code FL in the Mfg field, select Criteria again. The criteria value from the previous find is still there; to eliminate it, select the value and press Clear. Then enter the value FL (or fl) in the Mfg field and select Find Prev or Find Next. Repeat the appropriate Find

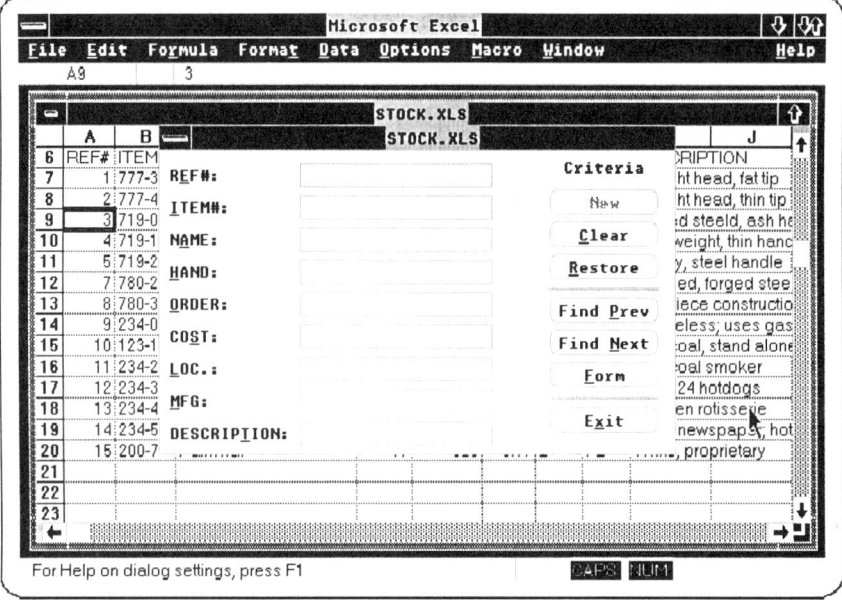

FIGURE 8.4. Data Form Criteria Dialog Box

button until you have found what you were looking for or have seen all records that match. You can place criteria in as many fields as you wish. You can use conditional operators, such as greater than (⟩) or less than (⟨). For example, you might use ⟩10.00 to find costs greater than 10 or ⟨20 to locate items that have fewer than 20 in stock.

Text criteria cause Excel to select records that begin with the given text. The criteria FL for Mfg will match FL, fl, Flour, or even FLIGHT. To specify an exact match use a formula in the form = " = FL" as the criterion. You need a leading equal sign, as well as one within the quotes.

Data Forms Summary

The data forms let you do a great deal in terms of maintaining and viewing your database. They are limited in what you do, however. Records are always added at the end and remain in the order in which you add them. And if you use forms for all your database work, you can print only the database as a whole. Suppose you want a listing of only one manufacturer. And suppose you want to save a copy of all the records you intend to delete. You'll find that you need to use the database commands a great deal in processing even very basic databases.

Later in this book, we'll show you how to customize forms to specify where each field appears and how large its text box is. Customized forms are extremely useful if you have inexperienced people working with your database.

SUGGESTED EXERCISE

1. Open a new worksheet and begin to create a database. Start the field names in row 7.
2. For each record use a last name, a first name, salary, phone number, zip code, and age. Create appropriate field names.
3. Enter two records of data below the field names. Just make up values.
4. Define the database to Excel. Check the Formula Define Name box to see the name Excel assigns.
5. Use Data Form to add three to ten records to the database. Again, make up any appropriate data values.
6. Use Data Form to change data in a few records and delete a record.
7. Use Data Form to locate any records with salary over $7,000. Try any with last names starting later than M in the alphabet. Try a Find with at least three criteria. Add a few records if necessary so the Find locates several records. Use the arrows to move among the found records.

What if It Doesn't Work?

1. Be sure you include one row of field names and several blank rows at the end in the range when you use Data Set Database to define the database. Otherwise the range won't be right and the form won't have the correct names.
2. If you decide to add records without using the data form, insert rows in the middle of the database range or redefine the range after you're finished.

SORTING RECORDS

When you work with data forms, the data records stay in the same relative position in the database. When you maintain the database or work with it as an Excel worksheet, you can use the Data Sort command to rearrange the records. In fact, you can use Data Sort to rearrange either rows or columns in any selected range. We'll consider sorting in database terms here, but the command can be used the same way to sort any range of data. When it sorts, Excel rearranges the selected range. You can restore the range to the condition it was in before the sort by selecting Edit Undo before you use any other edit commands.

Sort Sequence

Excel uses values in fields or cells to sort records. You can specify up to three fields at once. Within each field, Excel always uses the same sequence to sort records; you specify whether it should use an ascending or descending sequence. Excel sorts first numbers, then text, logical values, error values, and finally blank cells. Numbers are sorted algebraically; a positive value is larger than a negative value. Text values are sorted according to the sequence shown in Figure 8.5.

Excel does not distinguish between uppercase and lowercase in sorting. Text numbers are sorted before letters, and special characters are sorted where indicated in Figure 8.5. The space character sorts first, so the word Cat sorts before cathode, since space precedes h in the sort order. The logical value FALSE always precedes TRUE, and error values are sorted alphabetically. Blank cells sort last. If Excel does a sort on a field that may be empty, records containing the empty cells will be last in the result.

The sort is based on the complete contents of a cell. If you want to sort based on the value of a formula that isn't ordinarily part of the records, you must add a field with the appropriate formula to each record. You might add a temporary computed field at the right end of the database and copy the

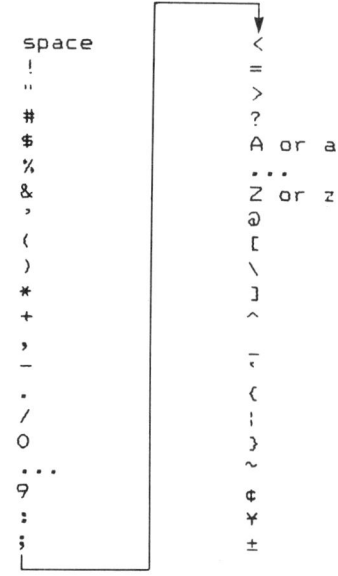

FIGURE 8.5. Sort Sequence

formula to each record. If you want to sort on part of a text field, say a zip code at the end of an address field or an area code in a telephone number, you can add a field that uses the appropriate text function (LEFT, MID, or RIGHT) to extract the portion of text, then sort on that field.

Starting a Sort

Before starting a sort, you must select the appropriate range. Strange as it may seem, the sort range is NOT the same as the database range! Remember that the database range includes one row of field names. You very seldom want to include that row in a sort, since you want to keep it at the very top of the column. So the thing to to do is define a name to refer to a range that includes all your database except the top row. Use a name like "sortdb" or "forsort" so you won't forget it. Then, before you do a sort, use Formula Goto and select your sort range name. Be sure it includes the entire rows and columns you want sorted. Only rows or columns within the selected range are affected. You can get a real mess if your sort range includes only 10 of the database's 12 columns. Those ten fields in each record will be sorted, but the last two won't. You can Undo a sort right away (with Undo Sort or ALT + Backspace) if you notice a problem, but it can be almost impossible to straighten out later. Many people feel safest if they do File Save As before a sort to create a temporary save file. Once you feel confident in your selected range, select Data Sort. Figure 8.6. shows the Data Sort dialog box. You'll generally sort by rows; the rows or records are rearranged based on values in the fields specified as keys. Sorting by columns rearranges the columns of the database; that is covered a bit later.

You can specify up to three keys for each sort. The first key is the most important. To sort in alphabetical order by name when first, middle, and last names are in separate fields, put the reference of the last name as the 1st Key, the first name as the 2nd Key, and the middle name as the 3rd Key. If you need more than three sort fields, first sort the entire sort range on the lesser keys, such as state or country. Then put the three most important categories on the final Sort dialog box.

Each key reference must be to a particular field, but it can specify any cell in the column. Excel uses the currently active cell as the default primary key. Figure 8.6 shows a reference to B7; any reference to a cell in the selected range in column B has the same effect. You can use absolute references if you prefer; Excel works a bit faster with absolute references.

When the keys are as you want them, choose OK and Excel sorts the records. Scan the sorted database before you do any editing; you can use the Edit Undo Sort command (or ALT + Backspace) to return to presort status.

170 ADVANCED EXCEL

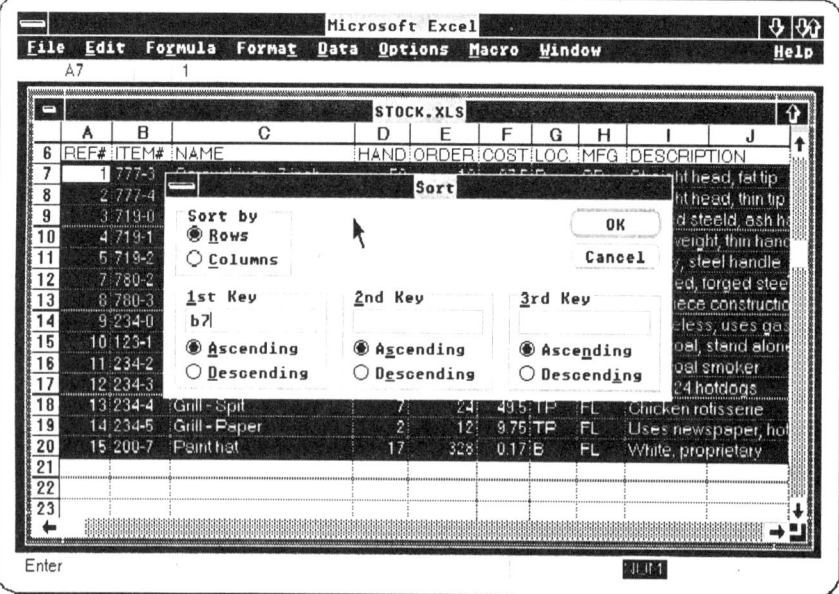

FIGURE 8.6. Data Sort Dialog Box

Rearranging Columns

You can use the Data Sort command to rearrange columns as well as to rearrange rows. To do this, first add a blank row within your sorting range. Enter a number in each field, indicating the desired order of columns. If each record has eight fields and you want to reverse the order, enter 8 in the first field of the new record, then 7, and so on through 1 in the rightmost column. If you want the third column to be first, the fifth second, and the rest in their current sequence, number the fields in the new record 3, 4, 1, 5, 2, 6, 7, 8. After the sort, the columns are rearranged. To rearrange columns in a database, use the complete database range; you want to include the field names in the rearranging. In fact, if you used more than one line for more descriptive names, include any extra lines in the sort range as well.

Once you have numbered cells in an otherwise blank row, use Data Sort. Select Columns to sort by columns. Reference any cell in the new, numbered record for the first key and choose OK. Excel rearranges the columns. Figure 8.7 shows the result in our sample database. Notice that the column widths are not adjusted by the operation. You'll have to format the column widths if you keep the arrangement. Edit Undo Sort restores the previous condition if you select exactly the same range before doing any other editing.

HANDLING DATABASES

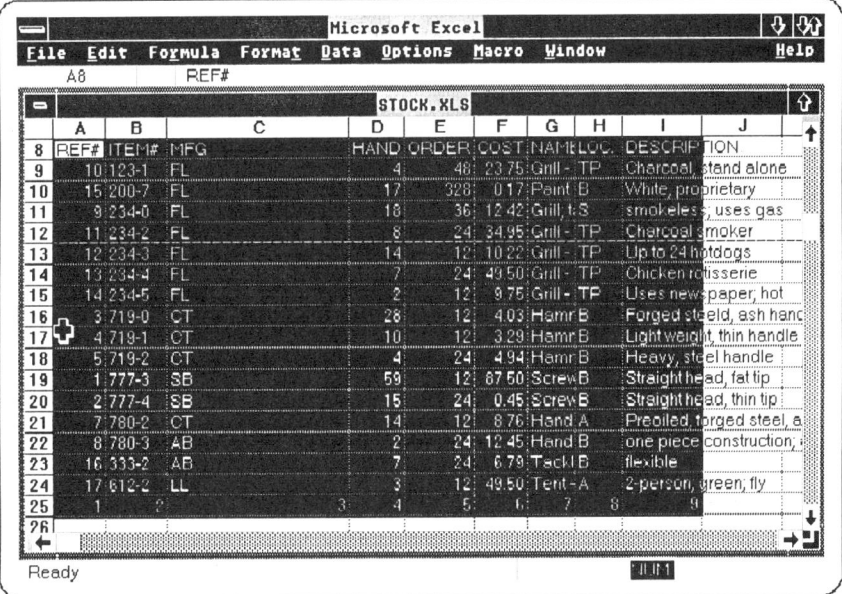

FIGURE 8.7. After Sorting by Columns

When to Sort

Sorting has many uses. You can use it to group the records you are interested in so that you can see them more easily. You can use it to prepare data for reports. Sorting is so easy you will probably find yourself sorting your data many times per session. If you want to be able to restore the database to a specific sequence, you can add a sequence field. Just leave it blank when you enter the original data. Then use the Data Series command to number the records. When you are finished sorting and rearranging for the session, sort by the sequence field and the original sequence is restored.

SUGGESTED EXERCISE

1. Sort the records in your database to put them in alphabetical order by name. Define a new sorting range, and use two keys in the Sort dialog box.
2. Sort the records by another field, such as age or zip code.
3. Rearrange the columns using the first blank row at the bottom of the database. Then use Edit Undo to restore the original arrangement.
4. Open file CARPOOL.XLS in the EXCELCBT directory. Save it as CARDATA.XLS in your current directory, then sort it based on area and arrival time.

What if It Doesn't Work?

1. If you have trouble sorting your database, try it again, using a field you know it should sort in. Be sure to set each key to be used as a single-cell reference. Be sure to sort by rows to rearrange records.
2. Be sure to select the entire range, including field names and the row that contains the desired sequence numbers of fields to rearrange columns.

USING THE CRITERIA RANGE

The Find, Extract, and Delete commands on the Data menu all require that you specify criteria, conditions for records to be selected. Excel requires that you define a criteria range on the worksheet. The criteria range must contain at least two rows; one has field names just as in the database itself, the other contains the criteria. Figure 8.8 shows a criteria range.

The field names you use must exactly match those in the database; you can copy them to the criteria range to minimize the chance of error. You don't have to use all the field names in the database, however. After they have been

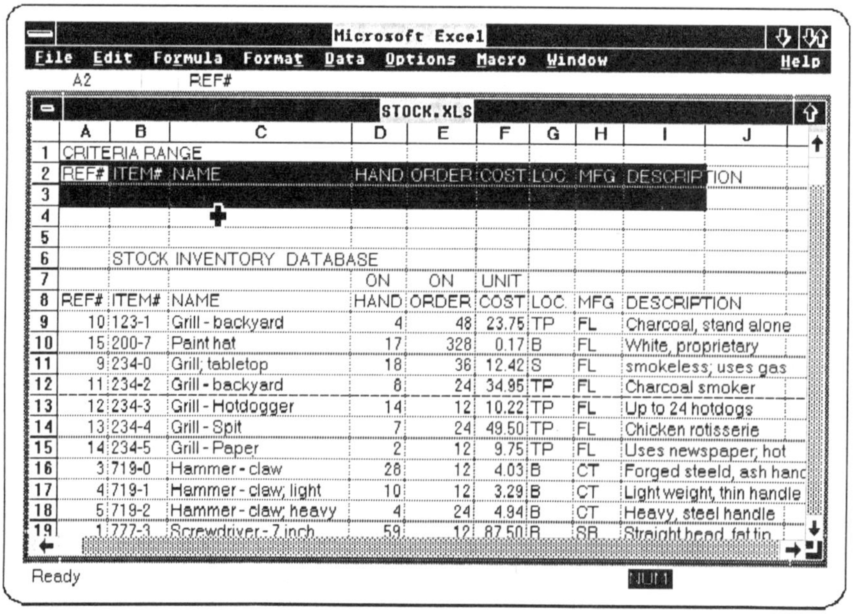

FIGURE 8.8. Criteria Range

HANDLING DATABASES

entered, select the row with field names and the blank row below it, as shown in Figure 8.8. Then use the Data Set Criteria Range command. Excel defines the name "criteria" to refer to the selected range.

To use the criteria range, just type the criteria under the appropriate field names. You can enter criteria for as many fields as you wish; records that match all the criteria will be selected. You don't need to include field names for fields you aren't selecting, but you can include them if you wish. Just leave the cell beneath the name blank if you don't want to specify a criterion. If you leave all the cells blank, all the records in the database will be selected. If you specify criteria for three fields, only records that match all three criteria are selected. Excel treats all the criteria in one row as AND functions.

If you want to specify more than one criterion for a single field, add additional rows to your criteria range. Additional values can be entered on the additional lines. For example, to select records containing exactly GL, CT, or CB in a field, you'll need three rows in the criteria range below the field name. On one row put ="=GL", on the next put ="=CT", and on the third put ="=CB". Excel treats these as OR functions; if any of the three values occurs in a given record, that record is selected by the criteria. Be sure to remove extra lines in the criteria range when you don't need them any more; a complete blank line in the criteria range matches every record in the database, effectively canceling out any other criteria you have specified. As in sorting and locating, Excel ignores the case in matching criteria.

Criteria in a criteria range can be simple, complex, compound, or calculated. The criteria in a data form are limited to the simple type.

Simple Criteria

Simple criteria are much the same in criteria ranges as in data forms. The criteria value CL matches any text string that starts with CL, regardless of case or what follows it within the cell. To match a text value exactly, use quotes, as in ="=CL". You can use wildcards in criteria range text values. The symbol ? identifies a single nonspecific character. "C?T" matches cat, CXTP, Catherine, and c-t-p. The symbol * identifies any group of characters; it can appear at the beginning, in the middle, or at the end of a text string. "*ing" identifies all text strings that end in ing. "P*NT" identifies such strings as punt, paint, painting, pliant, and piece of lint in blue. If you need to use * or ? as a specific character, precede it with a tilde; the criteria ="=WHY~?" matches the string WHY? or why?. You can use greater than (⟩) or less than (⟨) to select values later or earlier in the sort sequence for text values as well as for numbers.

```
   =    Equal to (use form ="=text")
   >    Greater than
   <    Less than
   >=   Greater than or equal to
   <=   Less than or equal to
   <>   Not equal to
```

FIGURE 8.9. Numeric Criteria Operators

Numeric values can be selected using any of the operators shown in Figure 8.9. For example, >100 selects all records in which that field contains a numeric value greater than 100. The criterion <>0 selects all records in which that field does not have a zero value.

You can select a range of values by repeating the field name in the criteria range. To select a range of zip codes between 92000 and 92100, use ZIP twice in the criteria range. Use >91999 in one and <92101 in the other; since Excel treats this as an AND condition, it will select the desired range of values.

Computed and Complex Criteria

Sometimes you want to find records based on more than a single field, or even a set of criteria. For example, suppose you want to find records where the total value (cost times hand) is greater than $2,000. Or you might need to find records in which the orders total more than the amount on hand. You might want to find customer records in which the amount owed is less than half the credit limit or on which the current payment is less than the amount due. You can use computed criteria to compare two fields in the record, do arithmetic, even compare values in different records in the database. Excel also lets you use values from outside the database range or from another worksheet. The criterion must be expressed in a form that Excel can reduce to TRUE or FALSE. It selects records that result in TRUE.

To use computed criteria, you have to provide an extra field in the criteria range; this field requires a unique name, one that does not appear in the database. If you add it in the middle of your criteria range, Excel adjusts the range automatically. In the cell below the new field name, put the formula, using cell references from the first record in the database. If the database begins on Row 5, you might use =D5*E5>2000. This will be TRUE if the value in the field in column D times the value of the field in column E is greater than 2000; all records for which this is true will be selected. A computed criterion must have a TRUE or FALSE result. When it is entered correctly, the value in the cell in the criteria range will be TRUE or FALSE, depending on the values in the first record in the database range. Figure 8.10 shows a criteria range with a

HANDLING DATABASES

[Screenshot of Microsoft Excel showing STOCK.XLS with formula =D9*F9>100 in cell I3, displaying FALSE result]

	A	B	C	D	E	F	G	H	I	J
1	CRITERIA RANGE									
2	REF#	ITEM#	NAME	HAND	ORDER	COST	LOC.	MFG	compute	
3									FALSE	
4										
5										
6		STOCK INVENTORY DATABASE								
7				ON	ON	UNIT				
8	REF#	ITEM#	NAME	HAND	ORDER	COST	LOC.	MFG	DESCRIPTION	
9	10	123-1	Grill - backyard	4	48	23.75	TP	FL	Charcoal, stand alone	
10	15	200-7	Paint hat	17	328	0.17	B	FL	White, proprietary	
11	9	234-0	Grill, tabletop	18	36	12.42	S	FL	smokeless; uses gas	
12	11	234-2	Grill - backyard	8	24	34.95	TP	FL	Charcoal smoker	
13	12	234-3	Grill - Hotdogger	14	12	10.22	TP	FL	Up to 24 hotdogs	
14	13	234-4	Grill - Spit	7	24	49.50	TP	FL	Chicken rotisserie	
15	14	234-5	Grill - Paper	2	12	9.75	TP	FL	Uses newspaper, hot	
16	3	719-0	Hammer - claw	28	12	4.03	B	CT	Forged steeld, ash hand	
17	4	719-1	Hammer - claw, light	10	12	3.29	B	CT	Lightweight, thin handle	
18	5	719-2	Hammer - claw, heavy	4	24	4.94	B	CT	Heavy, steel handle	
19	1	777-3	Screwdriver - 7 inch	59	12	87.50	B	SR	Straight head, flat tip	

FIGURE 8.10. Using Computed Criteria

computed criterion; you can see the result for the first record in the database as well.

Compound Criteria

You can use compound criteria to define what you want in each field. The AND, OR, and NOT functions let you do this in a single cell. (These logical functions are detailed in Chapter 5. You might want to review them before continuing.) Like the calculated criteria, the compound functions must be defined under a field name not a part of the database. Also, like the computed criteria, they result in a TRUE or FALSE value; Excel selects records that result in a TRUE value. Figure 8.11 shows a criteria range in which the AND and NOT functions are used.

Criteria References Outside the Database

Criteria can reference cells outside the database, but they must use absolute references to do so. If the reference is to a different worksheet, you must use an external reference that includes the name of the other worksheet. These references can be included in any criteria.

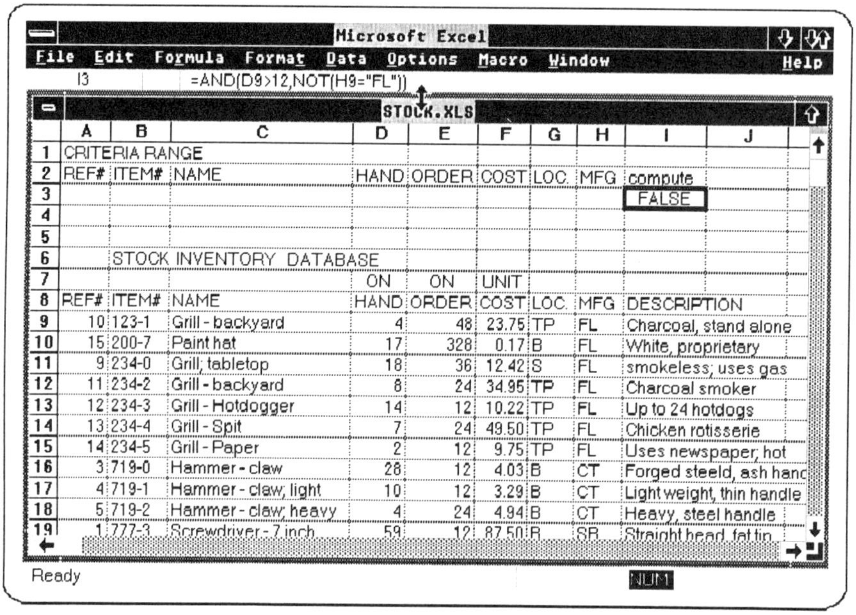

176 ADVANCED EXCEL

FIGURE 8.11. Compound Criteria

USING DATA FIND

You can use the Data Find command to locate records in a database that meet any set of defined criteria. First enter the criteria you want. To search the entire database, move the active cell outside the database; it can be in the criteria range if you like. If a cell in the database is active, the search begins at that point. Then select Data Find. If you want the search to start at the end of the database and move forward, press SHIFT while selecting Data Find. The first record with fields matching the criteria is selected. Figure 8.12 shows how you can move among other matching records. Notice that the up and down arrows on the keyboard or scroll bar move to the previous or the next matching record.

Keyboard	Record to Find	Mouse
Down arrow	Next matching	Click down arrow
Up arrow	Previous matching	Click up arrow
PgDn	Next, at least one screen down	Click below scroll thumb bar
PgUp	Next, at least one screen up	Click above scroll thumb bar
	Closest, in either direction	Drag scroll thumb bar

FIGURE 8.12. Moving Among Found Records

While you are in Find mode (the word Find appears in the status line) you can't move outside the database range. If you happen to accomplish this, Excel terminates Find mode. When you have examined the records to your heart's content, you can return to normal mode by pressing Escape, by selecting Data Find Exit, or by clicking outside the database. If you interrupt looking at records to edit one, you'll have to start the Data Find again.

EXTRACTING RECORDS

Often you want to collect all the matching records together rather than just look at them individually. The Data Extract command lets you do this. It uses the criteria entered in the criteria range, but instead of just letting you look at the matching records in context, it lists them where you specify. Extract doesn't remove anything from the database range; it provides a copy of matching records in another location.

The Extract Range

You tell Excel where to place the matching records by defining an extract range. The extract range is defined differently than the database and criteria ranges. Like them, though, it requires field names. And as in the criteria range, the field names you use must exactly match the names in the database. All you need to do is enter the field names of the fields you want copied; you don't need to use all the field names from the database; you don't need the same fields as in the criteria range. Data from matching records will be copied for the fields you specify, in the sequence you specify. You can use this technique to create a whole new database, a subset of the original one.

There are two ways you can define an extract range. If you know how many records will be extracted or if you want to limit it, you can select a range of the size you want; include the single row of field names, of course. Records that match the criteria will be placed in the range until it is filled. The other way is to define an unlimited extract range. This requires only that you enter the field names you want in the order you want, then select just that row. Then when you select Data Extract, any cells below the extract field names are cleared and extracted data fills as many rows as necessary. You'll probably find you want an unlimited range most of the time. So don't put any data you want to keep below the extract range field names. Place the extract range several rows below the end of the database or off to the right, well beyond the database itself. When you select the extract field names, you can't use SHIFT + Spacebar even if the rest of

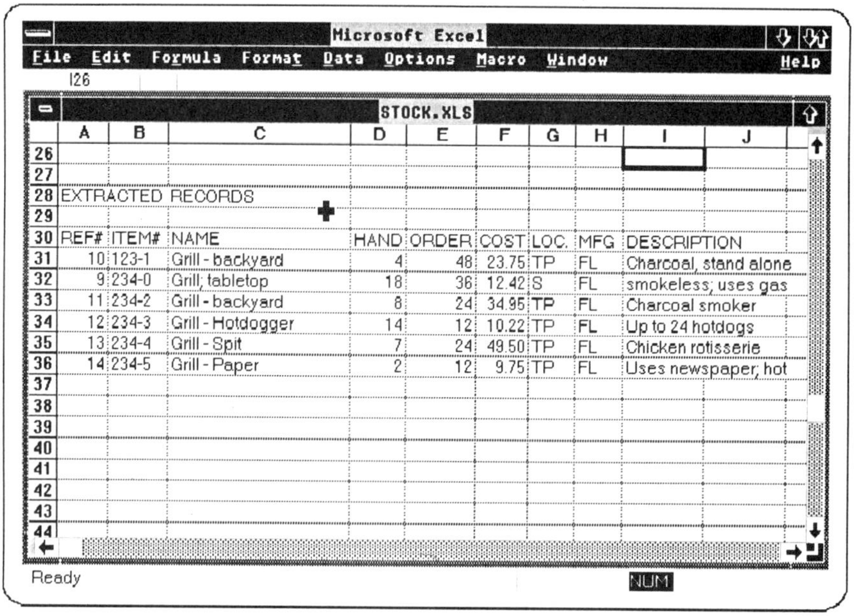

178 ADVANCED EXCEL

FIGURE 8.13. Extract Range

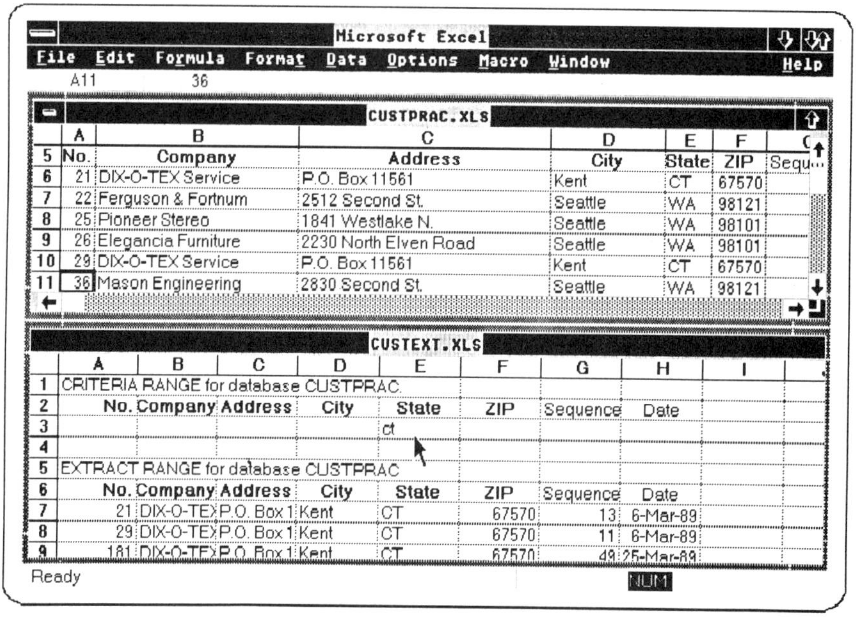

FIGURE 8.14. Extracting to a Separate Worksheet

HANDLING DATABASES

the worksheet is blank. Select just the names, with no empty cells included in the selection.

When you are ready to extract records, enter your criteria; be sure to erase (with Edit Clear or the Delete key) any old criteria values. Then select the limited extract range or the extract field names for an unlimited range. Finally, select Data Extract. Excel copies all records that match the criteria into the extract range (if it is unlimited) or fills it (if it is limited). They are still in the same sequence as in the database itself. Figure 8.13 shows an extract range containing extracted records.

You can process the records in the extract range as needed; you may want to print them, sort them, copy or cut them to another worksheet. You don't have to erase extracted data from an unlimited range. Next time you want to do an extract, just set your criteria, select the field names, and select Data Extract. Excel erases the old values and starts again. On the other hand, if you want to keep the result of an extract, be sure to copy it to a different location before you do another!

Extracting to a Different Worksheet

When a database gets large and unwieldy, you may want to extract records directly to another worksheet. You can accomplish this by defining the extract range and a criteria range on the target worksheet. First define the criteria range as usual, with the field names you need. When it is set, Excel assigns the range as the reference and assumes it applies the criteria to the Database range on the same worksheet. Since that's not true, you have to provide a definition for Database. Use Formula Define Name, and use the name Database. As reference, enter the external reference for the worksheet that contains the database. For example, you might use =INSBASE.XLS!Database as the reference. Now when you use the Data Extract command on the criteria range on this worksheet, the extracted records appear on this worksheet as well. Figure 8.14 shows the criteria and extract range on a separate worksheet; you can see that the actual database is separate.

DELETING SELECTED RECORDS

The Data Delete command erases all the records in the database that match the current set of criteria; this is a permanent delete, so Excel gives you an Alert message before completing the deletion. Since it's permanent, you might want to do an extract first and scan the result. Then you can use Data Delete with the same criteria to remove the unwanted records.

Using Data Extract first gives you another advantage. You can save the extracted records to different worksheet on which you accumulate deleted records. Every time you delete records from the database, first extract and copy or cut the extracted records to a storage worksheet. Then delete the records from the active database. Eventually, you will have a complete archive database containing all records removed from the active one. This can come in handy for various purposes. It is most useful, of course, if you discover you shouldn't have deleted some records after all. Regularly making backup copies of your active databases (and other worksheets) can also save much grief and pain. You only have to need these things once to become a convert.

SUGGESTED EXERCISE

1. Define a criteria range for your database, using all the field names and one blank row. Place it beginning in cell A1.
2. Enter criteria that will find at least three records in your database. After using Data Find, move through the found records.
3. Define an unlimited extract range several rows below the database range. Use Data Extract to pull out the records just found.
4. Change the values in the criteria range so that you can extract records of all salaries ranging from $10,000 to $20,000 (adjust the range so it has to ignore at least one at the low end and one at the high end). You'll have to add a salary field to the criteria range to specify the salary range.
5. Define a criteria range and extract range for CARBASE, off to the right of the database itself. Extract records for everyone in area 5 leaving before 9 A.M.
6. Experiment with more finds and extracts with both databases. Try deleting a set of records from one of them.

What if It Doesn't Work?

1. Be sure to clear old criteria before entering new ones. If your criteria range includes an entire blank line, all records are selected.
2. The extract range field names alone are selected for unlimited extract; if you select a range, only the number of records that fits in it are extracted.
3. If you try an OR condition, be sure to add a row to the criteria range and redefine it.

USING DATABASE FUNCTIONS

Excel provides a set of functions that work on databases; actually, they don't have to be applied to defined databases, but the worksheet ranges must be structured, as in standard databases, with a row of field names. These functions all have parallels in the standard set of functions. All start with D, followed by the rest of the function name, as in DSUM or DCOUNT. All have the same set of arguments: database, field, and criteria.

The *database* argument names the database or gives its range as a reference. If you used Data Set Database, you can use database as the name in the argument list. Or you can use any other defined name or a range reference. Be sure the reference or defined name includes one row of field names as well.

The *field* argument provides the field name or number. You can use the field name from the first row of the database; include it in quotes if it isn't a defined name. If you defined the field names, you won't need quotes. Excel also lets you use the column number; 1 refers to the first field, 2 to the second, and so forth.

The criteria argument provides the name or reference of the criteria range. If you used Data Set Criteria, you can use the name criteria. Otherwise use a defined name or a range reference that includes the appropriate field names.

Before the database function is issued, the criteria for record selection must be entered into the range. Then when the function takes effect, it operates on the specified field of each record in the database that meets the specified criteria. To cause the function to act on each record of the database, leave a complete blank line in the criteria range.

The Database Functions

DAVERAGE(database,field,criteria)   This function averages the value in the field column for each record in the database that meets the values set in the named criteria range. The result is an arithmetic mean; Excel adds all the appropriate values, then divides by the number of selected records.

DCOUNT(database,*field,*criteria)   This function counts the number of records that meet the criteria and in which the field cell contains a numeric value. If you omit the field value, DCOUNT counts the number of records in the database that meet the criteria.

DCOUNTA(database,*field,*criteria) This function counts the number of records that meet the criteria and in which the field cell is not blank. If you omit the field value, DCOUNTA counts the number of records in the database that aren't blank and still meet the criteria.

DMAX(database,field,criteria)   This function results in the largest value in field among the records in the database that meet the criteria. You might use it to find the product from a particular manufacturer (the criteria) that has the largest quantity on hand.

DMIN(database,field,criteria)   This function results in the smallest value in the field column among the records in the database that meet the criteria. You might use it to find out what item in the database sells for the lowest price.

DPRODUCT(database,field,criteria)   This function results in the product of the values in the field column of all records in the database that meet the specified criteria.

DSTDEV(database,field,criteria)   This function results in the estimated standard deviation of a population based on a sample, using the values in the field column of all records in the database that meet the criteria. Of course, the database must contain valid values if you expect a valid result from this function.

DSTDEVP(database,field,criteria)   This function results in the standard deviation of a population based on the entire population, using the values in the field column of all records in the database that meet the criteria. The database must contain valid values if you expect a valid result from this function.

DSUM(database,field,criteria)   This function results in the sum of the values in the field column of all records in the database that meet the criteria. If your database contains a total value in each record, you might want to use a DSUM function in preparing a report based on the contents.

DVAR(database,field,criteria)   This function results in the estimated variance of a population based on a sample using values from the field column of all records in the database that meet the criteria. As with the DSTDEV function, you need valid values if you expect this to work.

DVARP(database,field,criteria)   This function results in the variance of a population based on the entire population, using values from the field column of all records in the database that meet the criteria. As with the DSTDEVP function, you need valid values if you expect this to work.

Examples

To calculate the average cost in the entire database, first set the criteria range to include only the field names and one row of blank cells. Then use the formula =DAVERAGE(database,"cost",criteria); the value returned will be the average of the contents of the cost field in each record. If the field names have been defined as names, the quotes aren't needed. To calculate the average value in

HANDLING DATABASES

the same field in a subset of records, set the criteria to select the subset, then use the DAVERAGE function.

Using database functions in a worksheet saves work, but it has some side effects you must watch out for. Primarily, whenever you change the contents of the criteria range, every database function that depends on that range is recalculated. Of course, you can define additional criteria ranges and give them different names, specifying the different names in the appropriate database functions. If you don't want to bother using multiple criteria ranges, you can solidify values (with Paste Special) before changing the range.

For example, suppose you want to do a report on the STOCK.XLS database that shows the number of items for each manufacturer, and the average cost of each. Figure 8.15 shows how the report might look when printed. To create this report using database functions requires many, many steps. First, put in the title and other text as constants, then set FL in the MFG field as the criteria. In cell P6 place the function =DCOUNT (database,,criteria) and copy it to the four cells below; it places the same value in each. In cell Q6 place the function =DAVERAGE (database,"hand",criteria) and copy it to the four cells below it; it too places the same value in each.

At this point, only the values in cells P6 and Q6 are correct. To keep those values, copy each correct cell onto itself with Edit Paste Special Values. Then change the criteria range to reflect the next manufacturer, CT. The contents of the rest of the report change; the values in cells P7 and Q7 are now correct and can be pasted onto themselves. Repeat the process for the last three rows and the report is done. It seems like a lot of work for such a small database, but it makes a lot more sense for a database containing hundreds, even thousands, of records. And the process can be automated somewhat with macros, as you'll learn in Chapter 12.

	L	M	N	O	P	Q	R
1							
2				STOCK	SUMMARY	REPORT	
3							
4		Code	Manufacturer		# Items	Avg. Cost	
5							
6		FL	FarthingLutz		7	$20.109	
7		CT	Connecticut Jones		4	$5.255	
8		SB	Sterling Brands		2	$43.975	
9		AB	Allen Brothers		2	$9.620	
10		LL	Beantowners		1	$49.500	
11							
12							

FIGURE 8.15. Printed Report

SUMMARY

This chapter has covered the design, creation, and maintenance of databases on an Excel worksheet. You have seen how to use data forms to add and delete records and perform basic maintenance. You can sort records, or any range on the worksheet, based on fields within the range. You've learned to use the data commands along with the criteria and extract ranges to select and delete records, as well as to extract subsets based on current criteria. You've also learned to use the database functions to perform common operations on the entire database or a subset of it.

Later chapters in this book give you more advanced information on database processing. You'll learn to develop macros to simplify many operations and how to customize forms to make adding records and maintaining the database even easier.

9 USING CHARTS

Excel can easily create a chart from any selection of numeric data in a worksheet. The key to creating a useful chart lies in selecting the appropriate data, knowing what Excel will do with the data, selecting a chart style that reflects what you want to show, and then customizing the chart so that it communicates the information you desire in the best way possible. We'll look at the basic mechanics of creating charts in this chapter, then focus on how you can control and customize the result in the next.

BASIC CHARTING

To create a chart, select a range of data from any worksheet. The data must be numeric; you can include text for labels on either the top or the left of the numeric data. Then use the File New command to tell Excel to create a new file. In the resulting dialog box, select Chart, so that the new file will be a chart. Then Excel creates a chart from your selected data, using its default chart style. Figure 9.1 shows selected data and the default chart created on the screen.

Creating a basic chart is simple because Excel makes all the decisions. In order to create useful charts, you have to know how Excel makes those decisions. In this way, you can select data that will create a chart that shows what you want it to. You'll be able to provide labels along with the data in your selection, as shown in Figure 9.1, or add them later while customizing the chart.

CHART CREATION

When Excel creates a chart, it uses values from the selected range. The values form data series; each data series is a group of related numeric values that can be used as data points in a chart. In Figure 9.1, the numeric values in each row, such as B4:F4, form a data series. A chart can include more than one data

186 ADVANCED EXCEL

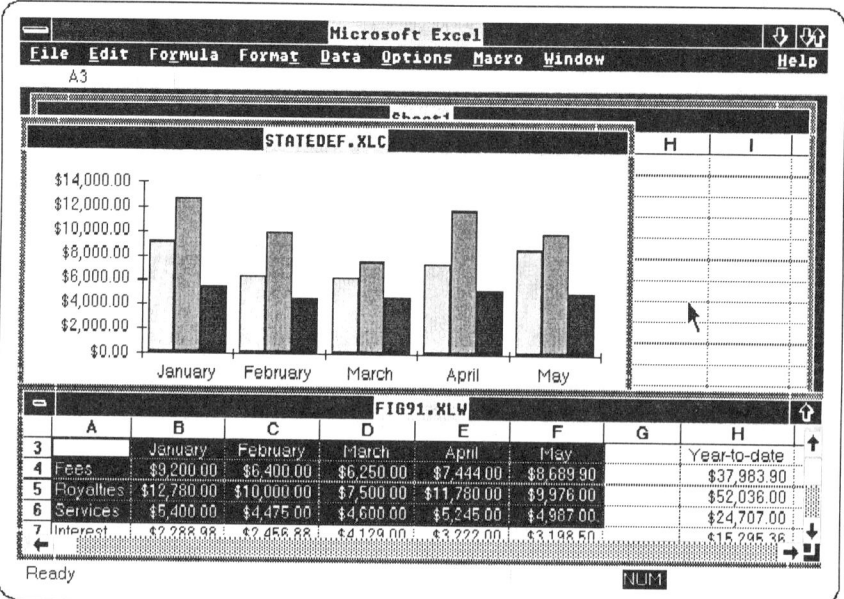

FIGURE 9.1. Selected Data with Default Chart

series; for example, the values in one row may be one series and those in a second another. If it contains only one row of data, it contains just one series. One type of chart, the pie, can use only a single series, but most can compare several series. Or the values in one row may be one series, those in a second another series, and those in a third still another series. Figure 9.1 includes three data series, one for each selected row of data. From your selection, Excel decides whether to use rows or columns as separate series. Whichever is chosen, the other is for separate categories. If your selection includes text values in the top row or in the leftmost column, they can be used as series and category labels in the chart.

When you create a chart, Excel links it to the worksheet containing the selected data with absolute external references. If you change the data in the worksheet, the change will be reflected in the chart. If you have stored the chart and worksheet on disk, then reopen the chart, Excel asks if it should update references. Since simple external references are used, updating can be done even if the worksheet isn't open.

Making the Selection

The shape of the selection determines whether the data series are in rows or columns. In most charts, as in Figure 9.1, the categories are listed on the horizontal, or category, axis. Let's consider the data values in the selection first, ignoring the presence of text names in either location. If it is more cells wide than it is tall, each row is treated as a separate series. Since the selection in Figure 9.1 is wider than it is tall (it contains five data columns) Excel uses the rows as the series.

If the selection contained only two columns of data, it would be taller than it is wide; in that case, Excel would use the columns as series. Excel always assumes you have more data points per category (one data point is from each series) than you have different categories, so the longer dimension becomes the series and the shorter the category. If the data is square, Excel uses the values in columns as categories and the rows as series.

Including Names in the Selection

You can include names in the left column and/or the top row in the selection to be charted. If you use names in both positions, the appropriate ones are included in the chart as category names and the others are treated as series names, to be used in a legend if one is created later. Look at the selection in Figure 9.1. Here the selection is wider than it is tall, and names are used in both positions. The upper left corner cell is blank. The names in the top row are used as category names in the chart, since each column is treated as a separate category. Notice that each of the three series is a different pattern on the chart; if you ask Excel to add a legend, you'll see that Excel uses the names from the left column to identify the separate series.

If names are included for either the top row or the left column but not the other, Excel uses those names as categories if appropriate, otherwise as names for series. Just because you select the names doesn't mean they are used as categories. In Figure 9.2, you can see a selection and the resulting default chart. Notice here that the selection is taller than it is wide, but the names included are from the top row. The chart shows numbers for the categories, since the category names weren't included in the selection. The selected names are treated as series names and will appear if a legend is added.

You can move and resize the chart window just as you do any other window. Excel may break your category names into two or more lines each to make them fit the default chart window size; just stretch the window lengthwise to make them read nicely. It is often convenient to arrange the windows on the screen so that you can see your worksheet selection at the same time that you can view the chart window, as we have done in these figures.

You'll see later in this chapter how to force Excel to use a different orientation of your data. In the next chapter, you'll learn to add legends, add labels, and otherwise customize charts to meet your needs.

188 ADVANCED EXCEL

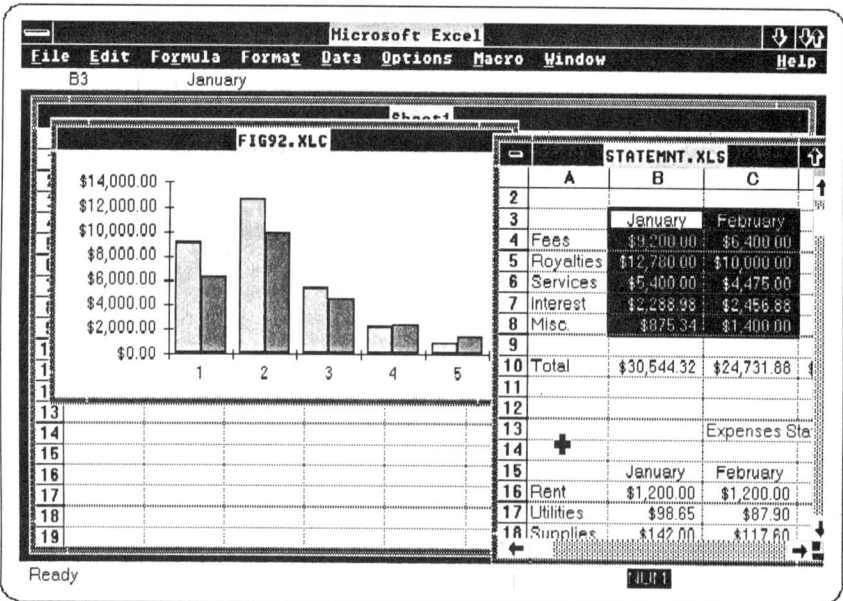

FIGURE 9.2. Sample Selection and Resulting Chart

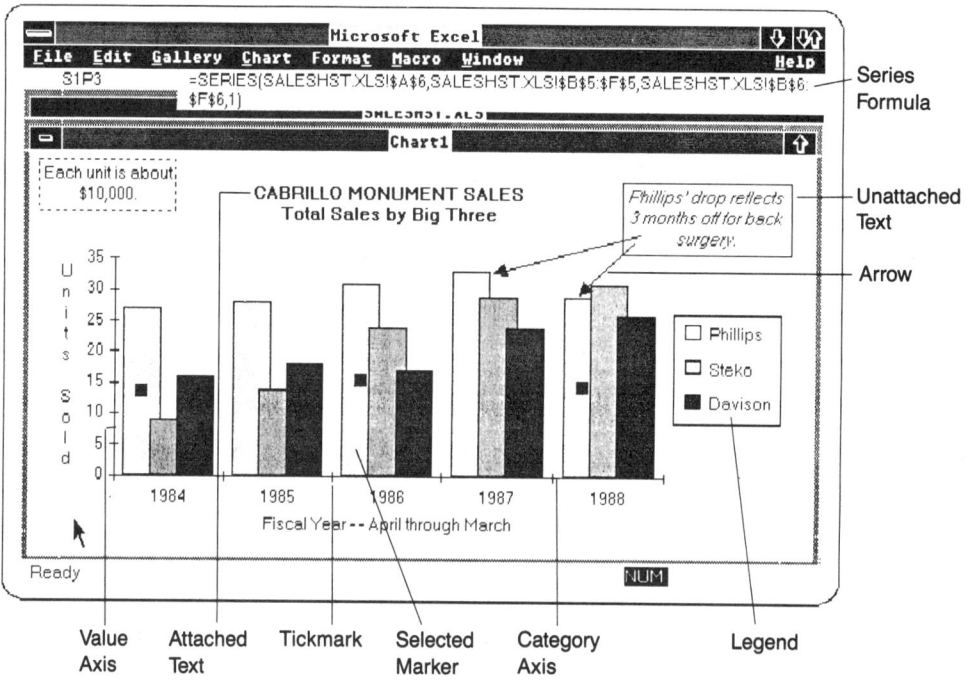

FIGURE 9.3. Chart Parts

CHART GEOGRAPHY AND TERMINOLOGY

Charts include many parts, each of which has a name and a function. Figure 9.3 shows a typical chart in which the parts are labeled. Some of the parts are involved in the default chart; you can find these in Figure 9.1 and Figure 9.2. Some are added or modified during customization. Most of the parts can be included in all charts; some can't.

The Elements of a Chart

The elements are similar, but not identical, from one chart type to another.

Chart The chart itself is everything inside the chart window below the title bar; it includes all the other elements.

Plot area The plot area includes the axes and any markers on them, and the area bounded by this. In a pie chart with no axes, the plot area includes the complete pie.

Axes Every chart except a pie chart has axes or reference lines. The vertical axis, called the value axis, includes numeric values calculated by Excel to show the range or scale of values in the data selection. The horizontal axis, called the category axis, contains labels generated by Excel; these labels are taken from the column or row adjacent to the data series. If no text labels are included, Excel just numbers the categories beginning with 1. In bar charts, the position of the value and category axes are reversed. A combination chart may have up to four axes.

Tick marks An axis includes tick marks for reference; these small marks are perpendicular to the axis and may cross it. If the chart includes drop lines or a grid, the lines all terminate at tick marks.

Markers Markers represent data series on a chart. A marker can be a column, a bar, a dot, or a symbol that marks one data point in a chart. All the data points that make up one series are usually the same color, pattern, or shape for identification; a chart that contains a single data series may have each point in a different color, pattern, or shape. If a small square appears within a marker, that means it is currently selected. If one marker is selected, the entire series is selected even if the square isn't in every marker of the series.

Chart Text Text in a chart is of two types, attached and unattached. Attached text is linked to some fixed chart object, such as the chart title, a category label, or an axis label. Unattached text is text you create and type. You can move it to the location you want on the chart.

Arrow You can add arrows on a chart if you wish, and position and size them as needed. They are unattached.

Legend Upon request, Excel creates a legend showing the marker used for each data series or category. It includes any names for the data series that were included in the original selection.

Series Formula When a series marker is selected, its formula appears in the formula bar. Excel creates this formula, which indicates where it gets data for charting the series. Interpretation and editing series formulas are covered in the next chapter.

Selecting Chart Elements

You can select any chart element, or object, by clicking on it with a mouse. On the keyboard, just press any arrow key, and some chart object is selected. The selected item is surrounded by six black or white squares. If they're white, that means the object can't be moved or resized with usual methods; there may be a menu selection to adjust it, however. If the selection squares are black, you can move and size the selected object at will.

To change your selection using the keyboard, use the arrow keys again. The left and right arrows select each object in turn, one class at a time. The up and down arrows move immediately to the next class. The classes, in order, are as follows:

Chart
Plot area
Legend
Axes (value, then category)
Chart text (attached, then unattached)
Chart arrows
Gridlines
Data series (first, second, etc.)
Drop lines
Hi-lo lines (for stock charts)

You can use the right and left arrows to go through all the objects in turn. Chart menu selections also let you select the entire chart or plot area.

The Chart Menu Bar

The other major feature of charts is the special menu bar present whenever a chart window is active. While some of the menus and many of the commands are the same as for worksheets, there are some definite differences. We'll overview the menus and commands here.

File The File menu contains exactly the same commands as for a standard worksheet. You can open, close, save and print charts as needed. The quality and type of installed printer determines the printed output of a chart.

Edit The Edit menu contains fewer commands than for a worksheet, but the commands it contains are familiar to you and work the same way: Undo, Repeat, Cut, Copy, Paste, Paste Special, and Clear. Later in this chapter you'll see how to cut, copy, and paste chart data.

Gallery The Gallery menu lets you select the type of chart you want and any variation on it. You can even set your preferred default chart type. We'll cover it in detail shortly.

Chart The Chart menu is used to customize charts. It also contains Protection, Calculate, and Short (full) menu commands. We'll cover customizing charts in the next chapter.

Format The Format menu lets you customize various aspects of the chart, as well as move and size specific parts of it. We'll cover the commands in detail.

Macro The Macro menu, while more limited than the worksheet Macro menu, lets you record and run macros; this topic is covered in detail in Chapter 12.

Window The Window menu lets you arrange, hide or unhide, and select open windows, much as in the worksheet menu.

In summary, use the Gallery menu to change to a different chart type. Use the Chart and Format menus to customize a chart. The remaining menus contain only commands identical to those in corresponding worksheet menus; use them as needed while working with charts.

SUGGESTED EXERCISE

1. Select a range five or six cells wide and two or three cells high. Include text on the top or left if convenient. Then create a chart (File, New, Chart).

192 ADVANCED EXCEL

2. Select another range three cells wide and five high. Again, use text if convenient. Create another chart. Compare the orientations of the two.
3. Change the size and shape of the chart windows for practice.
4. Take some time to create a few more charts for practice.

What if It Doesn't Work?

1. If you can't get Excel to create a chart, try a different selection. Select one row of about five cells of numeric data; be sure it's not text numbers. Then select File, New, Chart. If no chart results, check with your dealer.

TYPES OF CHARTS

While Excel uses a default chart type when it first creates one, you can change this to any other type. Figure 9.4 shows the Gallery menu. The various types of charts available to you are all listed here. We'll examine the charts that Excel offers and the prearranged variations on each. You can select any of the chart layouts in this section from the Gallery menu or dialog box once the default chart is created. You'll see that some types are more appropriate than others for various data selections.

Area Charts

An Area chart shows the data values according to how much area they cover in the chart. Figure 9.5 shows the dialog box that results from selecting Area on the Gallery menu. Every chart type results in the same general type of dialog box. There are a number of variations of chart layouts for you to select from. You can select Next to see a gallery of the next chart type or Previous to see the one before. Or you can select a chart variation and select OK. The chart is converted to that type and redrawn on your screen in the same window.

The area chart is most useful for showing the relative importance of values over time. It emphasizes the amount of change rather than the rate of change.

Each variation in the dialog box is a bit different. Variation 1 is a simple area chart using amounts as the vertical or value axis. Variation 2 is a 100% area chart; here all the data points at a single category location are treated as fractions of 100%. At each point, you can see the contribution of each portion to the whole. Variation 3 is a simple area chart with drop lines, so you can see what part corresponds to the category axis locations. Variation 4 includes both

USING CHARTS

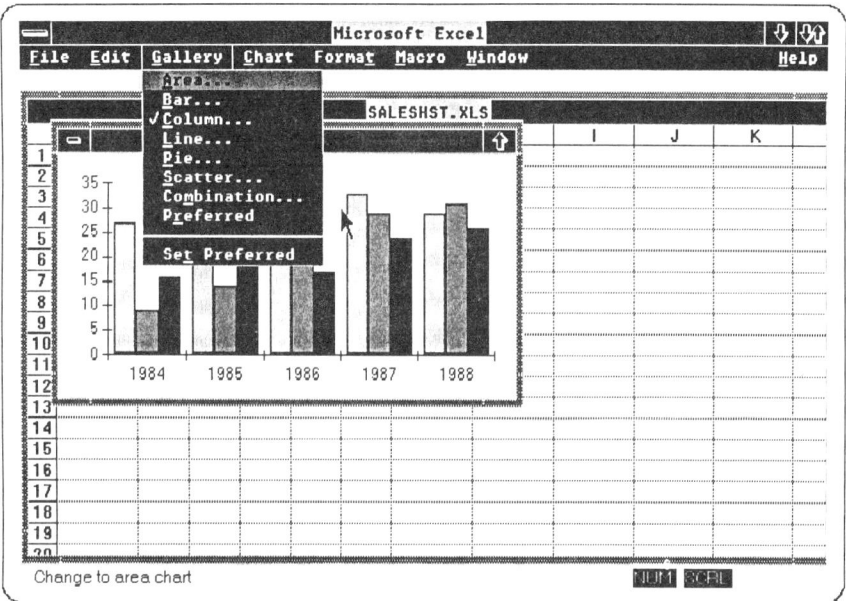

FIGURE 9.4. Gallery Menu

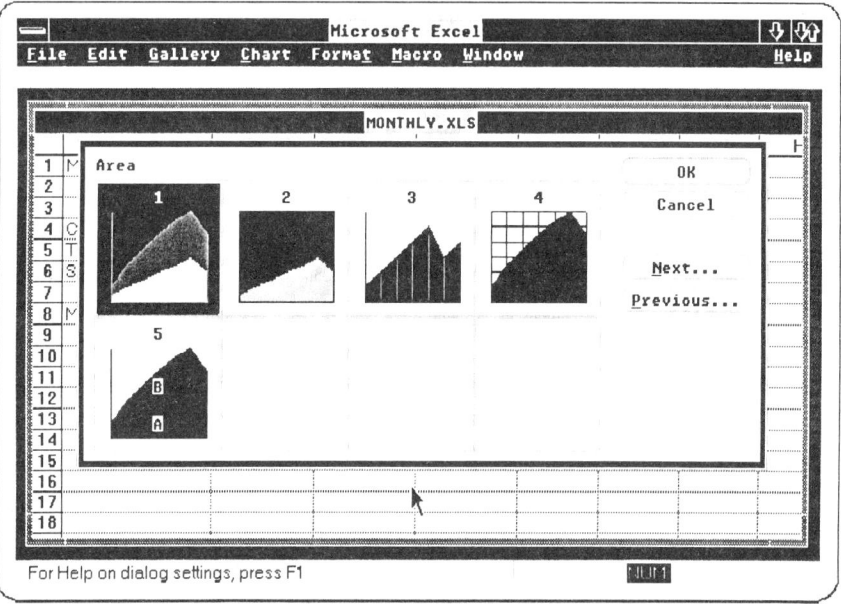

FIGURE 9.5. Gallery Area Dialog Box

vertical and horizontal gridlines for ease of reference. Variation 5 is another simple area chart, this time with the areas labeled using series names from the original selection. Figure 9.6 shows a screen with two area charts created using the same data selection. Variations 4 and 5 were used.

Bar Charts

A bar chart consists of horizontal bars extending from the vertical category axis. It is generally used to compare distinct items that don't form a continuum. Categories for a bar chart might be people, departments, years, or items. A bar chart can handle negative as well as positive values. When you select Bar on the Gallery menu, you see the dialog box shown in Figure 9.7. Notice that it contains Next and Previous buttons; these are present for every chart type.

Excel offers seven variations on the bar chart; all except 3 and 5 can handle both negative and positive values. Variation 1 is the simple bar chart; bars for each series are side by side in each category, with each series in a different pattern. Variation 2 lets you chart a single series using a different pattern for each category. Variation 3 uses a stacked bar; instead of the series being side by side for each category, they are stacked end to end. In variation 4, the series bars are overlapped rather than side by side; this gives a more compact and professional appearance to the chart, but is otherwise no different from the simple bar chart in variation 1.

Variation 5 is another stacked bar, but this one is done as percentages; the total stacked bar is equivalent to 100%. In variations 3 and 5, negative values are treated as positive. Variation 6 is the simple bar of variation 1 with vertical gridlines added for reference. The larger and more complex the chart, the more important gridlines can be. Variation 7 is another simple bar chart, this time with value labels added for documentation. Value labels are important for highlighting even small differences that may not show up well in a chart. Figure 9.8 shows two sample bar charts. The one on the left uses the overlapping variation 4. The one on the right uses value labels as in variation 7.

Column Charts

Column charts are similar to bar charts, but with the category axis on the horizontal rather than the vertical. Excel's default chart is variation 1 of the column chart. With column charts you have all the same variations as the bar charts, plus one. Figure 9.9 shows the Gallery Column dialog box.

USING CHARTS

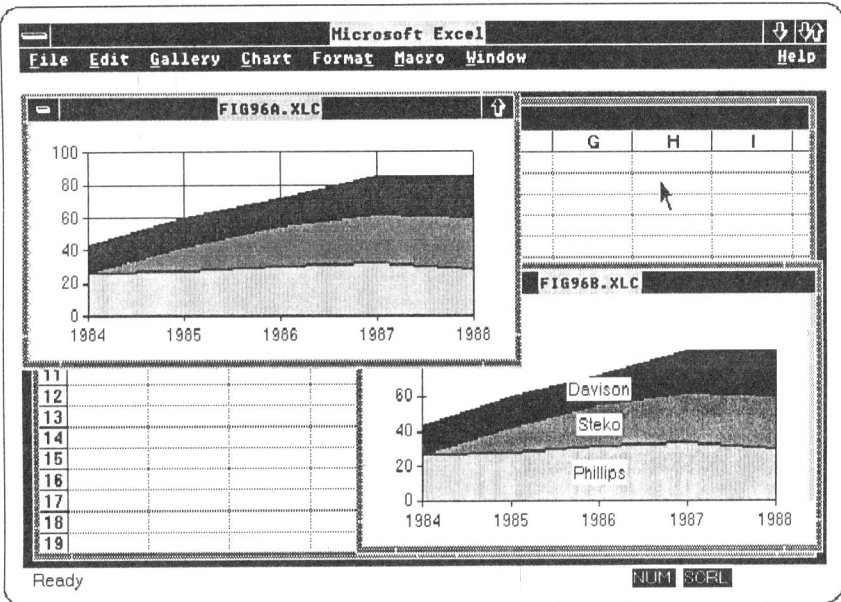

FIGURE 9.6. Sample Area Charts

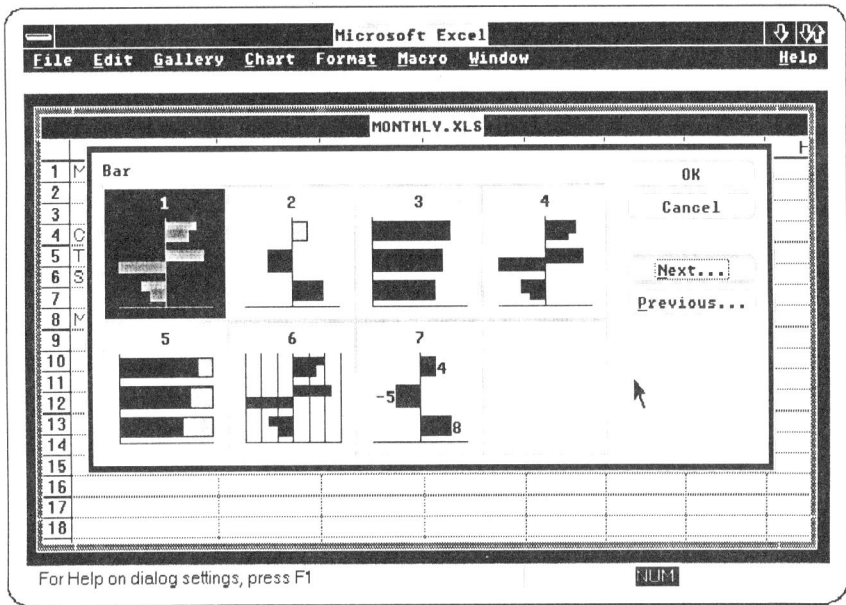

FIGURE 9.7. Gallery Bar Dialog Box

196 ADVANCED EXCEL

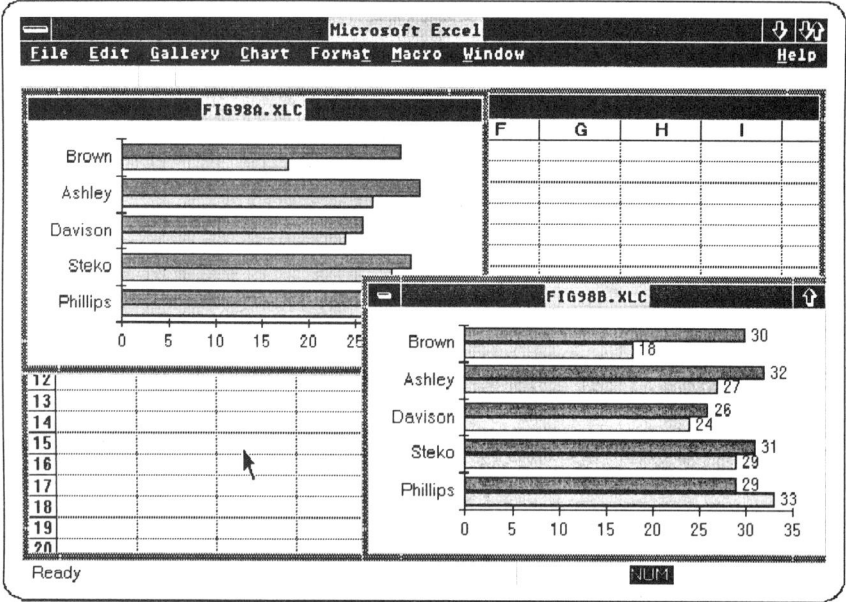

FIGURE 9.8. Sample Bar Charts

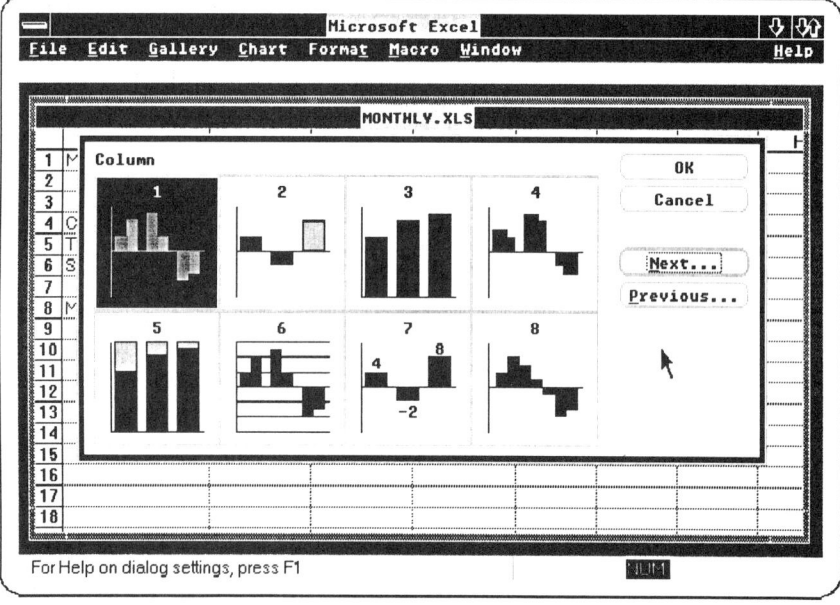

FIGURE 9.9. Gallery Column Dialog Box

USING CHARTS 197

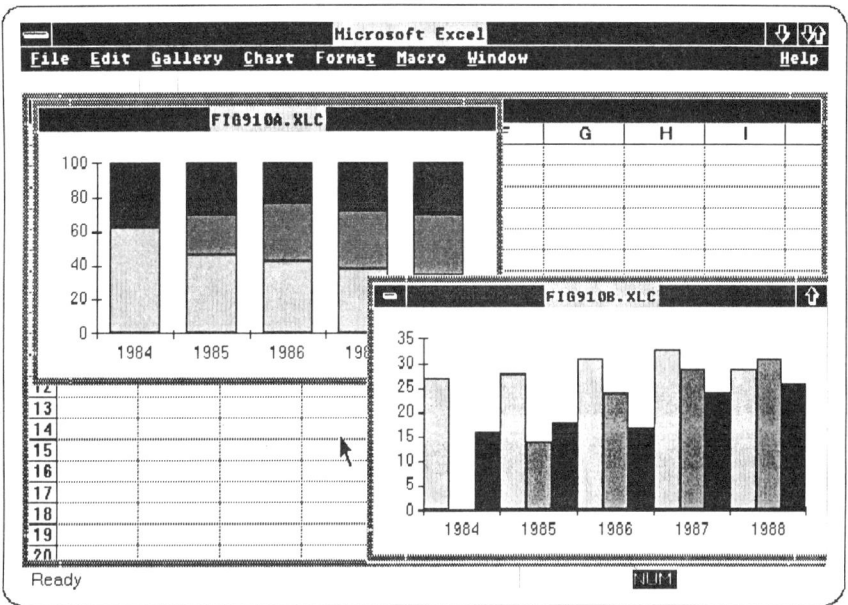

FIGURE 9.10. Sample Column Charts

Column charts, like bar charts, handle negative numbers; however, column charts are treated as positive in the stacked charts. Variation 1 is the simple column chart, with each series appearing side by side for each category in a different pattern. Variation 2 is used to show a single series with each category in a different pattern. In variation 3 the stacked bar for each category includes the appropriate proportion for each series. Variation 4 is much like variation 1, but here the data series are overlapped for each category, rather than side by side. Variation 5, like 3, is stacked, but here each category represents 100%; the amount for each series represents its part of the 100% total. Variation 6 uses horizontal gridlines for reference on the simple column chart. Variation 7 includes value labels for each data series.

Variation 8 is different from any in the bar gallery. It represents values as a step chart, with no space between the columns for one category and the next. You've already seen several variation 1 column charts. Figure 9.10 shows two more variations. The left chart is variation 5 with the 100% stacked columns, and variation 8 on the right shows the step chart with no space between the clusters of columns.

Line Charts

Line charts can be used to compare continuous trends over time or some other consistent increment. It can be used for many of the same sets of data as an area chart, but line charts focus more on time flow and rate of change, rather than the amount of change. As in the Area and Column charts, the category axis is at the bottom of the chart, with numeric values on the vertical axis. A line chart can include one or more data series; each is represented by a line or a series of markers or both. Figure 9.11 shows the Gallery Line dialog box.

Excel offers eight variations on the line chart. Variation 1 is the simple line chart, with lines and markers. A different marker is used for each series, in a distinct pattern, color, or shape. Negative values can appear on the line charts as well; the position of the category axis is adjusted if necessary.

Variation 2 uses only lines, with no markers; the lines appear in different colors if there aren't distinctive markers. Variation 3 uses only the markers, not connected by lines. Variation 4 is the basic line chart, this time with horizontal gridlines to make it easier to identify the value at each point. Variation 5 is like 4, with vertical gridlines added as well. Variation 6 is similar to 4, but it uses a logarithmic scale and gridlines; it is most useful when there is a very wide variation between the smallest and largest values on the chart.

Variations 7 and 8 are used primarily for stock quotations. Variation 7 is a hi-lo chart with markers at the high and low points, while variation 8 shows the high, low, and close points. You can use these variations with worksheet data from stock reports as well as from other worksheets.

Figure 9.12 shows two sample line charts, using variations 1 and 5.

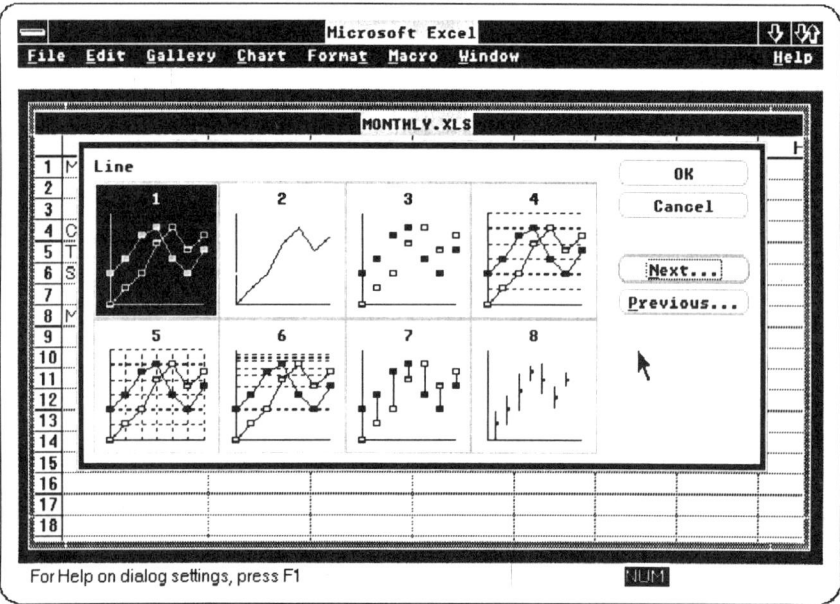

FIGURE 9.11. Gallery Line Dialog Box

USING CHARTS

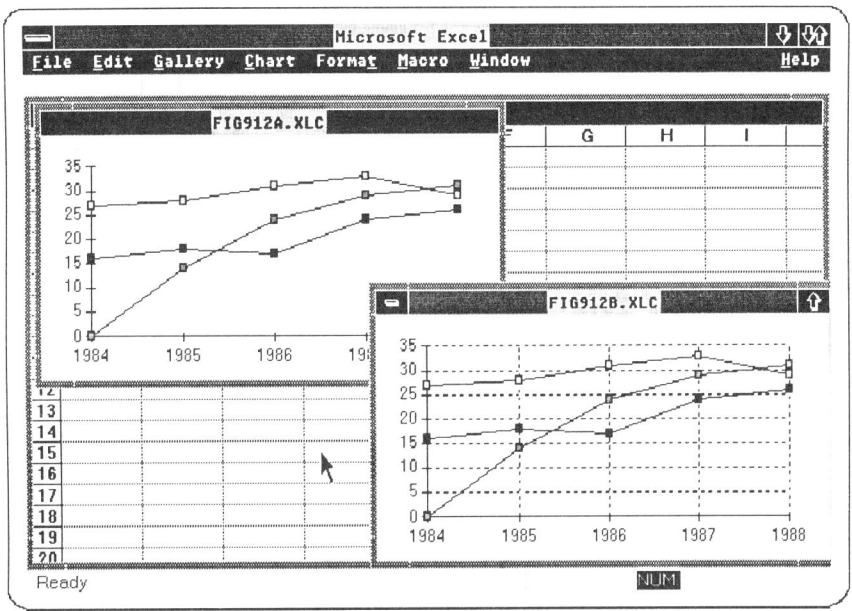

FIGURE 9.12. Sample Line Charts

Pie Charts

The pie chart deals with only one data series, showing the values of categories as proportions of the whole. The entire pie represents 100%; each slice of the pie is a category making up some part of it. You can't use more than one series in a pie chart; if the selected range includes more than one, Excel uses only the first. The pie is the only chart type that has no axes; it can't be used in any type of chart combination. Figure 9.13 shows the Gallery Pie dialog box.

Excel offers six pie chart variations. The first is the simple pie, in which each category is represented by a different pattern or color. In variation 2 the categories are all the same pattern, but category labels are included in the chart. Variation 3 has the first wedge exploded or set apart; the top or left value in the selection is considered to be the first. Variation 4 has all wedges exploded. Variation 5 is the basic pie chart with labels added, while variation 6 is the basic pie chart with percentages added. Figure 9.14 shows two sample pie charts, using variations 5 and 6. Notice that the series name appears above the chart when a single data series is used.

Scatter Charts

Scatter charts are used to chart a somewhat different assortment of values than the other charts. Points in a scatter chart are discrete values rather than

200 ADVANCED EXCEL

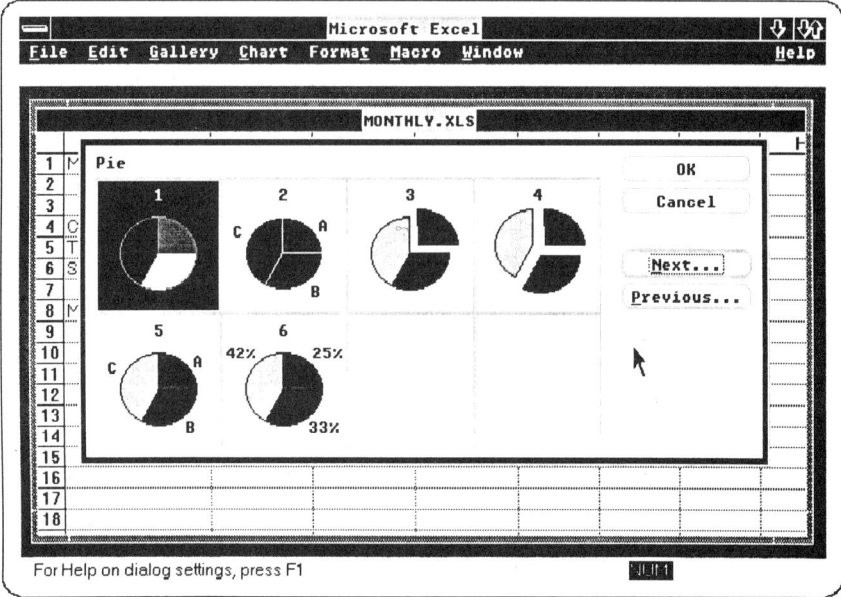

FIGURE 9.13. Gallery Pie Dialog Box

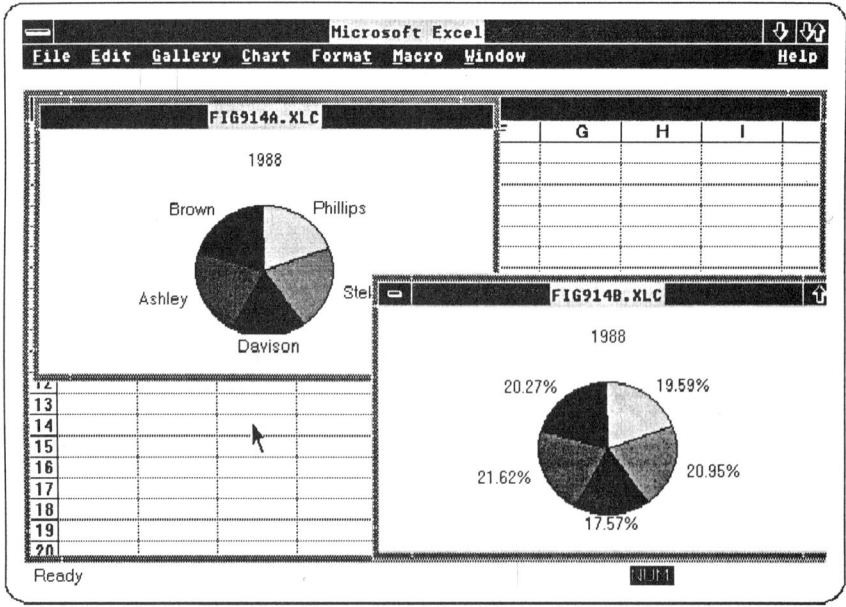

FIGURE 9.14. Sample Pie Charts

USING CHARTS

representations of continual data. There is no time or sequence involved. For example, a comparison of survey responses to the age of the respondent doesn't fit into any of the other chart types. It may show interesting results in a scatter chart. You may be able to identify patterns or see if variables are interrelated. Figure 9.15 shows the Gallery Scatter dialog box.

Excel provides five preformatted scatter chart variations. Variation 1 shows only the markers, with a different type for each series. Variation 2 is similar to 1, with the markers from the same series connected by lines. Variation 3 is like variation 1 with horizontal and vertical gridlines added. Variation 4 uses a semilogarithmic vertical axis and gridlines. Variation 5 uses log-log axes and gridlines in both directions. If you aren't comfortable with logarithmic axes, don't use variations 4 and 5. They're mostly used with scientific and/or research data. Figure 9.16 shows a sample scatter chart. This one is based on a selection of data resulting from a survey. Category labels don't appear on a scatter chart, since these charts generally use a great many categories. For readability, Excel just uses the sequence numbers to represent the different categories.

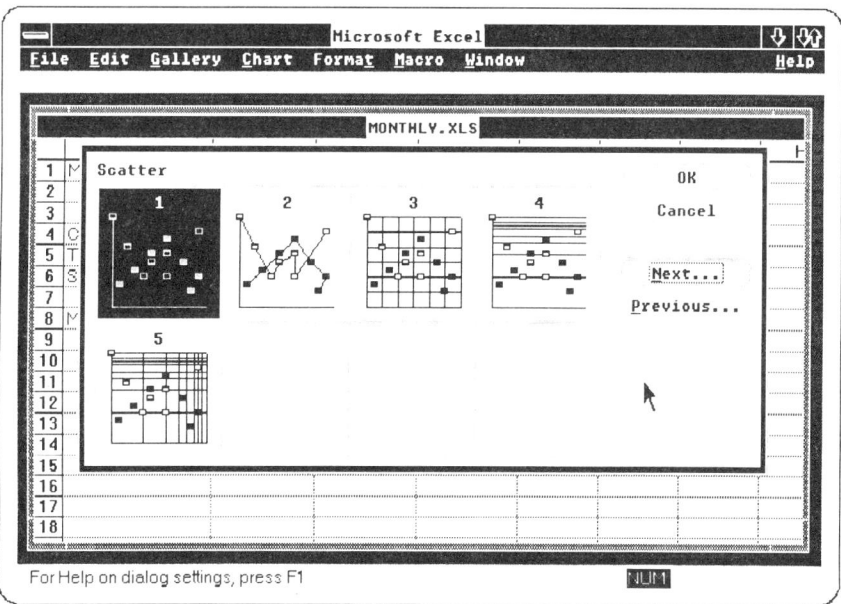

FIGURE 9.15. Gallery Scatter Dialog Box

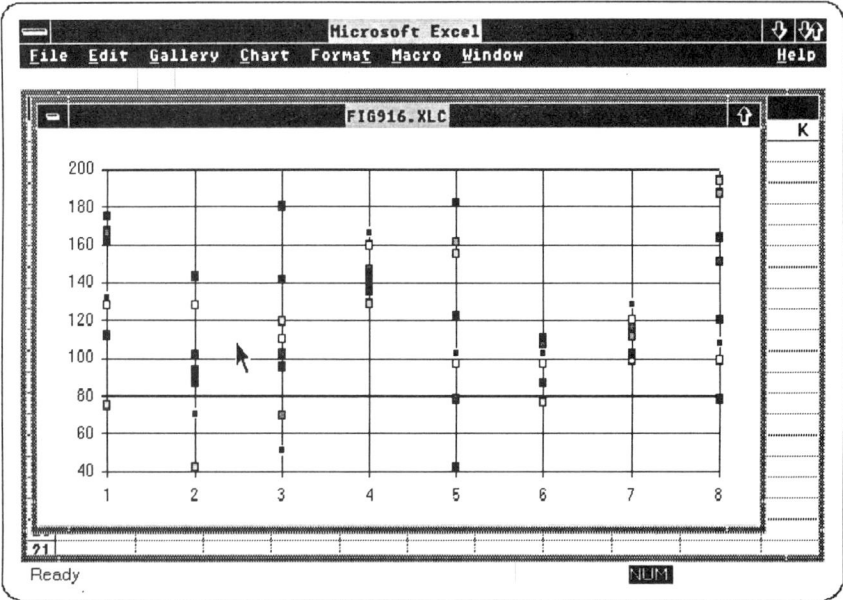

FIGURE 9.16. Sample Scatter Chart

Combination Charts

Excel allows you to combine chart types in several different ways. The easiest way is through the Combination option on the Gallery menu, which results in the dialog box shown in Figure 9.17. It modifies the active chart into a combination of two types of chart. If the selection includes an even number of data series, the first half are on the main chart (the one with standard axes) and the second half on the overlay chart. If the selection includes an odd number of data series, the larger number appears on the main chart.

Variation 1 is a line chart superimposed on a main column chart; the same axes apply to both portions of the chart. Variation 2 is another line chart over a main column chart, but this one uses opposing scales. Variation 3 shows two line charts with independent scales. Variation 4 is an area chart overlaid by a column chart. Variation 5 shows a high, low, close line chart overlaid on a column chart. You can change which data series appear in each form in any of these combination charts through the Format Overlay Chart command; that's covered in the next chapter. Figure 9.18 shows two combination charts, variations 1 and 2. While these use the same sets of data, notice that a third scale is added in variation 2.

USING CHARTS

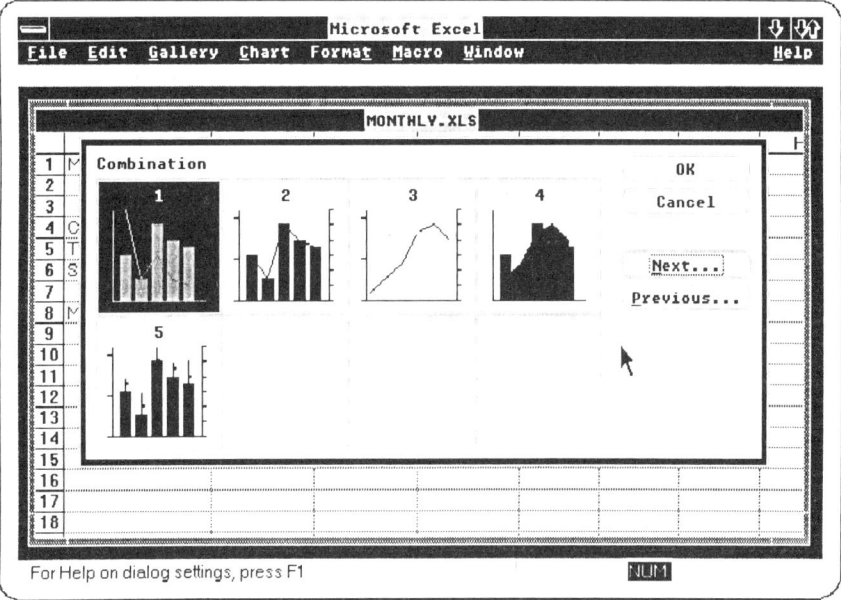

FIGURE 9.17. Gallery Combination Dialog Box

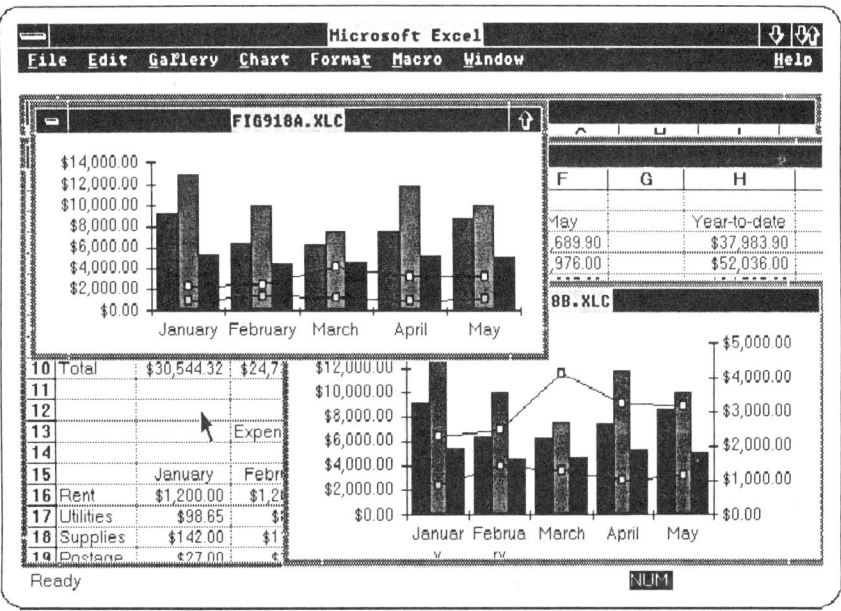

FIGURE 9.18. Sample Combination Charts

Setting a Preferred Chart Type

The Gallery menu includes a command that lets you change the default chart type that Excel creates when you request a chart. When the active chart is of the gallery type and variation that you want Excel to use, just select Set Preferred on the Gallery menu; any future chart requests in that session will be created in that format. To convert an already created chart to the preferred format, make it active and select Preferred from the menu. To make the new preferred setting carry over to later sessions, you can use File Save Workspace to save the settings; when you open the workspace later it is reestablished.

MODIFYING THE CHART LAYOUT

Before we get into customizing charts, let's consider the chart layout. You can now select and prepare the basic chart style you want. Excel does the work of putting it together. But sometimes you may want a different orientation of data in it, or you may have to use data from several worksheets in the same chart. You can solve the orientation problem by first doing a small chart, using just enough data to get the basic chart orientation correct, then paste in other data series, from the same or different worksheets, to the basic chart. Suppose you want to chart the area indicated in Figure 9.19, but you want the names in the first column used as category labels, so that you end up with three categories and five data series. If you select the entire region (with text), Excel creates a chart with the other orientation. So how can you force Excel to do it the other way?

First select a range that will give you the desired orientation, the names and a single column of data values. Create the chart. Now it looks like the leftmost chart in Figure 9.20. Then select the next two columns of data values from the worksheet. Use the Edit Copy command. Activate the chart and select the Edit Paste command. Excel adds the two new data series into the chart. Repeat the process again, selecting the last two columns in the region and pasting them into the chart. The result finally looks like the chart on the right in Figure 9.20. You have to paste the additional data series as two separate steps. If you paste the region made of four columns of three data values each, Excel switches the orientation, as it would if you created the chart originally with that selection. Each set of pasted values must have the same shape (tall or wide) for this to work. If you have data on several different worksheets, you can paste values into the same chart in much the same way. Paste Special can also be used in charts if you want to use the current values rather than the results of formulas.

USING CHARTS

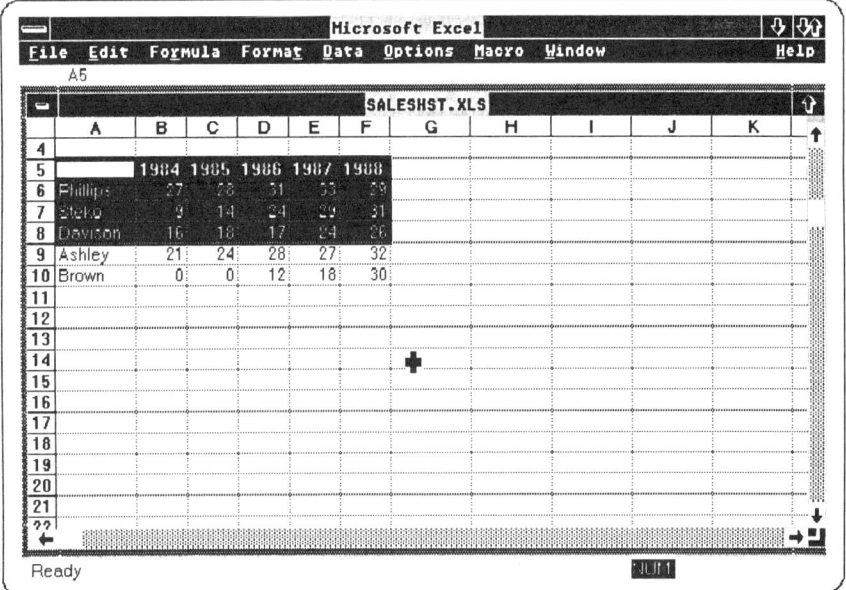

FIGURE 9.19. Region to Be Charted

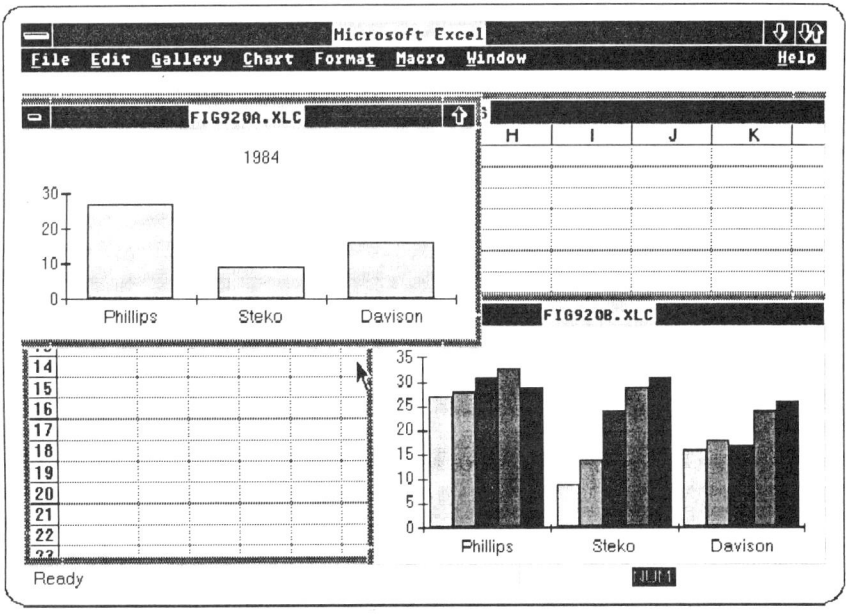

FIGURE 9.20. Initial and Expanded Charts

You can also use multiple selections from one or more worksheets to create a chart. The multiple selections, if considered in a block, must make up a perfect rectangle, just as a range does. Excel pulls it together (internally) and creates the chart, orienting it as if it actually were a single range.

PRINTING CHARTS

You can print charts just as you do any other file; just set the appropriate values and select File Print. The printed version may not be exactly what you see on the screen. Excel uses both your monitor and your printer appropriately. It may change the patterns in different data series for printing so the difference is more noticeable. If you don't like the printed effect, you can add patterns to the different markers. You'll learn to do this in the next chapter.

SUGGESTED EXERCISE

1. Select one of the default column charts containing at least three categories and two data series. Enlarge it to fill most of the screen below the title bar.
2. Try other chart forms. Use the Gallery menu to see how it looks in at least one variation of each chart type.
3. Convert another chart to various types. Take time to become familiar with the Excel chart types and the Gallery menu.
4. Print a few of your charts.

What if It Doesn't Work?

1. Some data selections don't make good charts of some types. If the data values are very different, for example, a column chart may look strange. Feel free to create additional charts with which you can experiment.
2. If the charts don't print well, you may have to customize the patterns in the markers. At this point, if you can tell it's a chart and can read the labels and axes you're doing fine. If the charts don't look like charts, you might want to check the installation of the printer or see your dealer.

SUMMARY

By now you can create charts for any selected worksheet range of numeric values. You can paste additional values into the chart for Excel to add. You can determine and control the orientation of the data in the chart.

You have also learned to use the Gallery menu to change the chart type to any of Excel's preformatted charts. In the next chapter, you'll learn to customize these charts and create even more types using additional Excel commands.

10 CUSTOMIZING CHARTS

Excel offers many features for customizing charts, primarily through the Chart and Format menus, shown in Figure 10.1. You can ask Excel to add a legend, modify the scale and labels on any axis, add gridlines at major points and minor points. You can add text, change text, move, format, and transform text on the chart; you can even add arrows to text blocks to point to parts of the chart. If you have an overlay chart, you can can customize both the main chart and the overlay separately if necessary.

Excel lets you use all its fonts in constructing charts; you aren't limited to four per chart as you are with worksheets. You can use any combination of patterns and colors that your screen can handle; when you print, Excel adapts the patterns and colors so you can see the differences on paper. In the rest of this chapter, you'll learn to use Excel's features to customize charts.

BEFORE YOU CUSTOMIZE

When you change chart types through gallery selections, you may lose any customization you have done to your chart. So before you begin customizing at

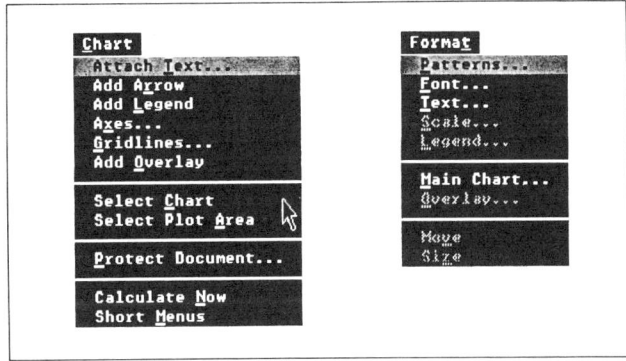

FIGURE 10.1. Chart and Format Menus

208 ADVANCED EXCEL

any level, be sure you have the basic chart format you'll want to work with; take time to save it under its permanent name. If you want to change the basic type after customizing is well under way, do it through the Format Main Chart method from the Format menu; this will keep your customization intact.

LEGENDS

A legend is the key to a chart; it identifies the different patterns used in markers that represent data series. If different patterns are used in a single data series chart, such as a pie, the legend can identify each point. Excel chooses the initial marker color, pattern, and shape; it uses these in the legend it produces when you select Add Legend on the Chart menu. Figure 10.2 shows the result in a typical chart. The series names used in the legend were selected as part of the original data selection; if no names were selected, Excel uses sequence numbers beginning with 1. To change the legend text, you have to edit the series formula; that's covered at the end of the chapter.

The legend in Figure 10.2 is in the default location. You can't move it with standard techniques. You select the legend by clicking on it with the mouse or by pressing uparrow or downarrow repeatedly until the legend is surrounded by

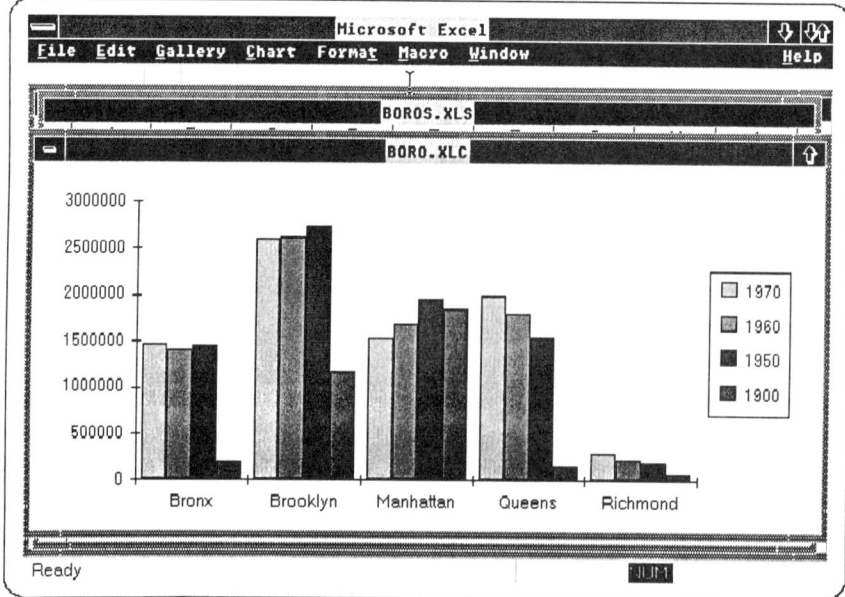

FIGURE 10.2. Chart with Legend

CUSTOMIZING CHARTS

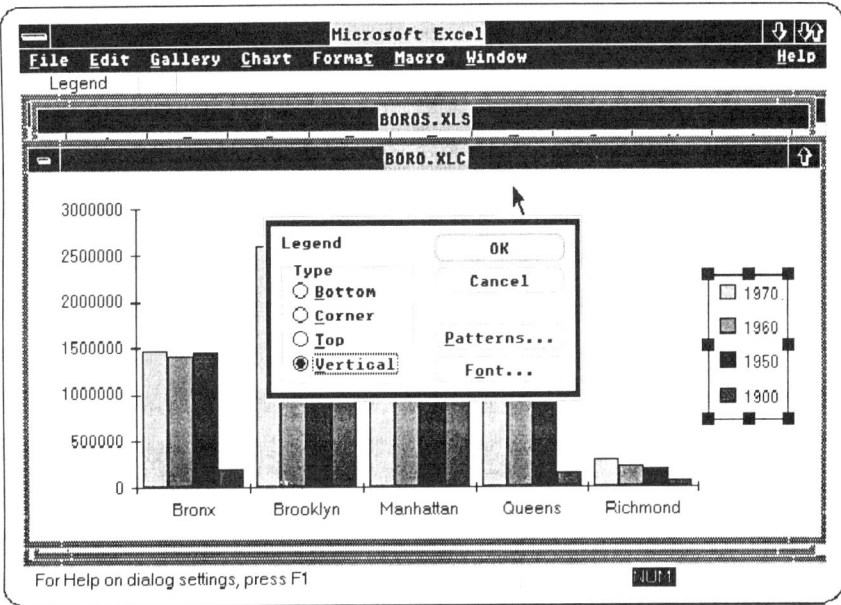

FIGURE 10.3. Legend Dialog Box

white squares. Then you can select Legend on the Format menu, which results in the Legend dialog box shown in Figure 10.3. In this box, you can specify a different location for the legend. You can place it at the top or bottom of the chart, in which case it is arranged horizontally and centered. Or you can place it in the upper right corner, where it has the same vertical arrangement as the default location. You have no other choices for legend location.

The other buttons in the Legend dialog box let you change the patterns (including colors and line style) and fonts used in the legend. Since the Patterns and Font choices appear in many chart formatting dialog boxes, we'll cover them in detail here. They are much the same no matter what route you use to reach them.

FONT FORMATTING

You can reach the Font dialog box by selecting Format Font or by selecting Font in any chart dialog box in which it appears. It affects all selected text, whether that's in the Legend box, the entire chart, or just in a piece of text. In fact, you can't select Format Font unless some text entity on the chart (or the chart itself) is selected. Figure 10.4 shows the basic Font dialog box. If you have selected an

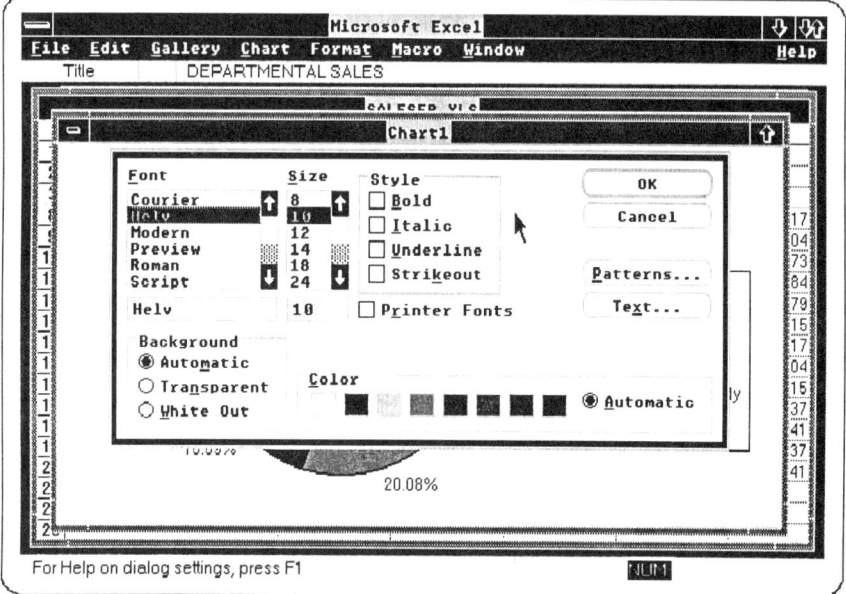

FIGURE 10.4. Format Font Dialog Box

axis it might be a bit different. We'll cover the differences later.

Notice that the two buttons on the right bring you to the Patterns dialog box (just as from the Legend dialog box) and to the Text dialog box. Either of these two buttons saves any changes and transfers you to another formatting dialog box. When you finally choose OK or press Enter, all the changes are applied to the selected part of the chart. The lower of the two buttons takes you to an appropriate formatting dialog box.

The fonts shown are pretty much the same as the ones you can use for display of worksheet data. The default for all chart text is Helvetica 10 point. You can change to a different font and size by selecting what you want. You can specify bold, italic, underline, and/or strikeout if appropriate. If you turn Printer Fonts on, the listing will show fonts your printer can handle; you have to decide whether you are customizing the chart primarily for display or for printing.

In the lower portion of the Font dialog box you can make background choices; the default is automatic, which means that Excel selects a background pattern for you. You can make the background transparent, which means you can see what underlies the selected portion. Or you can specify White Out, which means Excel uses a solid color, perhaps white, to obscure anything behind the selected portion without actually erasing it.

CUSTOMIZING CHARTS

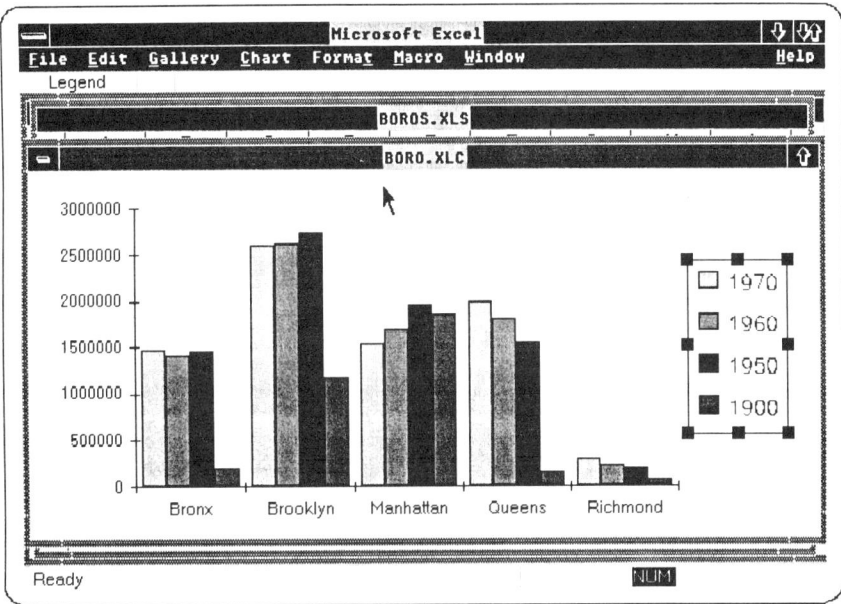

FIGURE 10.5. Chart with Fonts Changed

The Color box specifies the color of the text or whatever is in the foreground. The colors you see here can be used for selected text; if you leave it at automatic, Excel uses the default window text color.

When you print a chart, Excel does the best it can with your printer. It may not use the exact same patterns. It won't use the colors if you have a black-and-white printer. But it generally keeps everything readable and clear. If you use automatic color for your text, the characters always print out as black with a white background. Figure 10.5 shows the chart from Figure 10.2 with a different font in the legend.

The Font dialog box is much the same, no matter where you reach it from. You'll always see the Patterns button to save changes here and bring up the Patterns dialog box. You'll also see a second button. It may bring you to Text, to Scale, or to Legend.

CHANGING PATTERNS

When you select Format Patterns or use the Patterns button in another dialog box, you see the Patterns dialog box specific to the area currently selected.

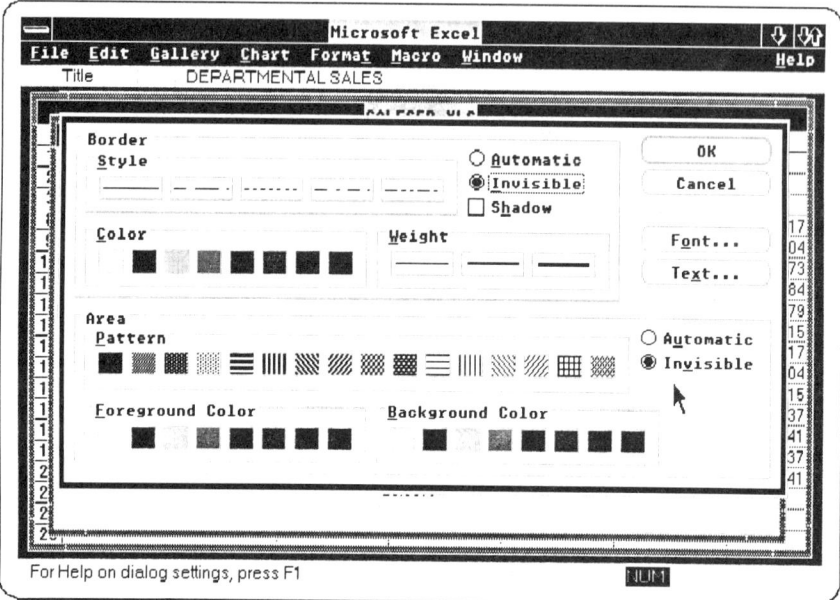

FIGURE 10.6. Format Patterns Dialog Box

Figure 10.6 shows the dialog box as it appears when a title is active. Notice that the two major sections are the Border and the Area. From here you can transfer to the Font dialog box or to another box, Text in this case.

Each selected area in a chart has a border, even if you can't see it. If you have selected the chart title, for example, you won't see a border; it's invisible. But Excel knows about it. The rightmost part of the Border section lets you specify how the border appears. Automatic means the border appears and Excel chooses its style, color, and weight. Invisible means there is no border. Shadow means the border has a shadow on the bottom and right edges. If you select invisible border, it doesn't matter what else you specify for it, because it won't show. The Style section lets you specify how the border will appear, whether as a solid line or some combination of dots and dashes. The Weight section lets you specify how heavy the line will be; if you choose medium or thick lines, the style must be solid. And finally, you can select the color for the border line. You'll see the lines in the Style and Weight sections change to the selected color. Automatic or Invisible is deselected as soon as you select a style, color, or weight for the border.

The Area section determines the appearance of the area inside the border; it too can be automatic or invisible. If it's visible, you can select a specific pattern; each is made up of a foreground color and a background color. As you select the colors, you see the patterns change to accommodate the current

CUSTOMIZING CHARTS

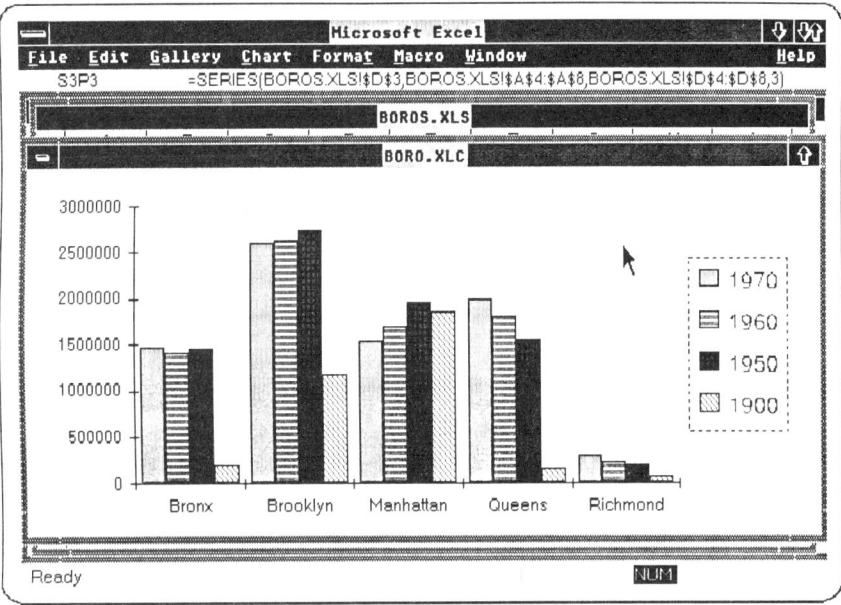

FIGURE 10.7. Modified Patterns

settings; the appearance reflects how the pattern will look in the selected area. The resulting pattern will fill the selected area, creating a background; any text is superimposed over the pattern, using colors selected in the Font dialog box. With a color monitor you can create almost any pattern you want.

Figure 10.7 shows the same chart as in Figure 10.5. Here we've changed the border in the legend as well as the patterns in the markers. We selected one marker at a time, then used Format Patterns to customize them. The effect appears as soon as you choose OK.

MODIFYING MARKERS

If a series marker is selected when you use the Format Patterns command, you can change the appearance of that marker in all its occurrences. If you want to change the appearance of your graph for printing, adding patterns to different markers can have a dramatic effect. Formatting markers involves only the patterns. Excel gives you the extra option of requesting an inverted pattern for a negative value. You can also specify that a given marker be invisible for security reasons. If you decide to do this, be sure to make the border and the area both invisible.

214 ADVANCED EXCEL

AXES

All charts except pie charts have axes; line, bar, column, and scatter charts have two each, while combination charts can have up to four. Each set of two axes includes a value axis and a category axis. The value axis is vertical except in bar charts. Excel calculates the value amounts and displays them using the format of the data itself; if the data has dollar signs, the values on the value axis will have dollar signs. The category axis is horizontal except in bar charts. By default, Excel shows the axes and the tick marks calculated by Excel. You can suppress either axis by selecting Axes on the Chart menu; then click on the appropriate axis to suppress it.

You can modify the scale on either axis. Just select the axis (click or use the arrows). Figure 10.8 shows the dialog box that results when the value axis is selected.

The box shows the minimum and maximum values Excel used, with the major and minor increments. You can change any of them, but be sure the values in the data series fall between the minimum and maximum values you choose. For example, you might want to use 0 as the minimum even if all the values fall between 5,000 and 10,000; this lets the chart show that the difference is not as large as it would appear with 5,000 as the minimum. A tick mark on

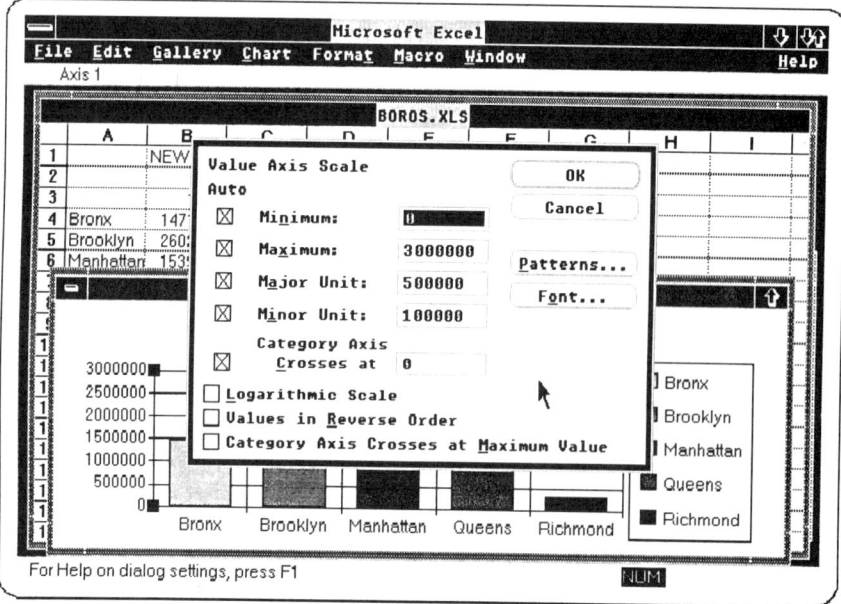

FIGURE 10.8. Value Axis Scale Dialog Box

CUSTOMIZING CHARTS 215

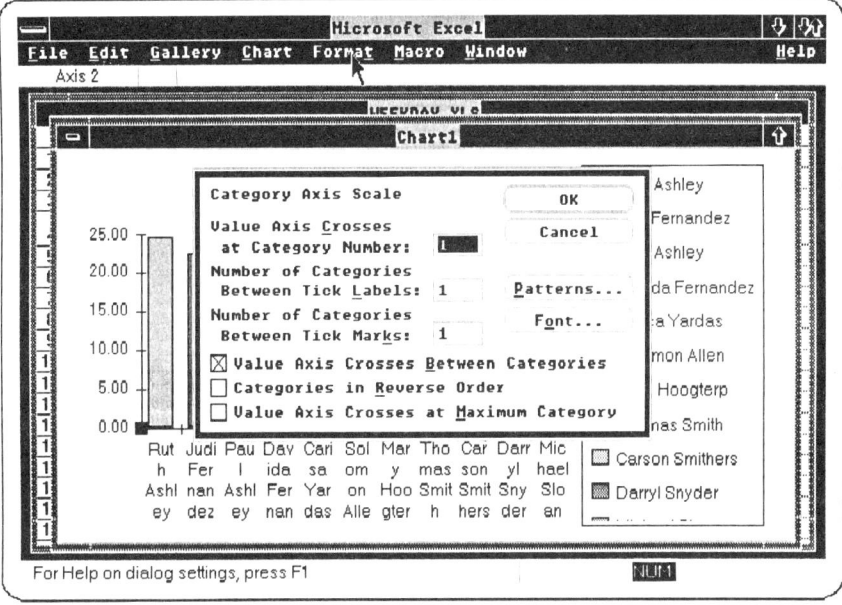

FIGURE 10.9. Category Axis Scale Dialog Box

the chart indicates the major unit, but markers can be placed at minor units as well. Notice that you can change where the other axis crosses this one, as well as specify a logarithmic scale or a reverse order of values.

Figure 10.9 shows the dialog box that results when the category axis is selected. As in the previous dialog box, you can change where the other axis crosses this one. You can also specify that the categories should be in reverse order. You can change the number of categories between tick marks or tick labels; this would be handy if you have a very large number of categories or a large number of data series to handle. You can also remove the cross (or tick mark) between categories on the axis.

The Scale option on the Format menu is available only when an axis is selected. From either Axis Scale dialog box you can access the Patterns and Fonts dialog boxes; these let you change the text and axis lines themselves for the selected axis. Some different options are available in the Patterns dialog box, as shown in Figure 10.10. Notice that you can't make the axis invisible. And you change the tick mark appearance rather than the area pattern.

The major tick marks cross the axis by default; you can make them appear just inside or outside the axis or be invisible. The minor tick marks, invisible by default, can be visible in any form. You can also specify how and where tick labels should appear. Notice that you can return to the axis scale dialog box from here or use the font dialog box for further axis formatting.

216 ADVANCED EXCEL

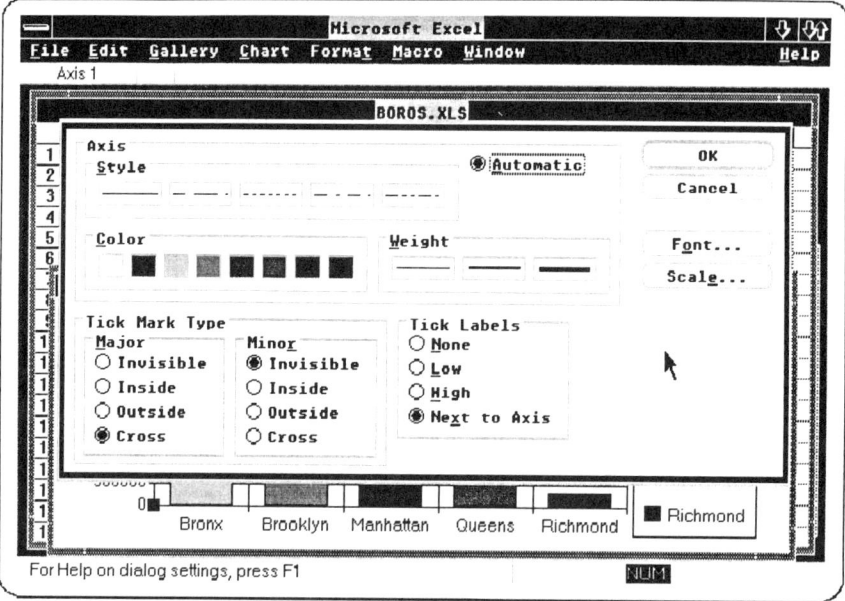

FIGURE 10.10. Axis Patterns Dialog Box

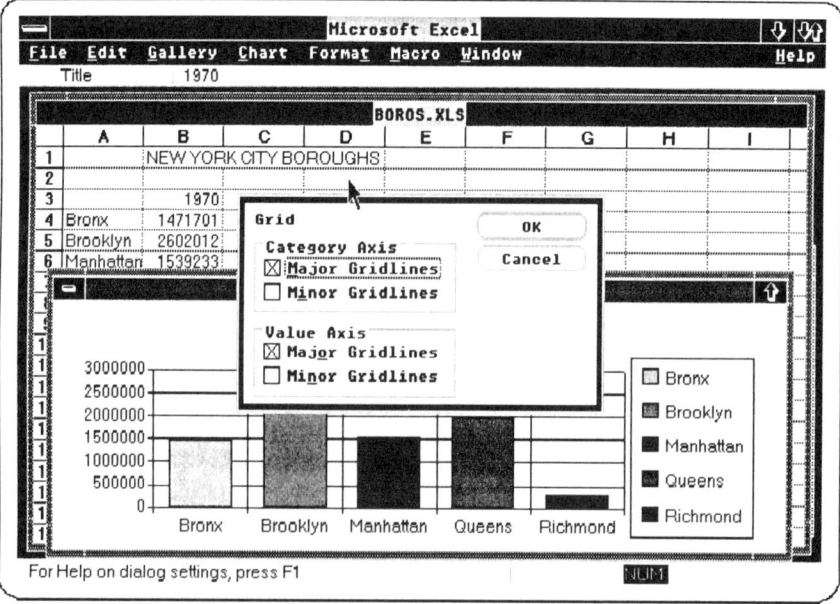

FIGURE 10.11. Gridlines Dialog Box

CUSTOMIZING CHARTS 217

GRIDLINES

You can cause gridlines to appear on any chart (except pie), whether or not they are part of the basic gallery selection. Just select Gridlines on the Chart menu. You'll see the dialog box shown in Figure 10.11. Notice that the chart on the screen shows major gridlines on both axes, as indicated in the dialog box.

Minor gridlines on the category axis are in the middle of each category field. On the value axis, the locations depend on the minor units specified in the Value Scale dialog box (see Figure 10.8).

SUGGESTED EXERCISE

1. Make a chart active that has category labels and had series names included in the original selection. If necessary, create a new chart with names on both the top and left.
2. Add a legend to the chart. Change the location of the legend by selecting it and then using the Format Legend command. Change the border and pattern to see how it looks.
3. Change the pattern of a marker. Notice that the change is reflected in the legend.
4. Modify the category axis; change the font and add minor tick marks.
5. Modify the value axis; use a different scale and color.
6. Print the chart to see how your modifications affect your printout. Decide what font/color/pattern combinations give you the effect you want.

What if It Doesn't Work?

1. Practice some more. Use a chart of your own devising and make it look snazzy.

TEXT IN CHARTS

Chart text comes in two forms, attached and unattached. Attached text is attached to some fixed chart element, such as the chart title, an axis, or a data point or series. Unattached text is just that; you can put it wherever you want. Excel handles the two types of text differently.

Attached Text

You can add, change, or delete attached text by means of the Attach Text command on the Chart menu. When you select Attach Text, you see the dialog

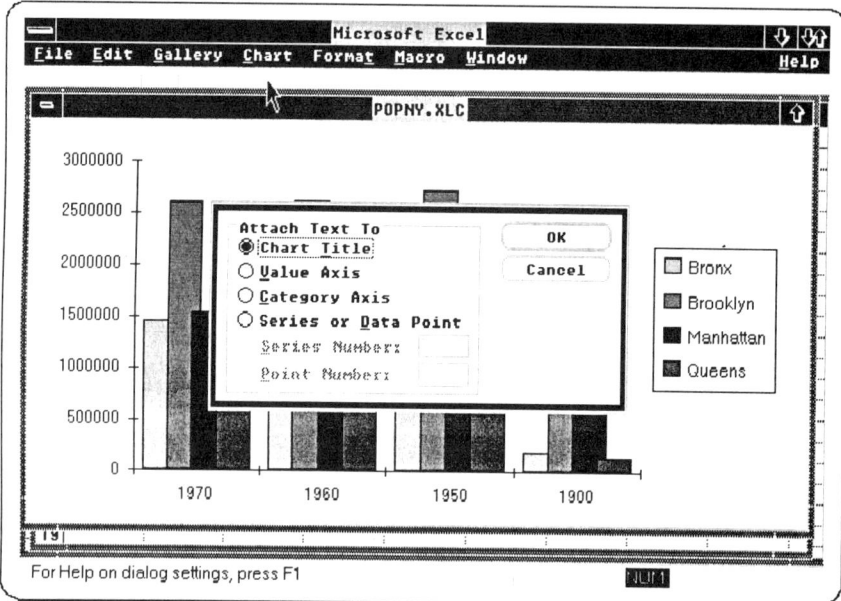

FIGURE 10.12. Chart Attach Text Dialog Box

box shown in Figure 10.12. You can select Chart Title even if the chart seems to have no title; Excel reserves an area centered above the chart itself for a title. Value Axis text appears to the left of the value axis labels, and Category Axis text appears below the category axis labels. We'll cover the Series and Data Point text a bit later.

When you select any of the first three items in the dialog box, dummy text appears in the appropriate location in the active chart, surrounded by six white squares; the white squares indicate that you can't move or size the text independently. You can, however, change its font, pattern, and alignment.

The dummy text for chart title is "title" in the center of the line above the plot area. For the value axis, "Y" appears to the left of the value labels. For the category axis "X" appears below any category labels. Once the dummy and squares appear, the dummy text also appears in the formula bar. You just type the desired text here. If you want to use more than one line, use CONTROL+Enter, since pressing Enter ends the entry. When you're finished typing, the text remains selected. You can then use the Format menu commands (Patterns, Font, and Text) to format the attached text. You've already seen the standard Font and Patterns dialog boxes (Figures 10.4 and 10.6); these are the same for text. Figure 10.13 shows the Text Alignment dialog box.

This box is used for both attached and unattached text. For attached text, you use the Vertical Text or Automatic Text fields. Vertical Text causes the

CUSTOMIZING CHARTS

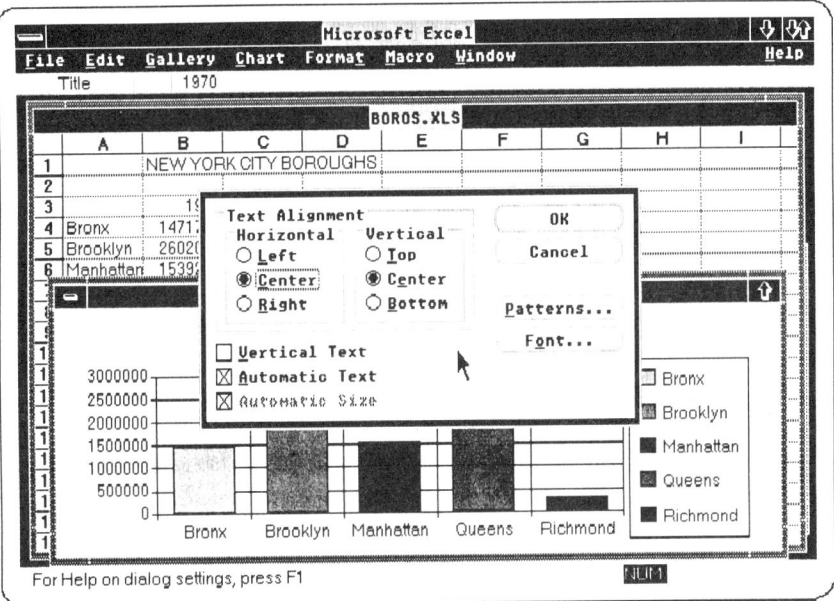

FIGURE 10.13. Format Text Alignment Dialog Box

selected text to appear vertically, one letter per line. You'll use it mostly for value axis labels; an example is in Figure 10.14. This figure also includes a chart title with a different pattern appearance. The Automatic Text field restores the text to whatever you entered originally. You can edit and modify any attached text by selecting it and editing it in the formula bar. If you change your mind, just turn on automatic text in the Text Alignment dialog box.

If you want to attach text, such as a label of the exact value at a point, to a series or data point within the chart itself, you can select the Series or Data Point option in the Attach Text dialog box (Figure 10.12). You'll have to tell Excel what series or data point you want to use. Excel numbers them (internally) from left to right in a column, area, line, or scatter chart, from top to bottom in a bar chart, or clockwise from the top (12 o'clock) in a pie chart. Remember that the chart may contain several series; each point in the same series has the same color or pattern or shape.

When a marker is selected, the reference area of the formula bar shows the current point as SnPn, indicating the series and point numbers. Each point is at a different location along the category axis. Series number 1 point number 1 refers to the first point in the first series, or the first one on the chart. Series number 3 point number 2 refers to the second data point in the third data series. When it knows what you are referring to, Excel uses the data value at that point as the dummy text at the appropriate location on the chart. You can

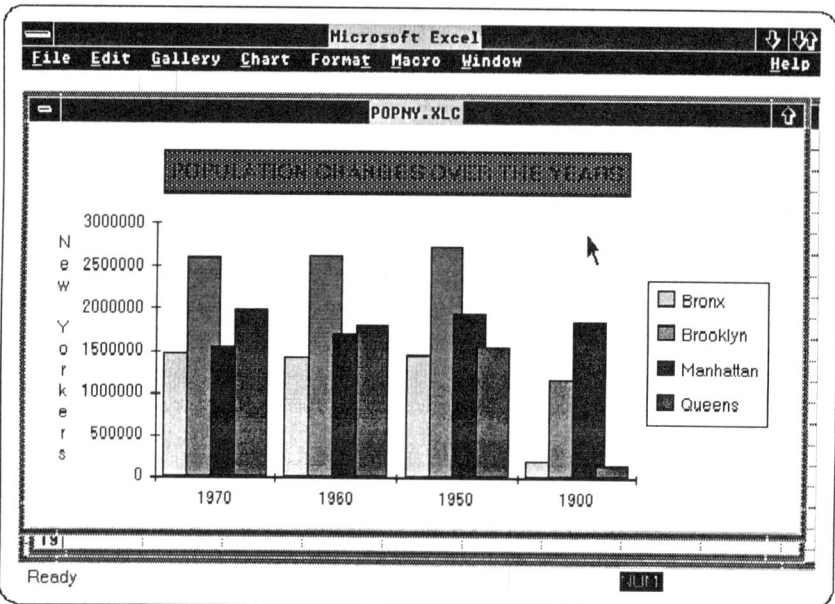

FIGURE 10.14. Effects on Attached Text

see instantly if you used the correct series and data point numbers or not. In most cases, you'll want to use that value as it is, so just press Enter; however, you can add to it or replace it if you want. You can then format the value, perhaps adding a border or changing the font, as you please. Once text is attached, you have some additional features available through the Text Alignment dialog box. Show value is the default; the data point value is shown as text. If you turn on Show Key as well, a segment of legend appears with the attached text. You can use Show Key without Show Value if you prefer.

The only chart in which you don't have to enter both numbers is the area chart. If you omit the point number here, Excel uses the series name for the specific series and places it in the area.

Unattached Text

You can use unattached text anywhere on a chart. Just start typing whenever no text is selected. Whatever you type appears in the formula bar; use CONTROL+Enter to start a new line. When you're finished, press Enter. The unattached text appears in the center of your chart, surrounded by black squares. Now you can move it or size it however you want. The location of the squares indicates the size of the area.

CUSTOMIZING CHARTS

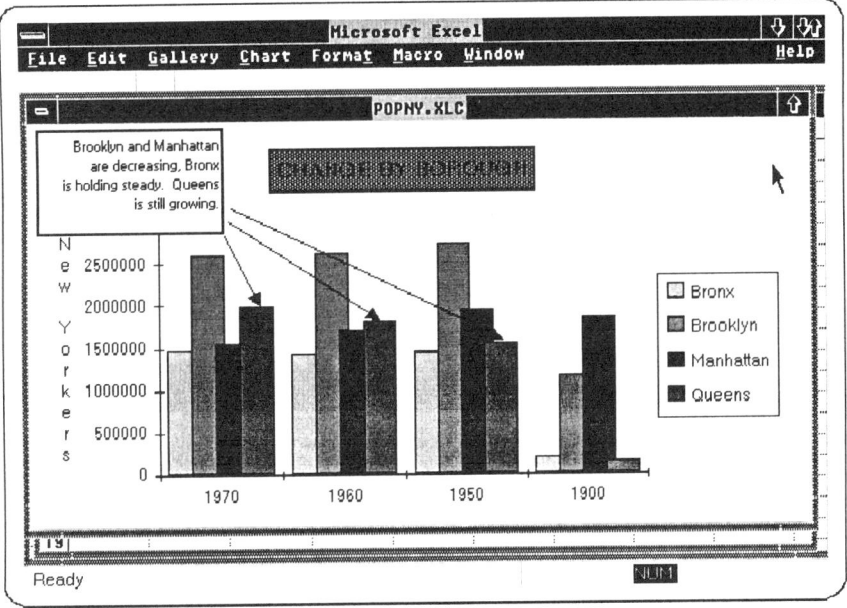

FIGURE 10.15. Unattached Text with Arrows

You can change unattached text easily; just select it and edit it in the formula bar. You can format it using the Patterns, Font, and Text Alignment commands, just as you do with attached text. In Figure 10.15, the unattached text in the upper right has been changed to a smaller font, enclosed in a medium border, and aligned at the right and the top.

Using Arrows

You can also see arrows added in Figure 10.15. Each is created with the Chart Add Arrow command. When you select the command, an arrow appears, with a black square at each end. You can position the two ends where you want. With the mouse, just click on the end you wish to move and drag it to the new location. With the keyboard, use the Format Move and Size commands when the arrow is selected. You can use Format Patterns to change the appearance of the arrow shaft and head. Figure 10.16 shows the Format Arrow dialog box. You just make the selections as usual and Excel modifies the selected arrow to meet your requests.

You can add arrows to any part of a chart; they don't have to be connected to text, although it makes sense to use them with text. While the arrow is selected, the command changes to Delete Arrow. When it isn't selected, you can add another arrow.

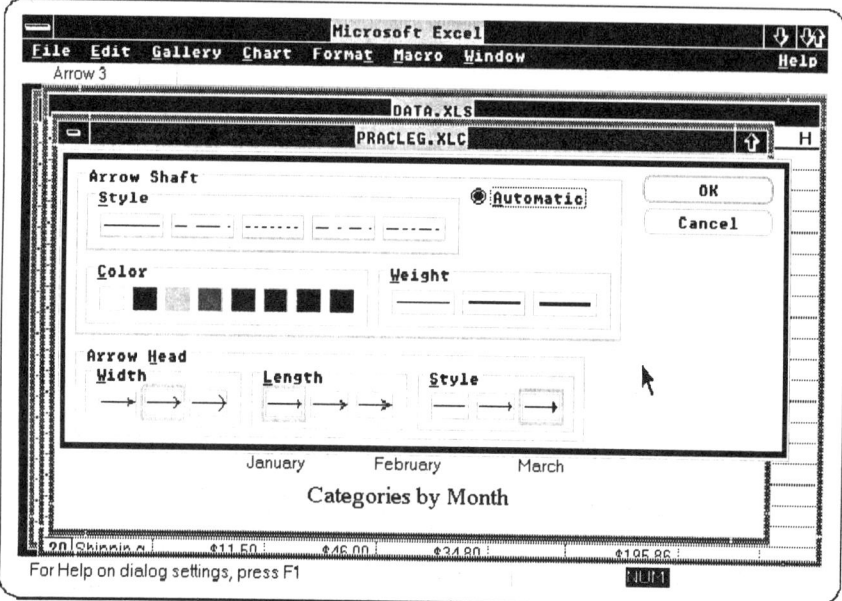

FIGURE 10.16.   Format Arrow Dialog Box

Linking Text to a Worksheet Cell

Instead of typing attached or unattached text as a constant value, you can tell Excel to take the value from some specific or named cell in any worksheet. For example, suppose you want to use the heading in the worksheet as the chart title; it is stored in INCOME.XLS, cell B4. After you select Attach Text and Chart Title, just type =INCOME.XLS!$B$4 and press Return. Excel creates a simple link and uses whatever is in that cell as the chart title. If you change it in the worksheet, the change will be reflected in the chart just as value changes are. You can also use links to reference comments or other entries in the worksheet as unattached text.

As long as the links are all to the same worksheet, Excel doesn't have to do much extra work. If you use relative references and create other complex links, it could take longer for your chart to be drawn.

CONVERTING CUSTOMIZED CHARTS

We mentioned earlier that you can't use gallery selections to change the type of a customized chart without losing some or all of your customizations. You can, however, use the Format Main Chart or Format Overlay command. When you

CUSTOMIZING CHARTS

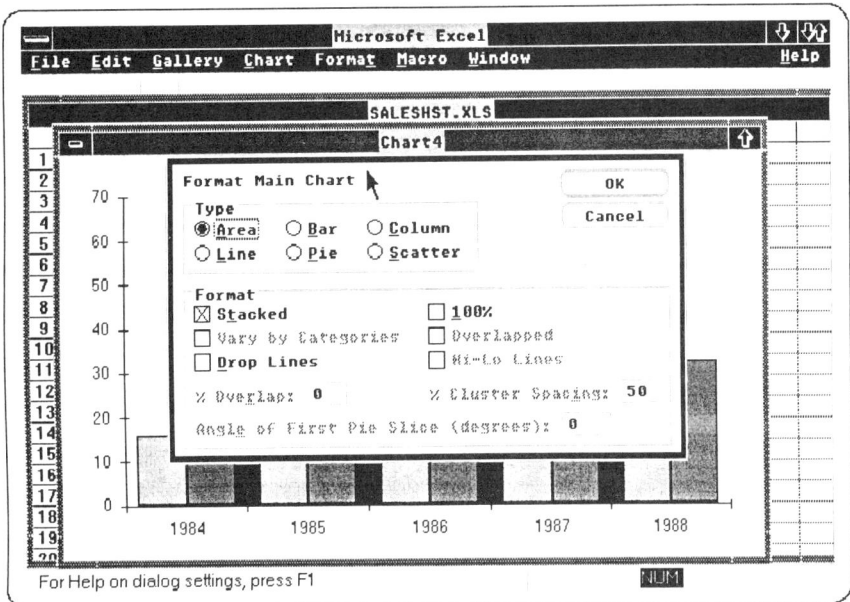

FIGURE 10.17. Format Main Chart Dialog Box

do, Excel converts the chart as you specifically request, keeping all your customizations intact. That means any text you added remains intact. Attached text is converted to the appropriate location on the converted chart. But unattached text and arrows are left where they are. You can move and resize as needed when you see how it looks. Figure 10.17 shows the Format Main Chart dialog box; the one for the Overlay is similar, but deals with an overlay chart. We'll deal with custom overlays shortly. Notice that you can select any of the six basic chart types here. You can specify whether columns or bars should be stacked, whether each should represent 100%, whether columns or bars should be overlapped, or whether the marker pattern should vary by categories. You can also specify drop lines or hi-lo lines for the appropriate types of charts. You can also modify the amount of overlap (you get 30% through the gallery) or the amount of cluster spacing (the gallery gives you 50% of the width of a bar or column). For a pie chart, you can modify the angle of the first pie slice; it starts at the very top (0 degrees) by default.

HANDLING OVERLAYS

The Format Overlay dialog box is similar to the one in Figure 10.17, but the available choices apply to the overlay type. In addition, you can change the number of the first series in the overlay portion. For example, if the selection had five series, Excel automatically puts three in the main chart and the last two in the overlay. In the dialog box, it would show that the first series in the overlay was 4; you can change that to 3, 5, or whatever is appropriate. Excel rearranges both charts so that all data series are shown.

If you want to add an overlay to a chart that doesn't have one, use the Chart Add Overlay command. Excel uses its internal rules and converts the top half of the series (rounded down) to a line overlay on your chart. By editing the series formula, you can change which data series are included in the overlay and which are included in the main chart.

THE SERIES FORMULA

We've been avoiding the series formula up to now. Excel automatically creates a series formula for each series to tell it where to get the data for the chart. Since the series formula contains external references to the original worksheet, you are asked if Excel should update a chart whenever you load one when the worksheet on which it is based isn't open. Whenever a data series is selected, you'll see the series formula in the formula bar. You can delete the series formula to remove the data series from the chart. You can edit this formula to change the effect.

The data series formula is really a function (SERIES). In Figure 10.18 a series formula shows in the formula bar, since a series marker is selected. Notice that the series formula begins with an equal sign (=) and has four arguments. Each argument contributes an important aspect of the chart contents; the first three are generally external references to the worksheet from which the chart was drawn. The first two may be omitted (with places marked by commas) if no series or category names were included in the original selection.

Series Name Argument

The first argument is the series name argument; it refers to the text field in the top or left edge of the series. If no series name was selected, no reference precedes the first comma. You can change the reference to a different cell or name if you like. Or you can use a quoted text value as the argument. Excel uses whatever is present as the first series argument to name the series in the legend. If you replace the first external reference in Figure 10.18 with "Projected

CUSTOMIZING CHARTS

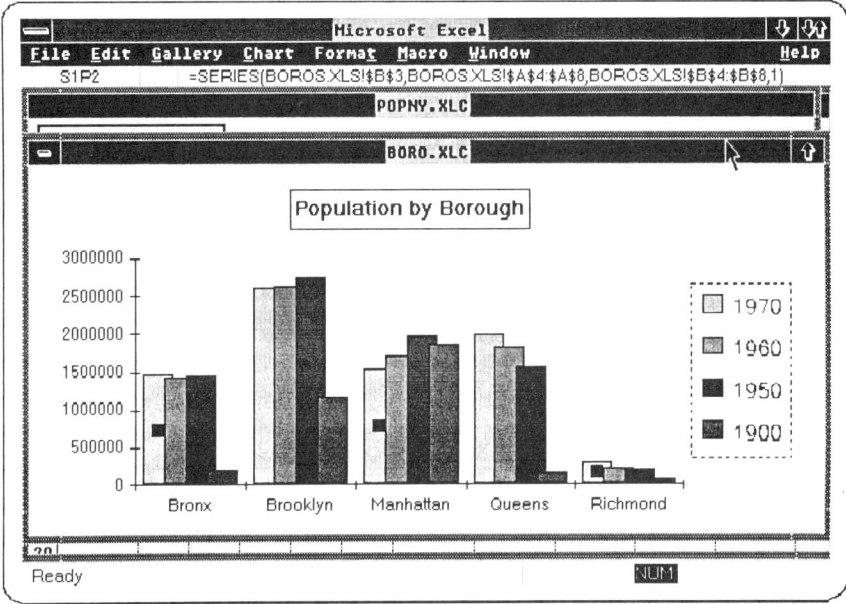

FIGURE 10.18. Series Formula

1990," then Projected 1990 replaces the first series name (1970) in the chart legend.

If you insert a series name for one series in a chart, you will probably want to do it for every series for consistency. Just select the different series markers one at a time and edit the first series argument.

Categories Argument

The second argument in the SERIES function specifies a range that contains the category names for the chart. This argument is an external reference to the range in the original worksheet selection that contains the category names. It is generally the same in each series formula for the same chart. If you didn't select category names, you can add them here, but only as a range reference. The easiest way to handle this is to add the category names you want (the exact number) in a range of cells in the same worksheet as the selection; you can use a format consisting only of a semicolon (;) to hide them if you like. Then edit the series formula to include an external reference to those names as the second argument. You can use pointing while editing the formula bar to pull in the external reference if you like. You need do this in only one series formula for the chart, since the same categories apply to each series.

Values Argument

The third argument gives the range that includes the values for the data series, one for each category. You can change this if necessary. Generally, you'll want to leave the values reference alone if Excel created the chart automatically.

Plot Order Argument

The final argument in the SERIES function specifies the plot order, which determines in which order the data series are included in the chart. You can rearrange them here. Just make sure the numbers start with 1 and aren't repeated. Figure 10.19 shows a chart in which we have changed the plot order and modified one of the series names. Notice the formula bar reflects the current status.

Another reason you might want to change the plot order arguments in series formulas for a chart is to control which series are part of the main chart and which are part of the overlay. By default, Excel uses the first half as the main chart and the second half as the overlay; the main chart may have one more series. You can change this by using lower numbers (1 through the midpoint) for

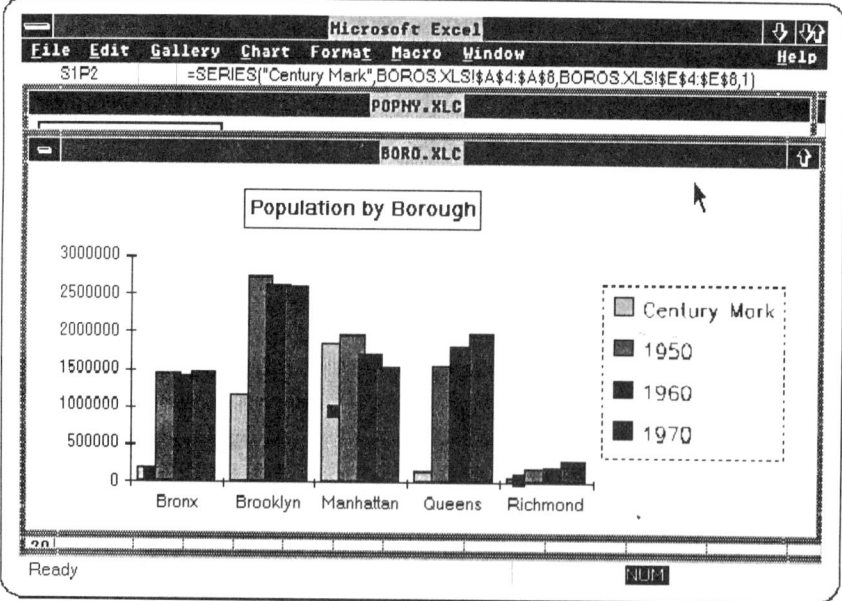

FIGURE 10.19. Modified Series Formula

CUSTOMIZING CHARTS

series to be in the main chart and higher plot order numbers for those to be in the overlay. The changes you make here have no effect on the worksheet itself.

Creating a New Series Function

If you want, you can create a series formula from scratch to design your own set of data for a chart. First you have to get an empty chart window. Just select a single empty cell on any worksheet, then select File New Chart. You'll get an empty chart window, and you can start typing your series function with =. The worksheets from which you gather data must be open at the time. You'll find it easiest to do this if you have sized and arranged the screen so that you can see most of the data you want while you are working with the chart. You can type the complete function and external references or use pointing to pull them in as needed. As with standard charts, Excel creates its default type first; you can change it at any time.

SUGGESTED EXERCISE

1. Add some attached text to a chart. Use a chart title, then format it to have a border and a patterned background. Change the font if you like.
2. Add axis labels; make the value label display vertically. Change the font and color if you like.
3. Add a note in unattached text. Remember to press CONTROL + Enter to start a new line. When it's ready, move it to an unused spot on the chart and format it. Try the alignment options.
4. Add an arrow or two and position them to point from the unattached text to specific markers.
5. Modify a series name in the series formula. Notice that it appears in the legend.

What if It Doesn't Work?

1. Try other text and formatting options. They should all work on screen.

SUMMARY

By now, you should be able to customize a chart to emphasize what you are trying to show with it. You can manipulate legends, chart titles, axis labels, and data point labels. You can add and format unattached text to explain parts of the chart. You can modify, or even build, a series formula to gain more control over what Excel does in building a chart.

11 USING DATA SERIES, TABLES, AND ARRAYS

In this chapter, we'll look at various ways you can enter and manipulate data in groups. Data series let you enter a single value or date and expand it to fill a range or to a certain point, changing the value by the amount you specify each time. Data tables let you play "what if" with figures. Other types of tables let you look up information and translate values based on the result of the lookup. Arrays are generally more mathematical but are often useful in standard worksheets as well. We'll cover the common uses of arrays and show you how to use the matrix functions to manipulate them. You'll also learn to handle arrays if you get one by accident, perhaps resulting from a Formula Paste Special command.

DATA SERIES

Suppose you need values from 1 through 250 in the first column of a worksheet. Or you need values from 10 through 400 in increments of 10. Or you need the dates, in one-week increments, for the next year. You can use the Data Series command from the Data menu to accomplish any of these.

To have Excel create a data series for you, enter the beginning value, then select the range (either in a single row or a single column) to hold the rest of the series. Next, select the Series command from the Data menu. The dialog box in Figure 11.1 results.

The first field specifies whether the generated data series will be placed in a row or a column; the default is whatever you have selected. If you are generating several identical series at once, you can have Excel fill several rows or columns. The type of series depends on what you have entered and what you want. If you enter a numeric value, Excel uses Linear as the default. If you enter anything it recognizes as a date, Excel uses Date as the default type. The Step Value field at the bottom of the dialog box tells Excel how much to increase each value in the series by. Use the default (1) to increment by 1. To increment by 2 or 1,000 or whatever, just enter the value in the Step Value field.

USING DATA SERIES, TABLES, AND ARRAYS

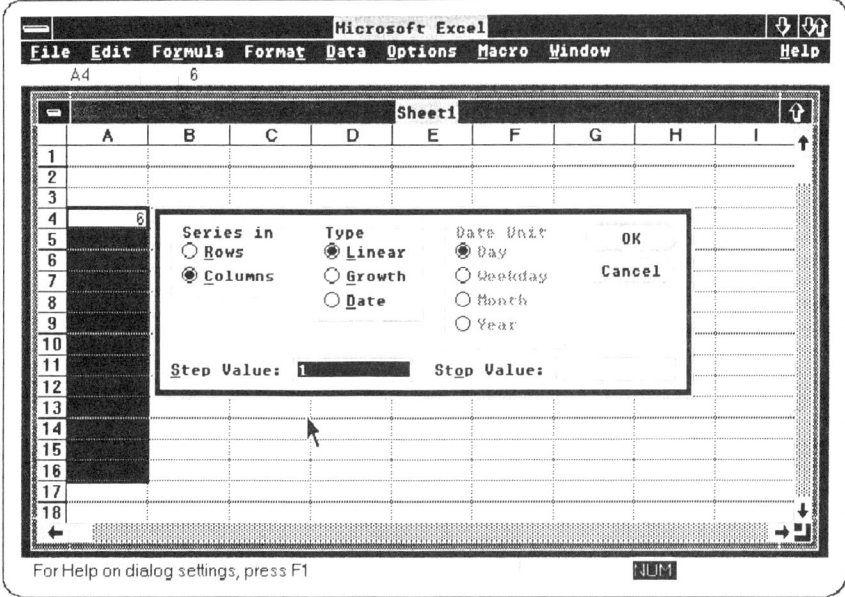

FIGURE 11.1. Data Series Dialog Box

The Stop Value field tells Excel when to stop. Ordinarily, Excel stops when the selected range is filled, but you can tell it to stop when a specific value is reached or exceeded. In that case, the series will stop when the stop value is reached or the range is filled, whichever comes first.

Excel creates a linear series by adding the step value to the first value and placing the result in the next cell; then it adds the step value to that result and places that result in the third cell, and so on. If you enter 20 in the first field and enter 10 as the step value, a linear type series contains 20, 30, 40, 50, and so forth until the range is filled or the stop value is reached.

A growth series is created by multiplying the value in each cell by the step value and placing it in the next cell. If you enter 1 in the first field and use 2 as the step value, a growth series contains 1, 2, 4, 8, and so forth.

If the first field contains a date in any format Excel recognizes, Excel uses the date series as the default, but any value can be handled as a date. When the date type is selected, you can select the date unit to increment values by day, weekday, month, or year. You must change the step value to increment by more than one unit. To increment by three-month intervals, select Month as the date unit and 3 as the step value. If the original value is 2/2/88 and you select weekday as the date unit and 3 as the step unit, the next three values will be 2/5/88, 2/10/88, and 2/15/88. The Weekday unit uses only Monday through Friday dates, ignoring Saturday and Sunday.

230 ADVANCED EXCEL

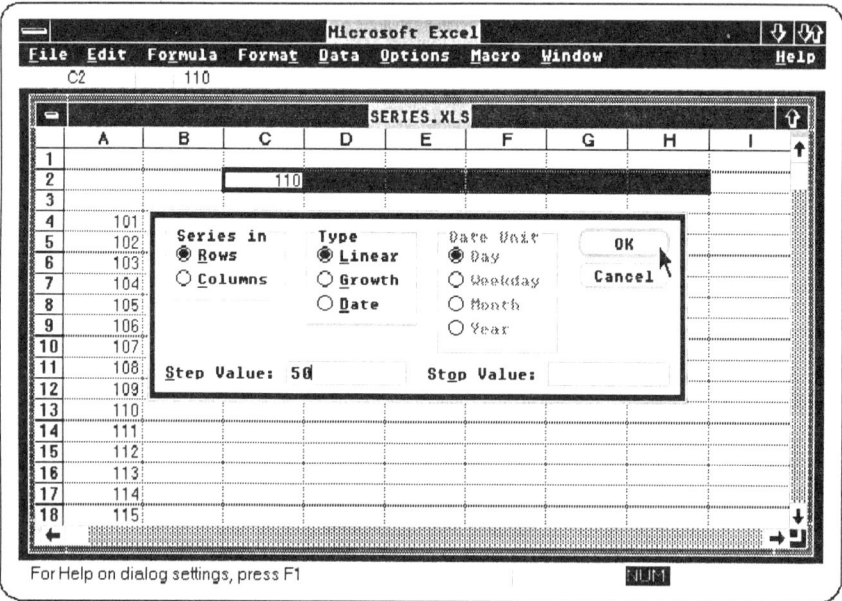

FIGURE 11.2. Numeric Data Series

Using Numeric Data Series

Figure 11.2 shows a worksheet that contains one data series generated by Excel and the preparations for another. The column was generated with a linear series using step increment 1. The row will contain a series of values from 110 through 360, as specified in the Data Series dialog box.

Using Date Data Series

Figure 11.3 shows a worksheet with a data series that shows the weekdays at five weekday increments (displaying all the same day of the week) and another showing the end of calendar quarters. The weekday increments required that the date unit be set at Weekday and the increment at 5. To use the end of calendar quarters, we entered the end of the first quarter, then used the Month date unit and an increment of 3.

Be sure to enter values Excel recognizes as dates if you intend to ask Excel to calculate date series. When you enter 1988 in the first cell, then ask Excel to increment by years, Excel considers 1988 as a date serial number and the next value is 2353, which is 365 days later. You can use YEAR functions to produce years if you need them, or treat 1988 at a numeric value and increment by 1.

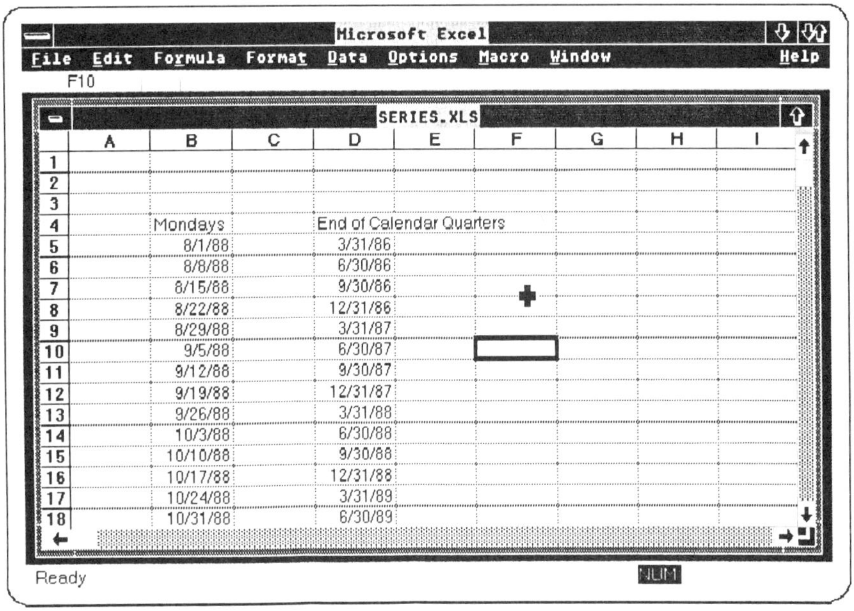

USING DATA SERIES, TABLES, AND ARRAYS 231

FIGURE 11.3. Date Data Series

DATA TABLES

Sometimes you want to know results in various circumstances. For example, suppose you are about to buy a house. You know the basic price of the house and the general range of possible interest rates. You can set up a data table so that Excel calculates what the monthly payment is at each of a number of interest rates. Once the basic table is set up, you can add more formulas to it, so that Excel uses the variable input value (interest rate) in more than one formula. Everytime you ask, Excel calculates the entire table.

If you want to vary more than one value, you can set up a two-input table, using much the same process. We'll look at one-input tables in detail and then continue with two-input tables. For all these, you use the Table option on the Data menu.

A One-Input Table

You can use a one-input table when you know all the values involved in a formula and want to see the effects of changing one of them. Figure 11.4 shows a completed and calculated one-input table to find the mortgage payment

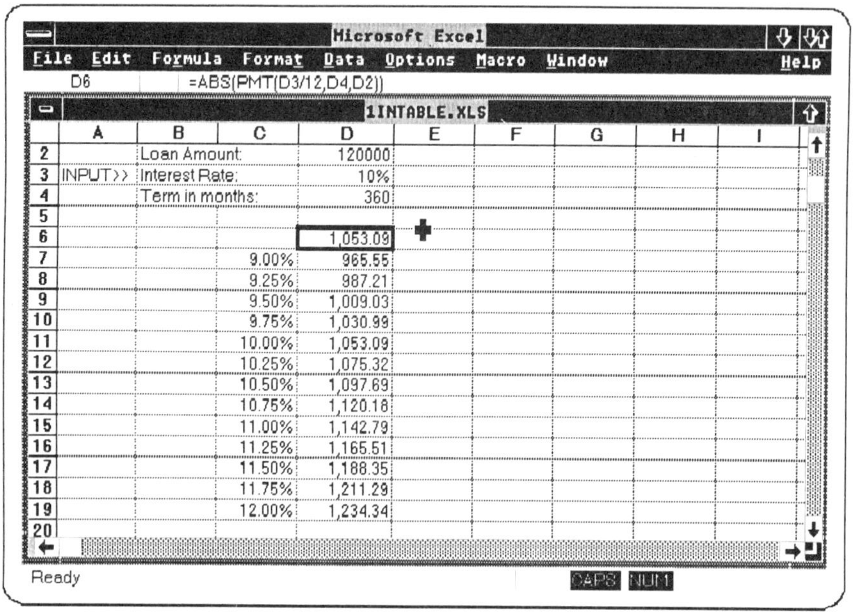

232 ADVANCED EXCEL

FIGURE 11.4. One-Input Table to Calculate Monthly Payments

(principal and interest only) on a specific house purchase with a specific loan amount. The input variable here is the interest rate.

The screen layout in Figure 11.4 shows more information than is actually required in a data table, but, as you'll see, it all is useful. The upper part of the screen includes the constant values for the formula; in this case, the loan amount, a sample interest rate, and the term of the mortgage in months. You could supply any values in the formula except for the input variable as a constant or a reference, even as a defined name. The input variable, here the sample interest rate, must be a reference. Excel substitutes any other interest rates you supply into the reference to this cell in the formula.

The formula appears here in cell D6; since that's the current cell, you can see the formula in the formula bar. We used the absolute value (to make it positive) of the PMT function which calculates a monthly payment given the interest rate, the term, and the full value. Notice that we divide the interest rate by 12 to get the interest rate per month. You could use all constant values in the formula except for the input cell reference; whatever function or formula you use in a table must refer to the input cell. The result of the formula here uses the value in the input cell (C3). Below the formula cell, the column to its left contains other interest rate values to be substituted into the input cell when the table is calculated. You can begin with the input cell itself empty, if you prefer, but then the result of the table formula may look strange, since it uses an input value of zero.

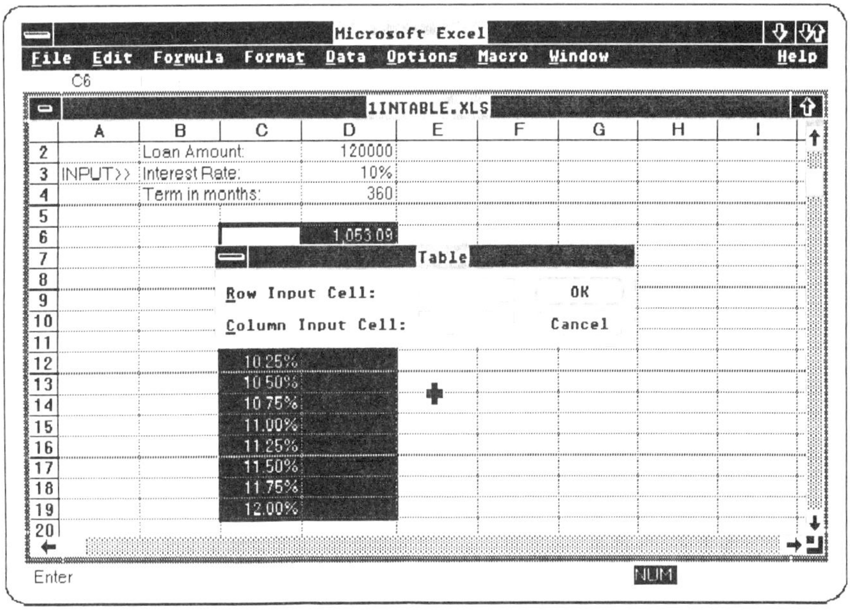

USING DATA SERIES, TABLES, AND ARRAYS

FIGURE 11.5. Data Table Dialog Box

When you're ready to calculate the table, select the range that includes the table formula and the list of values to be substituted into it and choose the Data Table command. You'll see the dialog box shown in Figure 11.5. You have to enter only one value, the reference of the input cell; this must be the reference included in the selected formula. You can use either relative or absolute reference here; in small tables it makes little difference, but absolute references are calculated more quickly and can speed up large table processing. The biggest problem is deciding whether it is a Row Input Cell or a Column Input Cell; in the example, it is a Column Input Cell, since the values to be substituted are in a column. If you have a two-input table, which we'll cover shortly, you'll use both values.

Once the table is calculated, you can't change individual parts of it. Excel creates an array formula using the TABLE function and the input cell reference. We'll cover arrays and array formulas later in this chapter. For now, you'll have to change the reference formula and recalculate the table to change it. You can delete the whole thing, but not just part of it.

Adding to the Table

A one-input table can calculate one or many formulas based on the one variable input value. Just enter all the sample formulas in a single row or column. To

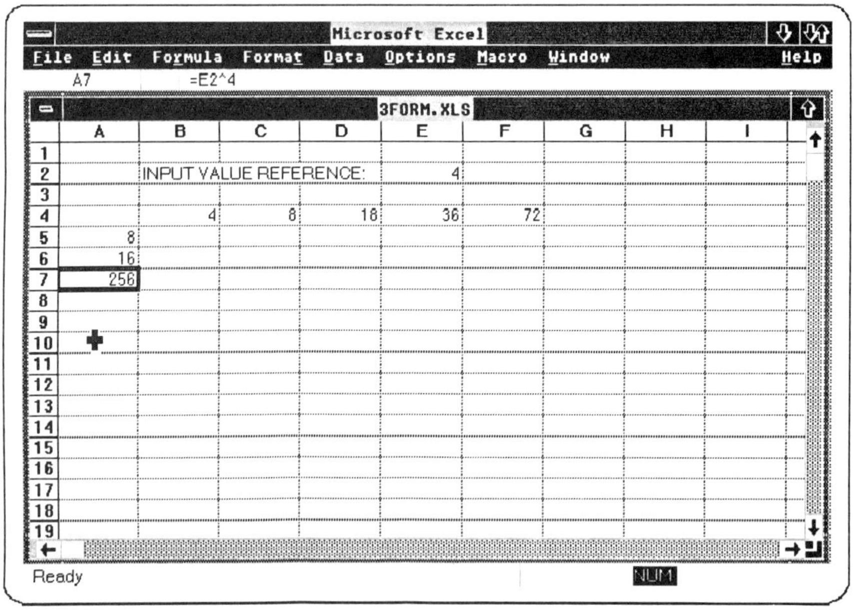

234 ADVANCED EXCEL

FIGURE 11.6. One-Input Table with Three Formulas

expand the table in Figure 11.4, add formulas in row 6 to the right of the first sample formula. Once the formulas are in a row, you can select the entire range and use the data table command again; all the formulas are calculated for each variable input value.

If you prefer, you can put the values to be substituted in a row and the formulas in a column. Arrange the formulas and the input cells so that they can form the top row and left column of a range that will contain all the calculated values. Figure 11.6 shows another sample one-input table. This one contains the values to be substituted in a row and formulas to be calculated in a column. In the data table dialog box, you'll have to enter the reference cell as a row reference. All the formulas will be given the same array table formula and then calculated at once.

A Two-Input Table

A two-input table is an expanded one-input table; you specify two input cells and use them both in a single formula. The range you select includes values to be substituted for one input cell in the column on the left and values to be substituted for the other input cell in the row on the top. When you choose the Data Table command, you enter the references for the row and the column.

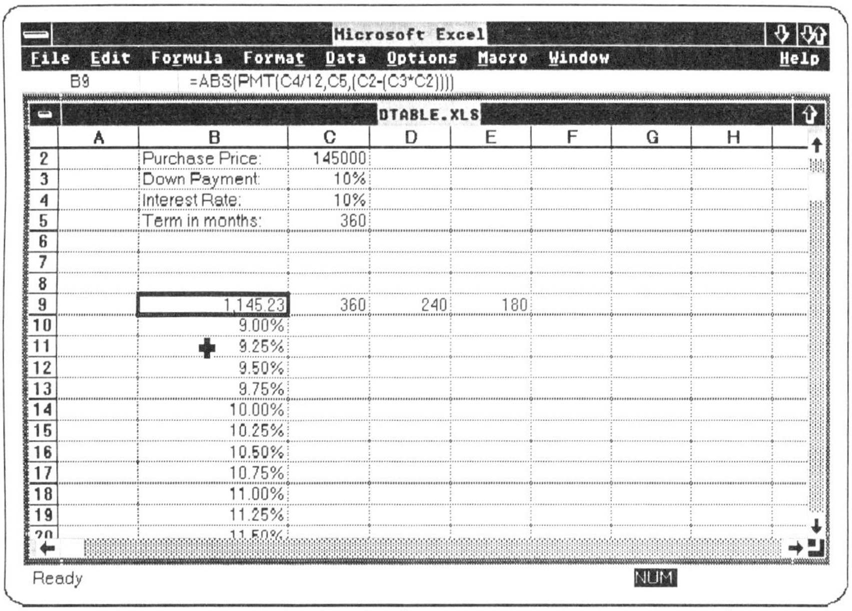

USING DATA SERIES, TABLES, AND ARRAYS

FIGURE 11.7. Two-Input Table Framework

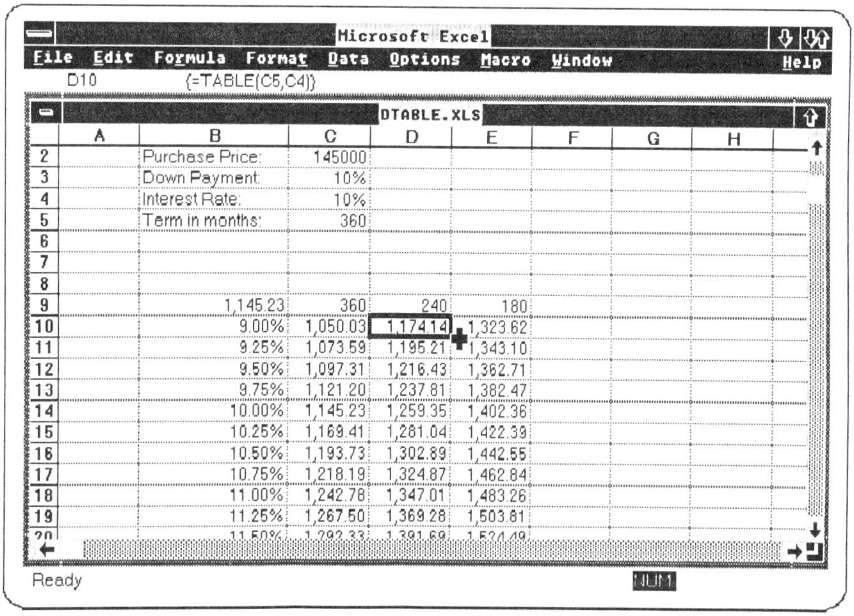

FIGURE 11.8. Two-Input Table, Calculated

Figure 11.7 shows the framework of a two-input table. This is similar to the one-input tables you've seen earlier, but here we're varying the purchase price as well as the term and using a constant 10% down payment.

In the two-input table, you place the formula in the corner cell, between the row input values and the column input values. That cell is selected in the figure. The row input cell is C5; it references the term of the loan, and the values to be substituted appear in the row at the top of the table. The column input cell is C4; it references the interest rate, and its values appear in the column on the left of the table. All the values calculated by Excel receive the array TABLE function formula, so you can't change or delete any of them individually. You can see the formula in Figure 11.8, which shows the calculated table. This same formula appears in every cell generated by the Data Table command.

To make changes, you'll have to redo the formula and calculate the result again. You can clear the entire area of the table, of course. To move the table, you can select its entire area and move it to another location or worksheet.

SUGGESTED EXERCISE

1. Bring up a new worksheet for practice; SHEET1 will do just fine.
2. Create a data series, starting with 25 and increasing by 25 each time. Remember to fill the first cell and select the desired range before using the Data Series command.
3. Create a series of dates, three days apart. Modify it to be a month apart.
4. Now create a one-input table to calculate the volume of a rectangular solid 3 by 4 inches on two sides. Use a data series to create input values from .25 to 4 inches in .25 inch increments. Use the formula =3*4*nn where nn is your input cell.
5. Modify the one-input table to add another formula, this one to convert the height to centimeters (nn*2.56). Calculate it again.
6. Convert the one-input table to a two-input table, so that only one dimension of the solid is a constant. You'll have to move the formula to the upper left corner of the table and modify it, then add a series of constants to the table.

What if It Doesn't Work?

1. If you have trouble with data series, press F1 to get help. If you have trouble with dates, be sure you are using a format Excel recognizes or the five-digit serial number.
2. If you have trouble with the data table, build a very simple one first, perhaps copying the one in the text. Then use it as a model.

USING DATA SERIES, TABLES, AND ARRAYS

LOOKUP TABLES

Excel offers another type of table too, this one for looking up data. You probably use lookup tables for many things outside of Excel. You may have a list of branch numbers with addresses, customer codes with names, tax tables, even telephone extensions and names. You can create any type of table in Excel, hiding the cells if desired, and look up information on them as needed with specific lookup functions. In this section, you'll see how to set up tables for lookup and how to use them to enter values into a worksheet.

Defining Lookup Tables

You can enter tables of data into a range in Excel. Excel can then look up values in the left column or top row and extract corresponding values in any other column or row in the table. Figure 11.9 shows three examples as entered into an Excel worksheet.

The table on the left is vertically arranged; the values to be looked up are vertical in a column at the left. You specify a number from 1 to 7 and get back the spelled-out day of the week. The table on the right is horizontally arranged;

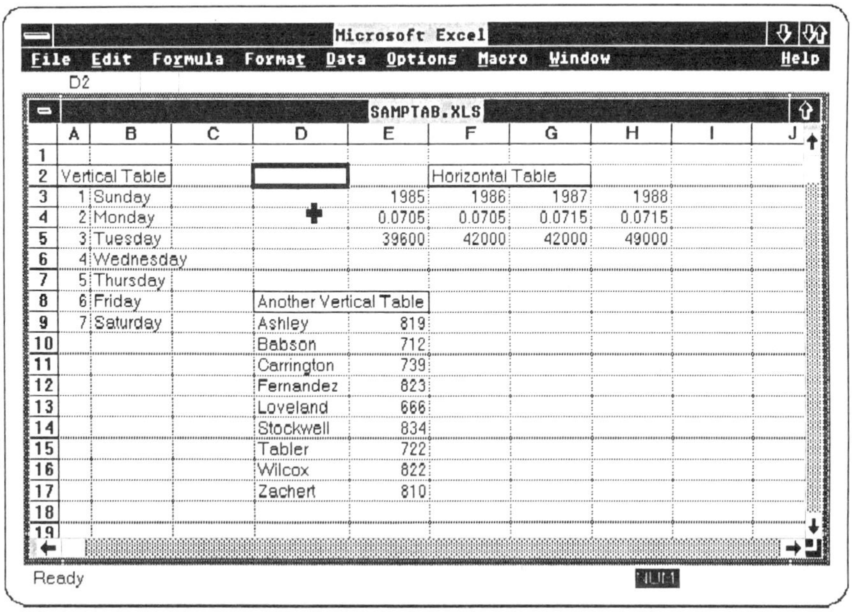

FIGURE 11.9. Lookup Tables

the values to be looked up are horizontal in a row at the top. This table names four consecutive years; the next row gives the FICA withholding rate and the next the maximum salary taxed. The table in the center is another vertically arranged one; this table uses names as lookup values with extension numbers as values to be returned.

The values in the search row or column must be numbers, text, or logical values in ascending order; the lowest value must be on the top or the left. Numbers are lower than letters (upper- and lowercase are treated the same); letters are lower than logical values; FALSE (0) is lower than TRUE (1). If the items are out of sequence, the lookup function will not work correctly. The search values in two of our samples here are numbers; the other table uses text.

HLOOKUP and VLOOKUP Functions

Most table lookup can be handled with the HLOOKUP (horizontal) and VLOOKUP (vertical) functions. Figure 11.10 shows the formats of both. The functions can use absolute or relative references or defined names to refer to any component.

The table on the left in Figure 11.9 has the lookup values vertically in the first column, so you use the VLOOKUP function to get the weekday name. The function looks something like this:

= VLOOKUP(WEEKDAY(B1),A3:B9,2)

In this case, the lookup value must provide a number from 1 to 7; the WEEKDAY function accomplishes this nicely. B1 contains an Excel date.

```
HLOOKUP(lookup-value,table-array,row-index)

VLOOKUP(lookup-value,table-array,col-index)

     lookup-value is the item or reference to match; must be
         text, numbers, logical, or reference

     table-array is complete reference of table; row or
         column containing lookup items must be in
         ascending sequence

     col-index is number of result column, from 1 to n

     row-index is number of result column, from 1 to n
```

FIGURE 11.10. HLOOKUP and VLOOKUP Functions

The center table also supports the VLOOKUP function. It could be written as = VLOOKUP("Loveland",D9:E17,2) or, more likely, use a reference to the name to be looked up.

The table on the right in Figure 11.9 includes the tax rate and maximum salary taxed by FICA for four years. To look up values, a function provides the year (or a reference to it), specifies the table range, and indicates 2 for the percentage or 3 for the maximum salary taxed. A function included on another worksheet would look something like this:

= HLOOKUP(G11,SAMPTAX.XLS!E3:H5,3)

In this case, the function returns the maximum salary taxed under Social Security for the year indicated in cell G11.

Both lookup functions identify an exact match or a value in the table that is not greater than the specified lookup value. The lookup value can be a constant, a reference, or a name. The table-array must be a range reference or an array constant; you'll generally use a range reference, but you'll see how to define array constants in the last part of this chapter. If the lookup value is invalid so function doesn't locate an appropriate value, it returns #N/A instead.

The row or column index specifies the number of the row or column in the range (or array) from which the function's result is to be taken. The index counts the first row or column, the one with the lookup values, as 1; if you omit the index, Excel uses 1, so you'll get the selected comparison value itself. That's not all bad, if it's what you expect, but generally you'll want to use at least column 2. You can use an expression to specify the index. For example, suppose you use data on the worksheet to calculate withholding and you use tax tables on a different worksheet to find amounts. You might include fields for gross pay, for the type of employee to decide whether to use married, single, or head-of-household tables, and for the number of declared dependents. Figure 11.11 shows part of one table. Here, notice that the comparison values are vertical in the left column. The rows represent numbers of dependents. Suppose the data records include named fields for "gross" and "dependents" but the chart selection is done elsewhere with an IF function. You can use this function to find the appropriate withholding in the table:

= VLOOKUP(GROSS,A6:L45,DEPENDENTS + 2)

The gross value is located in the left column; the largest value not greater than the gross value is selected in the table referenced by A6:L45. Then the value in the DEPENDENTS + 2 column is selected and returned to the cell containing the function. We added 2 to the dependents value to access the appropriate value from the table. A sample formula is included in cell A1 so you can see that an exact match of lookup value is not required.

240 ADVANCED EXCEL

```
                    Microsoft Excel
 File  Edit  Formula  Format  Data  Options  Macro  Window        Help
     A1              =VLOOKUP(800,A6:L40,3)
                           SAMPTAX.XLS
```

	A	B	C	D	E	F	G	H	I	J	K	L
1	7.5											
2												
3		TAX WITHHOLDING -- SINGLE, MONTHLY										
4				number of dependents								
5	MAX.	0	1	2	3	4	5	6	7	8	9	10
6	419.99	0.00	0.00	0.00	0.00	0.00	0.00	0.00	0.00	0.00	0.00	0.00
7	439.99	2.90	0.00	0.00	0.00	0.00	0.00	0.00	0.00	0.00	0.00	0.00
8	479.99	3.40	0.00	0.00	0.00	0.00	0.00	0.00	0.00	0.00	0.00	0.00
9	519.99	4.20	0.70	0.00	0.00	0.00	0.00	0.00	0.00	0.00	0.00	0.00
10	559.99	5.00	1.50	0.30	0.00	0.00	0.00	0.00	0.00	0.00	0.00	0.00
11	599.99	5.80	2.30	1.10	0.00	0.00	0.00	0.00	0.00	0.00	0.00	0.00
12	639.99	6.60	3.10	1.90	0.70	0.00	0.00	0.00	0.00	0.00	0.00	0.00
13	679.99	7.50	3.90	2.80	1.60	0.40	0.00	0.00	0.00	0.00	0.00	0.00
14	719.99	8.70	5.10	4.00	2.80	1.60	0.50	0.00	0.00	0.00	0.00	0.00
15	759.99	9.90	6.30	5.20	4.00	2.80	1.70	0.50	0.00	0.00	0.00	0.00
16	799.99	11.10	7.50	6.40	5.20	4.00	2.90	1.70	0.50	0.00	0.00	0.00
17	839.99	12.30	8.70	7.60	6.40	5.20	4.10	2.90	1.70	0.60	0.00	0.00
18	879.99	13.50	9.90	8.80	7.60	6.40	5.30	4.10	2.90	1.80	0.60	0.00
19	919.99	15.00	11.50	10.30	9.10	8.00	6.80	5.60	4.50	3.30	2.10	1.00

Ready

FIGURE 11.11. Tax Table for Lookup

The LOOKUP Function

Excel offers another function that acts on tables, LOOKUP. It works in a slightly different way; in fact it works in two different ways. You can use LOOKUP to return the value in the last cell corresponding to the lookup value or to return values when they aren't really in a compact table. As with HLOOKUP and VLOOKUP, LOOKUP returns #N/A if no matching value is found. Figure 11.12 shows the two formats.

```
LOOKUP(lookup-value,table-array)

LOOKUP(lookup-value,lookup-vector,result-vector)

      lookup-value must be text, numbers, logical, or a
            reference

      table-array is a range; lookup row or column must be in
            ascending sequence

      vectors are ranges with single row or column; lookup-
            vector is for lookup value; result-vector holds
            result values
```

FIGURE 11.12. LOOKUP Function

USING DATA SERIES, TABLES, AND ARRAYS

The first format operates on a table much like those you've seen with HLOOKUP and VLOOKUP. LOOKUP finds the lookup-value in the named table-array. You don't have to specify H or V, because LOOKUP decides where to look based on the shape of the named table-array. If it is taller than it is wide, LOOKUP looks in the first column for the lookup-value. If it is square or wider than tall, LOOKUP looks in the top row. It always selects the last value in the appropriate row or column as the result of the function.

The second format uses vectors. A vector is a range that includes cells in a single row or column; you might call it a one-dimensional range. You specify the lookup-value as usual, but you don't specify any particular table-array for it to look in. Instead you specify a lookup-vector, a range that includes a single row or column; Excel looks for a match (not greater than the lookup-value) in the lookup-vector. As in the other lookup functions, the lookup values must be in ascending sequence. Excel then finds the corresponding cell in the result-vector, another single row or column which must be the same size and direction as the lookup-vector, and returns its contents as the function result.

The LOOKUP function is handy to look up values that aren't in standard tables. It may come in handy for using nonadjacent lookup values and values to be returned from an already prepared worksheet as a table. Or you may even be able to locate information on different worksheets, since the lookup and array vectors need not be on the same one. Be sure to use external references if either vector is not on the active worksheet.

The MATCH Function

The MATCH function differs from the other lookup functions in that it returns the position of the lookup value in the table relative to the upper left corner, rather than a value. You can specify the type of match, which changes the sequence requirements of the lookup row or column. Figure 11.13 shows the format.

In the MATCH function, the lookup-value and table-array are specified much as in the lookup functions. Whether the lookup value is matched in the first row or the first column depends on the shape of the table-array as in the

```
MATCH(lookup-value,table-array,type-of-match)

    Types       Meaning
      1         Largest value, less than or equal
      0         First exact match
     -1         Smallest value, less than or equal
```

FIGURE 11.13. MATCH Function

LOOKUP function. If it's taller than wide, the first column is used, otherwise the first row. If you specify type 1 or omit the type, the match works much like a lookup; the values in the lookup row or column must be in ascending sequence. If you specify −1, they must be in descending sequence. If you specify 0, the values can be in any sequence; the function starts with the first cell and stops whenever it finds an exact match. And when you use 0, you can use the standard wildcard characters (? and *) in the lookup-value if appropriate. The first matching value is selected.

Remember that MATCH returns the position in a range rather than a value. You might want to use it to locate a position that you can then use in another function. The INDEX function discussion includes an example of MATCH.

The INDEX Function

The INDEX function locates a value in a range using relative positions. Figure 11.14 shows its usual format. Another, seldom-used format returns a reference rather than a value. We won't cover that one in this book.

The INDEX function returns a value anywhere in a given range if you can tell it the row and column of the cell. In formulas, you may often know one of these figures, but you seldom know both; if you do, you can reference the value yourself. The MATCH function returns a relative row or column, and you can use it to generate one or both of the position values needed in the INDEX function. Suppose you have a table of item numbers and descriptions stored at M7:N99 in ITEMS.XLS, with the item numbers in no particular sequence in column M and the descriptions in column N. If a user enters an item number in cell C8 on another worksheet, you want Excel to find the corresponding description and enter it in cell E8 on that worksheet. Here's the function you could place in cell E8:

=INDEX(ITEMS.XLS!M7:N99,MATCH(C8,ITEMS.XLS!M7:M99,0),2)

Look at the MATCH function first; it returns the row-number of the value that matches what was just entered in C8 in the item-number range of ITEMS.XLS,

```
INDEX(table-array,row-number,column-number)
    table-array is a range referring to the entire table
    row-number specifies a relative row in the table
    column-number specifies a relative column in the table
```

FIGURE 11.14. INDEX Function

using type 0 which requires an exact match but no sequence. The row number returned is used by the INDEX function, with the column number 2 provided as a constant. The INDEX function uses these to find the appropriate value in the complete table on the external worksheet.

Like the other lookup functions, INDEX returns #N/A if no value is found, in case either the row or column number is outside the range of the referenced table-array.

Lookup Table Summary

This has been a brief examination of lookup tables and the functions you can use to process them. You can now look up data, locate values in corresponding rows or columns, and find exact matches when needed. You can also extract the column or row position with MATCH and use it in an INDEX function to do more sophisticated processing.

ARRAYS IN EXCEL

An array is any rectangular arrangement of cells that you can refer to. You can use arrays to build formulas that give multiple results or that operate on a group of arguments arranged in rows and columns. The tables discussed earlier in this chapter can be considered arrays. In fact, Excel creates an array formula for data series that it creates.

Arrays come in two forms; the array range and the array constant. An array range is just a rectangle with a common reference, such as C3:F12; any range can be handled as an array, although it doesn't have to be. An array constant is a set of values that form a logical rectangle to use as an argument in a formula. An array constant of {2,2,2,2;4,4,4,4} specifies an array constant 2 by 4, the equivalent of two rows by four columns. You can use an array constant in any formula or function where you can use an array reference. Our discussion is concerned primarily with array ranges.

Occasionally, you'll find you have an array formula when you didn't expect one. For example, when you use a one- or two-input table, Excel creates an array formula, with the result that you can't edit or delete the individual affected cells. Suppose you need to use a range of formulas that use references from another worksheet. You can use Formula Paste Special to place the range where you want it. Excel also creates an array formula when you use Formula Paste Special to copy formulas. If you want to process the resulting cells independently, you might want to use Formula Paste Special on the target range, this time selecting Values in the dialog box. The resulting values in the cells are constants, not the result of an array formula.

Using Array Ranges in Basic Applications

You can use array ranges to perform operations on several fields at once; this not only saves time for Excel to do the operation, but also saves memory. For example, suppose you have data as shown on the left in Figure 11.15. You want to put the product of C3 and D3 in cell E3, the product of C4 and D4 in cell E4, and so on. Of course, you could select E3:E15, create a single formula (=C3*D3) in cell E3 and press CONTROL+Enter to enter it in all the selected cells, or you could copy it to the other appropriate cells; Excel creates an individual appropriate formula for each recipient cell.

Another option is to create an array formula to calculate the result. Select the entire range to hold the products, with cell E3 active. Then type =C3:C15*D3:D15 and press CONTROL+SHIFT+Enter. Excel automatically places braces ({}) around the formula and calculates C3*D3 for cell E3, C4*D4 for cell E4, and so forth. When you enter an array formula, you never

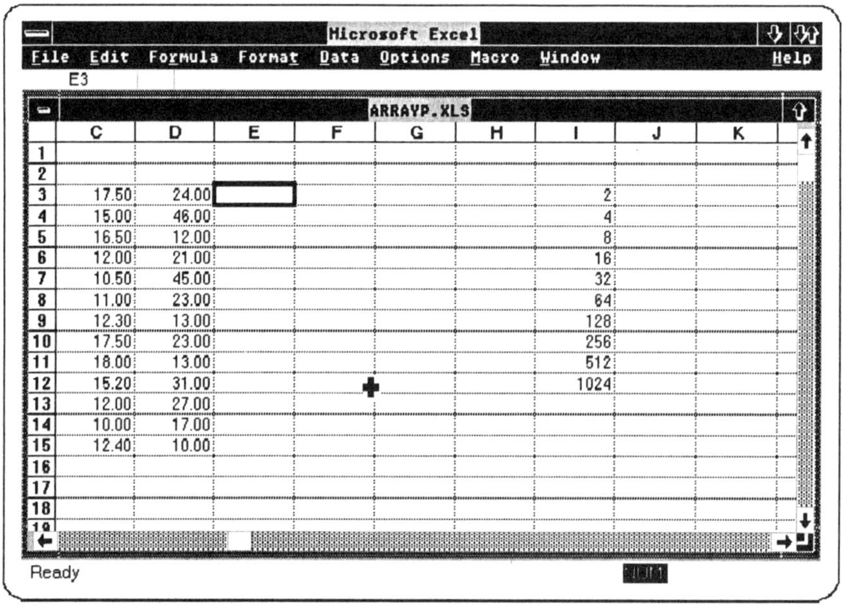

FIGURE 11.15. Sample Data for Array Processing

USING DATA SERIES, TABLES, AND ARRAYS

type the braces; Excel adds them for viewing or removes them when you press F2 to allow editing in the formula bar. If you type the braces, Excel treats your formula as text. And don't just press Enter; if you do, Excel doesn't realize it is an array formula and calculates the value for the active cell only. If you press CONTROL + Enter, Excel treats it as an ordinary formula repeated for each selected cell; you'll get the same result but each is a standard formula rather than an array.

Suppose you want to get a single result from a range. For example, how can you calculate the sum of the products calculated by the array formula just described? Select a single cell to hold the value and use the formula = SUM(C3:C15*D3:D15) and press CONTROL + SHIFT + Enter. Excel calculates all the individual products, finds the sum, and places it in the active cell. If you happen to use this formula and just press Return, Excel calculates a different value; it uses the value from each range that is in the same row or column as the active cell.

The data on the right in Figure 11.15 can also be handled with an array formula. Suppose you want to place the square root of each in the adjacent area to the right. Select the entire target range with the top cell active. Type the formula = SQRT(I3:I12) and press CONTROL + SHIFT + Enter. Excel adds braces to the formula and calculates the result for each of cells J3 through J12.

Using Array Formulas

When arrays are referenced in formulas or functions, you have to follow a few rules. If a single formula refers to more than one array, they must be the same size and shape. It will give a single result if a single cell is selected to hold that result. To edit the array range, select the entire range and edit it. To edit an array formula, select any cell that uses it, press F2, then edit it; be sure to press CONTROL + SHIFT + Enter when you're finished. Although you can't edit or delete the results of an individual cell produced from an array formula, you can format or copy individual cells. To clear the entire range, select it, then use the Edit Clear command. To convert it to constant values, use Formula Paste Special.

Mathematical Arrays and Matrix Functions

Arrays are fairly widely used in mathematical applications, where they are often called matrices (plural of matrix). If you work with mathematical arrays, you may find use for the built-in matrix functions provided by Excel. Figure

```
MDETERM(array)   determinant of the named array

MINVERSE(array)  inverse of the array

MMULT(array1,array2)   product of two arrays

TRANSPOSE(array) transposes the array
```

FIGURE 11.16. Matrix Functions

11.16 gives the basic function formats. Three of the matrix functions take one array (range or constant) as the argument and return an array in the specified format—the determinant, the inverse, or the transposition of the original array—using the cell containing the function as the upper left of the resulting array. The fourth function (MMULT) uses two arrays, returning a third array oriented as in the others. If you have never worked with matrices, you probably won't have to use these functions. If you do, you can find more details in the Functions and Macros reference documentation.

SUGGESTED EXERCISE

1. On a fresh worksheet create a set of data to use as a lookup table. A list of last names (about 10) in one column and phone numbers or account numbers in the second would be appropriate.
2. In another cell on the worksheet insert a sample value that matches one of the names in your table.
3. In another cell, create a formula using the appropriate function to use the reference name to look up the corresponding number in the table.
4. Create another lookup table. Use a data series command to create the lookup values 1000 through 9000 in a row, in even thousands. Place the text values "ONE" through "NINE" in the cell below each lookup value.
5. Create a lookup function to return the text value when you supply a constant of less than 9000 to show the next highest thousand.
6. Create a set of values in two columns (at least 4 values in each column) that can be multiplied together using an array formula. Select the appropriate number of cells in the next column and create an array formula to find all the products in a single operation and place them in the appropriate cells.
7. Examine the formulas for cells within the generated array; notice the braces that indicate an array formula. Try to edit one.

What if It Doesn't Work?

1. The first table needs VLOOKUP. The first argument gives the lookup value or a reference to it, the second references the entire lookup table, and the third specifies the column for the result.

USING DATA SERIES, TABLES, AND ARRAYS

2. The second table needs HLOOKUP; the arguments are as before. The Data Table command should create the lookup values nicely, but you can enter them individually if you prefer.
3. If you have trouble with your array formula, check the formula itself. You don't type the braces. Each operand should be one range, connected with the multiplication operator (*).

SUMMARY

In this chapter, you've learned to create data series of numbers or dates in the increment and style you want. You also learned to create data tables in which Excel uses a single array formula to generate a set of values depending on values you supply for input. Lookup tables are different; they aren't mathematical at all. You can use various lookup functions to reference data in lookup tables, give a lookup value. The result is the corresponding value from the row or column in which a match (or value not greater than) is located.

Excel uses array formulas for several functions you already know. You can define your own array formulas to process data that can be handled as arrays. The matrix functions help simplify array processing.

12 RECORDING AND USING MACROS

Excel offers an extensive macro facility that you can use to make your work even easier. A macro is a set of functions that generate instructions that Excel performs on request. The macro can operate as a function, in which case it is called a function macro, or it can operate by executing commands, much as a miniprogram, in which case it is called a command macro.

Once it is defined, a macro can be used to simplify your work. You use function macros just as you would any built-in functions. A command macro can be selected from a Macro Run list or run with a shortcut key (with CONTROL) that you specify when you define the macro.

One terminology problem you may have is the difference between *function macro* and *macro function*. A function macro is a macro that operates as a function; it has an argument list and returns a single value as a result. Every macro is made up of functions; they can use the worksheet functions you are already familiar with, many special macro functions that duplicate all keyboard actions, and more. The functions that make up a macro are called macro functions.

TYPES OF MACROS

A function macro sets up a new function that works much like the built-in functions on any worksheet. You can create a function macro to calculate a result using any other functions and formulas you need. For example, you could create a function to add three values and divide the sum by five, if that is a procedure you need. The name you assign your function macro can be used just like the names of built-in functions. We'll cover creation and use of function macros in the next chapter.

A command macro sets up a shortcut; it contains a series of commands that operate one after the other when you run the macro. You might set up a command macro to create a chart from a selected range and then add a title to

RECORDING AND USING MACROS

that chart. Or you might want a command macro to establish a set of fonts for a worksheet and apply them to certain cells. Command macros can do anything you can do at the keyboard or with the mouse, and a great deal more. The macro functions Excel makes available let you develop complete programs, with decision making and loops, if necessary, for the macros.

MACRO SHEET

Excel has three types of documents that it can handle: the worksheet, the chart, and the macro sheet. When you use the File New command, the resulting dialog box gives you a choice of Worksheet, Chart, or Macro for the type of file. The macro sheet is more like a worksheet than a chart.

Figure 12.1 shows a macro sheet containing a short command macro. The sheet looks much like a worksheet, with cells, gridlines, and row and column headings. The default status for macro sheets lets you view formulas rather than values in cells, as with worksheets. We've widened column A so you can see the entire command macro; here the first line of the macro includes its name and the additional lines contain macro functions. Notice that these functions, like

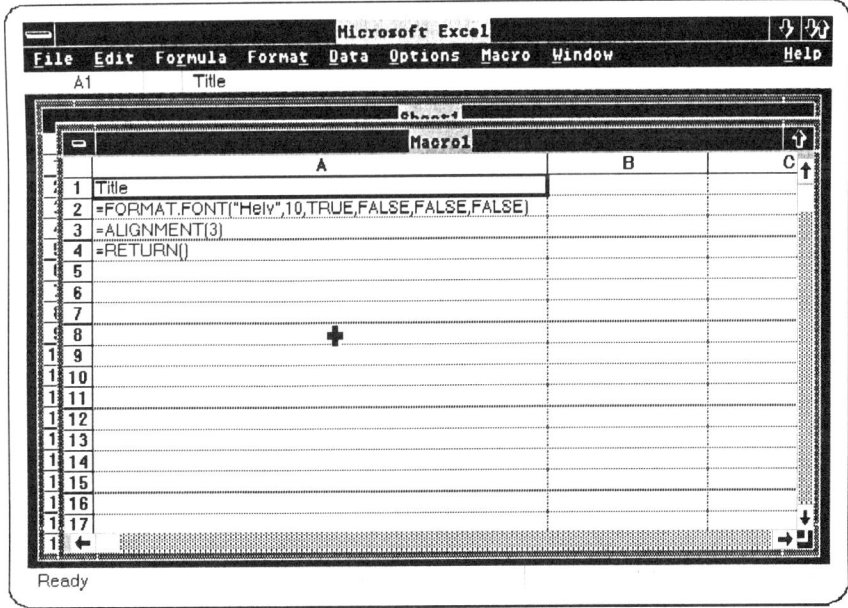

FIGURE 12.1. Macro Sheet with Command Macro

worksheet functions, contain argument lists. You can type macro functions on the sheet or let Excel create them with the macro recorder.

Cell A1 contains the macro name, Title. Each following cell contains a single macro function. Macro functions begin with an equal sign (=), just as worksheet functions do. The final function in each macro is RETURN; it returns control to the point where the macro was started. We'll cover the details of this macro later in this chapter.

The menus and commands available when a macro sheet is active are much the same as when a worksheet is active, so you can do the same editing and file manipulation you can do when you are editing worksheets. The only real difference is in the contents of a few dialog boxes.

In order for you to run a macro, the macro sheet must be open. It may be hidden (with Windows Hide) if you like, but Excel has to be able to find the macro. A single macro sheet can contain many macros, of both types. You might want to put all the macros you use with a particular application on the same macro sheet. If you have a set of generalized macros that you use with many applications or in developing worksheets, you might put them all on the same macro sheet. It really doesn't matter to Excel. As long as the macro sheet is open, Excel can locate the macros. Later in this chapter, we'll talk about organizing the macro sheet, documenting it, and formatting it.

MACRO FUNCTIONS

Every macro is made up of a series of functions, each in a different cell, as you saw in Figure 12.1. Basically there are two types of functions, those that perform an action and those that don't. A function that performs an action may set alignment, adjust the column width, select a range, or open a worksheet. One that doesn't perform an action may return a value or transfer control within the macro. Like all functions, these contain a name and an argument list.

What you do at the keyboard or with the mouse is perform actions; you select cells, issue commands, and type entries. Once you turn on the macro recorder, it traps your actions and converts them to macro functions as it creates a command macro for you. Later, you can edit or modify the functions in the recorded macro as you want. You can even add functions to make the macro more generalized or more useful to you.

All the macro functions are listed in Appendix A, divided into those that perform actions and those that don't. The command equivalent functions are equivalent to commands you select on menus or with shortcut keys. The other action equivalent functions let you scroll, select cells or worksheets, and perform other keyboard and mouse activities.

While you can type a command macro from scratch if you want, the easiest way to create one is with the macro recorder. Once started, the recorder keeps track of all your actions with the keyboard or mouse until you tell it to stop. You can then edit the resulting macro if you want to change it or add additional functions.

COMMAND MACROS

By now, you have probably found yourself performing the same series of actions in Excel many times. You've probably even said to yourself, "Boy, I sure wish there was a command to . . ." Whatever it was, you should be able to create a macro and use it like a command. For example, suppose you like to use the Info window with all the types of information displayed. That takes many steps, including at least five trips to the Info menu to turn on separate features. If you create a macro, you can do it all in one step. Or suppose you need to put the current formatted date and time in a cell, but you need it as a constant value rather than as a function that is recalculated regularly. A command macro can access the date and time with a function, apply a format, then use Edit Copy and Edit Paste Special to save only the value. You'll see a command macro that accomplishes this later in this chapter.

You can also create much more complex command macros. Suppose you have to regularly create a summary report from four separate worksheets, all formatted alike. You can create a macro to open the four worksheets, create a new one to hold the summary report, copy and consolidate what you need, create and title a summary chart, and, finally, print the worksheet with today's date. Your macro may make decisions, such as which of the four supporting worksheets to include in the final report. It may even add messages depending on the gross profit shown in the result or generate a chart to show the profit levels.

THE MACRO RECORDER

Excel's macro recorder automatically records your keyboard or mouse actions and generates equivalent macro functions that accomplish the same thing when

252 ADVANCED EXCEL

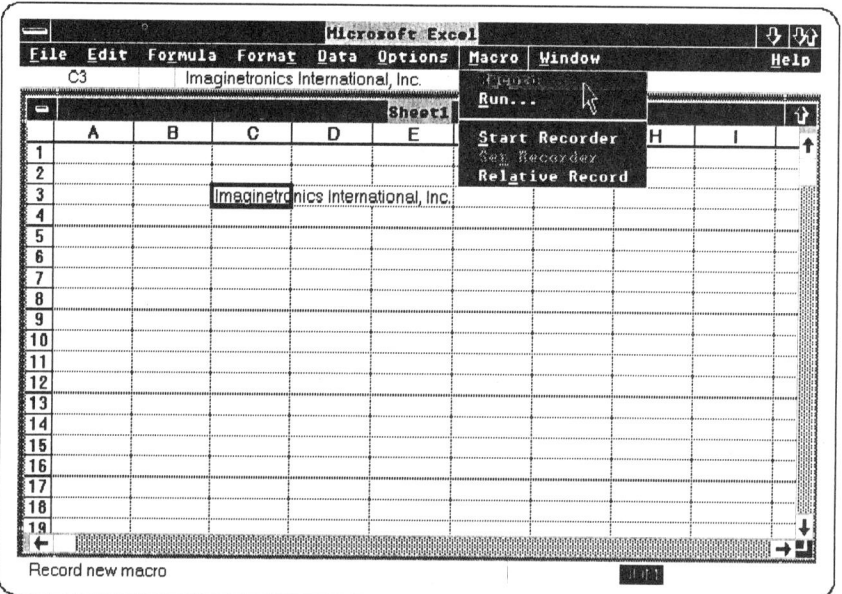

FIGURE 12.2. Macro Menu

you run the macro later. The Macro menu, shown in Figure 12.2, includes the commands you use to control the macro recorder.

With short menus, you see only the top two Macro commands, Record and Run. Macro Record is the easiest way to use the macro recorder; it is replaced with Stop Recorder whenever the recorder is actively recording actions. Macro Run lets you run a recorded macro. Set Recorder and Start Recorder give you more flexibility in recording macros; we'll get back to those commands shortly.

Relative and Absolute Recording

When you record a macro, Excel uses either relative or absolute references, depending on the setting reflected in the Macro menu; absolute references are the default. When the menu command is Relative Record, absolute references are in effect; you can select Relative Record to cause the recorder to use relative references. Relative references are in effect when the menu shows Absolute Record, which you can select to use absolute references. This doesn't affect all the macro functions, of course. Many functions, such as alignment and format, act on the current or selected cell or cells. When you select cells within the recorder, however, the relative/absolute status becomes important. If you start the recorder, then select cell A3 for formatting, Excel uses the absolute reference in the macro, because absolute references are the default. When you run the macro later, it works on cell A3. Check the status of relative/absolute record before starting the macro recorder.

The recorder always uses the R1C1 style of cell reference. If you see a notation such as R2C6 in a recorded macro, it means that Excel used absolute references. If you see R[+1]C[+1] in a macro, Excel used relative references. If you want a function that needs references to be useful from any cell in a worksheet, be sure the recorder will use relative references. If the menu says Absolute Record, it is currently using a relative form. If you want to be sure your macro refers to specific worksheet cells, you may want to use Options Workspace to switch to R1C1 reference style in the worksheet as well. This enables you to compare references in the worksheet and macro sheet directly.

If you want a macro to use relative references at some points and absolute references at others, you can use the Macro menu command during recording or you can modify some in the macro after it is recorded. If you want to use A1 style references, you can change them after the macro is recorded.

Recording a Basic Macro

Suppose you want to create a macro that will use a bold font for a text value in a cell and center the text. (This macro is shown in Figure 12.1.) First select the cell and type the text in it. Then use the Macro Record command. A dialog box appears, as shown in Figure 12.3. This dialog box suggests a macro name and shortcut key. You can accept the suggested ones or enter your own. The name you accept or enter here becomes the macro name; Excel defines it automatically. When you're finished, the macro can be run by selecting the name from the Macro Run command dialog box or by pressing CONTROL + the shortcut key.

Excel suggests macro names like Record1, Record2, and so on; you'll generally want to create your own. We'll name this one Title. You can use any standard Excel name; it must start with a letter, contain only letters, digits, and the . and _ characters. Upper- and lowercase letters are considered the same in Excel names.

The Key field names a shortcut key. Excel starts suggesting with a; you can use any digit or letter, except for e, i, n, or u. Case is critical in shortcut keys— A and a are different shortcut characters. We'll use T to stand for title. After we choose OK to accept the name and shortcut key, the dialog box disappears and the message Recording appears in the status line.

Now you can start performing the actions you want in your macro; you can use the keyboard, the mouse, or a combination. Excel converts whatever you do

254 ADVANCED EXCEL

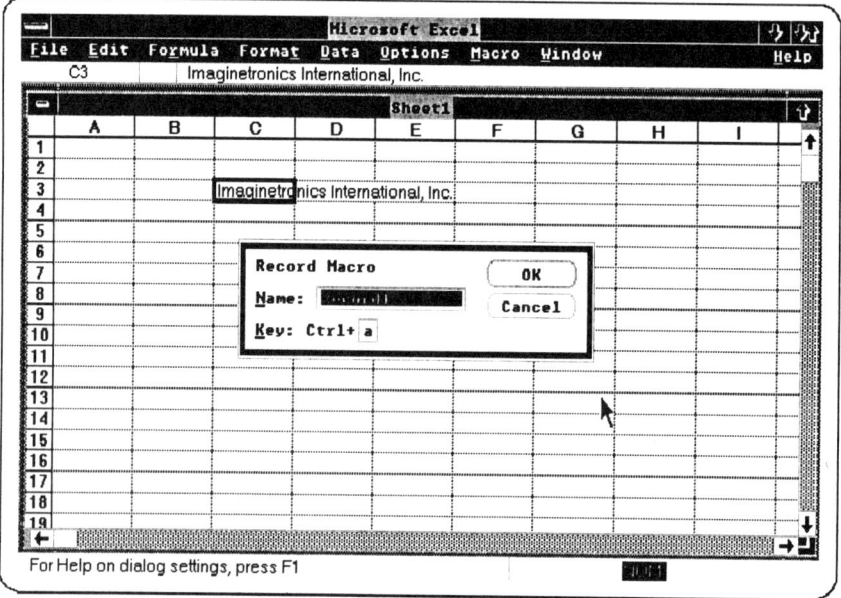

FIGURE 12.3. Macro Record Dialog Box

to macro functions and records them on a macro sheet. If no macro sheet is open, Excel opens one. To create the macro shown in Figure 12.1, we first selected Format Font and changed to the appropriate font for bold; that's number 2 on our system. Then we selected Format Alignment to center the text. Finally, we selected Stop Recorder from the Macro menu where it replaced Record. The Recording message disappeared from the status line.

The recorder records all completed actions except for Help selections. If you choose Cancel to remove a dialog box or stop an entry, the canceled entry won't appear in the recorded macro. If you use Edit Undo, however, both the previous action and the Undo appear in the macro; you can edit it later to remove excess commands. The recorder consolidates your selections; that is, if you make several different selections before performing a specific action such as formatting, the recorder uses only the final selection. The same is true of moving and sizing windows; you can do a great deal of selecting, moving, and sizing while the recorder is running, but only the final one before another action or the end of the macro becomes a permanent part of it.

Examining the Recorded Macro

Once you've recorded a macro, you may want to examine it. Check the Windows menu to locate the macro sheet and activate it; Excel uses names like

Macro1, Macro2, and so forth during each session. When you save macro sheets, you'll use different names; Excel adds an XLM extension.

The macro name you enter in the dialog box appears on the first line. The functions on the following lines replicate your commands. In Figure 12.1, the FORMAT.FONT function selects the font we selected in the Font dialog box. The ALIGNMENT function sets the alignment to 3, its code for Center. The RETURN function ends the macro; when you select Stop Recorder, the RETURN function is inserted. We'll talk about functions in more detail later. For now, just be aware that Excel has a different function for each keyboard or mouse action you might take. You can generally tell what the function's purpose is from its name, like FORMAT.FONT or ALIGNMENT, but interpreting the arguments generally requires investigating the documentation.

Another Macro

Let's examine the steps to create a longer macro. Suppose you want a macro to place the company name, in bold font and centered, in cell C2, then put the current date centered in cell C3 and make cell A5 active before ending the macro. Suppose you go through these steps:

1. Choose Macro Record and enter a name and shortcut key.
2. Select cell C1 and type the company name.
3. Discover you entered it in the wrong cell and choose Edit Undo, then select cell C2 and type the company name again.
4. Select the appropriate font and alignment.
5. Select cell C3 and type the function =NOW(), then format it as m/dd/yy.
6. Select cell A5, then choose Macro Stop Recorder.

Figure 12.4 shows the resulting recorded macro. Notice that it is in column B; when you choose Macro Record it always places the new macro in the next completely blank column. We've widened the column so you can read the entire functions. Later in this chapter you'll see how to control where macros are placed.

The macro starts with the name entered in the dialog box. Then you see a SELECT function followed by a FORMULA function. These functions were generated in response to step 2. The UNDO function and the following SE-

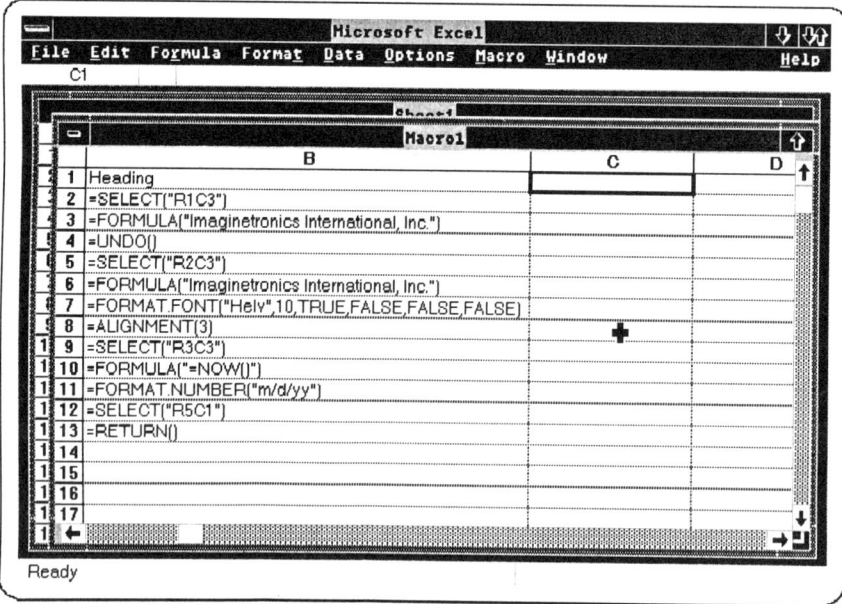

FIGURE 12.4. Sample Macro

LECT and FORMULA functions were generated by step 3. You can delete these three functions if you like; they will be repeated each time you run the macro and slow it down. The SELECT function makes a cell or range active in preparation for a command. Here the recorder is using absolute references. The FORMULA function enters data into a cell. Notice that it can include text, as in cells B3 and B6, or functions, as in cell B10. The FORMAT.FONT and ALIGNMENT functions are equivalent to Excel commands. All the functions in the recorded macro will be executed every time you run it.

RUNNING A MACRO

To run a recorded macro, you can select the macro name from the Macro Run dialog box or press its shortcut key with CONTROL. To run the macro from Figure 12.1, just select any cell containing text, then press CONTROL + T. The font and alignment are adjusted before your very eyes. If you select Macro Run, you'll see a dialog box like the one shown in Figure 12.5. The list box lists all the macros defined on all the open macro sheets. Here, the only open macro sheet is Macro1, and it contains the macros Title and Heading. Notice that Excel uses an external reference, since the macro is not defined on the active

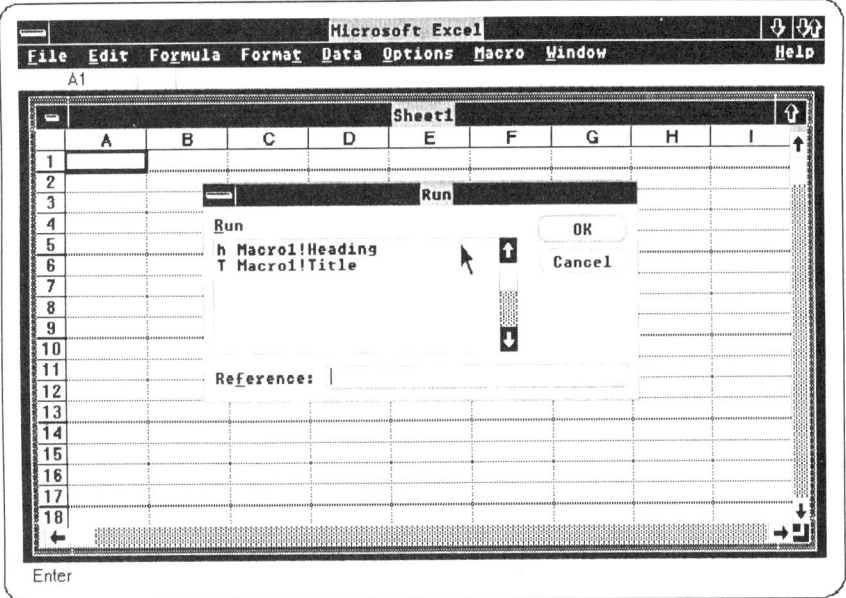

FIGURE 12.5. Macro Run Dialog Box

worksheet. The single character at the left edge of the list box is the shortcut character; we defined T as the key for quick use of the Title macro and h for the Heading macro. To run any macro, just select it in the Macro Run dialog box and choose OK or press the control key with the shortcut key.

EDITING A MACRO

A macro sheet can be edited just as a worksheet can. You might want to remove some functions. For example, suppose you used an Excel command, then removed it with Edit Undo as in the Heading macro. You can remove both the command and the Undo function from the resulting macro. If you like, you can use Edit Clear (or the Delete key) to remove functions; Excel just skips over blank cells in the macro. Or you can use Edit Delete and shift cells upward to maintain a solid macro.

You might also want to add additional functions to change or customize the effect of the macro. You'll learn to handle most of those in the next chapter. In general, editing a macro sheet is exactly like editing a worksheet. You can even create a macro from scratch by typing all the functions in yourself. In general, it's easier to record the basic macro, then modify it to meet your needs.

SUGGESTED EXERCISE

1. Bring up Excel so that the only open worksheet is an empty one. Select cell A3 and turn on the macro recorder.
2. Name the macro Practice and assign shortcut key P.
3. Type a report name in cell C3, then center it and use a bold font.
4. Select cell A5 and type "Administration."
5. In cells A6 through A9 type "Clerical," "Manufacturing," "Marketing," and "Distribution."
6. Adjust the width of column A so that the complete words are fitted in the column.
7. Stop the recorder.
8. Edit the macro to remove the "Distribution" cell.
9. Select cell C12 and run the macro using its shortcut key. Notice that it puts the report name in cell C12, but uses the same cells as before for other entries; that's because it is using Absolute Recording of cell locations.
10. Open a new worksheet, select cell A3 and run the macro from the Macro Run dialog box.

What if It Doesn't Work?

1. Your macro should start with the name Practice in cell A1. The FORMULA function sets up each text entry, and a SELECT function precedes all text entries except the first. The FORMAT.FONT and ALIGNMENT functions should look much like those in Figure 12.1.
2. If you have extra functions in your macro, don't worry about it. Use Edit Delete to remove them.
3. If your macro recorder doesn't work at all, try to create a new macro sheet first (File New Macro), then try again.

CONTROLLING RECORDED MACRO PLACEMENT

When you select Macro Record when no macro sheet is open, Excel opens a new one. It places the macro name you enter in cell A1 and places the macro functions in column A, one function per row. It uses absolute references for all cell references needed in the functions unless you change it to Relative Record on the Macro Menu.

If a macro sheet is already open when you select Macro Record, Excel starts the next macro in the next completely blank column; a second macro on Macro1 with Macro Record appears in column B. A third macro appears in column C, and so forth.

Controlling Macro Sheets

Macro Record automatically opens a macro sheet if none is open. Alternatively, you can open a new macro sheet with the File New command or open an existing one with File Open. If you use Macro Record to start recording, the macro will be recorded in the next completely blank column.

Setting the Recorder Range

You can force Excel to record macros in different parts of the sheet by setting a recorder range with the Macro Set Recorder range command to tell Excel where to put the macro, then using Macro Start Recorder instead of Macro Record to start the recording. When you use Macro Set Recorder, Excel creates a named range (Recorder) to hold the next macro recorded by the Macro Start Recorder command. The Macro Record command, however, continues to use the next blank column whenever you select it.

If you select a single blank cell before you choose Set Recorder, the macro recorder range begins there and continues to the bottom of that column. If necessary, it will then continue at the top of the next column. If you select a cell that isn't blank before choosing Set Recorder, the recorder looks down the column for the last nonblank cell and starts in the next cell. If it finds a cell that contains RETURN, it starts there, overlaying the RETURN function; this lets you use the recorder to extend a function.

If you select a blank range that extends over more than one column, macro functions will begin in the first column, continue to the second, and so forth, until the range is full. When a recorder range is full, the recorder stops and you see a warning message. If you select a range in which the first cell is not blank, Excel thinks the range is full and displays a warning message.

Before you set the recorder range, you must decide where on the macro sheet you want the macro to appear. For example, suppose you used Macro Record for the first macro. You decide you want all your macros to be in column A, so you can use column B for explanations of the commands. Select a cell a few lines below the recorded macro and type the name you intend to use for the new macro. Then select the next cell down and choose Macro Set Recorder.

When you control the placement of macros in a macro sheet by using Start Recorder instead of Macro Record, you must set a new recorder range for each macro; if you don't, Excel assumes you are adding to the former macro and just extends it. If you want your macro to extend over more than one column, you can select a range before setting the recorder.

Starting Macro Placement

As mentioned earlier, Macro Record always uses the next completely blank column, whereas Macro Start Recorder uses the recorder range. Another difference between the two is that the Macro Record command gives you a dialog box for the name and shortcut key and automatically defines them. When you use Macro Start Recorder, you have to provide and define the name and shortcut key before you can use the macro.

Once you have set the recorder range, you start the recorder with Macro Start Recorder. The Recording message in the status line appears immediately; you won't see a dialog box for the name. Complete the commands or movements needed for the macro, then choose Stop Recorder.

To create another macro on the same sheet, type the new macro name, then select the next cell down before setting the recorder range. Then return to the worksheet and record the macro. If you neglect to reset the recorder range, the new macro will be added to the earlier one, replacing the RETURN function and extending down the column or through the range.

MACRO NAMING

If you used Start Recorder to record your macro, you need to provide and define a name. If you didn't type a name in the macro sheet before recording, you can edit the macro sheet to add the name on the cell just above the macro. In either case, you must define the name with the Formula Define Name command before Excel will recognize it as a macro. Select the cell containing the name on the macro sheet and issue the command. Figure 12.6 shows the resulting dialog box. Notice that it lists all the named entities in the sheet that it knows about, including Recorder. Recorder is the name of the current recorder range. We used Macro Set Recorder with cell A7 selected, so the recorder range includes the rest of column A.

If you selected the cell containing the name before selecting Formula Define Name, that name and its reference appear in the box. You have to select the type of macro in the bottom part of the box, either function or command. If you select command, as we have here, you can also enter a shortcut key; the shortcut key is not required.

Once the name is defined, it will appear in the Macro Run list box along with its shortcut key whenever the macro sheet containing it is open. If you assign the same shortcut key to several macros, the one that appears first in the Macro Run list box takes effect.

RECORDING AND USING MACROS

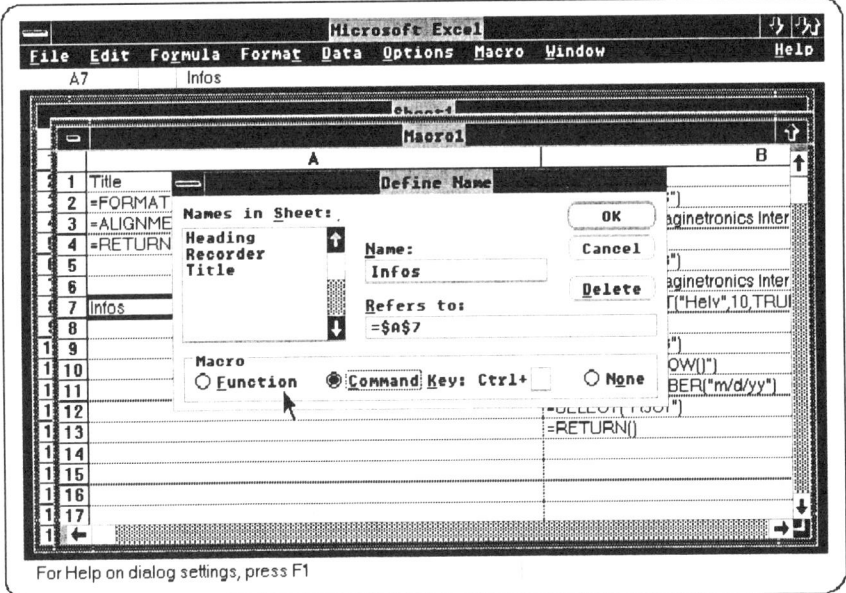

FIGURE 12.6. Formula Define (Macro) Name Dialog Box

FORMATTING THE MACRO SHEET

If you use macros to any great extent, you'll want to format and arrange your macro sheets so they are easy to read, easy to reference, and, above all, easy to modify. This generally means you want to use a nondefault format. Figure 12.7 shows a format many Excel users find acceptable. Notice that the macros themselves are stored in column B. Column A is used for names, both macro names and names of entities within the macros. Column C is used for documentation, explanation of any macro functions that aren't completely obvious. The first macro on this sheet opens the Info Window and turns on all its display features. The second macro creates a chart from the selected range of cells, changes its gallery type, then adds a title.

If you use this format, you'll record macros only in column B; that means you have to use Macro Set Recorder before each macro. And you'll have to use Macro Start Recorder to start recording each one. Finally, you'll have to define each macro name individually. The advantages are great, however. You can page through the macro sheet to find macros. You can delete or insert rows in editing macros wherever you want, since no row extends across more than one macro.

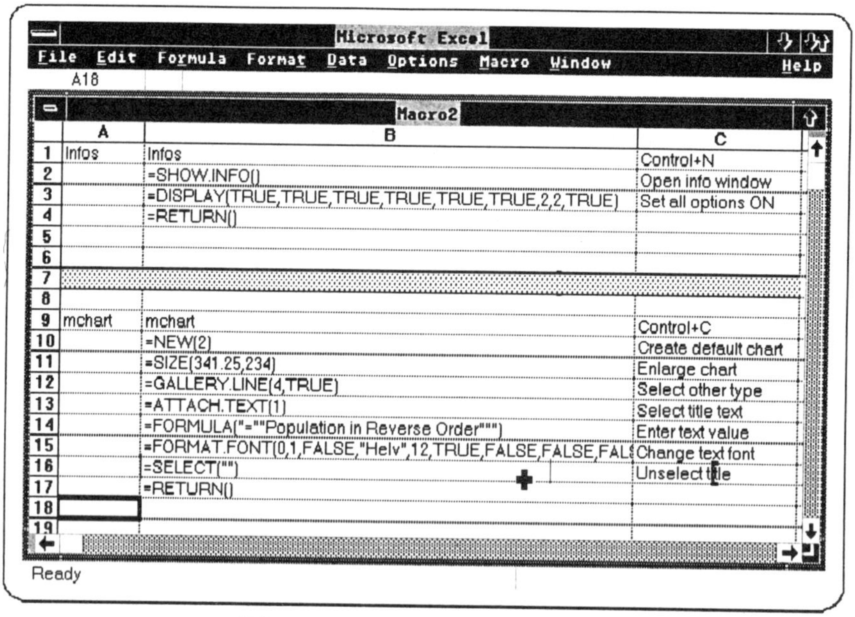

FIGURE 12.7. Formatted Macro Sheet

In the next chapter, you'll learn more uses for names in macros. As in worksheets, however, names make functions and formulas easier to read and understand. And they are more stable than references, since Excel updates them automatically.

DISPLAYING DIALOG BOXES THROUGH MACROS

You might want to provide a dialog box in a macro function rather than assume a default value and bypass it; you can do this by inserting a question mark at the end of the function name. For example, to cause the macro to stop at the Format Font dialog box, you can change the function to read =FORMAT.FONT?(. . . This causes the requested features to become the default, but not to take effect until the user chooses OK or changes the request. Appendix A indicates which command equivalent functions can be converted to dialog box functions. You can include as many dialog box functions as you want in a macro, but remember that the user has to react to each one. The dialog box functions must be edited; that is, you must insert the ? following the function name and before the argument list.

REFERENCING OTHER WORKSHEETS

Many macros reference other worksheets. Suppose you record a macro to open the Info window, turn on all the cell information fields, size both the original worksheet and the info window to show on the screen, activate the worksheet, and end the macro. Figure 12.8 shows the recorded macro. Here the ACTIVATE function references the original worksheet as a constant, since it is expected to be open on the screen. If you use this macro with another worksheet, it will open an info window, set all the display fields, and then activate the same BUDGET.XLS worksheet.

Notice the SIZE function in Figure 12.8. You never have to figure out the numeric arguments for the such functions as SIZE and MOVE; Excel does it automatically while the macro is recording. When you select the worksheet, Excel generates the ACTIVATE function. When you select the Info window, Excel generates the SHOW.INFO function. This macro activates a specific worksheet after opening the Info window; it assumes that the Info window was opened from BUDGET1.XLS. You'll see how to generalize it in the next chapter.

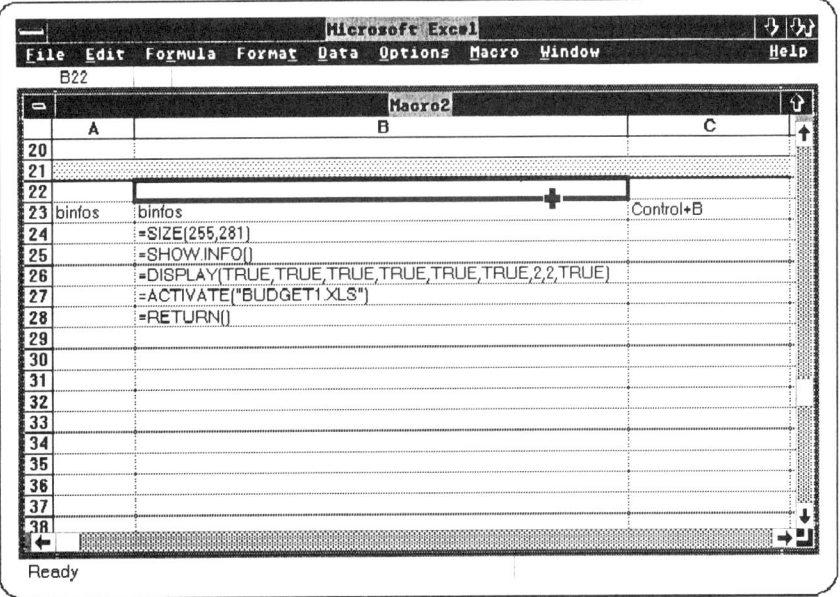

FIGURE 12.8. Recorded Info Window Macro

MACRO RUNNING ERRORS

Errors can occur when a macro is running, just as when you issue a command. If a macro function issues a command that is invalid, you'll see a message. If it tries to access a file that isn't open, as when you run the macro from Figure 12.8 on another worksheet when BUDGET.XLS isn't open, you'll see a message box like the one in Figure 12.9. The box tells you the macro cell where it encountered the error (Cell B27 on macro sheet Macro2) and gives you three choices. Halt stops the macro where it is; it doesn't undo any steps that are completed however. Step continues in the macro, but pauses after each function and displays a step box. Figure 12.10 shows the single step box. Continue tells Excel to ignore that function and continue with the macro. You must be aware that the results may not be as you expect. For example, in this macro, if Excel can't activate the worksheet, a following SIZE function would apply to the Info window instead.

The Step box shows the current cell in the macro being executed, the function in that cell, and the same three choices as in the macro error box. Stepping through the macro is a good technique for finding problems in a

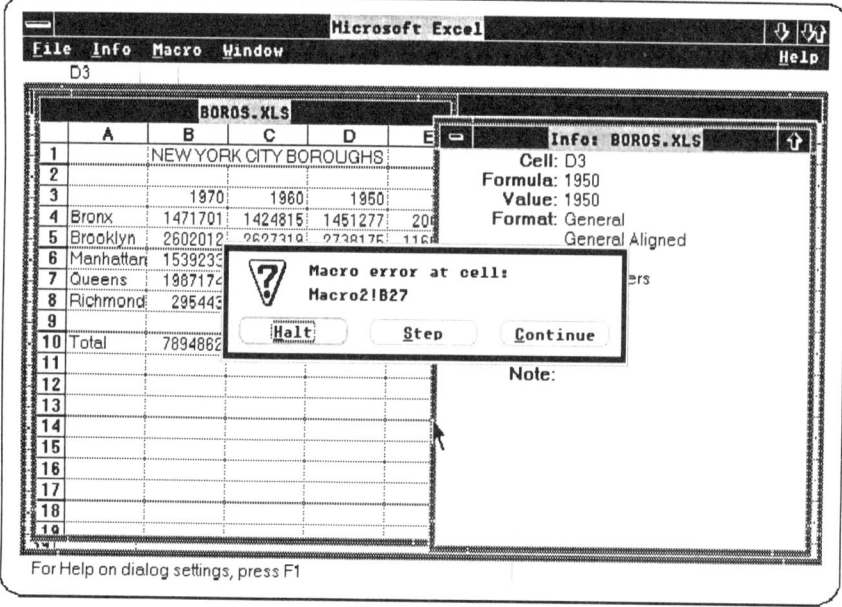

FIGURE 12.9. Macro Error Dialog Box

RECORDING AND USING MACROS

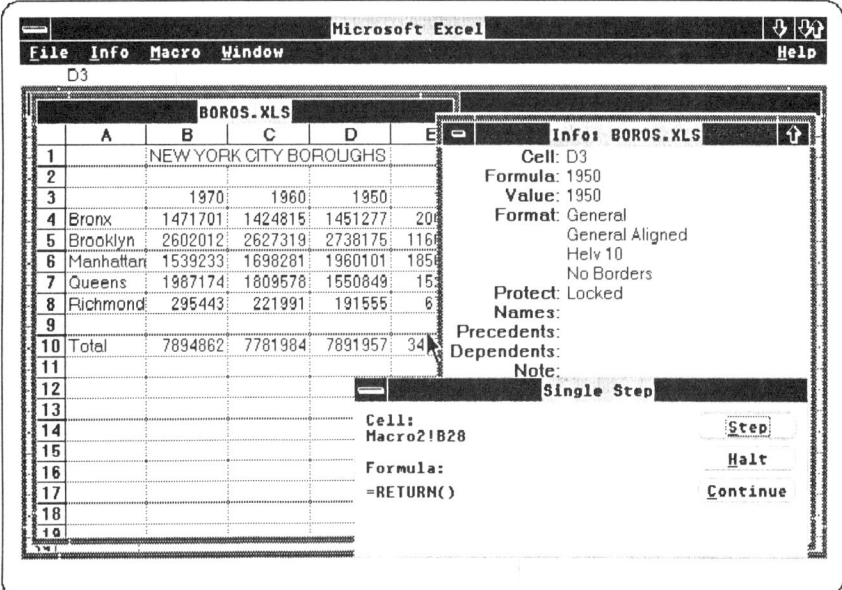

FIGURE 12.10. Single Step Dialog Box

macro, because you can see the effect of each function in the macro on the screen.

SAMPLE RECORDED MACROS

Let's look at a few more recorded macros so that you get a better feel for the types of actions they can perform. In the next chapter, you'll see how these macros can be modified to provide more flexibility or generality, whatever is needed. Figure 12.11 shows the printed text of a macro that generates the framework of a worksheet. This macro provides the title, adjusts column width, turns off gridlines, adds borders, and enters formulas before selecting an active cell for the first data entry. We've formatted the macro sheet and added documentation, leaving space for names to be added in column A.

Figure 12.12 shows a macro that can be used as soon as Excel is initiated and the macro sheet opened and hidden. It removes the active worksheet (Sheet1), opens a different worksheet and chart, arranges them on the screen, then adds a note to cell A1 of the worksheet giving the user's name as part of the ongoing documentation.

ADVANCED EXCEL

	A	B	C
1	Frame	Frame	Control+F
2		=FORMULA("WEEKLY WORKSHEET")	Title
3		=SELECT("R3C1")	column heads
4		=FORMULA("Number")	Number
5		=SELECT("R3C2")	
6		=FORMULA("Name")	Name
7		=COLUMN.WIDTH(23)	
8		=SELECT("R3C3")	Adjust width
9		=FORMULA("Hours")	Hours
10		=SELECT("R3C4")	
11		=FORMULA("Wage")	Wage
12		=SELECT("R3C5")	
13		=FORMULA("Pay")	Pay
14		=SELECT("R5C5")	
15		=FORMULA("=RC[-2]*RC[-1]")	Formula
16		=SELECT("R5C5:R21C5")	range to
17		=FILL.DOWN()	fill with formula
18		=SELECT("R5C1:R21C5")	
19		=BORDER(TRUE,FALSE,FALSE,FALSE,FALSE,FALSE)	Set outer border
20		=SELECT("R4C3:R21C5")	
21		=FORMAT.NUMBER("0.00")	Set number format
22		=SELECT("R5C1")	Select data cell
23		=RETURN()	

FIGURE 12.11. Worksheet Framework Macro

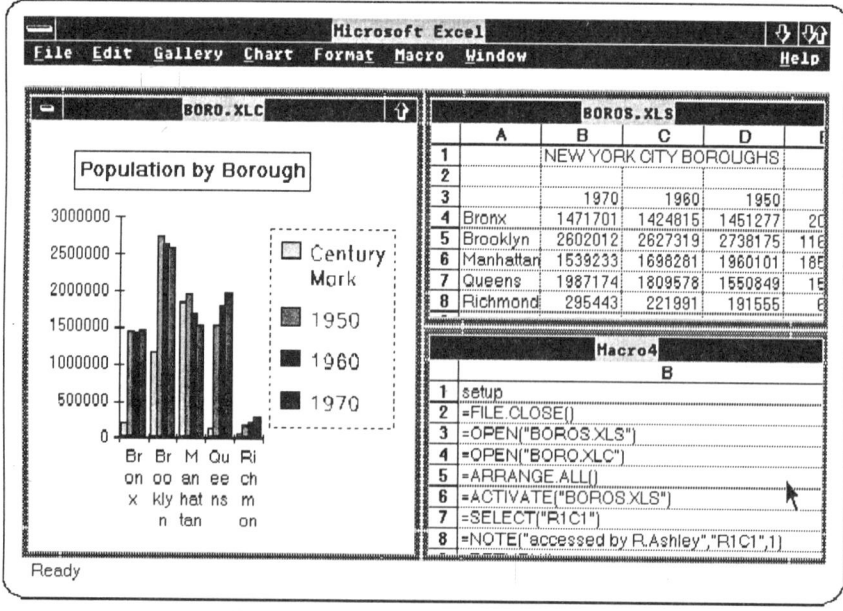

FIGURE 12.12. File Open and Note Macro

SUGGESTED EXERCISE

1. Create a new macro sheet and set the recorder range in column B. Use the name Prac2 in cell B1. Set the recorder so it will use relative references.
2. Start a new macro. Put a report name in cell C3, centered and in bold.
3. In cells A5 through A9 place "Administration," "Clerical," "Manufacturing," "Marketing," and "Distribution." Adjust the column width so that all values are displayed.
4. Make cell B5 active and stop the recorder. Activate the macro sheet, then define Prac2 and assign a shortcut key.
5. Examine the recorded macro; add the macro name and shortcut key in cell A1, then define the name. Modify the macro so it will display the Format Font dialog box with a bold font as the default. Return to the worksheet. Type a new report name in cell D12, then run the macro. Notice the result.
6. Enter numeric values between 500 and 1000 in cells B5 through B9 in preparation for a new macro.
7. Set a new macro recorder range a few rows below Prac2 in column B. Return to the worksheet and start the recorder.
8. Create a pie chart of the values. Add a title and legend. Then stop the recorder and examine the macro. Define the name and add documentation about the name and its shortcut key. If you have any extra functions, delete them.
9. Erase the chart generated while the macro was recording, and run the macro again. If it has any problems, correct the macro.

What if It Doesn't Work?

1. If you see any Macro error boxes, step through the macro until you figure out the error. Correct if obvious, otherwise wait till the next chapter, when you'll have more information.
2. Edit the macros if necessary. For example, if you used Edit Undo or repeated steps, correct them.
3. If you're still having trouble recording macros, create a few of your own. Use more than one worksheet. Try sizing and changing worksheets.

SUMMARY

Macros save a great deal of time in helping you perform operations with just a few keystrokes. Any series of operations you perform regularly is a good candidate for a macro. Excel provides a macro recorder to help you build macros by trapping your keyboard actions.

This chapter has covered recording, editing, and running basic macros using macro functions generated by the macro recorder. You've also seen how to manipulate the recorder to control whether references are relative or absolute and to determine where macros are placed on the macro sheet.

The next chapter focuses on using macro functions in creating more complex and more useful macros, including function macros.

13 MACRO DEVELOPMENT

In the last chapter, you learned to record and use basic command macros in Excel. You've seen many macro functions by this time. In this chapter, you'll learn to use many more macro functions in constructing both function and command macros. You'll learn to define and use function macros in any worksheet. You'll also see how you can program macros to make decisions and branch, much as in a small computer program. Keep in mind that you don't have to use all the features, but it's nice to know the features are available. If the macro programming features are a bit beyond your inclinations, you may be able to coerce a colleague into creating the macros you need.

MACRO FUNCTIONS

Every macro is made up of a series of functions, each in a different cell. You can use any of the worksheet functions in a macro. In addition, Excel offers hundreds more functions you can use only in macros, but we won't be covering the details of all of them in this book. When you use the Formula Paste Function command and a macro sheet is active, the list box contains all the macro functions in alphabetical order. Figure 13.1 shows the beginning of the list. If you turn on the Paste Arguments field before selecting a function, text indicating the type of its arguments will be included in the formula bar when the function appears there.

Appendix A lists all the macro functions, divided by type, as introduced here. You've already seen how the macro recorder generates command equivalent functions and the other action equivalent functions. You saw in the last chapter how to insert a ? symbol to cause the function to generate a dialog box. The Microsoft Excel Functions and Macros reference covers all the functions in detail in alphabetical order, including argument lists and examples. We'll overview them here so you can relate to the following discussions.

270 ADVANCED EXCEL

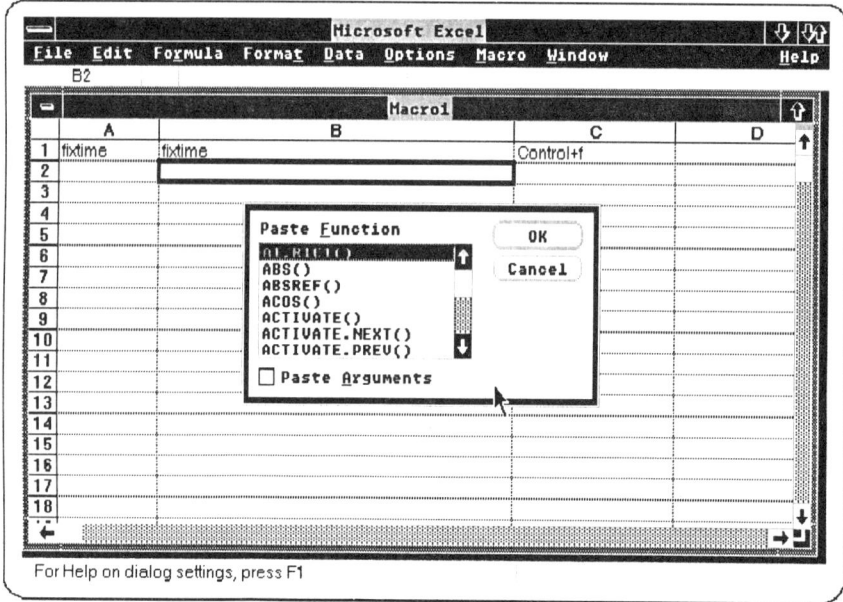

FIGURE 13.1. Formula Paste (Macro) Function Dialog Box

What you do at the keyboard or with the mouse is perform actions; you select cells, issue commands, and type entries. Command macros can contain functions that perform actions, but function macros cannot. These are the types of macro functions that perform actions:

Command Equivalent Functions These functions are equivalent to commands. Except for a very few, each command on each menu has an equivalent macro function that you can use in command macros. Appendix A lists the command equivalent functions arranged by menu and command; the reference manual treats these in alphabetical order. Like other functions, these have argument lists, which are also detailed in the reference manual. The argument lists provide all the information you would otherwise supply through a dialog box. Excel generates the appropriate argument list when you use the macro recorder to create macros. Figure 13.2 shows a command macro that uses mostly command equivalent macro functions. The column on the right can be used for explanations to help document the macro. This macro uses the worksheet NOW function to get the current date and time, then selects a specific format for it and adjusts the column width. Finally it copies the cell onto itself (in the PASTE.SPECIAL argument list, 3 means values), ends the copy, and returns control to the worksheet.

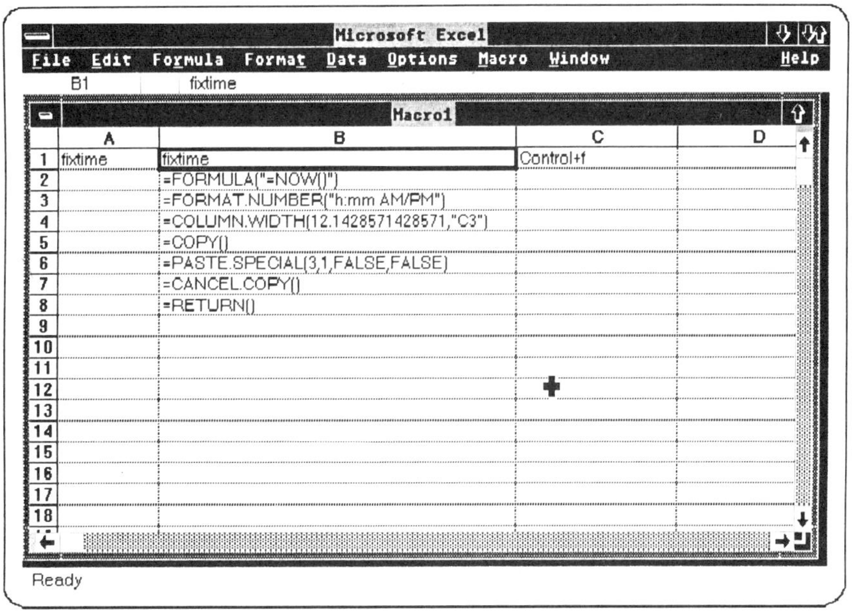

MACRO DEVELOPMENT

FIGURE 13.2. Macro with Command Equivalent Functions

Dialog Box Functions These functions are like the command equivalent functions, but with a question mark following the function name. The result is to execute the command, then display the dialog box that would result if you used the command yourself. The argument list sets up the default values to appear in the dialog box. The user can choose OK to accept those values or make any desired changes first. When OK is chosen, the macro continues. The macro recorder doesn't generate dialog box functions, but you can edit the macro produced by the recorder to insert the question mark after a function name. Figure 13.3 shows the macro from Figure 13.2 modified so the user can select any time format. When the FORMAT.NUMBER function is executed, the standard Format Number dialog box is displayed, with the specified format highlighted. The user can choose OK to accept it or select a different format.

Customizing Functions These are special functions that let you create customized menus and dialog boxes. You can use an INPUT function to get user input, add ALERT and MESSAGE information as needed, or use special functions to develop custom menu bars and dialog boxes, to handle text file input and output, or start other applications. The macro recorder doesn't generate customizing functions; you'll learn to use

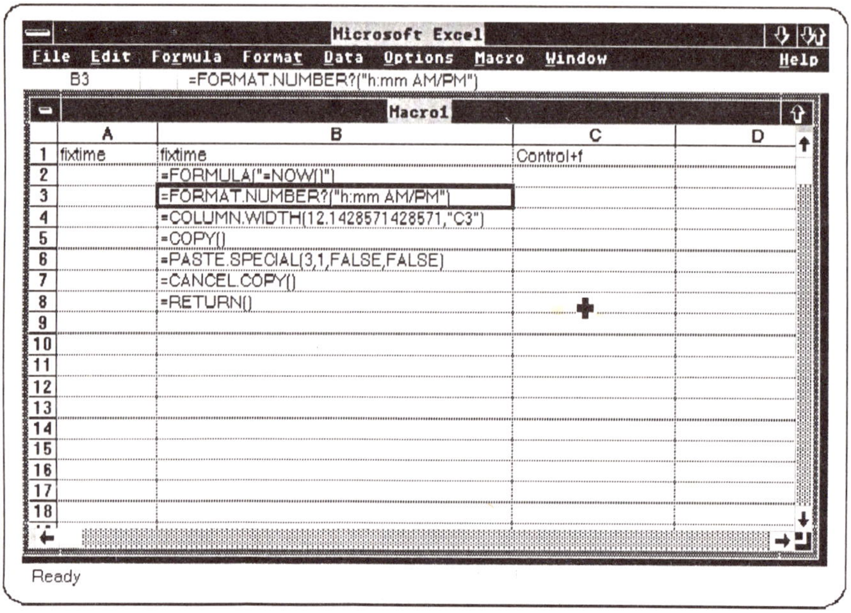

272 ADVANCED EXCEL

FIGURE 13.3. Macro with Dialog Box Function

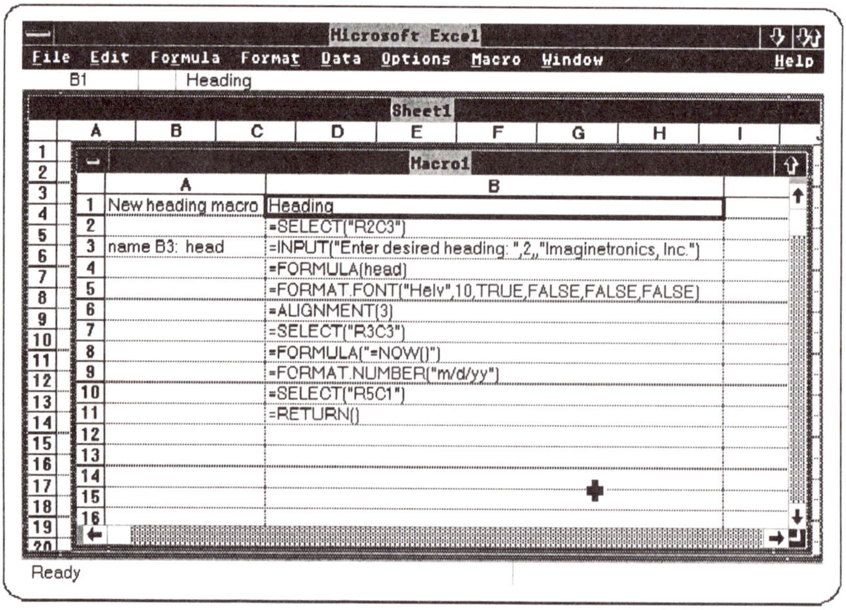

FIGURE 13.4. Macro with Customized Input

MACRO DEVELOPMENT

several of them in this chapter and the next. Figure 13.4 shows the macro from Figure 12.4 modified so that the user is asked to input the text before the font and alignment changes are applied. In this macro, the INPUT function creates a generic dialog box that looks like the one in Figure 13.5. The user can choose OK to accept the default or enter a different value. The FORMULA function places the value returned by INPUT in the current cell, where it is assigned a font and aligned as in the macro. We'll examine the INPUT, ALERT, and MESSAGE functions in more detail later in this chapter.

Other Action Equivalent Functions These functions perform actions that don't correspond to Excel commands; selecting cells, scrolling, cancelling marquees, and finding the next selected cell are all included here. The recorder generates these when you perform the action.

There are two types of macro functions that don't perform an action. These functions can be used in either function or command macros; only the RETURN function is generated by the macro recorder.

Control Functions These tell a running macro to do something other than continue performing functions in sequence. They may use a GOTO to

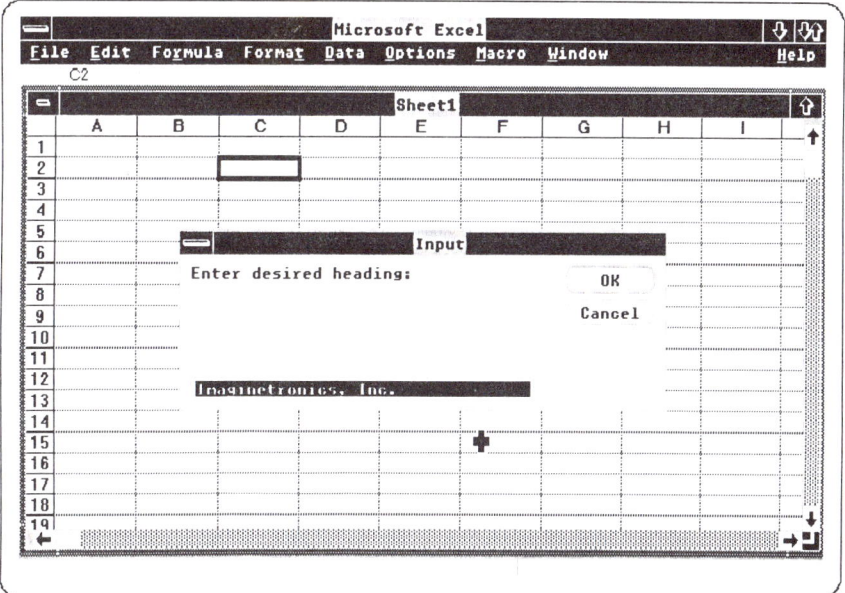

FIGURE 13.5. Resulting Generic Input Dialog Box

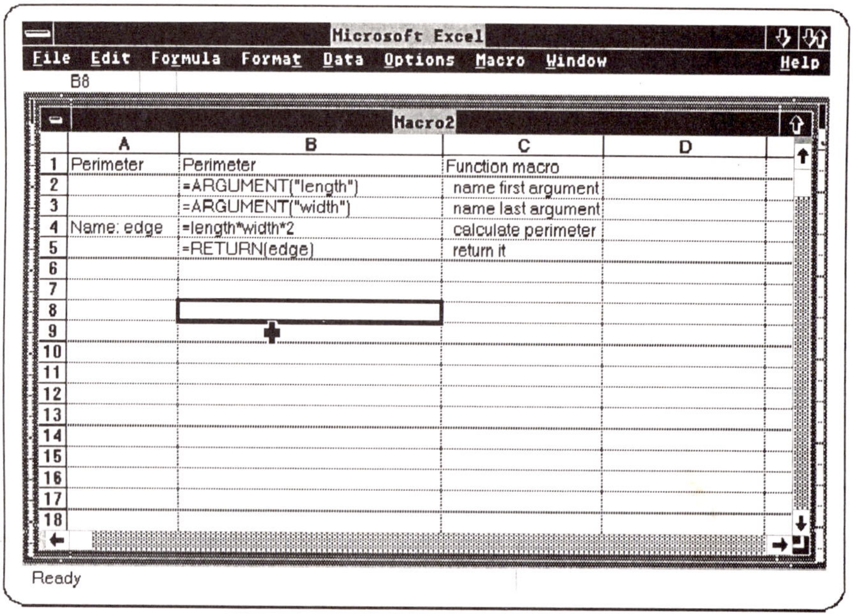

274 ADVANCED EXCEL

```
                      Microsoft Excel
File  Edit  Formula  Format  Data  Options  Macro  Window         Help
  B8
                            Macro2
        A              B                  C              D
1  Perimeter      Perimeter         Function macro
2                 =ARGUMENT("length")  name first argument
3                 =ARGUMENT("width")   name last argument
4  Name: edge    =length*width*2      calculate perimeter
5                 =RETURN(edge)        return it
```

FIGURE 13.6. Function Macro

transfer somewhere else, start a loop, or establish an argument value. The RETURN function returns control to the entity that started the macro. The RETURN function is shown in every macro you've seen so far. Figure 13.6 shows a function macro that uses ARGUMENT and RETURN macro functions.

Value Returning Functions These functions return values that you can use later in the macro; all the worksheet functions return values. In addition, you can get the reference of the active cell, an open worksheet, the contents of a cell, or convert text to a reference.

All the functions can be used in command macros. Function macros can use any worksheet functions as well as macro functions that don't perform any action.

FUNCTION MACROS

Function macros are made up of a series of functions that return a single value as the result. In a function macro you can use any worksheet functions and any macro functions that don't perform any action. Once defined, you use a macro function just as you do the built-in functions. It even appears in the Formula Paste Function dialog box, at the end of the list of built-in functions. If you press End when the function list box is active, the last function in the box is selected; you can use the uparrow to move upward and select a different one of your functions.

Designing a Function Macro

Before writing a function macro, you have to give it a bit of thought. First of all, make sure Excel doesn't already have a function that does what you want. If not, you have to make some decisions:

1. What value do you want the function to return? What data type is it?
2. What information will you supply to the function? What data types are these arguments?
3. What steps are necessary to get from the input (the arguments) to the output (the returned value)?

Excel uses a code for data types of arguments and results, as shown in Figure 13.7. You can combine the numbers except for 8 (Reference) and 64 (Array). A value of 6 means the argument (or result) can be either text or logical value.

If you don't select a specific or combined data type, Excel assumes the argument or result is either number, text, or logical, and converts it to one of those types if it can. If the value can't be converted appropriately, Excel uses the value #VALUE! instead.

Excel doesn't record function macros, so you start by opening a new or an

```
 1    Number
 2    Text
 4    Logical
 8    Reference
16    Error
64    Array
```

FIGURE 13.7. Data Code Types

existing macro sheet. Use the same type of formatting and documentation as for command macros. An easy and useful style is to put names in column A, macro functions in column B, and explanations in column C. Excel ignores cells that don't begin with the = symbol, so you can include names and extra information wherever you like. And you'll have to define the macro name and specify that it is a function macro on the macro sheet. The easiest way to do this is to type the name in the cell above the first line of the macro, select Formula Define Name, select Function macro, and choose OK.

Every function macro includes the ARGUMENT and RETURN functions. Many will need the RESULT function as well. Figure 13.8 shows the formats of these three functions. Notice that the ARGUMENT function has two forms.

The RESULT function is optional; you'll use it if the value returned is not the default data type (number, text, or logical). If you need RESULT, include it as the first function in the macro, immediately following the macro name.

The RETURN function specifies what value is returned; the value may be a reference or a name of a cell or range within the macro, often the cell just preceding the RETURN function as in Figure 13.6. If the function returns an array, the reference is a range reference. When used in a command macro, the RETURN function has no arguments, but one is required in a function macro.

A function macro can have from one to thirteen arguments; you need an ARGUMENT function for each one. The ARGUMENT function names the argument and may provide a place to store it on the macro sheet. The first form shown in Figure 13.8 is generally used; the second form includes a storage location within the macro for the argument, which isn't very often needed. You specify a name for the argument and a code for the data type if it isn't text, logical, or numeric. The name defines the value used as the argument; you use the name only within the macro. In Figure 13.6, the function macro has two arguments, length and width. No matter what values the user enters for the function, whether they are references, values, or whatever, the macro simply uses the names in calculating the desired result.

The ARGUMENT functions must be coded in sequence; that is, the first ARGUMENT function applies to the first argument in the function, the second ARGUMENT function applies to the second argument in the function, and so

```
ARGUMENT(name_text,data_type_code)

ARGUMENT(name_text,data_type_code,ref)

RETURN(reference)

RESULT(data_type_code)
```

FIGURE 13.8. Macro Functions for Function Macros

MACRO DEVELOPMENT

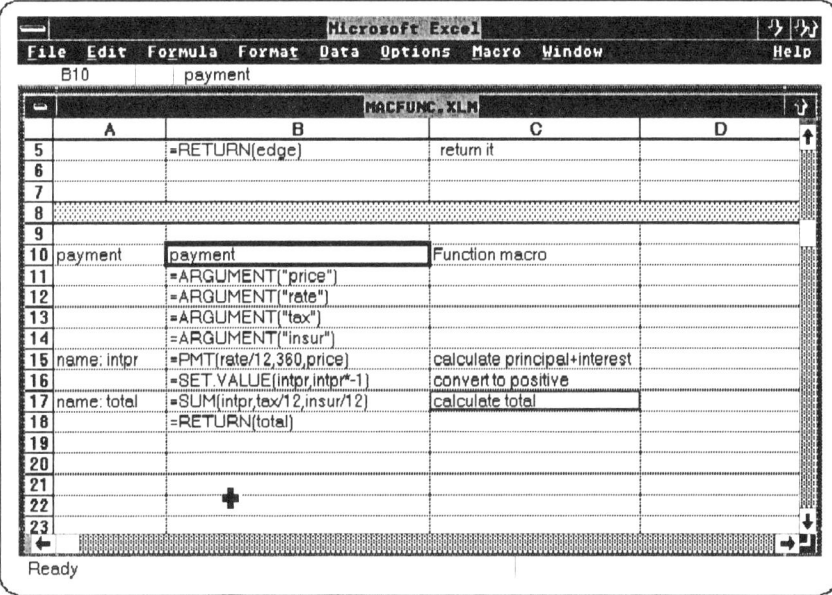

FIGURE 13.9. Function Macro with Four Arguments

on. If an argument is omitted when the function is used, Excel uses #N/A in its place.

Figure 13.9 shows a complete function macro that uses four arguments. The name has been defined so the function appears in the Formula Paste Function dialog box.

The function requires four arguments to calculate the monthly payment on a loan or mortgage. The first argument is the complete amount financed, the second the interest rate. The rate can be entered as a decimal or a percent (as in 9.5% or .095). The PMT function calculates the interest and principal for each payment; the name intpr is assigned to cell B15. The third argument is the yearly tax required and the fourth is the yearly insurance; both values must be divided by twelve and the resulting amounts added to the monthly principal and interest payment. Cell B17 (named total) adds the monthly values and produces a value that is returned when the macro ends.

SUGGESTED EXERCISE

1. Open a new macro sheet and create a function macro that will receive two arguments, the unit price and the quantity. The function will multiply the two and return the result with 6% tax added. First type the macro name, followed by two ARGUMENT functions.

2. Add a formula to calculate the desired result. Use the names assigned in your ARGUMENT functions in the formula.
3. Add a RETURN function.
4. Define a name for the macro; be sure to specify that it is a function macro.
5. Activate a worksheet and try out the macro by using it as a function. Use constant values for the arguments.
6. Type values into two cells in the worksheet and use references to those cells in the function. See if it still works.

What if It Doesn't Work?

1. If the function doesn't work at all, see if it is listed in the Formula Paste Function dialog box. (Press End when the list box is active.) If not, activate the macro sheet and check the Formula Define Name box. Be sure the reference for the macro name is listed as the cell containing the macro name, immediately preceding the first ARGUMENT function.
2. If the constant values work but the references don't try adding the type code for reference to the ARGUMENT function argument lists.

CUSTOMIZING COMMAND MACROS

In the rest of this chapter, we'll examine various macro functions and you'll see how you can use them to make your command macros more effective and easier to use. Some of these macro functions can be used in function macros as well.

NAMING IN MACROS

You already know how to define a macro name so that it appears in the Macro Run dialog box. You can use defined macro names to nest macros, or run them from within other macros. Just as you can use worksheet functions in macros, you can use function macros that you have created.

In a function macro, the ARGUMENT functions provide names for the values received from outside the macro. You can provide names for values in any macro by defining them while the macro sheet is active; Figure 13.9 includes examples of named cells. These names remain completely separate from names defined on worksheets or other macro sheets. You might assign a name to a cell that contains a worksheet macro that returns a value so you can refer to that value in later macro functions.

The layout we have been using for macros allows us to place names in column A, functions in column B, and explanations in column C. Placing a name in column A does not define it; you must use Formula Define Name separately for each name you define in the macro. In the following discussions, you'll see many applications for naming cells in a macro.

USER INPUT

Excel has an INPUT function you can use to allow the user to provide input during a macro. The INPUT function causes a standard dialog box to be displayed, as you saw in Figure 13.5. You can specify the title for the dialog box title bar, the prompt message within the dialog box, and a default value to appear in the input field. You can also tell Excel the type of input to expect and specify the location of the dialog box on the screen. The INPUT function takes from two to six arguments. It returns the value entered by the user. If the user chooses OK without entering anything, any default value supplied in the function is returned. Here's the format:

INPUT (prompt,type,*title,default,x_pos,y_pos*)

The prompt to appear above the input field is required, as is the data type. The prompt must be in text form; it tells the user what to enter. The type must be a number; you can use any of the types shown in Figure 13.7, using sums to allow more than one type of data input. You can also use 0; type 0 expects a formula to be entered and returns it in text form. If the value entered is not of the expected type, Excel tries to convert it. If it can't, the value #VALUE! is returned instead.

The title and default arguments are optional; if used, they must be quoted text. If you supply a title argument, it appears in the title bar of the dialog box; if not, the word "Input" appears there. If you supply a default argument, it appears in the input field; if not, the field is empty when the input box is displayed. The default is returned as the function value if the user chooses OK without making any changes.

The x_pos and y_pos arguments set the position of the input dialog box in the application window. If you omit x_pos and y_pos, the box appears in the center. If you include them, you specify the number of points (1/72 inch) from the left edge (x_pos) of the application window and/or from the top (y_pos) of it.

Figure 13.10 shows the input dialog box resulting from this function:
INPUT("Enter desired heading:",2,"TITLE FOR WORKSHEET",
"Imaginetronics, Inc.",180,150)

280 ADVANCED EXCEL

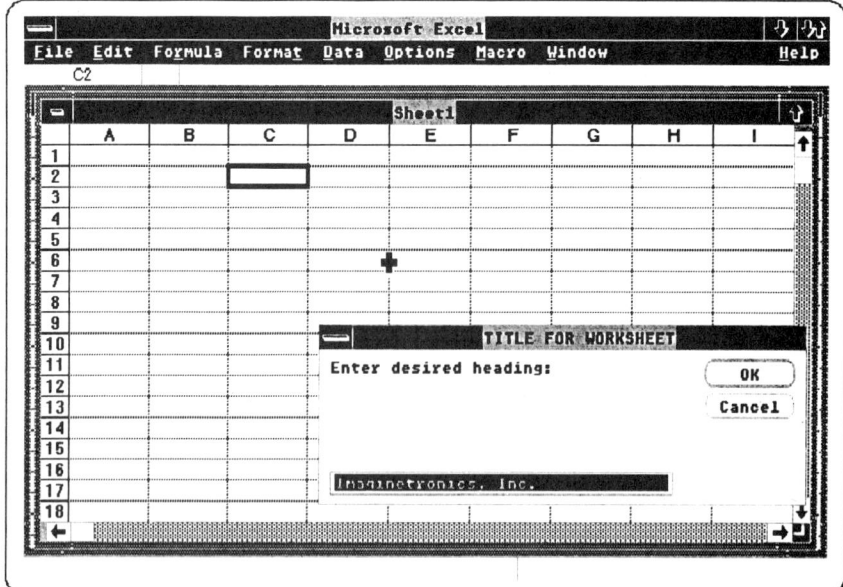

FIGURE 13.10. Positioned Input Dialog Box

Using INPUT Function Values

The INPUT function returns a single value, the default or whatever the user entered. You can use this value in a macro in several ways. You can reference the cell that contains the function. You can name the cell that contains the function, then use the name to apply to the returned value. Or you can include the INPUT function in another function, as in Figure 13.4.

Figure 13.11 shows two ways you can use INPUT values. Another way is to name the cell containing the INPUT function and use the name in later functions.

Figure 13.12 shows a macro in which the INPUT function is used to request several pieces of information from the user. Two different ways of referencing INPUT results are included. The cell containing the first INPUT function (B3) is given the name head; the FORMULA function in B4 uses the name to place

```
B6   =INPUT("How many do you want?",1)
B7   =FORMULA(Value*B6)

B12  =FORMULA(INPUT("How many do you want?",1)
```

FIGURE 13.11. Using Input Value

MACRO DEVELOPMENT

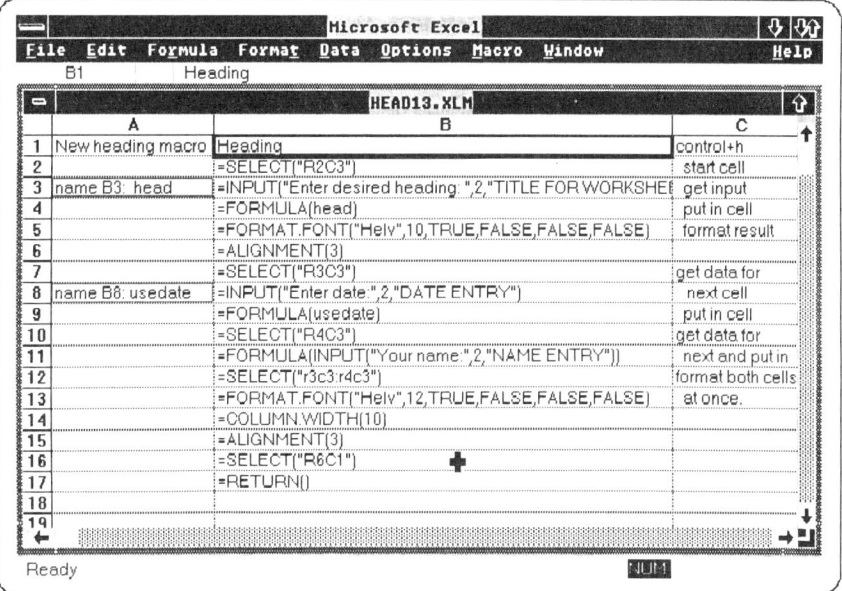

FIGURE 13.12. Macro with Multiple Input Functions

the contents in the last selected cell (R2C3). Cell B8 likewise is named and the name used in a FORMULA function. Cell B11 includes the INPUT function as an argument of the FORMULA function, so no name or reference is needed. In the next chapter, you'll see how to create a customized dialog box that lets the user enter more information at a time.

COMMUNICATING WITH THE USER

You can ask Excel to display messages in the status line, beep its alarm, or display special alert message boxes when appropriate. These techniques are especially useful when people other than yourself will be using your macros.

The ALERT Function

Excel offers the ALERT function to display one of three types of boxes requiring a response. You decide which one to use depending on the type of message and response you want. Figure 13.13 shows the three basic boxes.

282 ADVANCED EXCEL

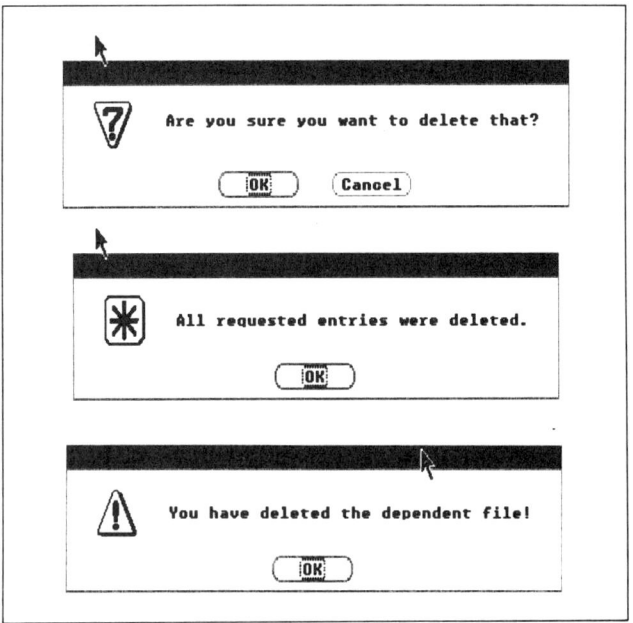

FIGURE 13.13. ALERT Function Variations

Notice that the symbol is different in each box. Only the first lets the user make a choice, to cancel the operation or continue. The second box is to present information; to make sure the user notices the information, we force him or her to choose OK. The third box is for error information, but the user isn't given any choice; we just want to make sure that the user knows what went wrong.

Here's the function statement format:

ALERT(message_text,type_number)

The type_number must be 1, 2, or 3, corresponding to the three types of ALERT dialog boxes shown in Figure 13.13. All return TRUE if the user chooses OK; box 1 returns FALSE if the user chooses CANCEL. Here are some examples:

=ALERT("Height must be between 40 and 80 inches.",3)
=IF(ALERT("Are you sure?",1),,RETURN())

The first example displays the message_text in a box of type 3, with the exclamation point icon. The next example uses the ALERT function as the logical test in an IF function. If the user selects OK, the macro will continue; if not, the RETURN function is executed immediately and the macro terminates. The ALERT function lets you give information on screen while the macro is running. It can use the response value if appropriate, as shown in the last example.

The MESSAGE Function

The MESSAGE function displays messages on the status line; it doesn't return a value, and the user gets to make no response. If you use MESSAGE, you might want to use an ALERT function early in the macro to tell the user to watch the status line for continuing messages. Here's the format:

MESSAGE(logical_value,*message_text*)

The logical_value must be TRUE or FALSE. If you use =MESSAGE(TRUE,"Now sorting the database"), the message appears immediately on the status line, no matter what you are really doing. It remains there until the macro removes it. You can remove a message in two different ways:

=MESSAGE(TRUE,"")
=MESSAGE(FALSE)

The first method replaces an existing status line message with blanks. The second removes the message and allows Excel to use the status line for its standard messages once again.

The BEEP Function

You might want to sound the alarm with a message to get the user's attention. You can do that with the BEEP function:

BEEP*(number)*

Number can be from 1 to 4, representing different tones on the computer bell. Most IBM PC, AT, and 386 compatible machines have only a single tone, however, so you might as well omit the number. You can use BEEP just before MESSAGE if you want. Or you might use it just before ALERT if the user might not be paying strict attention to the screen.

Macro Example

Figure 13.14 shows a macro that uses ALERT, MESSAGE, and BEEP functions to communicate with the user. Notice that the ALERT function requires the user to respond, but the MESSAGE functions don't. The final MESSAGE function (B17) clears the status line.

```
                          Microsoft Excel
File  Edit  Formula  Format  Data  Options  Macro  Window         Help
   B1            Heading
                          HEAD13.XLM
           A                       B                          C
1  New heading macro  Heading                         control+h
2                     =ALERT("You'll have to make three separate entries",2)  warn of input
3                     =SELECT("R2C3")                 start cell
4                     =BEEP()                         sound alarm
5                     =MESSAGE(TRUE,"Title for worksheet")   Status message
6  name B6: head      =INPUT("Enter desired heading:",2,"TITLE FOR WORKSHEE  get input
7                     =FORMULA(head)                  put in cell
8                     =FORMAT.FONT("Helv",10,TRUE,FALSE,FALSE,FALSE)  format result
9                     =ALIGNMENT(3)
10                    =SELECT("R3C3")                 get data for
11                    =MESSAGE(TRUE,"Date to appear in worksheet")  Status message
12 name B12: usedate  =INPUT("Enter date:",2,"DATE ENTRY")   next cell
13                    =FORMULA(usedate)               put in cell
14                    =SELECT("R4C3")                 get data for
15                    =MESSAGE(TRUE,"Name to appear in worksheet")  Status message
16                    =FORMULA(INPUT("Your name:",2,"NAME ENTRY"))  next and put in
17                    =MESSAGE(FALSE)
18                    =SELECT("r3c3:r4c3")            format both cells
19                    =FORMAT.FONT("Helv",12,TRUE,FALSE,FALSE,FALSE)  at once
Ready                                                      NUM
```

FIGURE 13.14. Communicating with the User

MACRO APPLICATION

It's no problem to create straightforward macros with single applications. You can do the basic operation with the recorder, then modify the recorded macro to include the features you want. But sometimes you want a more generalized macro that will operate under several different conditions. For example, in a worksheet, you generally have mailing information (name, address, city, state, postal code) in separate fields in the same row or database record. For creating mailing labels or addresses in letters or invoices, you want to rearrange those values. You might want to combine the city, state, and postal code into a single field. You certainly want to stack the values that represent different lines in the address.

Microsoft Excel's LIBRARY subdirectory includes macros that do this, then format the data into addresses and finally print labels or a list on paper. Although these macros are set up to work with a sample set of data, you can modify them to generate labels for other worksheets. The sample worksheet for this application is CUSTOMER.XLS and the macros are all stored on macro sheet LABEL.XLM; both are stored in the LIBRARY directory. We used a copy of CUSTOMER.XLS called CUSTMACS.XLS.

We'll examine the three macros included on LABEL.XLM in detail. In the

MACRO DEVELOPMENT

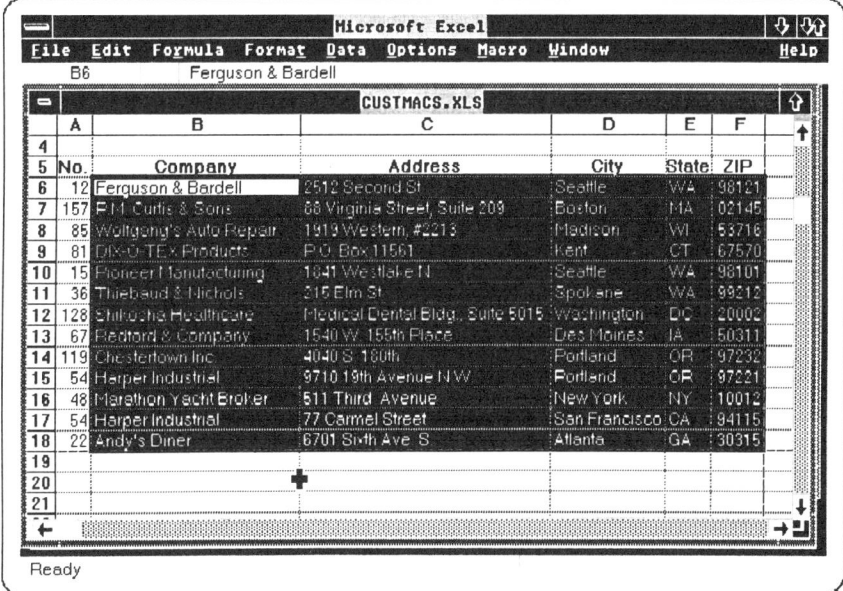

FIGURE 13.15. Data for Mailing Labels

process, you'll see how to get values from the current selection into the macro and use these values in performing operations. The macros we're discussing here don't use any complex programming, but you'll see that a loop is set up using an IF function and a GOTO function in the second macro.

The Sample Data

Figure 13.15 shows the sample data stored in CUSTMACS.XLS. The area to be used in the addresses is the range B6:F18. Before using the macro, you must select the range so that the upper left corner (B6) is the active cell.

The macro sheet (LABEL.XLM) contains three macros, Label.Setup (∧S), Label.Create (∧C), and Label.Print (∧P). We'll examine each in turn.

Setting up Labels

The setup macro inserts a new column for the concatenated line, then concatenates the three fields into it for each row, deletes the original last three columns, and, finally, adjusts the selection so it includes the lines to be included in the

286 ADVANCED EXCEL

	A	B
1	Label.Setup (S)	
2	Offset for mailing label concatenate address	
3	=SET.NAME("tmp",OFFSET(ACTIVE.CELL(),ROWS(SELECTION())-1,COLUMNS(SELECTION())-1))	Names the first line of data "tmp"
4	=SET.NAME("upper.left",ACTIVE.CELL())	Names the active cell "upper.left"
5	=STEP()	Causes the macro to step through its paces
6	=SELECT(OFFSET(ACTIVE.CELL(),0,2):OFFSET(ACTIVE.CELL(),ROWS(SELECTION())-1,2))	Selects column D for no. of rows in database.
7	=INSERT(1)	Inserts a blank column
8	=SET.NAME("bottom",OFFSET(ACTIVE.CELL(),ROWS(SELECTION())-1,0))	Names bottom cell of the selection "bottom."
9	=FORMULA.FILL("=RC[1]&"", ""&RC[2]&"" ""&RC[3]")	Combines City, State, & Zip in one column
10	=COPY()	Copies and
11	=PASTE.SPECIAL(3,1)	Pastes values only to blank column.
12	=SELECT(OFFSET(ACTIVE.CELL(),0,1):tmp)	Selects columns of Address, City, State & Zip
13	=EDIT.DELETE(1)	Deletes the cells
14	=SELECT(upper.left:bottom)	Selects the database.
15	=RETURN()	

FIGURE 13.16. Label.Setup Macro

label. Figure 13.16 shows the formulas in the macro as they look in the original condition as you received it. As we discuss each line, you'll see that you may want to make changes to accommodate more lines in an address or just to have a slightly different effect.

The first line of the macro gives its name and the shortcut key in parentheses; the second line gives a brief explanation of its effect. In the actual macro sheet, column B is used to provide a brief explanation of each function; don't put much faith in these. Look up the functions in the reference manual and try to figure them out first. The explanation for the very first function in this macro, for example, is completely inaccurate.

=SET.NAME("tmp",OFFSET(ACTIVE.CELL(),ROWS(SELECTION()) −1, COLUMNS(SELECTION())−1)) The SET.NAME function works like the Formula Define Name command but works only within the macro sheet; it specifies a name, "tmp," in this function, and a reference or value to be assigned to it. In this function, the OFFSET function returns the reference that defines the name "tmp."

The OFFSET function as commonly used has three arguments that it uses to determine and return a reference. The first argument is the basis from which the offset is calculated; in this case the ACTIVE.CELL is the reference point. Remember that the cell in the upper left corner must be active when you run this macro, so OFFSET originates at the upper left of the selected range. The second and third arguments give the row and column of the desired reference as offset from the origin. ROWS(SELECTION())−1 means to use the number of rows in the currently selected range and subtract 1 for the location of the desired

MACRO DEVELOPMENT

reference. If the −1 were omitted, the value here would be the number of rows in the selection (13 in the example); an offset of that much puts the reference in row 14, which is below the selected range. Since we are trying to identify the lower right corner of the selection, we have to subtract 1. COLUMNS(SELECTION())−1 does the same thing in the horizontal direction. In this case, it identifies column G and subtracts 1 to get back to column F. Cell F18 is assigned as the reference for the name "tmp."

= SET.NAME("upper.left",ACTIVE.CELL()) This SET.NAME function assigns the current value of ACTIVE.CELL (B6) to the name "upper.left." If this function were the first one in the macro, we could use "upper.left" instead of ACTIVE.CELL() in the OFFSET function used to name "tmp."

= STEP() The STEP function results in a dialog box like the one shown in Figure 13.17. It shows you the SELECT function in cell A6 about to be executed and lets you specify whether you want to Step (see the next step as well), Halt (end the macro here), or Continue (run rest of macro as normal). It is included in this macro so you can see how it works.

= SELECT(OFFSET(ACTIVE.CELL(),0,2): OFFSET(ACTIVE.CELL(), ROWS(SELECTION())−1,2)) This function selects a column in

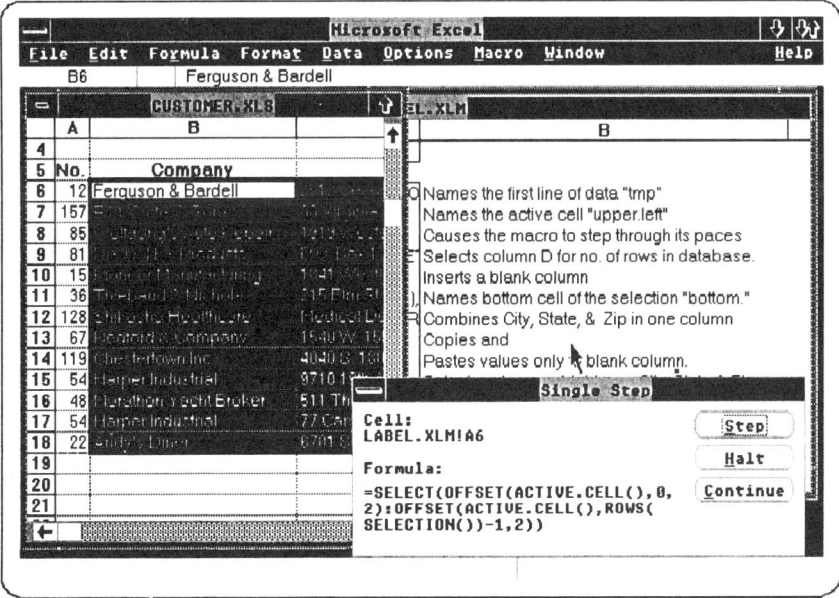

FIGURE 13.17. The Step Function Dialog Box

preparation for inserting a blank column. It selects column D of the selection. If you have a wider selection, say with a person's name as well as company and street, you could change the 2 to 3 in each place. Each reference in this function to ACTIVE.CELL actually refers to "upper.left" or B6, since no functions have changed that yet.

The function selects a range with two OFFSET functions. The first sets up a reference based on the active cell, in the same row (offset 0 rows) and two columns over (offset 2 columns). Since the active cell is B6, the returned reference here is D6. The second OFFSET again uses the active cell in B6 as the origin. It uses the bottom row (ROWS(SELECTION()) − 1 as in the first SET.NAME function) and two columns over (2 again), so the result is D18. This SELECT function selects D6:D18, the entire row D within the original selection.

=INSERT(1)   The INSERT function inserts new cells, shifting the selected cells to the right (1). The result is that the worksheet now has blank cells in the City column, and the City, State, and ZIP values have been shifted over one column to the right. At the end of this function, the inserted column of cells is selected, with the cell at the top (D6) active.

=SET.NAME("bottom",OFFSET(ACTIVE.CELL(),ROWS(SELECTION()) − 1,0))   This SET.NAME function assigns the name "bottom" to the cell at the bottom of the newly inserted set of cells. The reference is based on the current ACTIVE.CELL (D6), the bottom row of the selection (ROWS(SELECTION()) − 1), and the same column (0). We'll need this name later in setting the final selection.

=FORMULA.FILL("=RC[1]&"", ""&RC[2]"" ""&RC[3]")   This formula is equivalent to the Formula Fill command. The formula itself concatenates the values in the three columns to the right of the active cell in the same row, inserting a comma and space between the City and State values and a space before the ZIP value. The formula is then copied to the adjacent selected cells, just as in the command. The result is that the concatenated values are placed in all the inserted cells, so now each row of the original selection contains the city, state, and zip code in a single field.

=COPY()   The COPY function starts a copy of the currently selected range; that's still D6:D18, since it's unchanged by formula fill operations.

=PASTE.SPECIAL(3,1)   The PASTE.SPECIAL function is equivalent to the Formula Paste Special command; in this case it pastes values in the cells, replacing the formulas. This speeds up later use of the values in the labels.

MACRO DEVELOPMENT

=SELECT(OFFSET(ACTIVE.CELL(),0,1):tmp) This function selects the former contents of city and state fields so they can be deleted. There is a slight problem with the function as presented; it really should select the ZIP code column as well. When the name "tmp" was assigned to the lower left corner it was set at F18; Excel doesn't adjust that value when the column is inserted. To make this work correctly, you should return to the first SET.NAME function and remove the last " −1" so that cell G18 is assigned the name "tmp." At any rate, this function selects the range from the location in the same row as the current active cell (D6) and one column over, starting at E6 with the current value of "tmp" as the lower right corner.

=EDIT.DELETE(1) This function is equivalent to Edit Delete; it removes the selected cells and shifts any cells to the left.

=SELECT(upper.left:bottom) This function makes a new selection, from "upper.left" (that's cell B6) through "bottom" (that's cell D18). The result is a selection of the three columns that include what are now the three lines for the label, extending through the entire original set of records.

=RETURN() The RETURN function ends every macro. When control returns to the active worksheet, the modified label fields will all be selected and ready for the next macro.

Creating Labels

When the Setup macro is completed, the CUSTMACS.XLS worksheet looks like the one in Figure 13.18. Notice that the entire mailing area is selected with the active cell in the upper left.

The worksheet is now arranged so that the labels can be created. Although the column headed State isn't correct, it doesn't affect the label creation process. The LABEL.CREATE macro, shown in Figure 13.19, is used for the next phase. Basically, it creates a three-line label in the appropriate sequence for each row in the original data selection. We'll treat some functions, such as SET.NAME and OFFSET more briefly, since by now you know generally how these functions work.

The LABEL.CREATE macro includes a loop to handle each row in the range. Notice first that the function in cell A31 includes the GOTO function, which causes a branch back to cell A24. The macro performs the functions up to A24, then down to A31, then repeats the functions from A24 through A31 until the loop is broken. At that point, it performs the functions from cell A32 through the end of the macro.

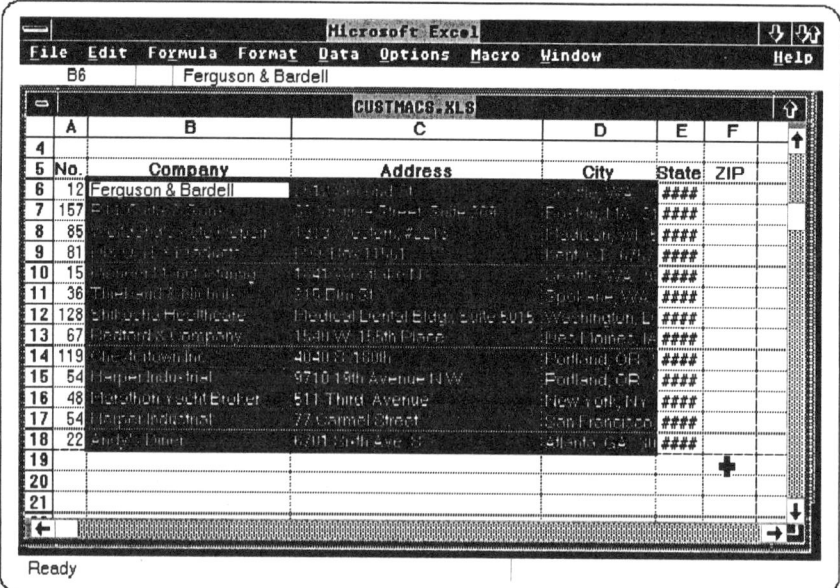

FIGURE 13.18. CUSTOMER Records after Setup

= SET.NAME("upper.left",ACTIVE.CELL())   This function assigns the name "upper.left" to cell B6.

= SET.NAME("row",ROWS(SELECTION()))   This function assigns the name "row" to the number of rows in the current selection; that's 13 in this case.

= SET.NAME("col",COLUMNS(SELECTION()))   This function assigns the name "col" to the number of columns in the current selection; that's 3 in this case.

= SET.NAME("counter",0)   This function assigns the name "counter" to the value 0. This name will be used to count loops as the macro proceeds.

= SELECT(OFFSET(ACTIVE.CELL(),0,0):(OFFSET(ACTIVE.CELL(), 0,col – 1)))   This function selects a range from the active cell (same row, same column) through two columns over (that's column D), so the selected range here is B6:D6, or the cells containing the information for the first label.

= DEFINE.NAME("temp",SELECTION())   This function assigns the name "temp" to the current selection on the worksheet. Note that SET.NAME assigns a name on the macro sheet, while DEFINE.NAME assigns a name on the worksheet that is running the macro. This function is at the beginning of the loop, so each time the macro

MACRO DEVELOPMENT

	A	B
17	Label.Create (C)	
18	Creates labels from a database	
19	=SET.NAME("upper.left",ACTIVE.CELL())	Names the active cell "upper left"
20	=SET.NAME("row",ROWS(SELECTION()))	Sets no. of rows in selection to be
21	=SET.NAME("col",COLUMNS(SELECTION()))	Sets no. of columns in selection to
22	=SET.NAME("counter",0)	Creates counter; sets it = 0
23	=SELECT(OFFSET(ACTIVE.CELL(),0,0):(OFFSET(ACTIVE.CELL(),0,col-1))	Selects first customer & address
24	=DEFINE.NAME("temp",SELECTION)	Gives name "temp" to first custom
25	=SELECT(OFFSET(ACTIVE.CELL(),counter*col+1+row,0):OFFSET(ACTIVE.CELL(),counter*col+col+row,0),OFFSET(ACTIVE.CELL(),counter*col+1+row,0))	Selects the area where label will b
26	=FORMULA.ARRAY("=transpose(temp)")	Transposes text
27	=COPY()	Copies and
28	=PASTE.SPECIAL(3,1)	Pastes values only to label area
29	=SELECT(OFFSET(ACTIVE.CELL(),-row-counter*col,0):OFFSET(ACTIVE.CELL(),-row-counter*col,col-1),OFFSET(ACTIVE.CELL(),-row-counter*col,0))	Selects next record of database to
30	=SET.NAME("counter",counter+1)	Increments the counter
31	=IF(counter<>row,GOTO(A24),)	Check: "Are we done yet?" If not,
32	=SELECT.LAST.CELL()	Selects last label cell
33	=SET.NAME("last.row",ROW(ACTIVE.CELL()))	Names row of last cell "last row"
34	=SET.NAME("label.area",OFFSET(upper.left,row,0):OFFSET(!A1,last.row,0))	Names "label area" as "last row" t
35	=SELECT(label.area)	Selects "label area" to prepare for
36	=RETURN()	

FIGURE 13.19. Label.Create Macro

branches back here, the name "temp" may be assigned to a different selection.

= SELECT(OFFSET(ACTIVE.CELL(),counter*col + 1 + row,0):OFFSET(ACTIVE.CELL(),counter*col + col + row,0),OFFSET(ACTIVE.CELL(),counter*col + 1 + row,0))   This function selects the location for the label to be placed. In this case, the range is in the same column as the current active cell. The first row is 0*3 + 1 + 13 or 14 rows below the active cell. The last row is 0*3 + 3 + 13 or 16 rows below the active cell. This allows three rows for the label to be placed in the new selected area.

= FORMULA.ARRAY(" = transpose(temp)")   This array function transposes the cells in "temp," where they are side-by-side, to the currently selected area, where they will be stacked in three cells in one row.

= COPY()   = PASTE.SPECIAL(3,1)   These functions replace the array formula with the values produced by it to solidify the label.

= SELECT(OFFSET(ACTIVE.CELL(), − row − counter*col,0):OFFSET(ACTIVE.CELL(), − row − counter*col,col − 1),OFFSET(ACTIVE.CELL(), − row − counter*col,0))   This function selects the next set of label information from the original set of records, in preparation for creating the next label.

= SET.NAME("counter",counter + 1)   This function changes the value of counter by adding 1 to it. You can write this function as counter = counter + 1 if you prefer. Remember that counter started at 0, so now after the first label is generated, it has a value of 1. After the thirteenth record is transposed into a label, counter will be set to 13.

=IF(counter<>row,GOTO(A24),) The IF function is a standard worksheet function. Its first argument is a logical test, the second tells what to do if the test is TRUE, the third what to do if the test is FALSE. Here the logical test says "the value of counter is not equal to the value of row." Since "row" was set to 13, this test will not be true until the thirteenth (or last) label is created. As long as there are labels to be transposed, the test is TRUE, so the macro jumps back to cell A24 and continues processing. In this case, no third argument is included, since we want processing to continue with the next function when the condition is false and all the labels have been created.

=SELECT.LAST.CELL() This function selects the last cell in the worksheet that contains a formula or value. We're getting ready to select a range for when we leave the macro.

=SET.NAME("last.row",ROW(ACTIVE.CELL())) This function assigns the name "last.row" to the row containing the active cell; that's the last row of the generated set of labels.

=SET.NAME("label.area",OFFSET(upper.left,row,0):OFFSET(!A1, last.row,0)) This function assigns the name "label.area" to the area that contains the generated labels in the worksheet. In this case, the range is from 13 rows below cell B6 through the last row containing label information. The range includes column A as well.

=SELECT(label.area) This function selects the area just named "label.area" to set it up for printing with the next macro.

=RETURN() This function returns control once again to the worksheet from which we are creating labels.

When control returns from the LABEL.CREATE macro, the labels are created in proper format on the same worksheet as the original one, but below it. The area is selected so that it can be printed on one-across labels. Or it can be printed on paper to see how it looks. You might want to adjust the spacing in the Create macro to allow more spacing between labels, depending on the needs of your label stock. If so, change the line we show in cell A25, changing 1 to whatever number of lines you want to separate your labels.

Printing Labels

Once the labels are created, you can use the third macro (LABEL.PRINT) to print them. You'll probably want to do this on paper a few times before you use actual labels. Figure 13.20 shows the complete macro.

MACRO DEVELOPMENT

	A	B
38	Label.Print (P)	
39	Prints on one-across labels	
40	=SET.PRINT.AREA()	Sets print area as "label area"
41	=PAGE.SETUP(,,0.4,0.4,0,0,0,0)	Sets up page parameters
42	=PRINT(1,,,1,)	Prints labels
43	=RETURN()	
44		

FIGURE 13.20. Label.Print Macro

=SET.PRINT.AREA() This function is equivalent to Options Set print area; it names the current selection as Print_area. This area will be printed when the worksheet is printed.

=PAGE.SETUP(,,0.4,0.4,0,0,0,0) This function is equivalent to the File Page Setup command; it sets various margins and features of the printed page. You can get the details in the reference manual if you want

---

Ferguson & Bardell
2512 Second St.
Seattle, WA 98121

CUSTMACS.XLS

P.M. Curtis & Sons
88 Virginia Street, Suite 209
Boston, MA 2145

Wolfgang's Auto Repair
1919 Western, #2213
Madison, WI 53716

DIX-O-TEX Products
P.O. Box 11561
Kent, CT 67570

Pioneer Manufacturing
1841 Westlake N.
Seattle, WA 98101

Thiebaud & Nichols
215 Elm St.
Spokane, WA 99212

Shikosha Healthcare
Medical Dental Bldg., Suite 50
Washington, DC 20002

Redford & Company
1540 W. 155th Place
Des Moines, IA 50311

Chestertown Inc.
4040 S. 180th
Portland, OR 97232

Harper Industrial
9710 19th Avenue N.W.

Page 1

FIGURE 13.21. Printed Output from Label.Print

to change it. As set up here, it will use default values except for a 0.4 inch left margin, and a 0.4 inch right margin.

=PRINT(1,,,1,)   This function is equivalent to the File Print command; it uses most of the established default values. The first 1 means to print all, and the second 1 means to print the worksheet only, not any notes.

=RETURN()   This function ends the macro and returns control to the worksheet.

You won't see the print dialog boxes on screen. Figure 13.21 shows the first part of a printed set of labels. There is one problem you might encounter. If column B is not wide enough to display the entire line, the line won't print completely. If you find this a problem, you can add a COLUMN.WIDTH function to the LABEL.PRINT macro at some point before the PRINT function. =COLUMN.WIDTH(34,!B:!B) sets the column width to 34. You may have to use a larger number if you have long address lines.

SUGGESTED EXERCISE

1. Open the sample worksheet CUSTOMER.XLS and the macro sheet LABEL.XLM. They are both stored in the LIBRARY subdirectory. Save CUSTOMER.XLS under another name so you don't damage the original file.
2. Select the range that includes the data for customer name and address, as shown in Figure 13.15.
3. Activate the macro sheet and examine the macros on it. Then return to the worksheet.
4. Run the LABEL.SETUP macro, using Macro Run and the dialog box. Note the result on screen.
5. Run the LABEL.CREATE macro. Notice the result on screen.
6. Run the LABEL.PRINT macro; just print it on regular paper or use preview to see how it looks.
7. Abandon the worksheet when you are finished; it will still be saved under the original name of CUSTOMER.XLS if you want to try modifying the macros.

What if It Doesn't Work?

1. If any of the macros seem to mess up the data on the worksheet, save the worksheet without saving changes, reload it, and try again. If anyone has modified LABEL.XLM or CUSTOMER.XLS, the macros may not work. Then again, they may work better!

SUMMARY

This chapter has shown you how to create and run function macros as well as how to customize and interpret command macros. Function macros are especially useful when you frequently need some function that is not included in the set of built-in functions. They must always be developed from scratch, using one ARGUMENT macro function for each argument in the function macro.

Customizing recorded macros involves editing them and modifying them by adding additional macros that are not generated by the recorder. We examined the set of LABEL macros in detail to give you an idea of how you can program macros to make selections and repeat a sequence of operations. If you are a programmer at heart, you can create branches and loops using additional functions. The Functions and Macros reference includes detailed instructions on all the functions that you can use in macros.

14 CUSTOMIZED EXCEL APPLICATIONS

When you begin developing your own applications, whether using Excel's database facility or standard worksheets, you can specify what appears in dialog boxes. You can create dialog boxes or data forms specifically tailored to your applications. You can add additional menu bars, place the menu names you want on them, and add commands to your own menus. You can even develop customized help windows to aid people in using the applications.

The basic process for defining a custom dialog box or data form is the same; the difference lies in what components are included, where you place the defined box or form, and how you access it. You can place a definition of a custom data form on the same worksheet as the database it refers to; it has fewer options than the customized dialog box. Through macros, you can display custom dialog boxes, interpret user input, and handle additional menu bars with their menus and commands.

We'll first deal with the general parameters for defining a custom data form or a dialog box since there are procedures common to both operations. You'll learn the basics of using the Dialog Editor to create the definitions; the Dialog Editor isn't available in versions prior to Excel 2.1, but its use greatly simplifies the process of defining data forms. Boxes can be defined quite adequately without the Dialog Editor, however.

Then, since custom data forms are easier to define and use, we'll deal specifically with these. In the latter part of this chapter, you'll learn how to define customized dialog boxes and use them in applications through macros, as well as how to define and use customized help and menus.

CUSTOMIZED BOXES

Before Excel can use a custom data form or dialog box, you have to define it in the format Excel expects. And Excel is very particular. You need a range that is

CUSTOMIZED EXCEL APPLICATIONS

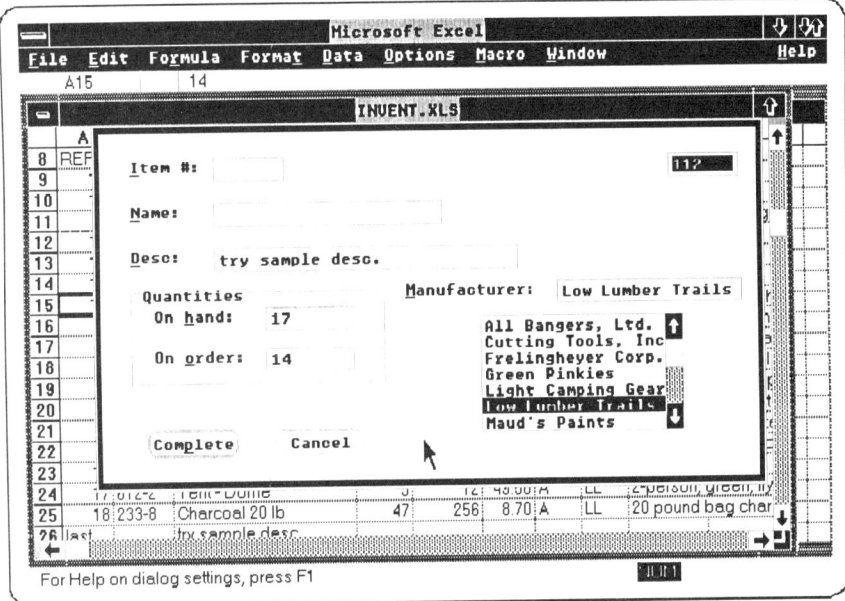

FIGURE 14.1. Typical Custom Dialog Box

seven columns wide and at least two rows tall, the first row for the box itself and one row for each object in the box. The Dialog Editor helps you define and locate the box and the various components within it, then creates the required range for you.

You've been using Excel's dialog boxes a great deal. You've probably noticed all the different objects that can appear in a box, including such objects as text, edit boxes for input, list boxes, check boxes, and various types of buttons. Figure 14.1 shows a custom dialog box. In defining such a box, you have to provide the location and size of each object that appears within its borders, either by specifying the coordinates directly or by placing the object through the Dialog Editor. You can also indicate or specify where on the screen the box will be placed. Later in this chapter you'll see how to define and process a dialog box like this.

A data form is a bit different, because Excel uses the same set of standard operation buttons on the right as in the default data form; you provide any text and edit boxes you need. Figure 14.2 shows a default data form along with a customized one for the same database. Later in this chapter, you'll see how to define and use such a form.

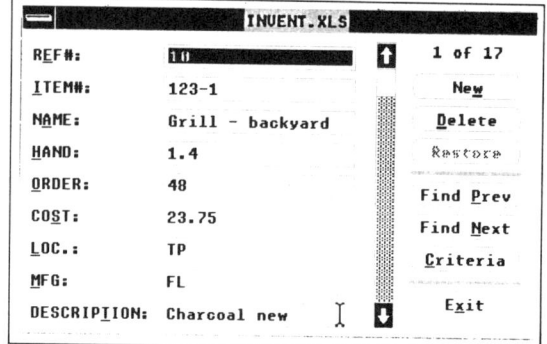

Default Data Form

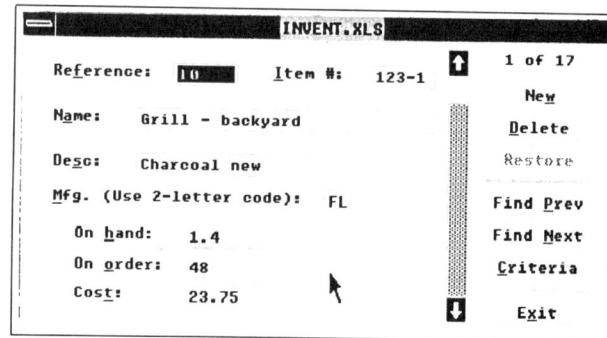

Custom Data Form

FIGURE 14.2. Default and Custom Data Forms

THE DIALOG EDITOR

Excel's Dialog Editor is available in Version 2.1; if you have an earlier version and expect to develop customized data forms or dialog boxes, you'll want to upgrade it. The Dialog Editor provides a visual way to design custom boxes onscreen and eliminates many of the problems inherent in developing custom boxes from scratch.

You access the Dialog Editor by selecting the Run command on the application control menu (or press ALT+Spacebar,U), then selecting Dialog Editor from the applications available. Figure 14.3 shows the resulting screen.

The box centered in the window is the default dialog box. In this box, you can use the Item menu to select any of the objects that can appear in dialog boxes; this includes all the objects you've seen in the dialog boxes Excel uses to communicate with you. You can use commands from the File menu to start over

CUSTOMIZED EXCEL APPLICATIONS

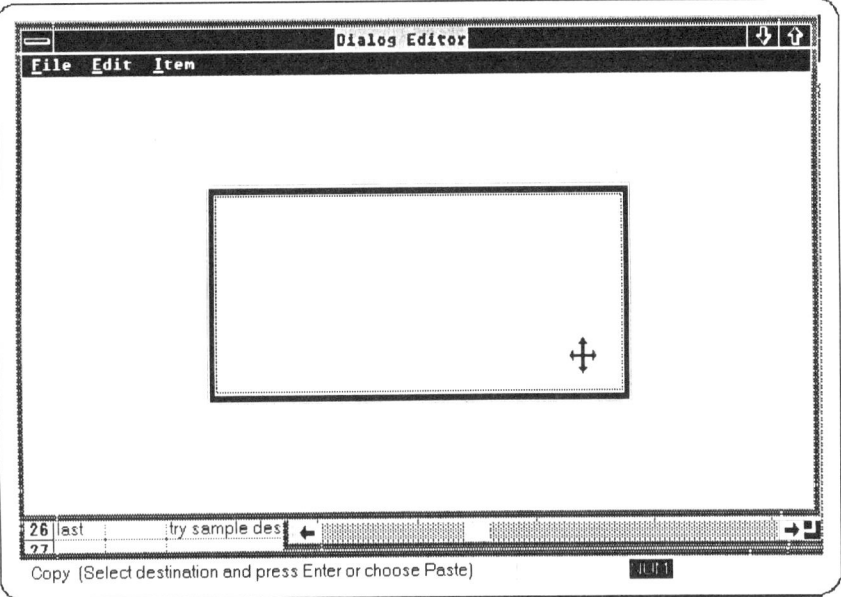

FIGURE 14.3. Dialog Editor Window

with a new, empty dialog box or return to Excel proper. You can use the Edit menu to modify, manipulate, and view various aspects of the box under development.

Selecting Objects

The Item menu presents six choices of objects, which together include all the items that can appear in dialog boxes. You select the item you want from the Item menu, choosing from a secondary menu if one is presented. The object appears in the box immediately, selected and ready for you to locate or customize. The first object is placed in the upper left corner of the custom box. Each additional object is placed immediately below the object that is selected when you create the new object. If you move an object and then add another, it is placed under the new location. If you select a different object and then add another, the added object is placed directly beneath the selected one, not the most recently added one. Each object is ready to be moved as soon as it is added to the box. The Item menu includes the following choices:

Button lets you select one of several button types. An OK or Cancel button can be specified as default (in effect when Enter is pressed) or

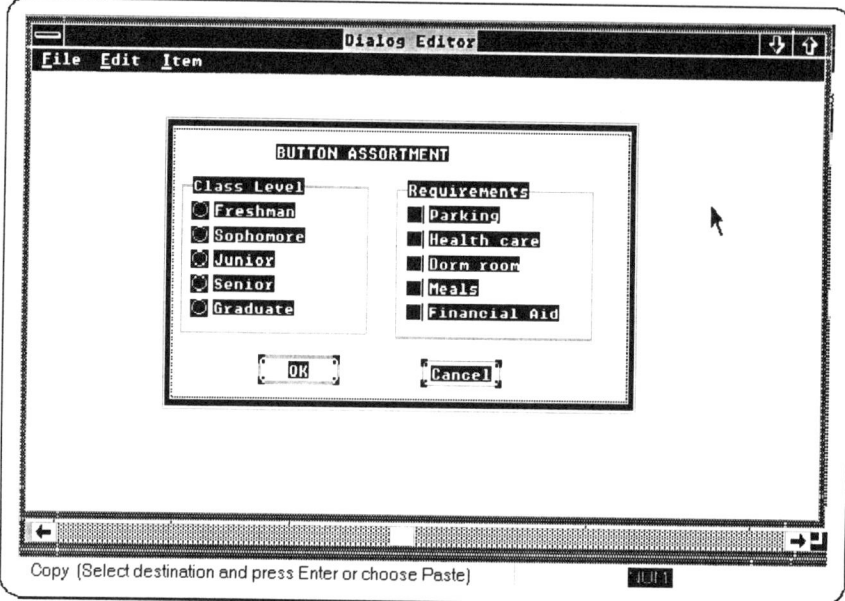

FIGURE 14.4. Dialog Box Button Assortment

not. An option button (as you've seen in the Alignment dialog box) can be specified; you'll usually use these in groups of which only one can be on at a time. A check box that can be either on or off can be selected. Figure 14.4 shows a dialog box under development that includes all four types of buttons; this figure shows how the dialog box appears in the Dialog Editor window.

Text lets you enter text that appears in the dialog box. You can enter as much or as little as you need. You'll probably need text preceding most edit boxes or list boxes that you put in the custom box.

Edit Box lets you select one of several types of edit boxes in which you or the user can enter data. You can choose from Text, Integer, Number, Formula, and Reference. Figure 14.5 shows a dialog box in development that includes several text and edit box objects.

Group Box lets you place a line around a group of objects in the dialog box. You might want to group related edit boxes or check boxes, for example. You must group a set of option buttons to let Excel know that only one of the bunch can be selected at a time. If you use a group box, you can select it before you create objects within it or create it later, after the objects you want to group are already positioned in the dialog box. Figure 14.4 shows group boxes around option buttons and check boxes.

CUSTOMIZED EXCEL APPLICATIONS

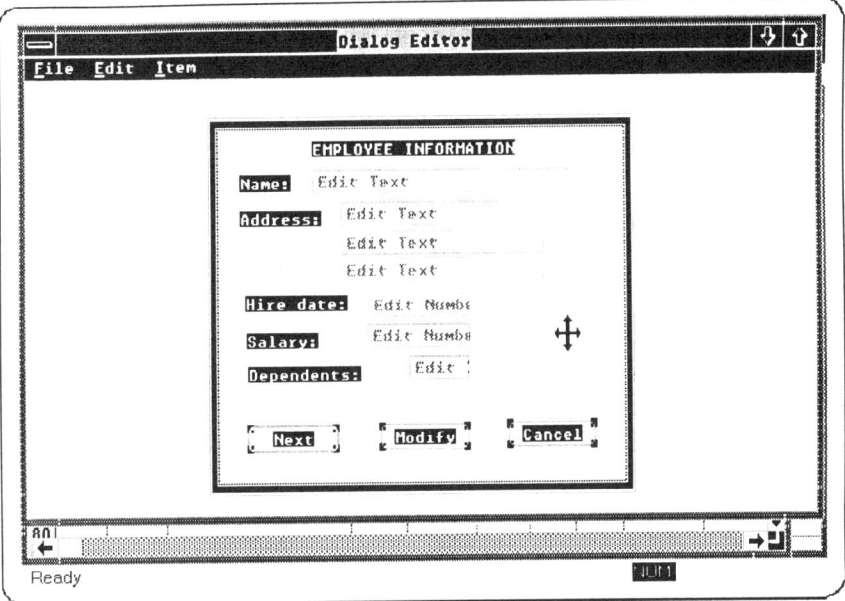

FIGURE 14.5. Text and Edit Box Objects

List Box lets you specify a list box, which will contain a list of items when the dialog box is displayed. It may be a list of manufacturers that the user can select from, for example. It may be linked to a preceding text edit box for display and editing of the selected value. You may also specify a linked File/Directory box here, in which case Excel provides the values for the box. The dialog box in Figure 14.1 includes a linked list box on the right.

Icon lets you specify one of three standard Excel Icons to appear in the displayed box.

Adding Text to Objects

In general, objects that include text can take any size text. The object takes up as much space as is needed to display the text. When the object appears in the dialog box, you just start typing the text; actually, you can type text into an object any time the object is selected.

Certain objects require or accept text as part of the object itself. The text object appears on the screen as a small area containing the word "text." When you start typing, your text replaces the default word. If you select the text object again later, you can add text to the end of your previous text or use backspace to delete characters from the end.

The group box appears by default with the word "group" in its top edge. When the group box is selected, you can replace the default word with your own text, as we have done in Figure 14.4.

To add text to buttons, just type when the object is selected. You can add text to any kind of button.

You can also add text through the Edit Info window, which we will cover a bit later.

Selecting, Moving, and Sizing Objects

When the selected object first appears in the dialog box, it is selected. You can select any object by clicking on it with the mouse or by moving to it with Tab and SHIFT+Tab, just as in a completed dialog box. You can select the entire box by clicking where there is no object or by selecting Select Dialog on the Edit menu. To select several objects at once, first select one object. With the mouse, use SHIFT+click to add objects to the selection. With the keyboard, use CONTROL+Tab until the next object to be selected is highlighted, then use CONTROL+Spacebar to add it to the selection. Once a multiple selection is established, you can delete or move it as a single entity.

Whenever an object is selected, you'll see a four-headed arrow that indicates that you can move the object by dragging it with the mouse or pressing the appropriate arrow keys. If you move the mouse to an edge of the object, you'll see a two-headed arrow that indicates you can change the size of the object with either the mouse or the arrow keys. The Edit menu includes a Resize command you can use to change size from the keyboard. All the objects are moved or resized in the same way. Excel doesn't give you a grid, so you have to "eyeball" the objects in lining them up onscreen. If you hold down the shift key while pressing arrows, you can keep the object in the same horizontal or vertical line; it restricts the orientation to the one indicated by the arrow you press first. In Figures 14.4 and 14.5, the objects have been sized and positioned.

Using the Dialog Editor Edit Menu

The Dialog Editor Edit menu, shown in Figure 14.6, contains many of the same commands as the standard worksheet Edit menu. You can undo some operations. You can cut or copy selected objects and repaste them or select Clear to

CUSTOMIZED EXCEL APPLICATIONS

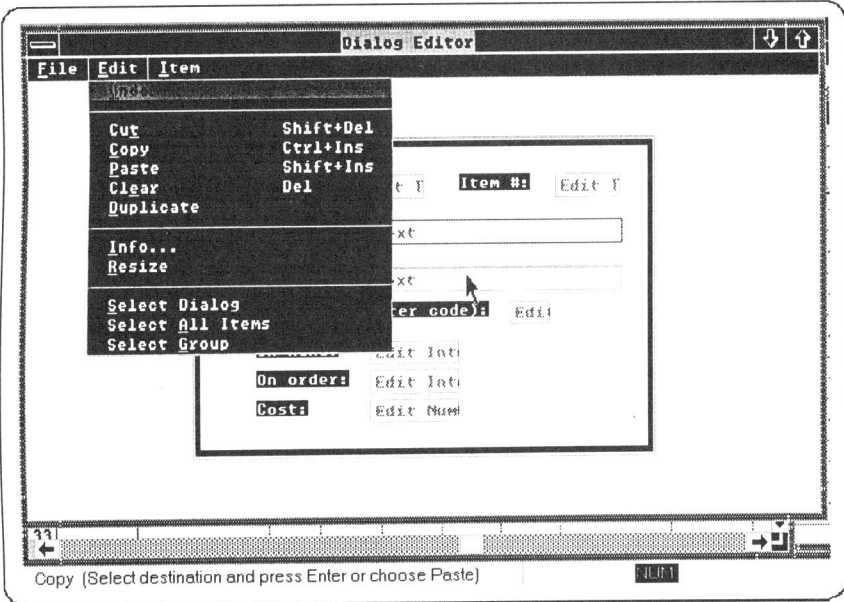

FIGURE 14.6. Dialog Editor Edit Menu

remove them from the dialog box. The Duplicate command repeats the selected object or set of objects in a single command, so it can replace the use of Copy followed by Paste. When you first enter the Dialog Editor, the Edit Paste command inserts a dialog definition range that you have previously copied to the Clipboard. Resize is used to change the size of the selected object.

The commands in the bottom section of the menu let you select the entire dialog box, all objects in it, or a group and all objects enclosed by it. These selections can all be made with the mouse as well. When you click within the dialog box where there is no object, the entire dialog box is selected.

The Info command brings up an information window on the currently selected object. Figure 14.7 shows a typical Info window for a text edit box. Notice that the object type is shown on the top line. You can change any of the values displayed here; they will be reflected in the dialog box being customized. If the field is marked as "Auto," it is in the default state; you can turn off the Auto check box if you want to change the value here. In the figure, the Height field is still in its original condition.

The X and Y fields give the starting position of the object, relative to the upper left corner of the dialog box. If you move the object, the X and Y coordinates change. We'll cover the measurement units and what they mean later in this chapter. Width and Height give the object's size in the same measurement units. If you used the default size, both will be marked as

ADVANCED EXCEL

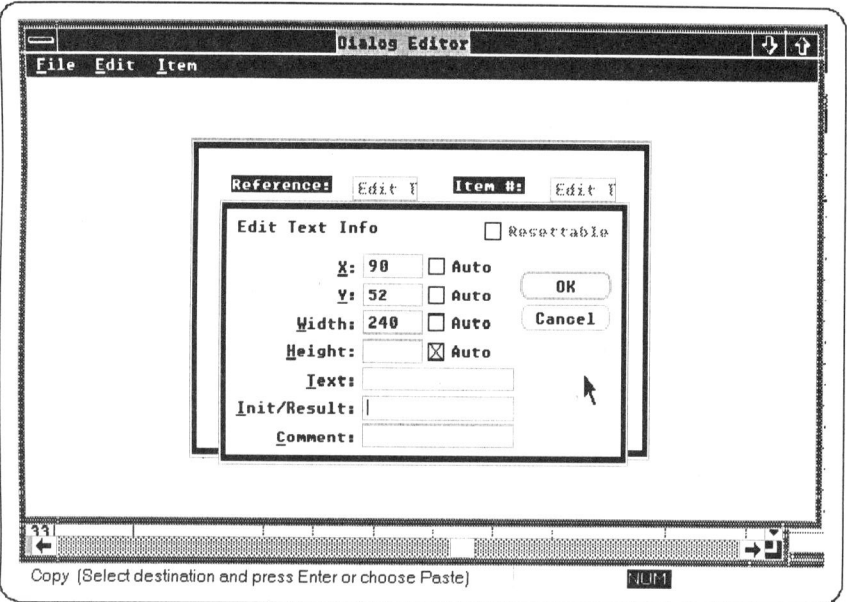

FIGURE 14.7. Dialog Editor Info Window

"Auto" and no values are shown. In this case, we changed the width in the box itself.

The Text field shows any text you entered for the object. Edit boxes don't recognize the Text field, so the field is empty. For a constant text or a button, you'll see the appropriate text here. You can change it if you wish.

The Init/Result field can contain a value that will appear in the field when the box is displayed. For example, if you want the initial value to be 00000, just add it through the Info window. If you are developing a customized data form, you'll enter the database field names for each input field in the Init/Result field. What you enter won't show up while you are in the Dialog Editor, but will display as you want when you use the dialog box from a worksheet.

The Comments field lets you add a note to the field. These are never displayed with the dialog box, but they are copied to the definition range with the rest of the information. In fact, if you use any comments, the Dialog Editor produces an eight-column range when pasted into a macro sheet or worksheet. This has the advantage of saving your comments where you probably want them. Excel will ignore this eighth column in processing the customized dialog box.

The Edit Info window shows you all the information about a given object at one time. You can edit the information here or continue to work with the objects on screen.

Saving the Dialog Box

The File Menu lets you specify a new empty dialog box on this screen or exit the Dialog Editor. If you select New or Exit, Excel asks if you want to copy the current dialog box to the Clipboard. If you respond No, the current work is lost. If you say Yes, the current work is copied and a new default box created or the Dialog Editor terminated. The Clipboard holds only one thing at a time, so you probably won't copy to it and then immediately create a new dialog box; take time to paste the Clipboard contents to a worksheet or macro sheet to save it before starting another.

To insert Excel's generated definition range, exit the Dialog Editor and activate the worksheet or macro sheet that you want to use. Select the cell at the upper left corner of the area where you want to place the range, then use the Edit Paste command. The range is inserted immediately and selected, just as with any paste operation. You might want to name the range (Formula Define Name) at this point to make it easy to reference again later. If Excel generated an eighth column (of comments), that's no problem; just include it in the named range.

We'll cover more specific ways to use the Dialog Editor as we continue in this chapter.

Converting a Range to the Dialog Editor

Once you have pasted the dialog box coordinates to a range, the Clipboard is empty and so is the Dialog Editor. If you want to make more changes through the Dialog Editor, you must copy the range back to it. Select the entire range, just as it appeared when you pasted it to the worksheet or macro sheet; if you've made any changes directly in the range they'll be included. Then use Edit Copy to place the range in the Clipboard. Enter the Dialog Editor as before. When the empty dialog box appears, select the Paste command from the Edit menu. A dialog box will be created for you to work with.

THE CUSTOM RANGE

The range required to define a data form or dialog box is seven columns wide. Each column contains a specific type of information. The Dialog Editor creates the range when you Paste a prepared data form or dialog box into a worksheet or macro sheet. Most Excel developers use an additional column on the right to label the contents of each row; they may also include an additional column for use in reestablishing initial values for the box after the original ones are overlaid. If you've added comments to the Dialog Editor items on the Edit Info screen, then copying the dialog box coordinates results in eight columns. Excel uses only the seven required columns, however. You'll find it helpful to include an additional row of labels above the definition range to remind you of the contents of each column.

The first row in the range gives information specific to the dialog box or data form being described. Each other row describes a single object to appear in the finished box. Figure 14.8 shows a sample defined range generated by the dialog box shown in Figure 14.2. You can change the values directly in the range if you prefer.

The first row of the range defines the custom data form or dialog box itself. Each other row defines a specific object in the box.

Column 1 of the definition range can be blank only in the first row of the range. For all other rows it contains a number from 1 to 20 that indicates the type of object the row describes. You don't have to enter the object type through the Dialog Editor, but knowing (or looking up) the object types helps you understand the generated range and helps you modify it. Data forms recognize only types 5, 6, 7, and 8, so that Excel can automatically interpret the user entries. Type 5 indicates text that won't change, 6 indicates a text edit box,

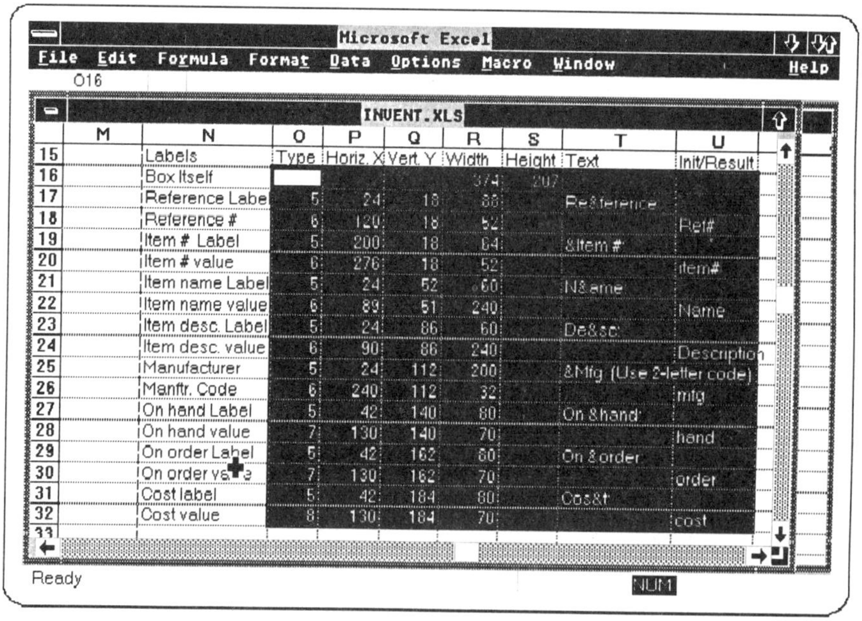

FIGURE 14.8. Defined Range for Data Form

7 indicates an integer edit box, and 8 indicates any number edit box. In Figure 14.8, only three of these four data types are used. The object types are described in detail later in this chapter.

Columns 2 and 3 correspond to the X and Y fields in the Edit Info window; they specify the position of the upper left corner of the box or object. Excel generates these values automatically if you use the Dialog Editor. If you blank the first row, Excel will center the box on the screen whenever it is displayed. Excel places the objects as you positioned them in the Dialog Editor. You can specify or change both horizontal and vertical positions for each object in the box. We'll explain the positioning units shortly.

Columns 4 and 5 correspond to the Width and Height fields in the Edit Info window; they specify the size of the object. You can specify or change both width and height for each object. If you left the object in its default size and shape, Excel doesn't specify a width and height. The object positioning units (to be covered shortly) are the same as in columns 2 and 3.

Column 6 corresponds to the Text field in the Edit Info window; it specifies any constant text that is part of the object. Excel brings over any text you entered in the Dialog Editor, as well as labels for buttons and check boxes. There's always text in column 6 for object type 5, since these are text labels and information in your data form or dialog box. Some other objects, such as buttons and group boxes, also require or allow text information.

If you want the users to be able to press Alt + character to select the input field associated with a text object, you must ensure that the text object immediately precedes the input field in the definition range. To specify the ALT character, type an ampersand (&) before the letter to be pressed; this is shown in Figure 14.8. You can do this when you first type the text, edit it into the text in the definition range, or insert it through Edit Info in the Dialog Editor. Be careful to use a different letter in each text. And don't use the ones that are used in the data form buttons (see Figure 14.2). You won't be able to see which character is underlined while in the Dialog Editor. You'll see the ampersand in the text in column 6 or in the Edit Info window.

Column 7 (Init/Result) contains the value to appear in a field when the box is first displayed. You can enter values through the Dialog Editor (Edit Info) or in the pasted definition range. For a data form, you put the name of the data field here, exactly as it appears in the first line of the database. Then when data is entered, Excel can relate it to the appropriate field in the database. For a dialog box, you put the actual value you want to use as the default. The user will be able to change it. For dialog boxes, this column will contain the results after the user completes the dialog box entry. The results overlay the initial values. If you're defining a dialog box, you might want to include an extra column and make it identical to the Init/Result column. Then, after the dialog box is processed, the macro can copy the extra column to column 7 and reestablish the initial values for the next time the box is displayed.

Screen Measurement Units

The position and size of boxes and objects are specified in horizontal and vertical screen units, as you've seen in the ranges generated by the Dialog Editor. You can modify the values in the range or determine them and enter them yourself. For example, you may not be sure if several text objects start in the same horizontal position. You can check in the generated definition range and see; if two start at position 84 and one at 85, just change the 85 to 84 to better align the group.

Horizontal screen units are 1/8 the width of a character in the system font; a full screen is about 620 units wide. Vertical screen units are 1/12 the height of a character in the system font; a full screen is about 400 vertical units high. If you use the full width of the screen, you can display up to 78 characters. If you use the full height of the screen with only text (no boxes), you can display about 33 lines. A text line must be at least 12 units high. An edit box must be at least 18 units high. In fact, these are the automatic default heights for text and edit boxes you position through the Dialog Editor.

Positioning

The positioning values (X and Y) specify the absolute position of an object's upper left corner in the box. A single line entry, such as text or an entry field box, is placed horizontally from that point. If the position fields are blank, Excel stacks your objects one after the other in the box, much as in a default data form.

While making changes in the definition range, keep in mind that a given position can contain only one thing. If you overlay positions, the last one specified appears on the screen. If your positions overlap, the constant text and field entry boxes you request may appear all jumbled on the screen. For example, suppose you want two objects, text and an edit box, to appear on the first line in the box. You can use 12 as the vertical position for both, since they should be on the same line. The horizontal position for the first could be 16 if you want it to be indented a bit from the box edge. But you have to consider the width of the first object in determining the horizontal position of the second. In calculating the horizontal position of later objects on the line, add the width of any preceding objects to any blank space you allow for spacing or alignment.

Better yet, copy the range back to the Dialog Editor and make the changes there where you can see what you are doing.

Vertical positioning works much the same way. Once you are past the first line, you have to add the height of preceding objects as well as empty space to arrange an attractive and readable display. You'll be able to accomplish this most easily through the Dialog Editor.

Sizing Objects

If you clear the Width and Height columns for the box specification row, Excel gives you a box large enough to hold all your entries. The Dialog Editor requires a width and height to display the box, however. You'll have to resize the box yourself if you paste a box with no specific width and height to the Dialog Editor.

You can specify the width and height of objects in the Dialog Editor or in the generated range. If you don't change the height for constant text, Excel uses 12 vertical units. For edit boxes, Excel uses 18 vertical units. If you use the default width for edit boxes, Excel uses the same standard width you see in default data forms (about 144 horizontal units). Of course, the user can type any amount of data into these boxes, since scrolling occurs automatically.

If you're designing custom forms or boxes, you'll probably want to change the default width of many objects. Using a short width for a state abbreviation gives a clue to the user that you expect a short entry. A longer edit box implies a longer entry. If the Auto box is checked in the Edit Info window, you won't be able to change that feature in the Dialog Editor until you select Auto to remove the check.

If you want to specify a height, use at least 12 for text objects and 18 for edit boxes. This allows Excel to draw the box around the area where the user's entry will appear. If you use smaller heights, they will overlay lines above them. If you use larger heights, the box will contain more space. Again, this is easier to see in the Dialog Editor than in the range.

CUSTOM BOX DESIGN

The major considerations in box design are what you want to include, where you want to put it, and the sequence in which the user entries are made. You'll also want to consider how easy it is for someone to read and understand what the box contains or what kind of data should be entered into it.

The easiest way to design a custom box is to sketch it first on paper. When you know approximately where everything goes, what text you want to use, and the sequence of data entry, you're ready to start defining it through the Dialog Editor.

When a custom box is in use, you use Tab and SHIFT + Tab to move among the fields. Excel uses the sequence of fields in the definition range to determine the sequence of movement. In generating the range, Excel remembers what was selected each time you chose a new object for the box. In the resulting range, it places the new object logically after the currently selected object. So if you have entered a list of four text objects and want an edit box associated with each, you can't just enter one edit box, move it opposite the first text object, and create the other text boxes under it. To associate each text object with the appropriate edit box, you select one text box, then create and position its associated edit box. Then select the next text box and create and position its associated edit box, and so forth.

PREPARING CUSTOM DATA FORMS

A custom data form uses the standard seven-column definition, with the top line for the data form definition and one line for each object in the form. Excel constructs the right side of the box using the central scroll bar and the standard set of data form buttons. When you use the Dialog Editor to generate the rest of the box, use a box that is not too wide; a square box works fairly well, since Excel adds the right side to it. You don't have to leave space for the buttons. Figure 14.9 shows a custom data form in development. Notice that it uses many text constants and input boxes as objects. The scroll bar and buttons will be the same as for a default data form.

The definition range for a custom data form goes on the same worksheet as the database, off to the right in some area that doesn't interfere. You can paste it here from the Dialog Editor. Then you assign the name "data_form" to the exact definition area, the seven columns with one row for the data form and one for each included object; if you included comments, this range may have eight columns. You may want to add extra rows and columns to label the required portions, but don't include any added labels in the named range. Figure 14.10 shows a defined area with the name definition dialog box. Notice from the highlighting that only the exact definition is selected.

Use the name "data_form" for the custom definition. Then whenever you use the Data Form command when your database is selected, Excel uses the custom data form instead of the default one. To restore the default data form, just delete the data_form name.

CUSTOMIZED EXCEL APPLICATIONS

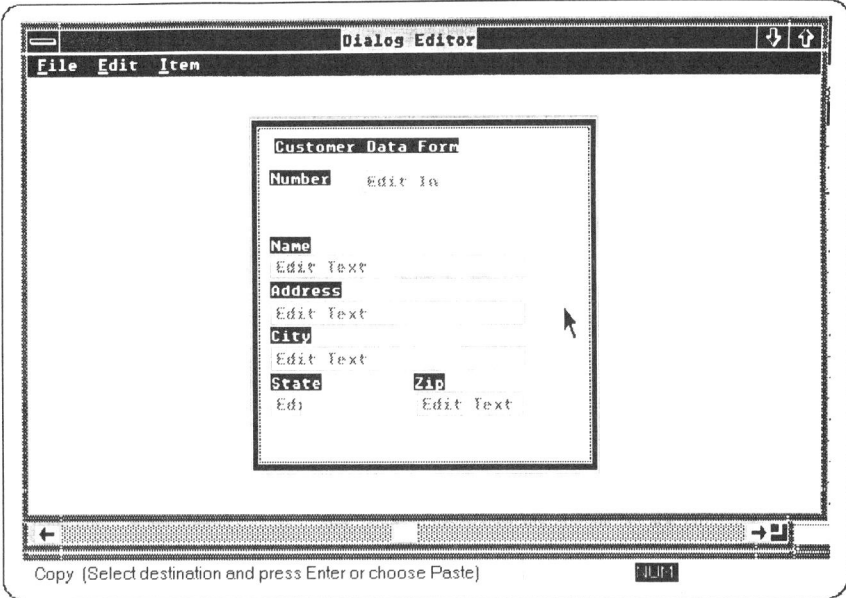

FIGURE 14.9. Custom Data Form

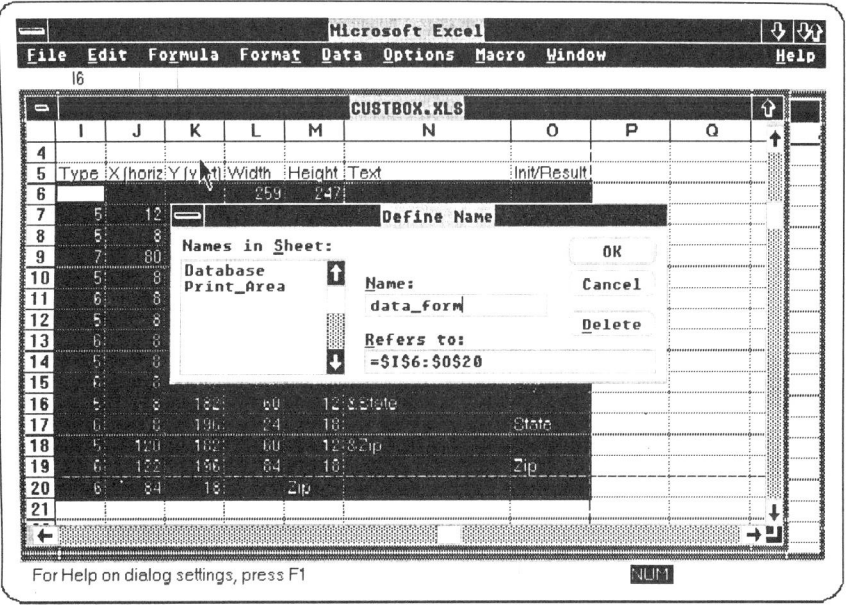

FIGURE 14.10. Naming a Custom Data Form

Developing Custom Data Forms

The easiest way to develop your own data forms is to use the Dialog Editor. You don't have to use the exact data field names as text constants. And use only text, text edit boxes, integer edit boxes, and number edit boxes as objects. If you use other objects, they'll appear in the Dialog Editor, but they won't appear in the custom data form itself. You don't have to use any buttons, because Excel supplies these. Enter the objects in the order the user will enter data. Be sure to add the exact field name in the Init/Result field through the Edit Info window for each edit box.

When entering text constants, you can select a character in each text label to be underlined, so that the user can move directly to the following edit box. Be sure not to use the characters that Excel uses in the buttons (W,D,R,P,N,C,X); you can use each letter only once, because Excel doesn't differentiate between upper- and lowercase letters in ALT key usage. If you don't care to add them while initially typing the text, you can insert the ampersands through the Edit Info window or in the generated range.

You don't have to include all the fields in a data form; just be sure to include the ones users have to deal with. If you include a computed field, the user won't be able to enter or change the data, but the value will be displayed as soon as Excel can calculate it.

Testing Custom Data Forms

When you are creating a custom data form from scratch, you can try it out after every few objects are entered into the definition range. If you use the Dialog Editor, you can safely enter more objects before testing it. Each time you modify the range size, however, you have to rename the reference definition for data_form so that all objects you want to appear are included and those you don't yet want aren't. It's a cyclical process, something like this:

    Prepare or modify a partial data form with the Dialog Editor
    Copy and paste it to an area on the database worksheet
    Redefine the data_form name to reference the form as currently ready to test
    Add the database field names in the Init/Result column if they aren't there yet
    Select the database (Formula Goto Database)
    Select Data Form
    Examine resulting data form

Note positions and sizes, then select Exit
Return to the Dialog Editor or defined form (Formula Goto data_form, copy, start Dialog Editor, and paste)
Make any needed changes
Return to top of list

You can develop temporary macros to speed up the process if you want. While in the definition range, start the macro recorder and provide a short name such as "tryout" and a shortcut key such as Ctrl+T. Then select the database and the Data Form command. Select Exit or press Escape, then stop the recorder. Now you can try out the customized data form by pressing your shortcut key immediately after naming the range or pasting it from the Clipboard. You can create a second macro to return to the definition range after leaving the data form if you like.

Using the Custom Data Form

Once it is defined and named, Excel uses a customized data form instead of the default form. You can perform any operation through it that you can through the default form. All the buttons and operations work the same. To return to the default data form, just delete the defined data_form name.

SUGGESTED EXERCISE

The instructions in this exercise ask you to use the database you created in Chapter 8. If you didn't create one then, use any database you have. Modify the instructions as needed.

1. Open the database you created during Chapter 8 and take a look at it using the default Data Form. Decide on a different arrangement of fields.
2. Set up a range off to the right of your database to use for the custom data form. Type in headings for the seven required columns.
3. Use the Dialog Editor to create the basic form with at least two text objects and associated edit boxes. Move and/or size at least two of the objects.
4. For each text field, specify one character indicated for ALT key access in the text column. For the edit boxes, use the Edit Info window to include the appropriate database field name in the Init/Result field.
5. Exit the Dialog Editor and paste the dialog box coordinates to the area beneath the labels you entered.
6. Define the name Data_form for the generated range. Then select the database and use the Data Form command to see how it looks.

7. Select the range again (Formula Goto Data_form) and copy it back to the Dialog Editor.
8. Make any necessary changes to your early objects, then add additional text and edit boxes to your data form definition. Repeat steps 3, 4, 5, and 6.
9. When the data form looks right, use it to add a record to your database. Notice that all the buttons work just as they do in the default data form.

What if It Doesn't Work?

1. Check name definition if the form doesn't appear at all. Be sure the range includes seven columns. Don't include the headings or any labels preceding the generated range.
2. If the Tab key doesn't move through the edit boxes as you expect, you probably didn't create the objects in the correct order. You can use the standard Edit commands to insert, delete, cut, and paste to adjust the lines in the generated range.
3. If no values appear in the database, make sure you used the actual field names in the Init/Result column.

CUSTOM DIALOG BOXES

If you want to process data from a worksheet that is not structured as a database or perform operations not included on the default data form, you can design customized dialog boxes. The basic procedure is much the same as for custom data forms, but you can use all the objects available through the Dialog Editor. You can define your own buttons to process or cancel the input. And you have to handle the user input yourself in order to place it appropriately in the worksheet. Custom dialog boxes are displayed and user entries processed through the use of command macros.

The macro function that displays a custom dialog box is DIALOG.BOX (definition-reference). The definition reference is the same as the one you define as data_form for a custom data form. It is generally seven columns wide, although if the Dialog Editor generates eight columns, you can use that range. The definition range contains one row for the box itself and one for each object within the box. For a customized dialog box, however, the definition range should be placed on the same macro sheet as the macro that uses it, although a customized dialog box can be referenced by many macros. In this section of the chapter, we'll cover the object types in detail and see what values you can specify within Dialog Editor or the definition range. Then we'll look at some ways you can design and develop the dialog box reference. We'll also look at ways to process the dialog box and any of its user entries in the rest of the macro so that the data appears in the worksheet as required.

USING THE OBJECT TYPES

You've already seen how to use text objects and edit boxes. Text objects are type 5 in the generated definition range. Types 6 (text), 7 (integer), and 8 (number) are edit boxes for various forms of input; each results in a box for user input that accepts the designated type of value. In defining a customized dialog box, you can use up to 16 different data types in addition to these basic ones; they can all be selected from the Dialog Editor Item menu or entered directly into the definition range. All the types, in numerical sequence, are described in this section. Use only the ones you need in any given application. Each customized dialog box is limited to 64 different objects, only 32 of which can return a value to the Init/Result field.

OK and Cancel Buttons

These objects produce buttons of the same size and shape as typical OK and Cancel buttons. Just select OK or Cancel on the Item Button menu; you can specify one button as the default, to take effect when the user presses Enter. When the user selects any OK or Cancel button, the dialog box closes and control returns to the macro. You can include text in any of these buttons by typing it while the button is selected or by typing it in the Text field of the Edit Info window or the definition range. An ampersand (&) indicates a character to be underlined for use with the ALT key, just as with any text. OK and Cancel buttons have a standard size. You can override the length by typing longer text directly into the object. If you enter longer text through the Edit Info window or into the definition range, the text is centered in the button; if it is too long, characters at the beginning and end aren't displayed. If you don't change the text value, OK or Cancel appears in the button. Figure 14.4 showed the default OK button and standard Cancel button. Figure 14.11 includes a default Cancel button with standard OK button; both buttons include nonstandard text.

> **Type 1 The default OK button.** This button is displayed, as in the typical dialog box, with a thick dark border; it is chosen if you press Enter. When selected, this button causes any entries in the dialog box to be placed in the Init/Result column (column 7) of the defined range,

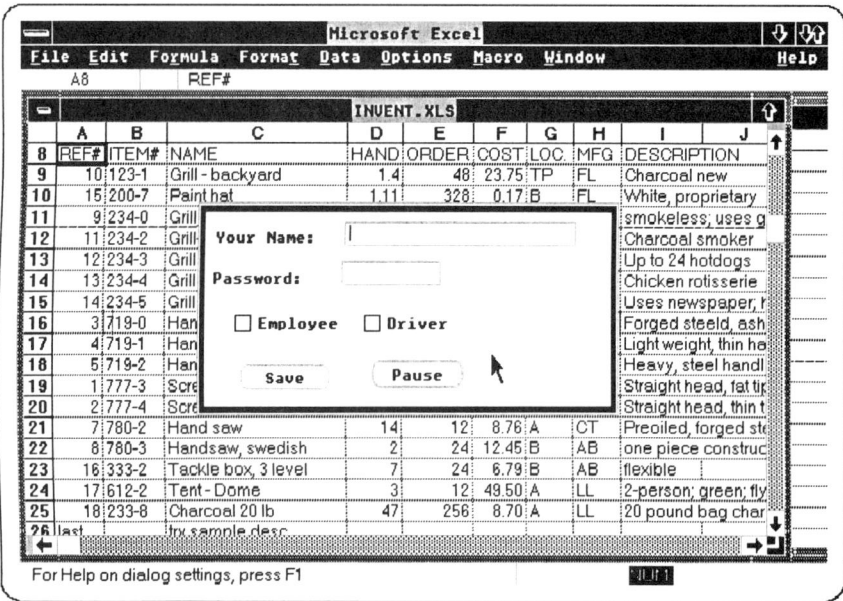

FIGURE 14.11. Nonstandard Button Types

overlaying any initial values there. To create this button through the Dialog Editor, select OK while the Default box is checked.

Type 2 The standard Cancel button. This button doesn't have a thick border. Pressing Esc has the same effect as selecting it directly. It doesn't enter any values into the Init/Result column, and it abandons any user entries on the screen. The Default box must not be checked if you want to create this button. If the box already includes a default OK button, the Default box is automatically turned off.

Type 3 A non-default OK button. This button has the same general effect of type 1, of placing input values in the Init/Result column of the range. But it must be selected deliberately. Pressing Enter doesn't select a Type 3 button. Be sure the Default box is not checked to create this button.

Type 4 A default Cancel button. This button has a thick dark border and is chosen if the user presses either Enter or Esc. It doesn't enter any values into the Init/Result column. The Default box must be checked to create this button.

Text and Edit Boxes

You've already seen how to use types 5 through 8 in creating custom data forms. They work exactly the same in dialog boxes. Values entered in edit boxes are

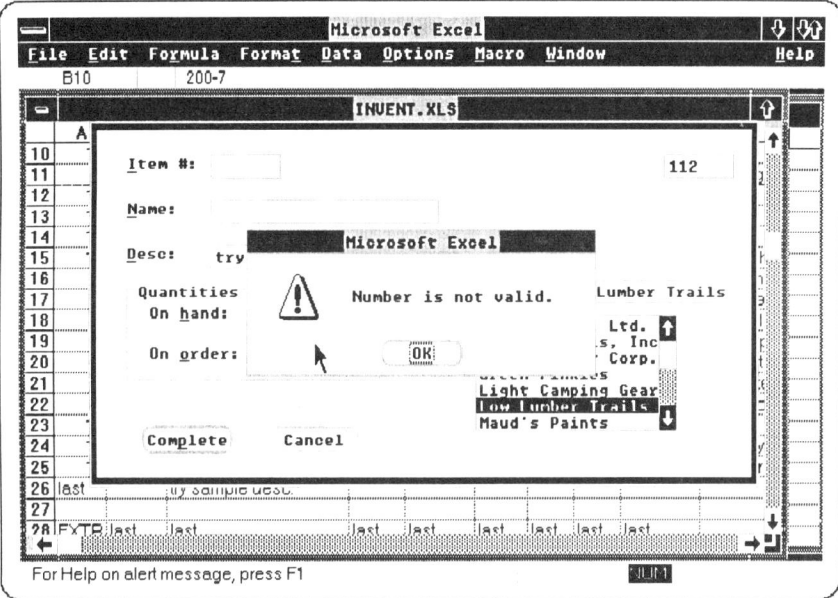

FIGURE 14.12.   Macro Error Box

placed in the Init/Result field for that object when an OK button is selected. Excel never alters the definition rows that describe type 5 objects; it simply displays the text in the appropriate location. Excel ignores any values in the Text field for types 6 through 10, as well as any values in the Init/Result field for type 5. Any initial values must be in the formula bar representation of the required format. Figure 14.12 shows a typical error box that appears if the wrong type of data is entered in one of these fields.

> **Type 5   Fixed text.** The fixed or constant text appears just as you enter it through the Dialog Editor or in the Text field (column 6) of the definition. You'll use it to label fields, give information, and generally make the dialog box easy for people to use. Each dialog box is limited to 1024 constant text characters in all.
>
> **Type 6   Text edit box.** This box represents an input field that will accept only text and displays the formula bar representation of whatever it entered. It treats whatever is entered as text, whether you want it to or not.
>
> **Type 7   Integer edit box.** This box represents an input field that accepts only integers—from −32765 to 32767. It uses the formula bar representation of what is entered. If the user enters anything else, Excel sends a message that the number is not valid when the OK button is selected. The integer edit box is selected, and the user can make a correction.

318   ADVANCED EXCEL

> **Type 8   Number edit box.** This box represents an input field that will accept any number values, even in scientific notation, and display the formula bar representation. It can handle decimal points, signs, and dollar signs and will ignore commas. The same message as for type 7 appears if non-number values are entered.
>
> **Type 9   Formula edit box.** This box represents an input field that accepts only formulas. Each must begin with an equal sign (=) just as in the formula bar. Any references in the definition range must use the R1C1 style, but Excel converts these for display to the current workspace style.
>
> **Type 10   Reference edit box.** This box represents an input field that accepts only references. In the definition range, the references must be in the R1C1 style, but Excel converts them for display to the current worksheet style. You can use individual cell references, ranges, or multiple selections.

Option Buttons and Check Boxes

Many dialog boxes use option buttons and check boxes, which you can find in the Dialog Editor on the Item Button menu. Option buttons are generally in a group; only one can be on at a time. For example, in an academic application you might have option button objects labelled Freshman, Sophomore, Junior, and Senior. You need an additional object to group them so that Excel knows that only one of the group can be on at a time. The group box item creates this group and puts a visible line around the group. Check boxes are a bit different; each is a toggle, but any could be on or off. You might use one for "Over 21," one for "Parking," and one for "Employed"; any or all might be checked for a given student. These too could be grouped to make the dialog box easier to read. You saw examples of these data types (11 through 14) in Figure 14.4. Figure 14.13 shows the definition range that describes that dialog box.

> **Type 11   Option button group.** This object isn't apparent in the displayed box, but it must precede each set of option buttons. If you define a group box and place it around a set of option buttons, this object is automatically placed in the range. Only one of the option buttons in a group (following a type 11 object) may be selected at a time. If the user selects one that is off, any on option is turned off automatically. In the Init/Result field, you can specify the sequence number of the button to be selected by default. If you leave column 7 blank or use 1, the first button is selected. If you don't want any button selected, enter #N/A.

CUSTOMIZED EXCEL APPLICATIONS

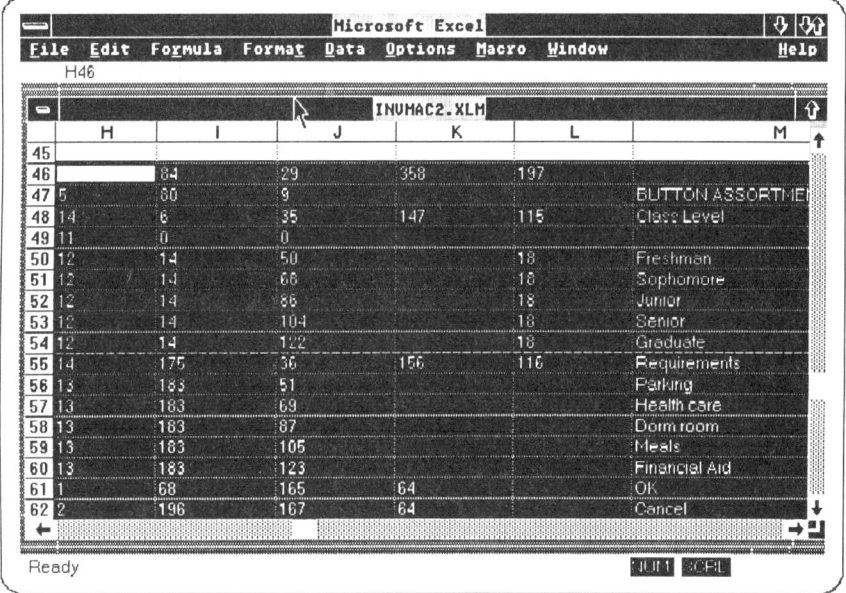

FIGURE 14.13. Definition Range for Option Buttons and Check Boxes

After the dialog box is entered, the value in the Init/Result field for object type 11 indicates which of the set of option buttons was turned on.

Type 12 Option button. You need a type 12 object for each option in a group; these should immediately follow the type 11 object. The text field specifies the text next to each displayed button. You can type these labels directly in the Dialog Editor or add them into the definition range.

Type 13 Check box. This is a toggle field; selecting it turns it on if it is currently off or off if it is currently on. Each check box is independent. The text that follows the check box appears in the Text field. TRUE in the Init/Result field means the object is checked; FALSE or no entry means it is not. Use #N/A to grey the box and make it unavailable. After the box is entered, the Init/Result field contains the final status of the box.

Type 14 Group box. This is a box that you can use to group anything in a dialog box. You must use the group box object to group option buttons in the Dialog Editor. It is also useful to group a set of check boxes, data entry fields, or a block of constant text. It can have text in the top edge; an entry in the Text field determines this. If you aren't using the Dialog Editor, you'll have to use a width and height for the group box. Excel

320 ADVANCED EXCEL

expects you to use all the sizing and positioning values to get objects to appear correctly within a type 14 box.

Text List Boxes

It's often convenient to use a list box in a dialog box. For example, you may want to let the user select from a list of items rather than enter the values. You can specify two different types of customized list boxes, as shown in Figure 14.14. The text preceding each list box is associated with it by its position; it must be already entered and selected when you create the list box through the Dialog Editor so that it appears on the line before the list object in the generated definition range. Excel limits you to a total of four list boxes in a dialog box.

> **Type 15 List box.** The standard list box contains a list of items. The Dialog Editor gives you a default size box that shows about six items in the list; you can resize it if necessary. You provide the list contents in a separate range elsewhere on the macro sheet. In the Text field (through

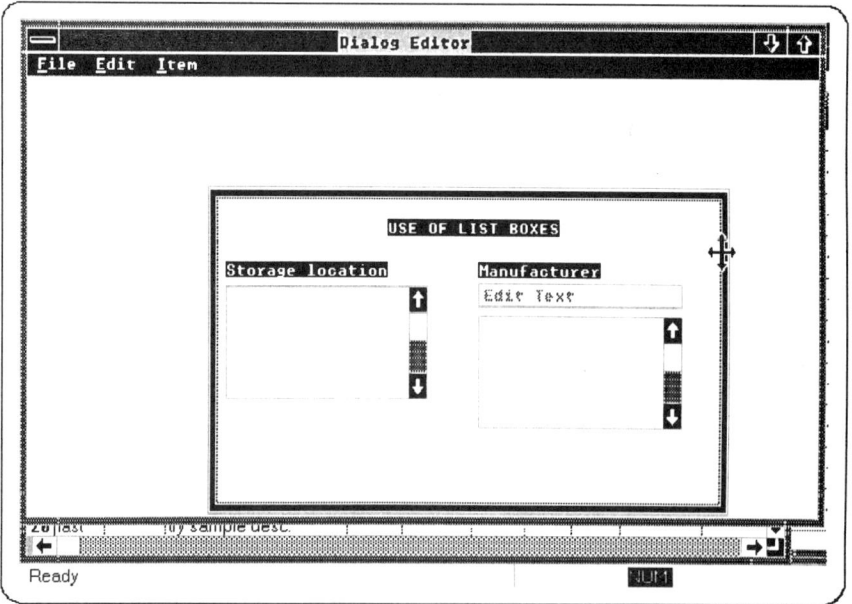

FIGURE 14.14. List Box Examples

CUSTOMIZED EXCEL APPLICATIONS

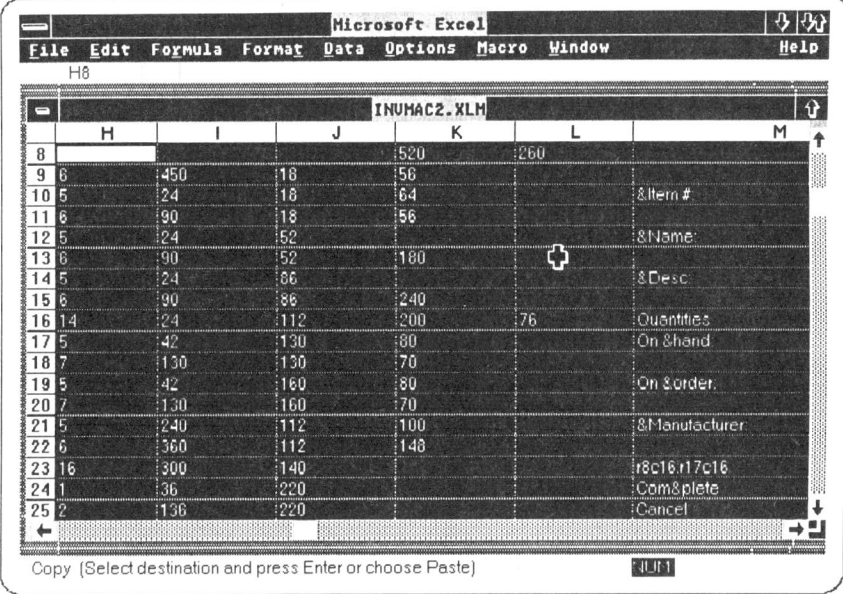

FIGURE 14.15. Defined Range with Linked List Box

Edit Info or in the generated range) you add a reference to the range that contains the contents of the list; the reference can be to a named range or in R1C1 style. If the reference is empty or not valid, nothing appears in the list box. By default, the first item in the list is highlighted when the dialog box is first displayed. To cause a different item in the list to be selected, enter its sequence number in the Init/Result field; use 1 for the first item, 2 for the second, etc. Use #N/A in this field if you don't want any list item selected when the dialog box is displayed. After an OK button is pressed, the text of the selected list item is placed in the Init/Result field.

Type 16 Linked list box. This looks and works just like the regular list box, but it is linked to a text edit box which must immediately precede it. When you select the linked list object from the Item menu, the preceding edit box is automatically generated as well. The selected item from the list appears in the box when the dialog box is first displayed, and it receives a different value if you change the selection in the box. You prepare the list and select a default value to appear in the text box just as you identify a default for the standard list. Figure 14.15 shows a defined range (the first six columns) that includes a linked list box. Notice that the reference range in the sixth column is in R1C1 style.

322 ADVANCED EXCEL

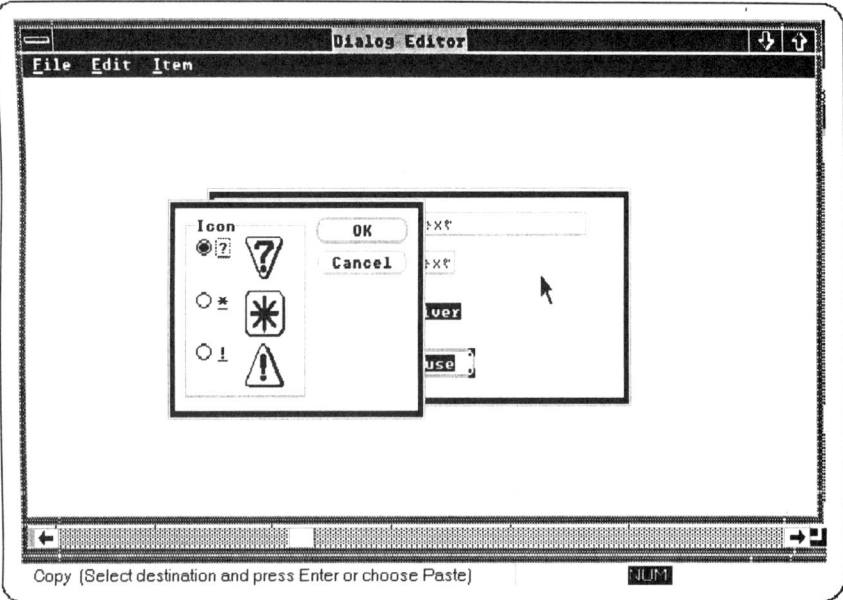

FIGURE 14.16. The Item Icon Menu

Icon Graphic

One of Excel's standard icons can appear in your customized dialog box, as shown in the Item Icon menu in Figure 14.16. You can use a question mark, asterisk, or exclamation point in the icon.

> **Type 17 Icon.** When you select the desired icon, it appears, and you can then move it. You can change the default size through the definition range or the Edit Info window. Remove the "Auto" check from width and height, then use screen measurement units representing the size you want. Some systems show only the standard size, so you might want to experiment with resizing icons before you use them. The Text field in the generated range shows 1 for a question mark, 2 for an asterisk, or 3 for an exclamation point to indicate which icon you requested.

Handling Files, Drives, and Directories

You can handle changing files, drives, and directories through your own dialog boxes, much as Excel does in the standard File Open dialog box, shown and

CUSTOMIZED EXCEL APPLICATIONS

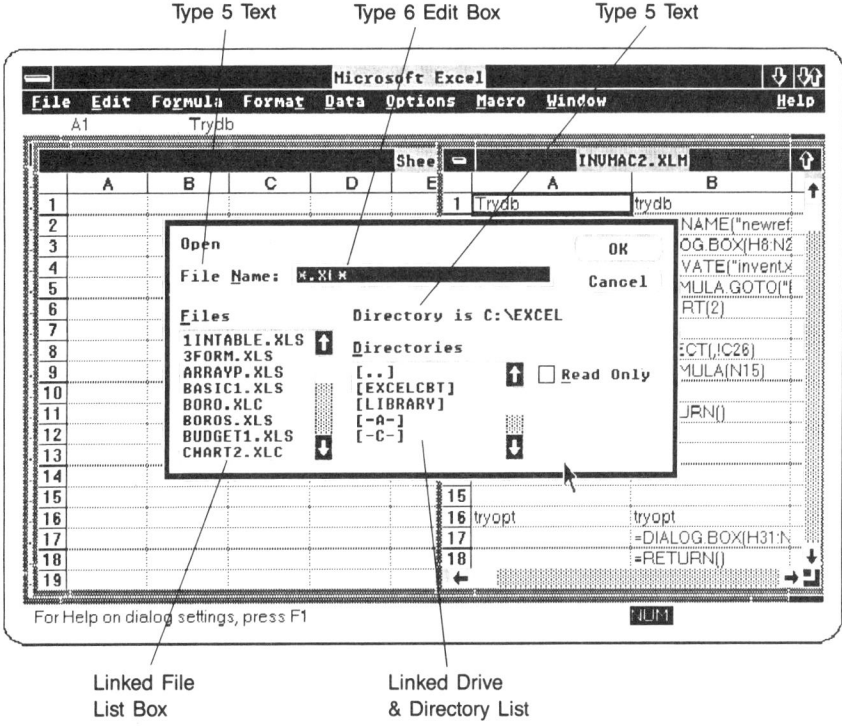

FIGURE 14.17. Components of File Handling

labeled in Figure 14.17. You can use the file list box and the drive and directory list box, along with the directory text and a few standard type 5 text boxes, to achieve the same options in your boxes. The file list box and the directory list box are always used together, in this order.

Type 18 **Linked file list box.** When you select Linked File/Directory on the Item List Box menu, you get three objects. The first is a text edit box (Type 6 object) that will hold the file name or an entry such as *.XLM to limit the files that are listed. The text edit box precedes the linked file list box in the Dialog Editor and in the definition range. You don't have to provide a list of files for this list box, since Excel uses the ones in the current directory; any entry in the text column is ignored. Excel uses a default size for the list box; you can change it if you like. Once generated, this box works just like the file list box in the standard Excel dialog boxes. The linked file list box is followed by a drive and directory list box (type 19). If a file is selected, it appears in the Init/ Result field for the linked text edit box after the dialog box is accepted.

Type 19 Linked drive and directory list box. This box follows the linked file list box. It lists the available drives and directories. If you use a standard text object (type 5) immediately following this box, it displays the name of the current drive and directory; Excel updates this even though it is entered as "constant" text. You can change the drive and/or directory with entries in the text box immediately preceding the linked file list box (type 18). Excel ignores any entries in the Text or Init/Result field for this object. You can position and size the drive and directory list box as needed. It must follow the file list box in the definition range.

Type 20 Directory text. This text displays the name of the current directory, but it doesn't change after the dialog box is displayed. When you select Linked File/Directory in the List Box menu, a check box for "Tracking Text" becomes available; just turn it on to generate this object. The type 20 object will immediately follow type 19 in the dialog box definition range, but it can be positioned anywhere in the dialog box. Any entry you make in the text field is ignored, but a selected directory may appear in the Init/Result field after the dialog box is accepted. Use a type 5 text item immediately following the type 19 object if you want Excel to update the current directory.

DEVELOPING A CUSTOMIZED DIALOG BOX

The development of a customized dialog box begins with a design. You examine the worksheet application that the box will be used with and decide what to include in the dialog box. You don't want to include too much information and data, or the user will become confused. Similarly, you don't want to omit information the user needs or the dialog box won't be useful. Once you know what you want, use the Dialog Editor to place the objects. Be sure to consider sequence here; to associate an object with text, enter and select the text first, then immediately add the associated edit box or list box. You can add most Init/Result values through the Edit Info window or directly into the generated definition range. When you copy a range back into the Dialog Editor, it is copied in its current form.

The dialog box will be displayed and processed through a macro, so the easiest place to put the definition range is on the same macro sheet. You can open and name a new macro sheet and copy a developed dialog box to it even before the macro is written. But you'll want at least a basic macro to display the dialog box while you're developing so you can check your progress.

Testing the Customized Dialog Box

You test a partial or complete customized dialog box by running a macro that includes the DIALOG.BOX macro function. The easiest way to do this is to include a very basic macro on the same macro sheet as the definition range. The macro can include just three lines; the macro name, the DIALOG.BOX function, and the RETURN function. If you name the range generated each time you paste from the Clipboard and use that name in the DIALOG.BOX function, you won't have to modify the DIALOG.BOX function every time you change the size of the definition range, since the name specifies the complete range. Be sure and define the name of the macro and give it a shortcut key so that you can use it easily.

While testing a customized dialog box, be sure and check it frequently. Use Tab each time you test to make sure the sequence is what you need. It's very easy to get a dialog box in a mess and not be able to tell where you went wrong.

SUGGESTED EXERCISE

For this exercise, develop a dialog box for one of your worksheets. Select one that can include text and number input as well as a list box. If you can, include a set of option buttons or check boxes as well.

1. Sketch out your dialog box on paper so you know about where each object should go.
2. Open a new macro sheet and enter the seven column headings beginning in Column G.
3. Enter the Dialog Editor and create several fields, associating text with edit boxes. Enter an initial value for one of the edit boxes.
4. Copy the dialog box to the Clipboard, then paste it into the macro sheet below your labels. Define the name TEMP for the range as pasted.
5. Create a short macro, placing its name in cell B1, =DIALOG.BOX(temp) in cell B2, and =RETURN() in cell B3. Define the name as a command macro and assign a shortcut key.
6. Activate the worksheet and use the shortcut key. If you get an error box, note the cell that caused the problem before you try to fix it. Notice the initial value you requested. Try Tab to see if the edit boxes are selected appropriately. If you used &, try the ALT key combination to select the associated edit box.
7. Copy the range back to the Clipboard and paste it into the Dialog Editor. Add a list box and a set of option buttons or check boxes. Put appropriate text with the buttons. Then copy the dialog box to the macro sheet and name the range just as before to replace the name with the new reference.
8. Try it out again. Type a list of ten items in a range on the macro sheet and

reference that range in the text field for the list box. See what happens when you use the dialog box now.
9. Make additional changes and try more object types and combinations if you want.

What if It Doesn't Work?

1. If the dialog box itself doesn't appear or if it is a very strange size and shape, check your macro. The DIALOG.BOX function must name the range just as generated by the Dialog Editor.
2. The problems that aren't obvious with objects generally come down to position/size conflicts. Try allowing more space between objects. Go back to the Dialog Editor and try to move things a bit. If an object won't move, check the Edit Info window and remove any Auto check that inhibits moving.
3. If you have trouble with a text list box, make sure you entered a list of values and referenced the range in the Text field of the row that applies to that object. A sequence number in the Init/Result field indicates the item to be selected.
4. If you have trouble with option buttons, be sure the type 11 (option group) object immediately precedes the list of buttons. If not, insert a row of cells and add it. The only other entry you need for the type 11 object is a sequence number in the Init/Result field to indicate which button is selected.
5. The Init/Result field for check boxes can contain TRUE (checked), FALSE or blank (not checked), or #N/A (greyed).

Processing Customized Dialog Box Input

After the user chooses OK to return control to the macro following the DIALOG.BOX function, the definition range contains any entered or selected information. The macro can refer to any of those values; often, it copies them into the worksheet from which the macro was originally run. The values can be copied from the Init/Result column with command equivalent macros (SELECT data to be copied, COPY, SELECT new location, PASTE) or with the FORMULA function.

To copy a value from the definition range into the original worksheet, you must first activate the original worksheet with ACTIVATE(worksheet.name) and locate the appropriate place for the values. One way to do this is to include a dummy last row of cells with your data, assigned a name such as LAST.ROW. Then the macro can follow the ACTIVATE function with FORMULA.GOTO("LAST.ROW") to select the named range and INSERT(2) to insert a new row and shift cells down. At this point the macro contains these commands:

```
                macroname
                    =DIALOG.BOX(H8:N25)
                    =ACTIVATE("INVENT.XLS")
                    =FORMULA.GOTO("LAST.ROW")
                    =INSERT(2)
```

Now you can SELECT a cell in the newly inserted row to receive a value and use the FORMULA function to insert a value from a cell in the macro. The next few commands might be these:

```
                    =SELECT(,"RC[1]")
                    =FORMULA(N11)
                    =SELECT(,"RC[1]")
                    =FORMULA(N13)
                    =SELECT(,"RC[1]")
                    =FORMULA(N15)
```

Once all the values you want copied to the worksheet are ready, you can end the macro and return control to Excel. The macro can perform any other operations you need done. One frequent operation is to restore certain Init/Result values to their original status for the next display of the dialog box. You can do this with the SET.VALUE function.

The SET.VALUE function uses two arguments, a reference and a value; if the reference is to a range, the value must be an array of the same size and shape. You can use it to restore the original Init/Result values, as in SET.VALUE(G12,"") to erase the value in cell G12. SET.VALUE(N22,"Low Lumber Trails") restores the original setting for the linked list in Figure 14.1.

CUSTOMIZED HELP

You can develop customized help to accompany custom dialog boxes and data forms; once developed, you can specify the help reference in the upper right corner of the definition range. Then the referenced help window will be displayed when F1 is pressed while the box is active.

You can develop custom help files through Excel or using your word processor. You need a text file with ASCII data that Excel can read. If you use Excel, you can justify the help information for each topic, then use the File Save As command to create a text file. The file can contain any number of help topics, each preceded by an asterisk and a help topic number on a separate line. Figure 14.18 shows the structure of a help file.

You can include as many help topics as you like in any sequence in a single

328 ADVANCED EXCEL

Format:

```
*topic_number  comments
line of help text
line of help text
...
*topic_number  contents
line of help text
line of help text
...
```

Example:

```
*201  Help for inventory dialog box

        General
Enter the full value for all fields except
for the manufacturer.  Select the appropriate
manufacturer code from this list:

        AB    Allbright Plastics
        CC    Connecticut Confectionery
        LL    Low Lumber Trails
        GP    Green Pinkies, Inc.
        FR    Freylinghauser Corp.
        MD    Maud's Plants

*222  Help for Mailing List Application
...
```

FIGURE 14.18.   Customized Help File

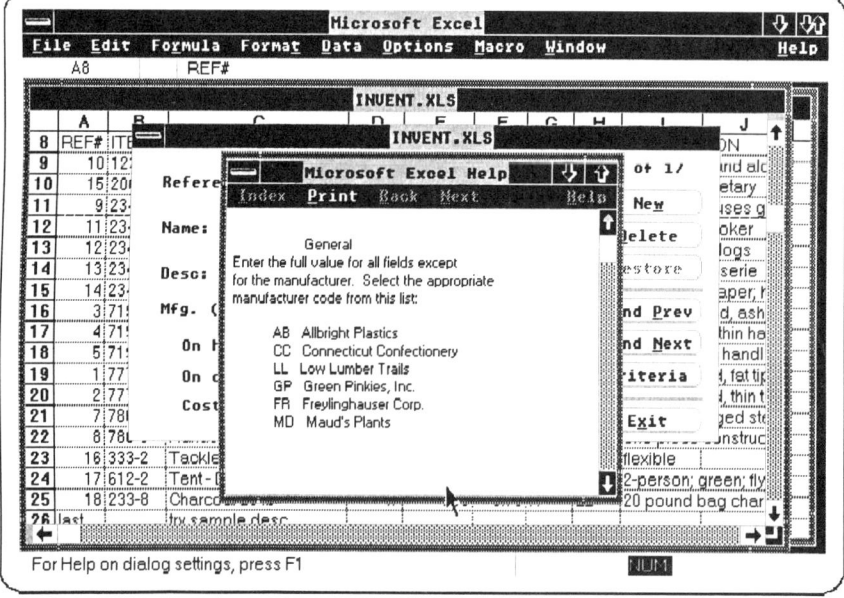

FIGURE 14.19.   Customized Help Display

file. The reference includes the name of the help file (with a path if necessary) in this format:

file_name!topic_number

If your help file is named DBHELP.TXT, you could reference topic 12 by typing DBHELP.TXT!12 in the upper left corner of a custom data form or dialog box. Figure 14.19 shows customized help for the custom data form shown in Figure 14.2.

OTHER CUSTOMIZING

As you've undoubtedly noticed, Excel has several built-in menu bars; Figure 14.20 lists the menu names on each. You can add up to 15 additional menu bars. You can add or remove menus on new or built-in bars, and you can add or remove commands on new or built-in commands.

```
Worksheet and macro sheet -- full and short menus
        File
        Edit
        Formula
        Format
        Data
        Options
        Macro
        Window
        Help

Chart document -- full and short menus
        File
        Edit
        Gallery
        Chart
        Format
        Macro
        Window
        Help

Nil menu bar (nothing open)
        File
        Help

Info menu bar
        File
        Info
        Macro
        Window
        Help
```

FIGURE 14.20. Built-In Menu Bars

Excel provides several functions specific for use in customizing menus. We'll overview them here; be sure to check the Excel Functions and Macros documentation before actually using these functions in your macros.

You can use ADD.BAR to add a new, empty menu bar; it returns the reference number of the bar, which you can name for use in referring to the new menu. You then use that number in the ADD.MENU function, which adds a menu to the specified bar; it references a definition range that includes the menu name, command names, and even status line messages and help topics if you want. You can use ADD.COMMAND to add individual commands to built-in menus or to added ones. A menu is always added at the right end of the bar, except for a help menu. A command is always placed at the bottom of the menu. When you're ready to use the new bar, use SHOW.BAR to display it.

The DELETE.COMMAND and DELETE.MENU functions remove built-in or added commands or menus. You can use ENABLE.COMMAND or DISABLE.COMMAND to make individual commands available or unavailable, depending on the needs of your application. You can use CHECK.COMMAND to add or remove checkmarks in a menu.

You may find it useful to use the REMOVE.COMMAND function to prevent users of applications from performing some actions. Take time to review the Excel documentation on all the customized menu control functions before you use them in a macro.

SUMMARY

In this chapter, we've examined in detail how to develop and use customized data forms and dialog boxes through the Dialog Editor. You've learned a great deal more about macro usage in the process. We've also touched on customized help, which is fairly easy to set up, and customized menu bar and commands, which aren't. If you have an application that can use the benefits of custom menus, however, it is worth the time to practice with the application.

15 PROTECTING AND CONTROLLING DOCUMENTS AND CELLS

Many documents must be protected, either from access by unauthorized people or from inadvertent change. This chapter covers various ways in which you can protect documents. It also covers ways to set up a document so that some cells can be changed and others can't.

The second part of this chapter deals with functions accessed from the application control menu by selecting the Run command. You'll see how to reach the areas for handling additional printers or fonts, removing excess ones, and modifying port and communications assignments. Changing various Excel defaults is also covered; you'll see how to modify the beep, the border width, and various screen colors and formats.

PROTECTING DOCUMENTS

You will often want to protect documents from access or change by other users. You can protect documents at several levels. The highest level protects from any access at all; the next level allows access but not any changes; another level allows changes only to certain cells but protects others from changes. Once a document is protected, its contents cannot be changed, since all cells are locked by default. You'll see how to unlock specific cells in this chapter.

Preventing Document Access

When you save a file, you can supply a password. The document can then be accessed only when the identical password is entered. When you select File Save As, Excel gives you a dialog box that includes an Options button. Select Options to expand the dialog box so it appears as shown in Figure 15.1. The former worksheet name appears in the upper text box. The File Format group includes the Normal button, which requests normal Excel document format for

332 ADVANCED EXCEL

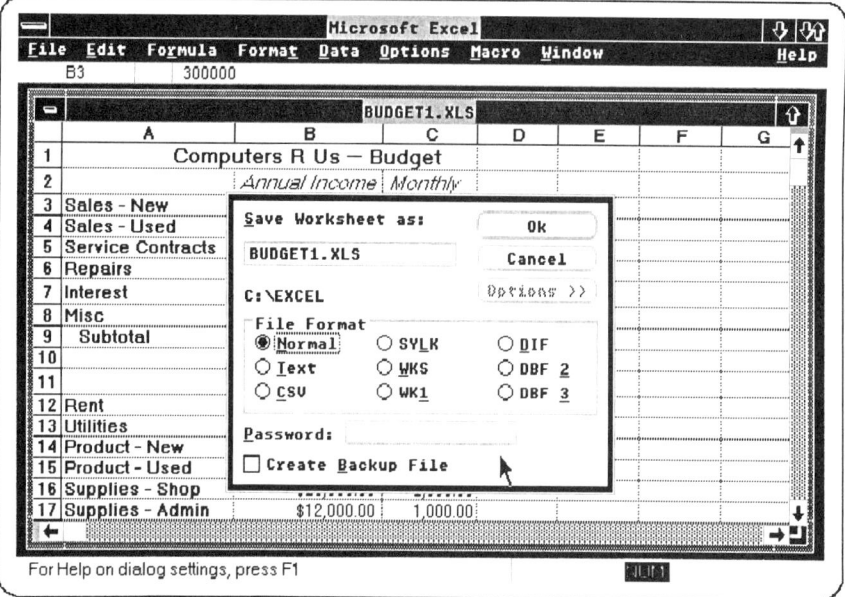

FIGURE 15.1. Establishing Password Protection

storage. To protect the document, type a password in the Password field near the bottom of the box. Any time someone tries to open that file, the password will be requested.

Once access is achieved, the entire document is available; it can be changed at will unless additional protection has been applied.

Passwords

A password can be up to 16 characters long. You can use any combination of letters, numbers, and symbols. Excel discriminates between upper- and lowercase letters. Once you use a password to protect a document, you must use the identical password to gain access to it. Depending on how much security you want, you might need a backup system to keep track of your passwords. If you use password protection just so mistakes aren't made by accident, you can keep your passwords on paper and look them up if necessary. If you need more extensive security, you won't want to store written passwords anywhere they can be seen by others. You might want to designate a person who is above reproach, such as the company president or security chief, to maintain a hard copy list of passwords. If you forget a password, you won't be able to access the file. Excel has no means of telling you what password applies to which file.

To prevent people from guessing your passwords, don't use the same password for more than one file. And don't use very common passwords such as your first name, your mother's maiden name, or your office extension. To make it easier to remember passwords but hard for others to figure them out, you might always capitalize the second or fifth letter, or use a symbol such as + in a certain position.

Accessing a Protected File

When you try to access a password protected file, Excel displays a dialog box like the one in Figure 15.2. You type in the password and press Enter, then you'll see the file just as if it weren't protected. Whether or not you can change the cells depends on whether or not additional protection is in force. If the document has been additionally protected, then the default cell protection status of Locked is in force.

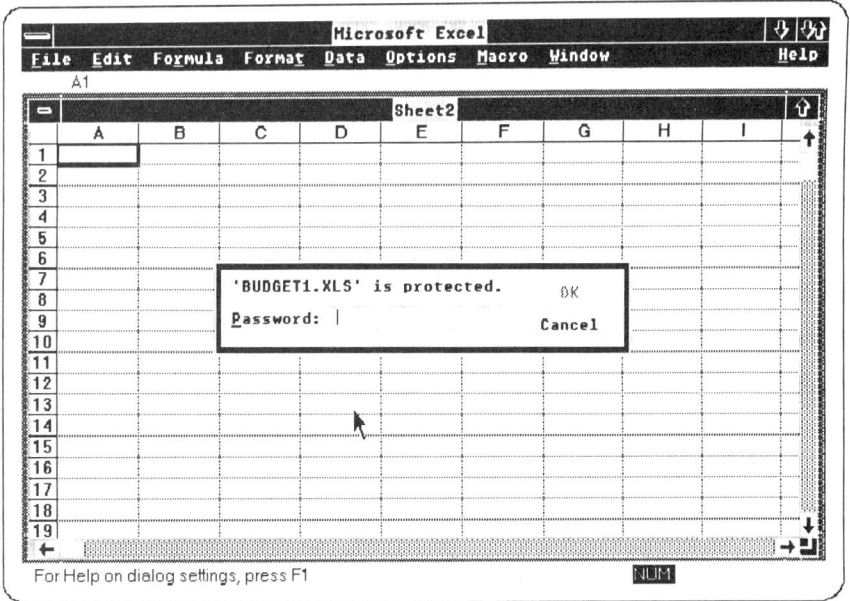

FIGURE 15.2. Accessing a Protected File

Removing Document Protection

You can remove document protection with the File Save As command or from the Options menu. The Options menu shows Unprotect document when the active document is protected. Once you can see the Password field, erase the current password. The password protection is gone. You can use a similar technique to change the password.

Protecting a Document from Changes

You can also protect a document without saving it as a separate step. You can select the Options Protect Document command while the document to be protected is active. You'll see the dialog box shown in Figure 15.3. Here again you can enter a password. You can also select either (or both) Contents or Windows to be protected. Contents refers to the document contents, to what is in each cell. Windows refers to the window as it is currently configured: the size, location, and panes in it. You can use Protect Window to keep users from seeing other parts of the worksheet or to make absolutely sure the window size isn't changed. If you use Options Freeze Panes before protecting a window, you can even prevent scrolling in the displayed window. If you protect both Con-

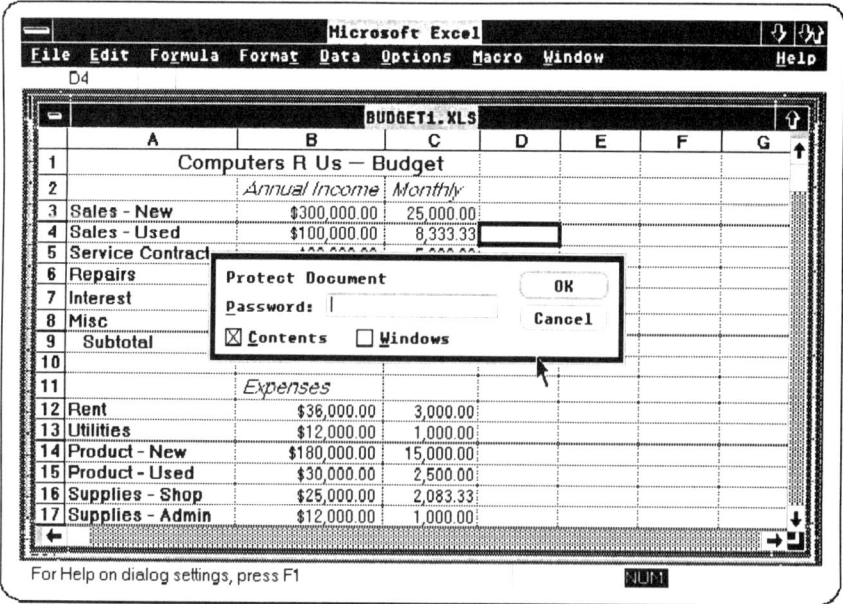

FIGURE 15.3. Options Protect Document Dialog Box

tents and Windows, you have absolute control over what the users see on the screen and over what they can do with it.

If you try to make changes to a protected cell, you'll see a message: "Locked cells can't be changed." To remove the password change protection, select Unprotect Document from the Options menu and enter the same password again. Protection is removed immediately.

Protecting without Passwords

When you protect a document without providing a password, the contents cannot be changed unless you "unprotect" it. If you want to prevent others from changing a worksheet, but not from seeing it, you can protect without a password. If you do this, anyone can just change the protected status in order to make changes. Protecting without passwords protects against inadvertent changes, but provides no protection against changes by any Excel user. When you try to change cells in a worksheet protected without a password, you'll see a message like the one in Figure 15.4.

To remove the protection, just select Options Unprotect Document. If no password was assigned, the protection is removed instantly.

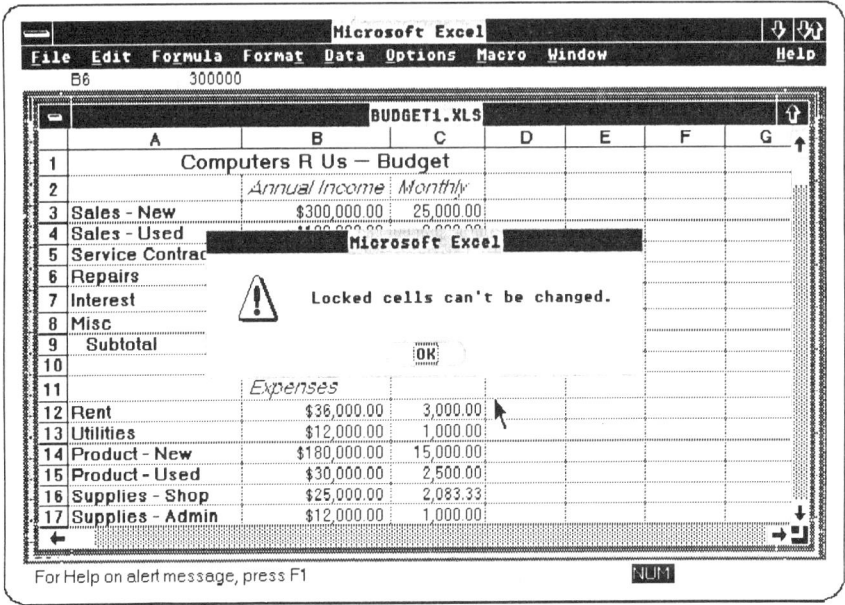

FIGURE 15.4. Protected Mesage

CONTROLLING CELL PROTECTION

By default, all cells in a worksheet have locked status; that means that if the worksheet itself is protected from change, then all the cells in it are also protected from change. You can "unprotect" some or all the cells in a worksheet before applying protection at the document level; then the unprotected cells can be changed by the user.

Unlocking Cells

You can unlock individual cells in a document so they can be changed while the document as a whole is protected from change. The document must be in an unprotected state when the cells are unlocked. To unlock cells, first unprotect the document. Then select the cells you wish to unlock and use the Cell Protection command from the Format menu. You can use multiple selection to select all cells to be unlocked. Excel gives you a dialog box like the one in Figure 15.5.

When you select the Locked check box, it is turned off and the cells are unlocked. They can be changed even if the Document containing them is protected.

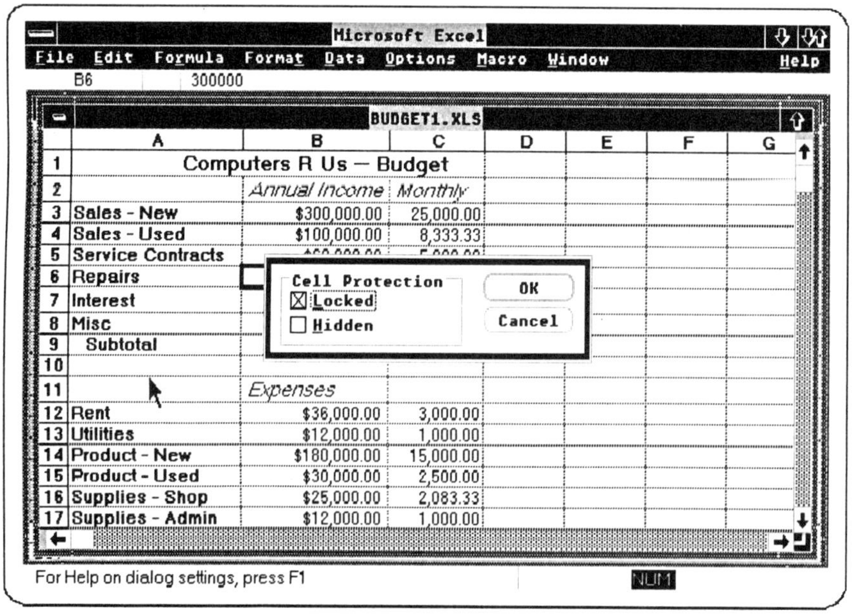

FIGURE 15.5. Cell Protection Dialog Box

PROTECTING AND CONTROLLING DOCUMENTS AND CELLS

The Hidden check box controls whether or not the formula for a cell is displayed in the formula bar while the cell is active. You may want to prevent users from seeing formulas; if so, turn on the Hidden check box to hide the formulas. When a "hidden" cell is selected, nothing appears in the formula bar.

Allowing Selected Changes

Suppose you want users to be allowed to make changes to certain fields in a database but not others. You want this to be true whether the users work with the data base directly or use default or customized data forms. How can you do this?

The first step is to open the document and select the cells you want to allow changes in. Select the entire range, including the field name through the last row in the database for each field. Then use the Format Cell Protection command and turn off the Locked check box. Finally, use the Options Protect Document command and assign a password.

When the user opens the document, the protected fields (the ones you did not unlock) cannot be changed. If data forms are used, the locked fields appear but are not surrounded by edit boxes. Figure 15.6 shows a data form in which

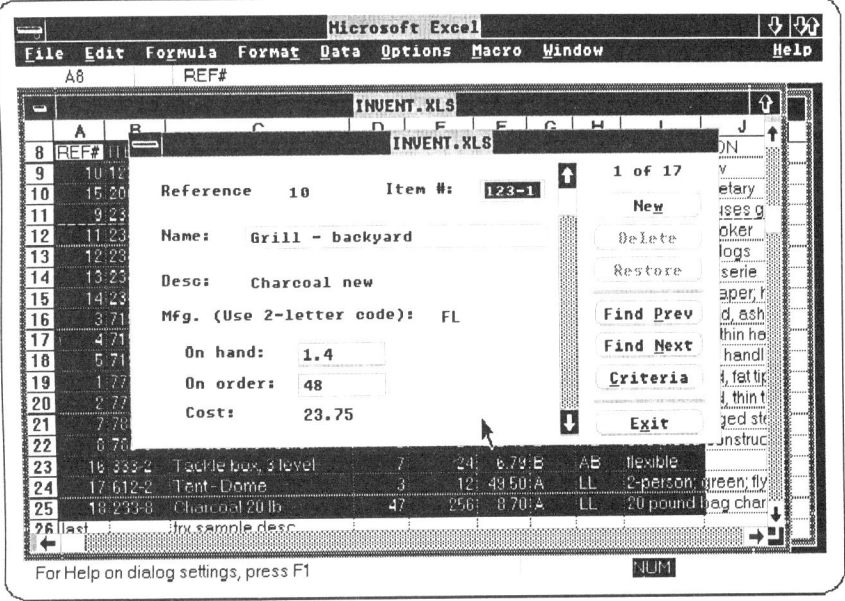

FIGURE 15.6. Data Form with Locked Data

several data fields do not have boxes. These are the locked fields. Only the fields that have boxes can be entered directly.

Even when adding new records, you can't enter data in locked fields. When Excel adds rows to the database for new records through data forms, it maintains the protection format of the rest of the database. If you add additional lines to the worksheet in the middle of the database, Excel perpetuates the protection pattern, just as it maintains formats for different fields.

Protecting Charts

You can protect charts from access or changes much as you can protect worksheets. If you assign a password when you save a chart, that password is required whenever it is accessed. You can protect a chart from changes with the Protect Chart command from the Chart menu. It results in a dialog box exactly like the one shown in Figure 15.3. Again you can protect the contents of the chart or the window in which it is displayed.

There is no equivalent of the cell protection feature with charts; you must protect the entire chart to protect any part of it. As with other documents, you can use a password or not as you prefer. If the protection is against inadvertent changes only, the password isn't necessary.

SUGGESTED EXERCISE

1. Open a worksheet you don't really care about (in case you can't access it again) and save it using the File Save As command. Assign a password you will remember easily, such as aaa. Close the document.
2. Open the same document. Enter the password to gain access.
3. Protect the entire document from changes with the Options Protect document command. Don't bother with a password for now. Then try to change a cell.
4. Remove the change protection. Then select a range of cells and unlock them, using Format Cell Protection. Protect the document again. Now try to change the cells that you unlocked.
5. Remove the document protection, then set the hidden feature for a cell that uses a formula to produce the cell contents. Protect the document again and note the result.
6. Remove both access and change protection from the document before ending the exercise.

What if It Doesn't Work?

1. If Excel lets you change cells in step 3, the default cell locking may have been changed. Remove the protection, then use the Format Cell Protection command to ensure that all cells in the worksheet are locked.

PROTECTING AND CONTROLLING DOCUMENTS AND CELLS

2. If you can't use your password to access the file or change the protection status, give it another try. Remember that Excel notices case in passwords, so use the same exact characters as when you first entered the password. If you still can't reuse the password, you must have forgotten the sequence of characters you used. Make a more specific note next time. We warned you to use a worksheet that wasn't important.

USING EXCEL CONTROL FUNCTIONS

Throughout this book, we have been working with Excel as it is currently set up. You can use commands on the application control menu (ALT + Spacebar) to adjust the size and position of the application window, as well as to close it. You've seen how to use the control Run command to access the Dialog Editor. In this chapter, we'll examine the other functions you can accomplish through control Run. Figure 15.7 shows the dialog box resulting from selecting control Run.

You've already learned to use the Dialog Editor. We'll cover the others in this chapter.

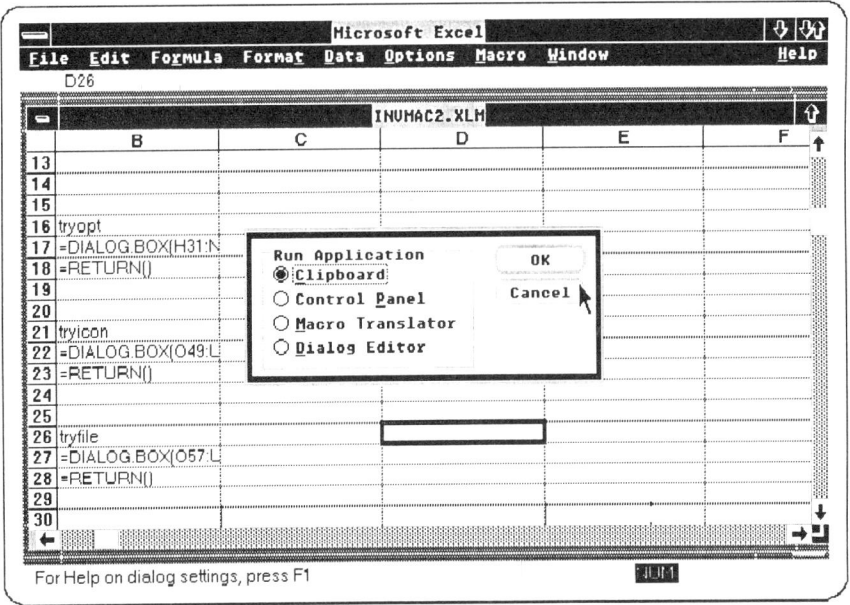

FIGURE 15.7. The Run Application Dialog Box

Running the Clipboard

The Clipboard holds data or references being copied or moved from one place to another. When you use the Dialog Editor, you copy its results to the Clipboard, then paste that into the desired worksheet. If you use the full Windows, you can use the Clipboard to copy data from one application to another. Whenever you use a copy or move command within Excel, a reference to the selected range is stored in the clipboard until the operation is finally completed. That's why you can paste the same data in several different locations. But when you cancel the operation with Escape, or start a new cut or copy operation, the data is removed from the clipboard. Figure 15.8 shows how the Clipboard looks if you select Control Run Clipboard when it contains data to be copied.

The lower part of the Clipboard window contains a description of the data being copied. In this case, it's a range 18 rows by 7 columns. The upper part of the clipboard contains flags that may possibly be needed in the operation. When the clipboard is not in use, it contains only the message "Clipboard is empty." Excel uses the Clipboard just fine without your ever looking at it.

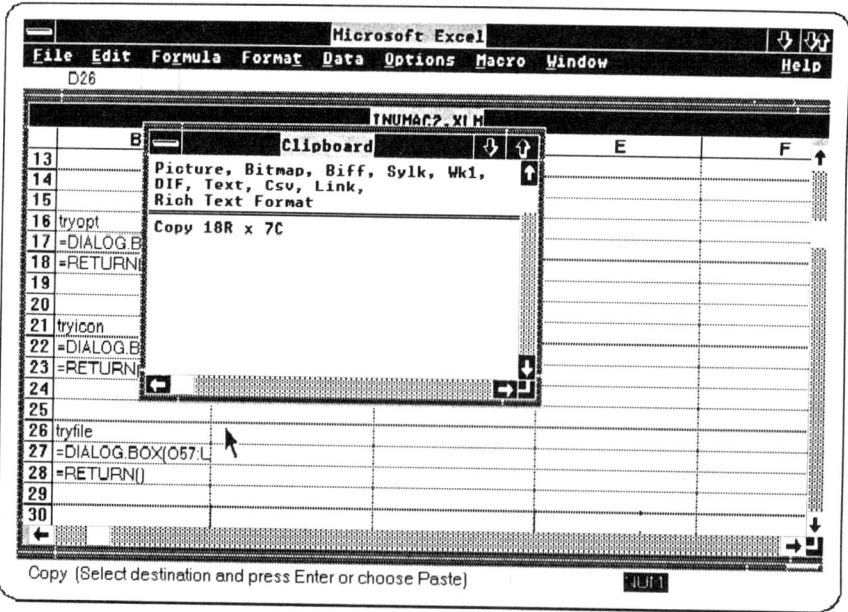

FIGURE 15.8. Clipboard Window in Use

Running the Control Panel

When you select Control Panel from the application control Run menu, you see a display like the one in Figure 15.9. This shows the current time and date, both of which you can adjust. You can also change the cursor blink rate and the double click speed in this display.

From this display, you can access three additional menus. We'll look at them shortly.

Adjusting Control Panel Fields. Use the Tab key to set one of the four fields (Time, Date, Cursor Blink, or Double Click) active.

When the Cursor Blink field is active, the thumb spot blinks at the current blink rate. You can change the speed by dragging the thumb spot in the scroll bar in the appropriate direction or by repeatedly pressing the appropriate arrow key. You can't make it stop blinking completely.

When the Double Click field is active, its thumb spot blinks at the current cursor blink rate. If you've been having trouble with double clicks, you might want to make the acceptable time gap between the clicks higher or lower. To do

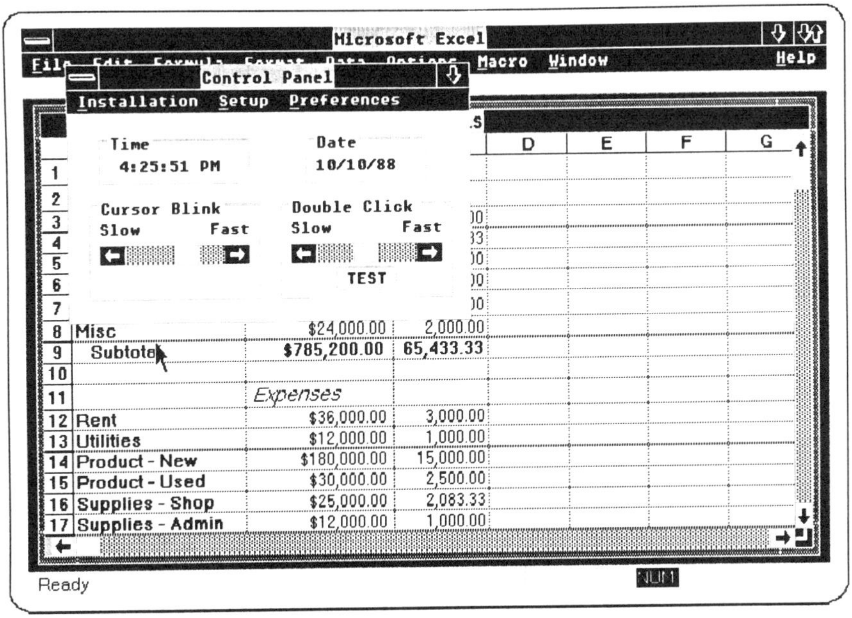

FIGURE 15.9. Control Panel Display

that, just move the thumb spot in the appropriate direction. You can test it by double clicking on the TEST spot to select or unselect it. If Excel interprets your action as a double click, the status of TEST changes; otherwise, it doesn't. You can keep changing the double click setting until you find one that is comfortable for you.

To change the Time or Date field, make it active. Use Tab to move to the field. One part of the field is active at a time; use right or left arrow keys to move to other parts of a Time or Date field. You can change first the hour or year. When that is satisfactory, use the right arrow key to activate the next part to be adjusted. The setting you make here affects the current Excel session, but it doesn't affect the system clock. You might want to adjust the settings here to cause them to be used in certain applications. The next time you start Excel, it will once again use the system clock.

Control Panel Installation Options. Figure 15.10 shows the Control Panel Installation menu. From here, you can add and delete printers and fonts as well as exit the Control Panel and find out its version number. Procedures for adding printers and fonts here are very much as during installation, so we won't cover it. Check your installation instructions and be sure you know the names of the ports and fonts to be used.

If you want to delete a printer or font, Excel shows you a listing of the

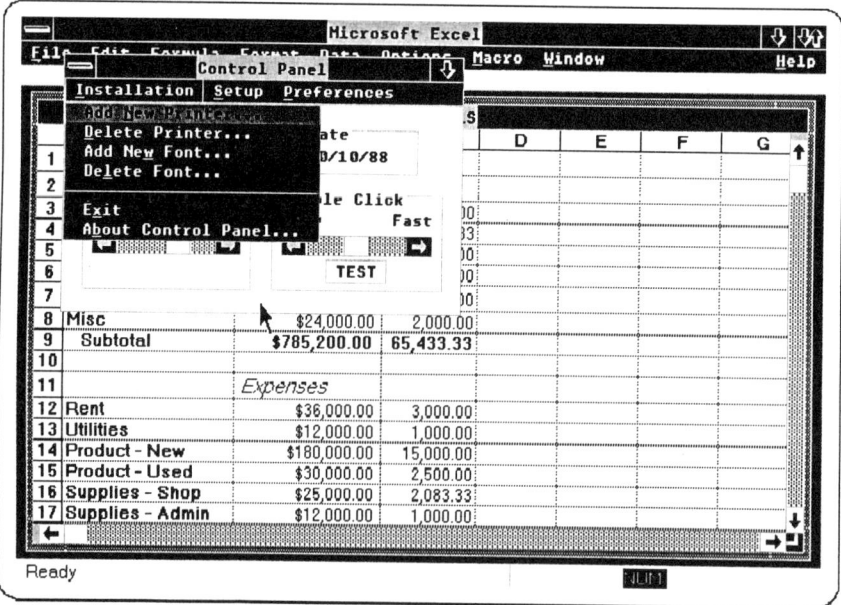

FIGURE 15.10. Control Panel Installation Menu

PROTECTING AND CONTROLLING DOCUMENTS AND CELLS

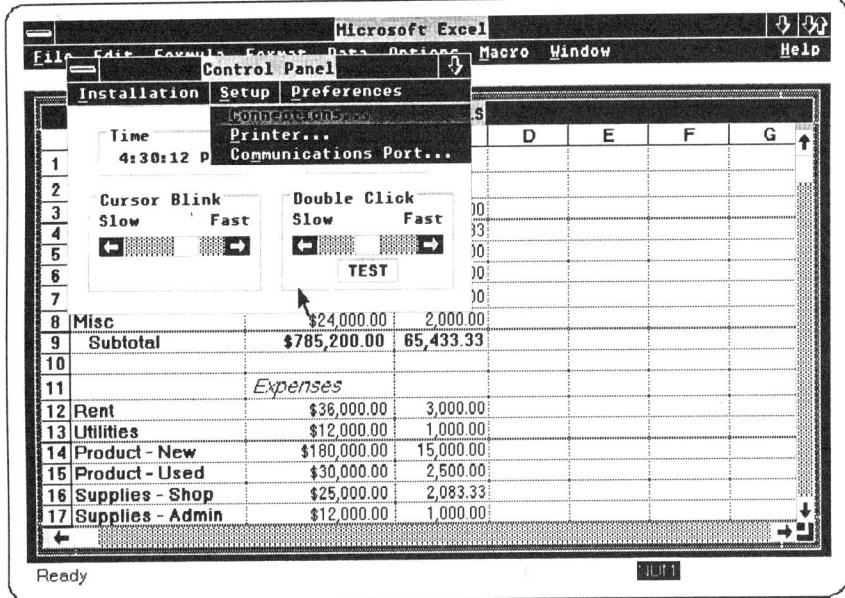

FIGURE 15.11. Control Panel Setup Menu

currently installed printers and fonts for the selected printer. Just select what you want to delete, and it's gone.

Control Panel Setup Options. Figure 15.11 shows the Control Panel Setup menu. You can adjust port connections to any currently installed printer, change the current printer to another installed one, or adjust settings on a communications port.

In most cases, you won't have to touch the setup options once Excel is installed the way you need it.

Control Panel Preferences. Excel lets you specify your preferences in various areas through the Control Panel and puts them into effect. Figure 15.12 shows the Control Panel Preferences menu.

Adjusting screen colors is the most dramatic change you can make through this menu. Figure 15.13 shows the resulting dialog box, but it looks quite different on screen. The default colors are shown in their appropriate positions in the sample window on the right. The list box includes all the different parts of the Excel window that you can change the colors of.

This dialog box has three buttons; OK accepts the changes and puts them into effect. Cancel cancels the changes, puts the colors back as they were when you accessed this dialog box, and returns to the previous menu. Reset puts the colors back as they were when you accessed this dialog box and leaves you in it to try again. There is no way you can get back to the default colors except by

344 ADVANCED EXCEL

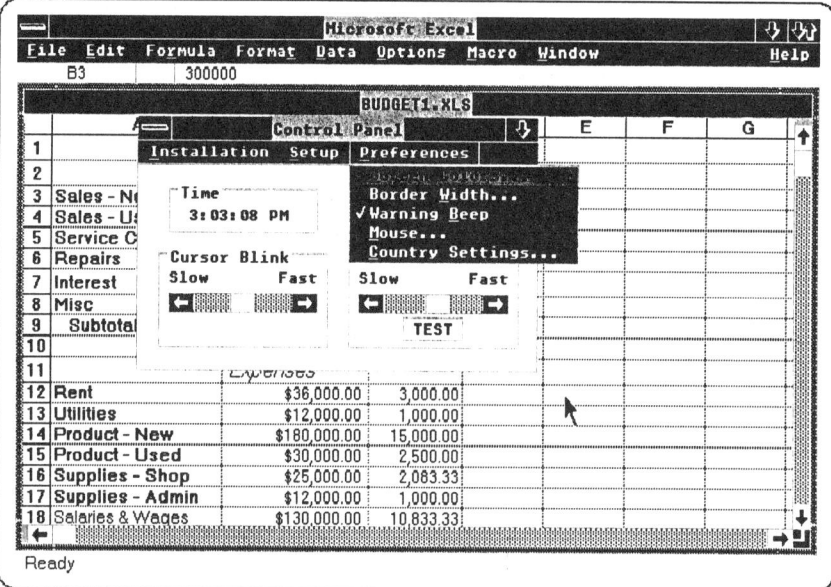

FIGURE 15.12. Control Panel Preferences Menu

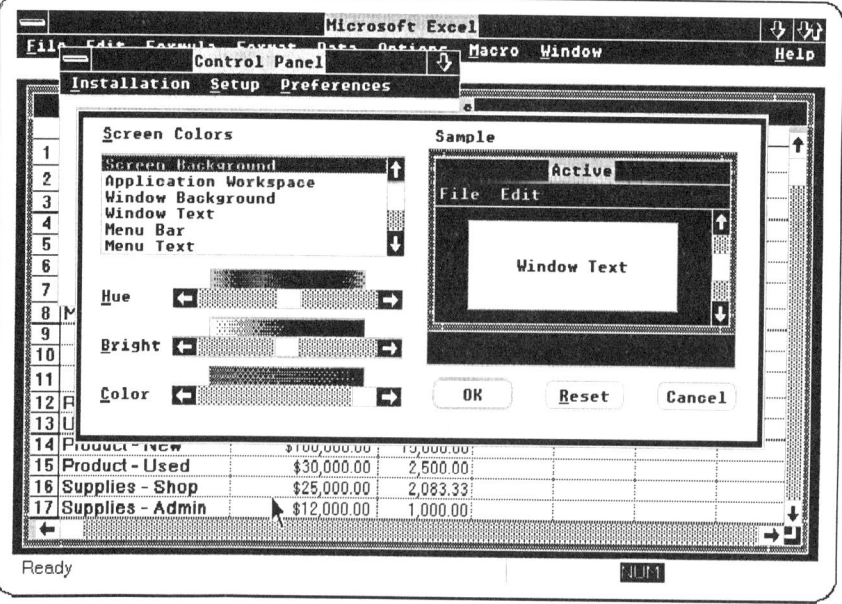

FIGURE 15.13. Screen Colors Dialog Box

reinstalling Excel. It's a good idea to draw a picture of the thumb settings for the Hue, Bright, and Color bars before you make any changes and store it in a file cabinet somewhere.

The three color bars interact with each other. They affect the selected window component selected in the Screen Colors list box. First select the component, then set Hue, then Color, then Bright for the best control. If you are trying to make major changes, try setting all three thumbs to the middle and see the effect. Then vary them. The big color decision is whether you want a dark or light background. From there, you have to consider readability; for example, a white background needs dark text and gridlines so you can see it on the screen.

The Border Width preference lets you change the width of the standard window border. The default width is 5; use a smaller number to use a smaller border; this might be useful if you like to be able to see several windows on screen at once since less space is needed for border, but the smaller borders are harder to grab with the mouse for moving and resizing windows. Whatever you set here affects all the active windows.

You can select Warning Beep to turn the Beep on or off (it's a toggle) for all applications. Like border width, the beep has one setting for all windows.

The Mouse preference presents you with the dialog box shown in Figure 15.14. Here you can make the other mouse button active or change the way Excel reacts to its speed.

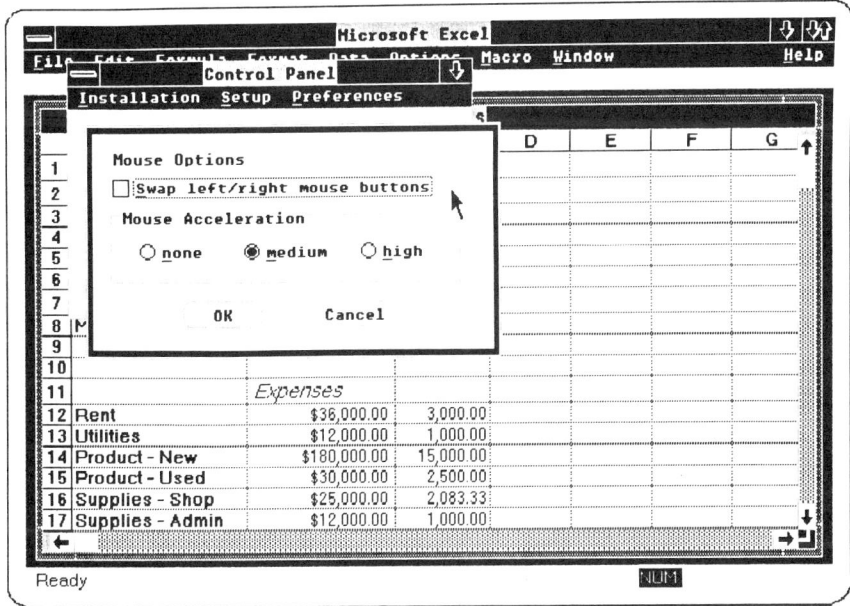

FIGURE 15.14. Mouse Preference Dialog Box

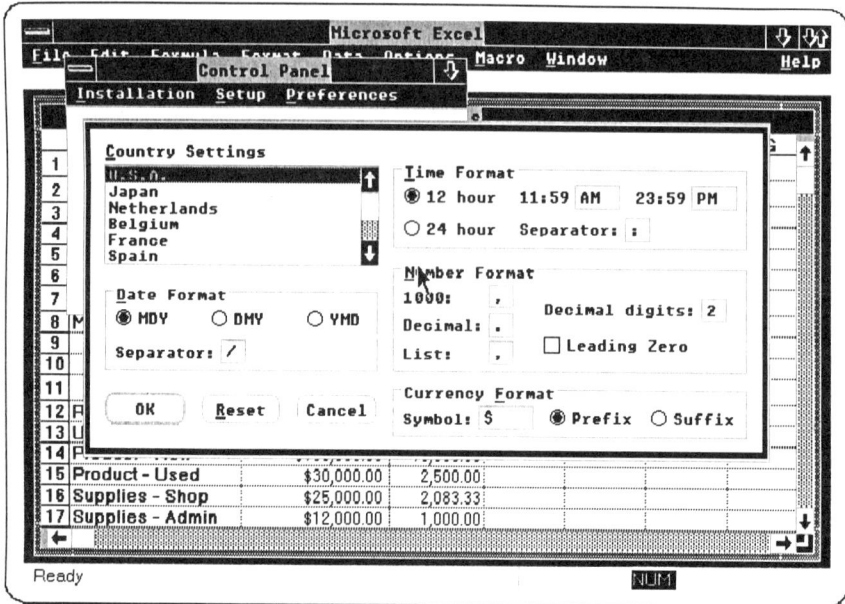

FIGURE 15.15. Country Settings Preferences Dialog Box

The Country Settings preference lets you change the way Excel handles date, time, and number formats according to a specific country. The U.S.A. is the default, as shown in the dialog box in Figure 15.15.

If you change to another country in the list box, you'll see the defaults for that country. You can change any specifications you want; just activate the field and type your preference. As with the other preferences, this one affects all your Excel documents. If you want a single worksheet prepared in a different country's formats, you can set the preferences, prepare and print a worksheet, then reset them. If you do this very often, you can create a macro to handle the procedure for you.

Macro Translation

The macro translation command helps you translate Lotus 1-2-3 or Multiplan macros into Microsoft Excel format. First open the worksheet containing the macro to be translated. Then use the application control Run command and select Macro Translator. In the resulting window, you can select either Lotus 1-2-3 or Multiplan for the translation mode.

Next you'll see a dialog box like the one in Figure 15.16. Here you select the open file that contains the macro to be translated. Then you see a similar dialog

PROTECTING AND CONTROLLING DOCUMENTS AND CELLS

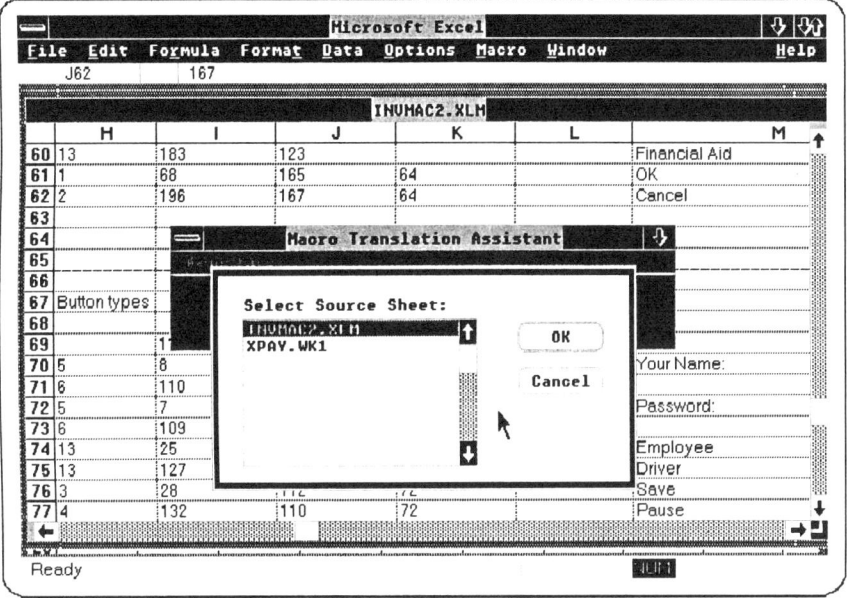

FIGURE 15.16. Translation Selection Dialog Box

box that lists the macros on that sheet; you select the one (or more) to be translated and choose OK.

The Macro Translation window displays messages as the translation proceeds, and it creates a new macro sheet to hold the translated macro. Finally, you'll see a completion message. At your request, Excel will close the Macro Translator and offer to open the appropriate translation file and run the translated macro. If you decline, you can examine the macro on the macro sheet.

You can obtain additional information about the Macro Translator through the Help system.

SUGGESTED EXERCISE

1. Examine the empty Clipboard from the application control menu.
2. Select a range on a worksheet and start a copy (CONTROL + Ins). Then examine the Clipboard again. Use the Clipboard's control menu to cancel it, then cancel the copy operation.
3. Examine the control panel. Adjust the cursor blink rate. Test your double click.
4. Examine the Preferences menu. Change the border width and see how it affects the displayed worksheet border. Reset the border width however you want.

5. Examine the Screen Colors window. Make a few changes and see how they affect the displayed sample window. Press Reset to restore them to the original way unless you really want to change them at this time.

What if It Doesn't Work?

1. Don't worry about these functions. If you haven't needed them up to this time, you can probably get along without them a while longer.
2. If a displayed window doesn't go away when you press Esc, use the Close command on its control menu.

SUMMARY

The protection features covered in this chapter are useful in worksheets at all levels. You can now protect all or part of your documents from changes and require a password for access.

Using commands from the document control Run menu is not required as often. You will probably set these values just once and work with Excel using those settings as defaults. If necessary, however, you can now change the colors, affect how the mouse works, modify the time and date settings, and alter other features of Excel and Windows.

A MACRO FUNCTIONS

Excel provides hundreds of functions specifically for use in macros, in addition to worksheet functions. This appendix lists them all and gives a brief description of each. They are divided here by type of function. *The Microsoft Excel Functions and Macros* reference manual treats them in detail, in alphabetical order. You can find information about arguments and usage there.

Command Equivalent Functions

Menu	Command	Macro Function	Dialog Box
Worksheet Menus			
File			
	Close	FILE.CLOSE	
	Close All	none	
	Delete	FILE.DELETE	?
	Exit	QUIT	
	Links	OPEN.LINKS	?
		CHANGE.LINK	?
	New	NEW	?
	Open	OPEN	?
	Page Setup	PAGE.SETUP	?
	Print	PRINT	?
	Printer Setup	PRINTER.SETUP	?
	Record Macro	none	
	Save	SAVE	
	Save As	SAVE.AS	?
	Save Workspace	SAVE.WORKSPACE	?
	Unhide Window	UNHIDE	
Edit			
	Clear	CLEAR	?
	Copy	COPY	
	Copy	COPY.PICTURE	
	Cut	CUT	
	Delete	EDIT.DELETE	?

Menu	Command	Macro Function	Dialog Box
	Fill Down	FILL.DOWN	
	Fill Left	FILL.LEFT	
	Fill Right	FILL.RIGHT	
	Fill Up	FILL.UP	
	Insert	INSERT	?
	Paste	PASTE	
	Paste Link	PASTE.LINK	
	Paste Special	PASTE.SPECIAL	?
	Repeat	none	
	Undo	UNDO	
Formula			
	Apply Names	APPLY.NAMES	?
	Create Names	CREATE.NAMES	?
	Define Name	DEFINE.NAME	?
		DELETE.NAME	
	Find	FORMULA.FIND	?
	Goto	FORMULA.GOTO	?
	Note	NOTE	
	Paste Function	none	
	Paste Name	LIST.NAMES	
	Reference	none	
	Replace	FORMULA.REPLACE	?
	Select Special	SELECT.SPECIAL	
Format			
	Alignment	ALIGNMENT	?
	Border	BORDER	?
	Cell Protection	CELL.PROTECTION	?
	Column Width	COLUMN.WIDTH	?
	Font	FORMAT.FONT	?
		REPLACE.FONT	
	Justify	JUSTIFY	
	Number	FORMAT.NUMBER	?
	Row Height	ROW.HEIGHT	?
	Text	FORMAT.TEXT	
Data			
	Delete	DATA.DELETE	?
	Exit Find	DATA.FIND	
	Extract	DATA.EXTRACT	?
	Form	DATA.FORM	
	Parse	PARSE	
	Series	DATA.SERIES	?
	Set Criteria	SET.CRITERIA	
	Set Database	SET.DATABASE	
	Sort	SORT	?
	Table	TABLE	?

APPENDIX A

Menu	Command	Macro Function	Dialog Box
Options			
	Display	DISPLAY	
	Freeze Panes	FREEZE.PANES	
	Full Menus	SHORT.MENUS	
	Protect Document	PROTECT.DOCUMENT	?
	Remove Page Break	REMOVE.PAGE.BREAK	
	Set Page Break	SET.PAGE.BREAK	
	Set Print Area	SET.PRINT.AREA	
	Set Print Titles	SET.PRINT.TITLES	
	Short Menus	SHORT.MENUS	
	Unfreeze Panes	FREEZE.PANES	
	Calculation	CALCULATION	?
	Workspace	WORKSPACE	?
Macro			
	Absolute Record	none	
	Record	none	
	Relative Record	none	
	Run	RUN	?
	Set Recorder	none	
	Start Recorder	none	
	Stop Recorder	none	
Window			
	Document	ACTIVATE	
	Arrange All	ARRANGE.ALL	
	Hide	HIDE	
	New Window	NEW.WINDOW	
	Show Document	SHOW.INFO	
	Show Info	SHOW.INFO	
	Unhide	UNHIDE	

Special Chart Menus and Commands

Menu	Command	Macro Function	Dialog Box
Gallery			
	Area	GALLERY.AREA	?
	Bar	GALLERY.BAR	?
	Column	GALLERY.COLUMN	?
	Combination	COMBINATION	?
	Line	GALLERY.LINE	?
	Pie	GALLERY.PIE	?
	Preferred	PREFERRED	
	Scatter	GALLERY.SCATTER	?
	Set Preferred	SET.PREFERRED	
Chart			
	Add Arrow	ADD.ARROW	

ADVANCED EXCEL

Menu	Command	Macro Function	Dialog Box
	Add Legend	LEGEND	
	Add Overlay	ADD.OVERLAY	
	Attach Text	ATTACH.TEXT	?
	Axes	AXES	?
	Calculate doc	CALCULATE.DOCUMENT	
	Calculate Now	CALCULATE.NOW	
	Delete Arrow	DELETE.ARROW	
	Delete Legend	LEGEND	
	Delete Overlay	DELETE.OVERLAY	
	Gridlines	GRIDLINES	?
	Select Chart	SELECT	
	Select Plot Area	SELECT	
Format			
	Legend	FORMAT.LEGEND	
	Main Chart	MAIN.CHART	
	Move	FORMAT.MOVE	?
	Overlay	OVERLAY	
	Patterns	PATTERNS	
	Scale	SCALE	
	Size	FORMAT.SIZE	?
	Text	FORMAT.TEXT	
Info			
Window			
Commands			
	Cell	DISPLAY	
	Dependents	DISPLAY	
	Format	DISPLAY	
	Formula	DISPLAY	
	Names	DISPLAY	
	Note	DISPLAY	
	Precedents	DISPLAY	
	Protection	DISPLAY	
	Value	DISPLAY	

Control Menus

Application
Control

	Close	QUIT	
	Maximize	APP.MAXIMIZE	
	Minimize	APP.MINIMIZE	
	Move	APP.MOVE	?
	Restore	APP.RESTORE	

APPENDIX A **353**

Menu	Command	Macro Function	Dialog Box
	Run	none	
	Size	APP.SIZE	?
Document Control			
	Close	CLOSE	
	Maximize	FULL	
	Move	MOVE	
	Restore	FULL	
	Size	SIZE	
	Split	SPLIT	

Customizing Functions

Function	Action
ADD.BAR	Adds a custom menu bar
ADD.COMMAND	Adds a custom command
ADD.MENU	Adds a custom menu
ALERT	Displays an ALERT box
APP.ACTIVATE	Starts another application
BEEP	Beeps
CALL	Calls Microsoft Windows Library
CANCEL.KEY	Changes the Escape key effect
CHECK.COMMAND	Marks a command
DELETE.BAR	Removes a custom menu bar
DELETE.COMMAND	Removes a custom command
DELETE.MENU	Removes a custom menu
DIALOG.BOX	Displays a custom dialog box
DISABLE.INPUT	Stops input to Excel
ECHO	Toggles screen update
ENABLE.COMMAND	Toggles graying of custom commands
ERROR	Specifies action in case of error
EXEC	Starts another application
EXECUTE	Performs a command in another application
FCLOSE	Closes a text file
FOPEN	Opens a text file
FPOS	Returns position in open file
FREAD	Reads characters from a text file
FREADLN	Reads a line from a text file
FSIZE	Returns size of a text file
FWRITE	Writes characters to a text file
FWRITELN	Writes a line to a text file
HELP	Displays a custom Help topic
INITIATE	Opens channel to another application
INPUT	Displays simple dialog box for input

Function	Action
MESSAGE	Displays message in status line
ON.DATA	Runs macro when data is sent to Excel from another application
ON.KEY	Runs macro when specific key pressed
ON.KEY	Runs macro when specific key pressed
ON.TIME	Runs macro at specific time
ON.WINDOW	Runs macro when a window is changed
POKE	Sends data to another application
REGISTER	Accesses Microsoft Windows library
RENAME.COMMAND	Changes name of a command
REQUEST	Returns data from another application
SEND.KEYS	Sends key sequence to another application
SET.NAME	Define name as a specific value
SET.VALUE	Enter value in a cell
SHOW.BAR	Display a menu bar
STEP	Single-step through a macro
TERMINATE	Close channel to another application
WAIT	Stop a macro

Other Action Equivalent Functions

A1.R1C1	Displays the A1 or R1C1 references
ACTIVATE	Selects a window
ACTIVATE.NEXT	Selects the next window
ACTIVATE.PREV	Selects the previous window
CANCEL.COPY	Cancels the marquee
COPY.CHART	Copies a picture of chart
DATA.FIND.NEXT	Finds next matching record in database
DATA.FIND.PREV	Finds previous matching record in database
DELETE.FORMAT	Deletes a number format
DIRECTORY	Changes directory; returns path name
FORMULA	Enters a formula into a cell, or text into a chart
FORMULA.ARRAY	Enters an array formula in document
FORMULA.FILL	Fills range with formula
FORMULA.FIND.NEXT	Finds next cell, as in dialog box
FORMULA.FIND.PREV	Finds previous cell, as in dialog box
HLINE	Horizontally scrolls by columns
HPAGE	Horizontally scrolls, one full window
HSCROLL	Horizontally scrolls by percentage or column number
SELECT	Selects an item on a chart
SELECT	Selects a reference
SELECT.END	Changes the active cell
SELECT.LAST.CELL	Selects cell at end of document
SHOW.ACTIVE.CELL	Displays the active cell
SHOW.CLIPBOARD	Displays the clipboard
STYLE	Changes font
UNLOCKED.NEXT	Moves to next unlocked cell

APPENDIX A

Function	Action
UNLOCKED.PREV	Moves to previous unlocked cell
VLINE	Vertically scrolls by rows
VPAGE	Vertically scrolls, one full window
VSCROLL	Vertically scrolls by percentage or row number

Functions That Don't Perform Actions

Control Functions	
ARGUMENT	Describes arguments to function macro
BREAK	Breaks out of loop
FOR	Starts loop with NEXT or WHILE
GOTO	Jumps to another cell
HALT	Stops macro
NEXT	Ends FOR-NEXT loop
RESTART	Removes return addresses from stack
RESULT	Specifies data type of function macro's return value
RETURN	Returns control to whatever started macro
WHILE	Starts WHILE-NEXT loop

Value-Returning Functions	
ABSREF	Absolute value of a cell
ACTIVE.CELL	Reference of the active cell
CALLER	Reference of cell that started macro
DEREF	Value of cell in a reference
DOCUMENTS	Name(s) of an open document
FILES	Name(s) of file in a specific directory
GET.BAR	Number of the active menu bar
GET.CHART.ITEM	Location of a chart element
GET.DEF	Name matching a definition
GET.DOCUMENT	Information about a document
GET.FORMULA	Contents of a cell
GET.NAME	Definition of a name
GET.NOTE	Characters from a note
GET.WINDOW	Information about a window
GET.WORKSPACE	Information about the workspace
LINKS	Names of all linked documents
NAMES	Array of defined names on document
OFFSET	One reference offset from a given reference
REFTEXT	Converts a reference into text
RELREF	Relative reference
SELECTION	Reference of selection
TEXTREF	Converts text into reference
WINDOWS	Name(s) of window(s) on screen

INDEX

References to figures that illustrate an index topic are printed in boldface type.

A1 reference style, 71
Absolute recording, 252
Absolute reference, 40, 71, 73
Access, prevention, 331
Access protected file, 333
Action equivalent functions, 273
Activate worksheet, 139
Active cell, in selection, 34
Add Arrow, 221
Adjustment, cell, 40
Alignment, cell contents, 50, 51, **52**
Alignment, chart text, 219
ALT key, 4, 10, 11
Annuity functions, 106
Application window, 5, 6
Apply Names, **82**
Area chart, 192-194, **195**
Areas, multiple, 140
Argument list, 99
Arguments, 32
Arithmetic, 31
Arithmetic operators, 96
Array, 243-246
Array, mathematical, 245
Array constant, 243
Array formula, 243, 245
Array functions, 246
Array range, 243
Arrow, **188**, 190
Arrows, 221, **221**
Attached text, 217-220, **218-220**
Axes, **188**, 189
Axes, modify, 214
Axis, category, **215**
Axis, value, **214**
Axis labels, 218
Axis pattern, **216**

Bar chart, 194, **196**
Beep, changing, 345
Border, cell, 61
Border, chart element, 212
Border, worksheet, **7**
Border width, setting, 345
Built-in formats, 30
Built-in functions, 23, 39. *See*
    Functions, worksheet
Built-in menu bars, 329
Button, Dialog Editor, 299, **230**,
    315-316, **316**

Calculation, **47**
Calendar design, 103
Cancel box, **28**
Categories, chart, 186
Categories argument, 225
Category names, 187
Cell, 73
Cell, move, 42
Cell information, 85, 86
Cell information functions, 109
Cell Protection, **336**
Cell protection, selective, 337
Center, 51
Change link, 153
Chart, 185-227, **188**
Chart, area, 192-194, **195**
Chart, bar, 194, **196**
Chart, categories, 186
Chart, column, 194-197, **197**
Chart, combination, 202, **203**
Chart, create, 185
Chart, default, **186**
Chart, format font, **210**
Chart, gridlines, **216**, 217

Chart, line, 197, 198, **199**
Chart, patterns, 211, **212-213**
Chart, pie, 199, **200**
Chart, scatter, 199-201, **202**
Chart, series, 186
Chart element, select, 190
Chart format menu, 207
Chart menu, 207
Chart orientation, 187, 204
Chart overlays, 223-224
Chart text, **188**, 190
Chart title, 218
Check box, dialog box, 319
Check box, formula bar, 14
Clear cell, **44**
Click, 4
Click, double, rate, 341
Clipboard, 156, **340**
Close file, 21
Close files, all, 21
Close window, 13
Color, screen, 343, **344**
Color format, 56
Colors, charts, 210, 212
Column, insert, 46
Column, select, 36
Column chart, 194-197, **197**
Column differences, 92, **93**
Column headings, **8**
Column headings, display, 65
Column headings, print, 131
Column width, 35, **37**
Columns, rearrange, 170
Columns, sort, 170
Combination chart, 202, **203**
Command equivalent functions, 270
Command macro, 248, 251

357

358 ADVANCED EXCEL

Commands, custom, 330
Comparison operators, 96
Complex external reference, 146
Concatenation operator, 97
Constant, array, 243
Context help, 15
Control functions, 339
Control functions, macro, 273
Control menu icon, 6, **7**
Control menus, **13**
Control panel, 341–346, **341**
Convert, charts, 222
Convert range to Dialog Editor, 305
Copy, 40, **41**
Copy, destructive, 41
Country settings, **346**
Create Names, 78, **79**
Criteria, compound, 175, **176**
Criteria, computed, 174
Criteria, Data Form, 165
Criteria, external references, 175
Criteria, simple, 173
Criteria operators, 174
Criteria range, **172**
CSV files, 154, **155**
Cursor blink rate, 341
Custom box definition, 306
Custom dialog box, 296
Custom forms, 296
Custom range, 306
Custom range, comments, 304
Custom range, Init/Result, 304, 307
Custom range, size, 303, 307
Custom range, start position, 303, 307
Custom range, text, 304, 307
Custom range, type, 306
Customizing functions, 271
Cut, 42

Data Delete, 179
Data entry, 28, 33
Data Find, 176
Data Form, 163–167, **164**
Data Form, adding records, 164
Data form, custom, 296–313
Data Form, deleting records, 165
Data Form, locating records, 165
Data Form, moving in, 164
Data form, name, 310, **311**
Data series, chart, 185
Data Series, date, 228–230, **231**
Data Series, growth, 229

Data Series, linear, 228–230, **230**
Data Series, nonchart, 228, **229**
Data Sort, 167, **170**
Data Table, 231
Data types, macro, 275
Database, 159–184
Database, creation, 161
Database, definition, 162
Database, design, 160
Database functions, 181
Database subset, 177
Date, change, 342
Date functions, 101
Dates, 31, 101
DDE, 156–157
Decision-making functions, 112
Default fonts, 68
Define Name, 77, **78**
Define Name, macro, **261**
Definition range, data form, 310
Delete, records, 179
Delete Arrow, 221
Delete cell, **45**
Delete file, 21, **22**
Dependent info, 87
Dependent worksheet, 146
Dependents, 89
Depreciation functions, 105
Design, custom box, 309
Design, function macro, 275
Design, worksheet, 27
Dialog box, 13
Dialog box, moving cursor in, 14
Dialog box display, macro, 262
Dialog box figures
  Alignment, Chart Text, 219
  Alignment, in cells, **52**
  Apply Names, **82**
  Area Chart, **193**
  Arrow Format, **222**
  Attach Text, **218**
  Bar Chart, **195**
  Borders, Format, **61**
  Calculation, **47**
  Change Links, **153**
  Column Chart, **196**
  Column Width, **37**
  Combination Chart, **203**
  Country Setting, **346**
  Create Names, **79**
  Customized, **297**
  Data Form, **164**
  Data Series, **229**

Data Table, **233**
Database Form, **164**
Define Name, **78**
Define Name, Dialog Editor, **311**
Define Name, Macro, **261**
Delete File, **22**
Display, **63**
Edit Clear, **44**
Edit Delete, **45**
File Open, **14**
File Save, **23**, **24**
Find, **90**
Font, Chart, **210**
Font, Worksheet, **67**
Format Numbers, **55**
Gallery, Area, **193**
Gallery, Bar, **195**
Gallery, Column, **196**
Gallery, Combination, **203**
Gallery, Line, **198**
Gallery, Pie, **200**
Gallery, Scatter, **201**
Generic Input, **273**
Glossary, **17**
Goto, **74**
Gridlines, Chart, **216**
Help About, **12**
Help Index, **16**
Input, Generic, **273**
Legend, **209**
Line Chart, **198**
Links, **148**
Links, Change, **153**
Macro Error, **264**, **317**
Macro Record, **254**
Macro Run, **257**
Macro Translation, **347**
Main Chart, **223**
Mouse Preference, **345**
New File, **21**
Note, **84**
Numbers, Format, **55**
Open File, **14**
Page Setup, **131**
Paste Function, Macro, **270**
Paste Function, Worksheet, **100**
Paste Name, **81**
Paste Special, **43**
Patterns, **212**
Patterns, Axis, **216**
Pie Chart, **200**
Print, **127**
Printer Setup, **125**

INDEX

Protect Cell, **336**
Protect Document, **334**
References, Update, **151**
Replace, **91**
Run Application, **339**
Save, File, **23**
Save, File Options, **24**
Save, Workspace, **25**
Scale, Category Axis, **215**
Scale, Value Axis, **214**
Scatter Chart, **201**
Screen Colors, **344**
Select Special, **88**
Sort, **170**
Step, **265**
Translation, Macro, **347**
Update References, **151**
Worksheet, Save, 154, **332**
Workspace, Options, **72**
Workspace, Save, **25**
Dialog box functions, 271
Dialog boxes, custom, 296-310, 314-327
Dialog Editor, 298-309
Dialog Editor Info window, 303, **30**
Directories, 18
Disk output, ASCII, 154
Disk output, non-Excel, 155
Display formulas, 64, 98, **142**
Display modifications, 62
Document, protection, 334
Double click rate, 341
Drag, 10
Duplicate, in Dialog Editor, 303
Dynamic Data Exchange, 156-157

E, 56
Edit Box, Dialog Editor, 300, **301**, 316-318
Edit cell, **29**
Edit Clear, 44
Edit Delete, 45
Edit menu, 38
Elements, chart, **188**, 189
Elements, chart, selecting, 190
Ellipsis, 11
Enter box, **28**
Enter data, 28, 33
Enter key, 11
Equal sign, 30
Error, macro, 264, **317**
Error messages, 95

Escape key, 11
EXCEL.EXE, 5
Exit, 24
Extensions, 18, 19
External reference, 146, 147
External reference, criteria, 175
External reference, macro, 263
Extract range, 177, **178**
Extracting records, 177

F1, 11, 15
F2, 28
Feature Guide, 15
Field, 159, 160
Field name, 159, 161
Field name, definition, 162
File Links, 147, **148**
File name, generic, 20
Files, through Dialog Editor, 322-324
Fill alignment, 51
Fill cells, 39
Financial functions, 105
Finding data, **90**
Fixed-width font, 66
Font, 65, **67**
Font, chart, 206, 207
Font, default, 68
Font, fixed-width, 66
Font, proportional, 66
Font, replacement, 68
Footer, print, 132
Format, general, 54
Format Arrow, **222**
Format info, 87
Format Main chart, 222-223
Format menu, 50, **51**
Format menu, chart, 207
Format Overlay, 223-224
Format pictures, 57
Format sections, 57
Formula, 30, 31, 95
Formula, array, 243, 245
Formula, display, 64
Formula bar, **7**, **28**, 95
Formula bar, edit, **29**
Formula info, 87
Formulas, display, 98, **142**
Freeze panes, 143-145
Full menus, 48
Full windows, 5
Function Keys, 10
Function macro, 248, 274-277

Function macro, arguments, 276, **277**
Function syntax, 99
Functions, worksheet
  ABS, 115
  ACOS, 122
  AND, **114**
  AREAS, 109
  ASIN, 122
  ATAN, 122
  ATAN2, 122
  AVERAGE, 117
  CELL, 109, **110**
  CHAR, 119
  CLEAN, 119
  CODE, 119
  COLUMN, 110
  COLUMNS, 110, 287
  COS, 122
  COUNT, 117
  COUNTA, 118
  DATE, 100, **104**
  DATEVALUE, 101
  DAVERAGE, 181
  DAY, 101
  DCOUNT, 181
  DCOUNTA, 181
  DDB, 106
  DMAX, 181
  DMIN, 182
  DOLLAR, 119
  DPRODUCT, 182
  DSTDEV, 182
  DSTDEVP, 182
  DSUM, 182
  DVAR, 182
  DVARP, 182
  EXACT, 119
  EXP, 115
  FACT, 116
  FALSE, 112
  FIND, 119
  FIXED, 120
  FV, 107
  GROWTH, 118
  HLOOKUP, 238-239
  HOUR, 102
  IF, 112, **113**, 292
  INDEX, 242
  INT, 116
  IPMT, 107
  IRR, 108
  ISBLANK, 108
  ISERR, 108

Functions, worksheet (*continued*)
  ISERROR, 109
  ISLOGICAL, 109
  ISNA, 109
  ISNONTEXT, 109
  ISNUMBER, 109
  ISREF, 109
  ISTEXT, 109
  LEFT, 120
  LEN, 120
  LINEST, 118
  LN, 116
  LOG, 116
  LOG10, 116
  LOGEST, 118
  LOOKUP, 240
  LOWER, 120
  MATCH, 241
  MAX, 118
  MDETERM, 246
  MID, 120
  MIN, 118
  MINUTE, 102
  MINVERSE, 246
  MIRR, 108
  MMULT, 246
  MOD, 116
  MONTH, 102
  N, 111
  NA, 111
  NOT, 114
  NOW, 102, 270
  NPER, 107
  NPV, 108
  OR, 114
  PI, 116
  PMT, 107
  PPMT, 107
  PRODUCT, 116
  PROPER, 120
  PV, 107
  RAND, 116
  RATE, 107
  REPLACE, 120
  REPT, 121
  RIGHT, 121
  ROUND, 117
  ROW, 111
  ROWS, 111, 286
  SEARCH, 121
  SECOND, 102
  SERIES, 224
  SIGN, 117
  SIN, 122
  SLN, 106
  SQRT, 117
  STDEV, 118
  STDEVP, 118
  SUBSTITUTE, 121
  SUM, 118
  SYN, 106
  T, 111
  TABLE, 233
  TAN, 122
  TEXT, 121
  TIME, 102
  TIMEVALUE, 102
  TRANSPOSE, 246
  TREND, 119
  TRIM, 122
  TRUE, 112
  TRUNC, 117
  TYPE, 111
  UPPER, 122
  VALUE, 122
  VAR, 118
  VARP, 118
  VLOOKUP, 238–239
  WEEKDAY, 102, **104**
  YEAR, 102
Functions, macro
  ACTIVATE, 263
  ADD.BAR, 330
  ADD.COMMAND, 330
  ADD.MENU, 330
  ALERT, 281–283, **284**
  ALIGNMENT, 256
  ARGUMENT, 276
  BEEP, 283, **284**
  CHECK.COMMAND, 330
  COLUMN.WIDTH, 294
  COPY, 288
  DEFINE.NAME, 290
  DELETE.COMMAND, 330
  DELETE.MENU, 330
  DIALOG.BOX, 314
  DISABLE.COMMAND, 330
  EDIT.DELETE, 288
  ENABLE.COMMAND, 330
  FORMAT.FONT, 256
  FORMAT.NUMBER?, 271
  FORMULA, 255
  FORMULA, 280, **281**
  FORMULA.ARRAY, 291
  FORMULA.FILL, 288
  INPUT, 279, **280**
  INSERT, 288
  MESSAGE, 283, **284**
  OFFSET, 286
  PAGE.SETUP, 293
  PASTE.SPECIAL, 270
  PASTE.SPECIAL, 288
  PRINT, 294
  REMOVE.COMMAND, 330
  RESULT, 276
  RETURN, 255, 276
  SELECT, 255
  SELECT, 287
  SELECTION, 290
  SELECT.LAST.CELL, 292
  SET.NAME, 286
  SET.PRINT.AREA, 293
  SET.VALUE, 327
  SHOW.BAR, 330
  SHOW.INFO, 263
  SIZE, 263
  STEP, 287
  TRANSPOSE, 291
  UNDO, 255

General format, 54
Generic dialog box, 279, **280**
Generic input, macro, 273, 279
Glossary, 17
Goto, 73, **74**
Gridline, display, **64**
Gridlines, chart, **216**, 217
Gridlines, print, 133
Group Box, Dialog Editor, 300, **300**, 319

Header, print, 132
Help, customized, 327–329, **328**
Help file reference, 329
Help files, 327, **328**
Help glossary, 17
Help Index, 15, **16**
Help system, 15–17
Hidden cells, 337
Hidden value, format, 57
Hide window, 151
Hierarchy, operations, **97**
Horizontal lookup tables, 238

Icon
  Control menu, 6, **7**, **8**
  Dialog Editor, 301, **322**, 322
  Maximize, 6, **7**
  Minimize, 6, **7**

INDEX

Pointer, **9**
Macro, **282**
Info, print, 128
Info menu, **86**
Info window, **86**
Info window, Dialog Editor, 303, **304**
Information functions, 108
Input variable, 232
Insert column, 46
Insert row, 46
Insertion point, **29**
Installation, 4
Installation, modify, **342**
Intersection operator, 97
Investment functions, 106
Item menu, Dialog Editor, 299–300

Justification, 52, **53**

Key, macro, 253
Key, sort, 168
Keyboard, 4, 10
Keyboard, help, 15

Label macros, 284–294
Landscape, **126**, **130**
Left alignment, 51
Left-handedness, 10
Legend, **188**, 190
Legend, 208, **209**
Line chart, 197, 198, **199**
Link, chart text, 222
Link, establish, 147, 149
Link, find, 147, 152
Link, redirect, 152, **153**
Link, remove, 152
Link, to chart, 186
Linked worksheet, opening, 150
Linked worksheet, saving, 150
Linking, 145
List box, **14**
List Box, Dialog Editor, 301, **317**, **320–321**
Locating records, 172
Locked cells, 336
Logical functions, 111
Logical operators, 113, 114
Logical return functions, 108
Lookup functions, 238
Lookup table, 237–243
Lotus 1-2-3, 15, 155, 156, 346

Macro, edit, 257
Macro, Run, 250, 256, **257**
Macro communication, 281
Macro function, 248, 250, 269–274, 349–355. *See also* Functions, macro
Macro name, 253, 260
Macro placement, 258–260
Macro Record, 252, 253, **254**
Macro recorder, 251
Macro sheet, 249, **249**
Macro sheet, format, 261, **262**
Macro translation, 346, **347**
Macros, 248
Magnification, 129, **131**
Main chart, convert, 222–223
Margins, print, 133
Marker, modify, 213
Marker labels, 219
Markers, **188**, 189
Marquee, 40
Mathematical functions, 115
Matrix functions, 246
Maximize, 6, **7**
Measurement units, screen, 308
Memory, 11, **12**, 27
Memory layout, 23
Menu bar, 6, **7**, 86
Menu bar, chart, **188**, 191
Menu bars, built-in, 329
Menu bars, custom, 330
Menu, 11
Menu figures
  Chart, **207**
  Control, **14**
  Dialog Editor Edit, **303**
  Edit, **38**
  Edit, Dialog Editor, **303**
  File, **19**
  Format, **36**, **51**
  Format, Chart, **207**
  Gallery, **193**
  Help, **12**
  Info, **86**
  Macro, **252**
Minimize, 6, **7**
Mouse, 4, 9
Mouse, changing, **345**
Mouse pointer, **8**, 9
Move between worksheets, 139
Move cell, 42
Move to cell, 73
Move window, 13

MS-DOS window, 5
Multiplan, 15, 346
Multiple selection, 74, **75**
Multiple selection, moving in, 75, 76

Name, macro, 253, 260
Name, move to, 83
Names, 76
Names, define one, 77
Names, define several, 78
Names, delete, 80
Names, edit, 80
Names, external references, 146, 149
Names, info, 87
Names, list, 80, **81**
Names, macro arguments, 278
Names, macro cells, 278
Names, macro references, 278
Names, paste, 80, **81**
Names, using, 80
Naming in macros, 278
Naming rules, 77
New file, 20, **21**
Nonwindows data, 156
Note info, 87
Notes, 83, **84**
Notes, create, 84
Notes, delete, 85
Notes, edit, 85
Notes, print, 85, 127
Notes, scrolling, 88
Number formats, 54, **55**
Number values, 30

Object, manipulation, 302
Object types, 315
One-input table, 231–234, **232–234**
Open file, 19
Operator hierarchy, **97**
Operators, criteria, 174
Operators, formula, **96**
Option buttons, 318–319
Orientation, 126
Orientation, chart, 187, 204
Outline, 61, **62**
Overlay, convert, 223–224

Page breaks, 135, **136**
Page Setup, 131
PageDown, 10
PageUp, 10
Panes, 142, **143**, **144**
Parentheses, 97

Password, 23, 332
Paste, 40
Paste, chart, 204
Paste arguments, 101
Paste Function, **100**
Paste Function, macro, 269, **270**
Paste Links, 148
Paste Names, 80, **81**
Paste Special, 150
Paste Special, 42, **43**
Paste Special, Formats, 43
Paste Special, Formulas 43
Paste Special, Skip blanks, 43
Paste Special, Transpose, 43
Paste Special, Values, 43
Pattern, axis, **216**
Patterns, chart, 211, **212–213**
Pie chart, 199, **200**
Plot area, **188**, 189
Plot order, **226**
Point size, 65
Pointer icons, **9**
Pointing, 33
Pointing, 97
Portrait, **126**
Ports, 4
Position, box or object, 303
Positioning units, 308
Precedent info, 87
Precedents, 89
Preferred chart, 204
Preview, 128, **129**, **130**
Print chart, 205
Print file, 126, **127**
Print formulas, 99
Print info, 89, 128
Print notes, 85, 127
Print preview, 128, **129**, **130**
Print spooler, 137
Print titles, 135
Printer fonts, 65, 68
Printer Setup, 124, **125**
Printer setup changes, **343**
Printing, 126 ff
Print_area, 134
Priority, print, 138
Proportional font, 66
Protect Document, **334**
Protection, cell, 336
Protection, charts, 338
Protection, document, 331
Protection, document, removing, 334
Protection info, 87

Queue, print, 137

R1C1 reference style, 71, 253
Range, 33, **34**, 73
Range, array, 243
Range, selection, 33
Range, sort, 169
Range entry, 42
Range operator, 97
Rate of return functions, 107
Recalculation, 47
Record, 159
Recorder range, 259
Redirect link, 152, **153**
Reference, absolute, 40
Reference, external. *See* External reference
Reference, relative, 40
Reference operators, 96
Reference setting, **72**
Reference style, A1, 71, 73
Reference style, R1C1, 71, 73
Region, current, 92
Relative recording, 252
Relative reference, 40, 71, 73
Remove cells, 45
Remove Page Breaks, 136
Repeat, 39
Replacing data, 90, **91**
Restore data record, 163
Restore window size, 13
RESUME.XLS, 24
Right alignment, 51
Row, insert, 46
Row, select, 36
Row differences, 92
Row heading, display, 65
Row headings, **8**
Row headings, print, 131
Row height, 36, **37**
Run, 13
Run-time Windows, 3

Save, dialog box, 305
Save file, 22
Save file as, 22, **23**, **24**
Save other formats, **154**
Save workspace, 25
Scale, axis, 215
Scatter chart, 199–201, **202**
Scientific notation, 30
Screen colors, 343, **344**
Screen fonts, 65, **67**, **69**

Screen layout, 23
Scroll bar, **8**, 9
Scrolling notes, 88
Select, column, 36
Select, from list, 17
Select, range, 33
Select, row, 36
Select Special, **88**, 92
Selective cell protection, 337
Series, chart, 186
Series formula, **188**, 190
Series formula, chart, 224–227, **225**
Series marker, 213
Series name, 187
Series name argument, 224
Set Database, 163
Set Page Breaks, 135
Set Print Area, 134
Set Print Titles, 135
Set Recorder, 259
Shading, 62, **63**
SHEET1, 18
Shift cells, 45, 46
Short menus, 48
Shortcut, keyboard, 10, 17
Shortcut, macro, 248
Shortcut key, macro, 253
Show Info, 85
Simple external reference, 146
Size, box or object, 303
Size window, 13
Sizing objects, 309
Sort, 167–171
Sort keys, 168, 169
Sort range, 169
Sort sequence, 168
Special paste operations, 43
Split window, 13
Spooler, 137
Spreadsheet, 27
Standard width, 36
Start Recorder, 259, 260
Statistical functions, 117
Status bar, **7**
Stop Recorder, 252
Subdirectories, 18
Subset, database, 177
Supporting worksheet, 146, 147
Suppress zeros, 65
Symbols, format, 55

Table, lookup, 237–243
Table, one-input, 231–234, **232–234**

INDEX

Table, two-input, 234–236, **235**
Text, 30, 31
Text, attached, 217–220, **218–220**
Text, chart, 217–222
Text, chart, alignment, 219
Text, Dialog Editor, 300, **300**, 316–317
Text, unattached, 220–221, **221**
Text functions, 119
Text operators, 96
Thumb, **8**, 9
Tick mark, **188**, 189, 214, 215
Time, change, 342
Time functions, 101
Title bar, 6, **7**, **8**
Trigonometric functions, 122
Tutorial, 15
Two-input table, 234–236, **235**
TXT files, 154, **155**
Type size, 65
Type style, 65
Typeface, 65

Unattached text, 220–221, **221**
Undo, 38
Unfreeze panes, 145
Unhide window, 151
Union operator, 97
Unprotect Document, 334

Value info, 87
Value returning functions, macro, 274
Value types, 30
Variable, input to table, 232
Variables, 132
Vector, 241
Vertical lookup tables, 238

Window,
   Application, 5, 6
   Close, 13
   Dialog Editor, **299**
   Document, **8**
   Executive, **5**
   Info, **86**
   Move, 13
   MS-DOS, **5**
   Print Spooler, **137**
   Restore, 13
   Size, 13
   Worksheet, **7**
Window panes, 142, **143**, **144**
Windows, arranged, **141**
Windows, full, 5
Windows, multiple, 140
Windows, run-time, 3, 6
Windows 2.0, 3

Windows data transfer, 156–157
Worksheet functions. *See* Functions, worksheet
Worksheet, dependent, 146
Worksheet, empty, 18
Worksheet, supporting, 146, 147
Worksheet window, **7**
Workspace, 23, **25**
XLM extension, 254

Zero values, 65
Zoom, 129, **131**

Symbols

,   56
0   55
\#   30, 54
$ 56
%   55
*   56
\+   56
\-   56
:   56
=   30, 95
\   56